Approaches to Canadian Politics

Approaches to Canadian Politics

Editor
John H. Redekop
Department of Political Science
Wilfrid Laurier University

Prentice-Hall of Canada, Ltd., *Scarborough, Ontario*

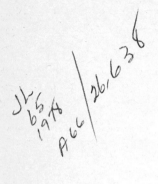

Canadian Cataloguing in Publication Data

Main entry under title:

Approaches to Canadian politics

Includes bibliographies and index.
ISBN 0-13-043729-8

1. Canada - Politics and government - Addresses,
essays, lectures. I. Redekop, John Harold, 1932-
JL65 1978.A66   320.9'71   C78-001131-7

Prentice-Hall, Inc., Englewood Cliffs, New Jersey
Prentice-Hall International Inc., London
Prentice-Hall of Australia, Pty., Ltd., Sydney
Prentice-Hall of India Pvt., Ltd., New Delhi
Prentice-Hall of Japan, Inc., Tokyo
Prentice-Hall of Southeast Asia (PTE.) Ltd., Singapore

ISBN 0-13-043729-8

Cover design: Vita Churchill

  2 3 4 5 W 82 81 80 79

Phototypeset by Eastern Typesetting Company
Printed and bound in Canada by Webcom

Contents

Preface

This book is designed to fulfill four basic objectives: (1) to describe, illustrate, and evaluate sixteen different ways of interpreting Canadian politics; (2) to stimulate interest in Canadian politics; (3) to enrich students' knowledge of Canadian politics by introducing them to new approaches; and (4) to demonstrate that no single approach can by itself generate an adequate, let alone balanced, explanation of the subject. Additionally, reading this volume should help students to recognize and make allowance for biases and to understand the strengths and the weaknesses, the potential and the limitations, of each approach as they encounter it in their studies.

These sixteen original and generally brief essays should be of considerable help to those instructors and students who have spent tedious hours scouting libraries and bookstores for suitable material to illustrate the large number of noteworthy approaches. My own students will, I trust, find this wide-ranging single volume much more useful than the previous list of scattered sections and first or last chapters. While each chapter is self-contained and can profitably be read by itself, the significant benefits of assessing the inter-author comments and of general comparison will be largely missed if the book is not read in its entirety.

The authors do not assume that readers come to this volume with substantial knowledge about Canadian politics; all chapters have been written with the beginning student in mind. Our aim is to help the student to understand and integrate the numerous ways in which substantive material is presented, be it in this book or elsewhere. Given this thrust and the usage of familiar categories, the beginning student should have no difficulty in relating these chapters to his other readings in politics. While the book may have many uses, it is intended to be used primarily as a main or auxiliary text for courses in Canadian and introductory politics. The annotated bibliographies at the end of each chapter should be helpful for students as well as instructors.

It is with much pleasure that I thank the contributors for their diligence and cooperation and the departmental secretaries, Arvis Oxland, Pat Moonah, Joan Dawson, and especially Doris McPhee, for their many hours of typing and retyping. Finally, it would be a serious omission not to mention the invaluable assistance of Luba Welykopolsky, Book Production Editor at Prentice-Hall of Canada.

John H. Redekop
December 13, 1977

Introduction

What is the best way of studying Canadian politics? Unfortunately there is no simple or straightforward answer to this question. As we shall shortly see, the field of Canadian politics is torn between differing conceptions of what the study should encompass, what are the really important questions, and which approach is the most useful. Instead of talking about different approaches, we could speak of orientations, interpretations, or perspectives.

Like so many terms in political science, the word "approach"—the generic term used in this book's title—has various meanings. As used here, it refers to a way of looking at and explaining politics, in this case Canadian politics. An approach gives a logical framework for inquiry and spells out what particular emphasis is considered important and, consequently, the criteria for deciding what data, questions, or problems are of greatest relevance. Every approach has a particular focus and scope, but not every one necessarily constitutes a full-fledged theory, be it descriptive, prescriptive, or explanatory. While not all approaches come to grips with the full gamut of Canadian politics, the sixteen selected for inclusion in this volume have all been described—if not here then elsewhere —either as explanations of the major features of Canadian politics or as explanations that show why some major component is critically important for a proper understanding of the whole.

Though there are references to "methodological approaches," there is a basic distinction between approach and method. If, as suggested above, approaches consist largely of convictions or assumptions concerning what is important and the attendant criteria for selecting problems and relevant data, then methods are the procedures for collecting and utilizing data. Given this distinction, it follows that methods are secondary and should be seen as instrumental to the larger and more fundamental questions of approaches. Accordingly, knowledge of approaches is both more important than, and should be antecedent to, knowledge of methods, significant though the latter obviously is.

If the authors were addressing themselves primarily to questions of methodology within the discipline, then our first concern would be: *"How* should I study Canadian politics?" However, in the present volume the more inclusive and more basic questions to which all the authors address themselves are: *"What* should I study in Canadian politics in order to get at the heart of the matter?" and, "How useful is this particular approach?" Only incidentally do we concern ourselves with techniques and alternate methodologies. This book was not intended to deal with phenomena such as laws, scientific method, models, mid-range theories, behavioralism, structure-functionalism, game theory, or inductive and deductive logic. Our purpose is neither to analyze techniques or methodologies, nor to develop broad theories about politics in general. Our aim, rather, is to present and assess alternative views of how we can acquire a broad and balanced knowledge about political affairs in Canada. Additionally, it should be emphasized that this book does not deal specifically with segments or divisions of Canadian politics, nor with problems or themes, although some of the topics treated here have often been dealt with in that manner.

Of course, the contributors, all experts in their areas, have not ignored the standard political science methodologies; they are discussed or even used in the various chapters but they are not analyzed as ends in themselves. In similar fashion, the writers use commonplace political science notions such as centrality of power, the significance of values, the nature of social cohesion and cleavages, the importance of decision making, the dynamics of conflict resolution, and the role of influence and authority. Although we may use all these ideas and many more, we focus neither on their relative strengths or weaknesses nor on the scope of their utility. The point bears repetition: we are not much concerned with the usual, broad methodological questions but with the much more specific question of what is really important in the study of Canadian politics.

Let me illustrate this point. The significance of environment, broadly defined, has been a major bone of contention among political scientists for a long time. In this book we do not debate the issue but acknowledge that environment is consequential, at least to some degree. Accordingly, in Part One, five writers assess the significance of five different dimensions of the environment as keys to understanding Canadian politics. Similarly, without asserting exactly where any one of us stands in the continuing controversy about studying values, we note the obvious fact that ideas play a noteworthy part in Canadian politics. Thus, in Part Two, two scholars with related, though distinct, perspectives evaluate the extent to which such an emphasis can help us to understand the broader subject.

Part Three deals with structures. In earlier decades, the description of structures dominated the literature. Now the relevance of description is hotly debated; let the debate continue. In the meantime two contributors who believe that the study of structures is still useful explain why they hold that view and draw our attention to the supposed centrality of certain structural arrangements.

Part Four treats processes, sometimes defined as the dynamics of a political system. We could have evaluated many processes, but we limited ourselves to three that have come to be considered central in Canadian politics.

Part Five focuses mainly on political actors and their power. For decades, indeed centuries, political writers have debated the utility of the concepts of power and powerful groups. This volume does not join that ongoing debate. Rather, assuming that power is an important, if not basic, concept, we ask who actually exercises great or ultimate political power in Canada and to what extent an understanding of each of the four hypotheses analyzed provides us with knowledge about the entire political system.

The sixteen chapters all deal with Canadian politics, but they do not begin with the same set of assumptions, although every one of us obviously has to begin with some sort of assumptions. However, they all reflect the view that description by itself is inadequate and that not everything in a political system is of equal importance; but that is where the agreement ends. Different basic perspectives lead equally competent experts to give sharply different views of what belongs at the core of our study. But all contributors agree that no single approach is sufficient to explain all that we ought to know about the topic. There is some consensus that alternate, even competing, approaches complement each other and can be equally useful, although perhaps for different purposes. Students should recognize that each approach throws light on important insights. Readers will soon note the considerable overlap, especially in certain sections; this is intentional and should serve to clarify differences in interpretation.

For our purposes we have defined politics very broadly. In its most comprehensive meaning it refers to the art and science of government as well as to those structures, organizations, and activities through which individuals or groups of people seek to achieve power, freedom, economic rewards, or other benefits. More than two thousand years ago, Aristotle defined politics as those arrangements and relationships found in more or less self-sufficient communities. Half a century ago, Max Weber said that politics involved the enforcement of law and order in a specific territory by a dominant authority employing coercion, threatening to do so, or at least capable of doing so. More recently, Harold Lasswell has argued that politics involves the shaping and sharing of power having the purpose of determining who gets what, when, and how. In a similar vein, David Easton asserts that the essence of politics is the production and authoritative allocation of values, both tangible and intangible. For the present, we will include all of the above emphases in our working definition of Canadian politics. As our study progresses we will doubtless want to reassess and revise certain aspects.

The approaches presented here were selected mainly because, either implicitly or explicitly, they are all found frequently in textbooks and scholarly articles dealing with Canadian politics. Doubtless, additional approaches might have been included to good advantage. For example, chapters dealing with communications theory, Freudian analysis, and the legal approach (which would have been included if this book dealt with American politics) would have added interesting perspectives but, given space limitations, a line had to be drawn somewhere. Several readers suggested that a chapter on quantification should be included but it seemed to me that quantification is not really an approach but rather a tool with which one may test certain kinds of approaches and theories.

It might be argued that the sixteen topics represent an arbitrary, not entirely logical, selection; I trust that is not the case. They were chosen in the belief that they reflect usage and, as Vernon Van Dyke once put it, "that it is more significant to comment on usage than to devise an entirely logical classification scheme."

The theoretical coherence and unity of this volume derive from the fact that all the contributors address themselves to the same question: "How significant is the given approach in the study of Canadian politics?" They all delineate a specific approach; they all assess the strengths and weaknesses of their approach; most of them raise questions about other approaches as well as respond to questions raised about their particular approach; and all the illustrations involve Canadian politics. Moreover, all contributors present a macro-perspective.

The variety of approaches presented in the following pages demonstrates once again the rich diversity and vitality in the study of politics. It also reminds us of the absence of any general agreement on approaches or widespread acceptance of any single integrating or synthesizing theme.

In assessing the various approaches, readers may want to keep several questions in mind: Does the approach adequately explain the important changes and developments in Canadian politics? Does the approach deal with major questions or does it concentrate on details? Given the dynamic and changing nature of Canadian politics, is the approach becoming more useful or less useful? Is the scope and generality of an approach adequate? Is its scope tortuously extended or not? Is the approach compatible with existing knowledge and earlier approaches and, if not, then is the more recent approach clearly more useful and convincing? Does the approach allow for modification and reformulation in the light of new findings? Finally, and very generally and subjectively, which approach provides the greatest enlightenment?

In order to make this book as readable as possible, an effort has been made to avoid scholarly jargon and rhetoric. We have tried to be direct, concise, and simple. Our hope is that you will find as much satisfaction in reading these chapters as we had in writing them.

J.H.R.

Approaches to Canadian Politics

Part One:

The Environment Shapes Canadian Politics

Environment, or setting, refers to the various forces that influence the political system. These range from such tangible factors as geography to such intangible phenomena as historical development. In this section, five experts demonstrate, or speculate, how certain environmental factors have affected Canadian politics.

Without suggesting that human decisions have been dictated or determined by inanimate nature—a naive dictum that must not be allowed to discredit a responsible geographic emphasis—the first chapter shows how Canadian politics has been affected by mountains, rivers, borders, and anything else that can be depicted on a map. The vast reaches of the impenetrable and seemingly inexhaustible North, the crowded cities near the American border, and other geographical factors such as distance, watersheds, and population clusters, obviously play important roles. Perhaps it is true that geography, more than anything else, has shaped Canadian politics. Professor Whebell raises many basic questions about the physical environment.

The second chapter, while acknowledging the significance of geography, asserts that the truly important factor is not Canadian geography per se but the relationship with our giant neighbor to the south, the only country with which Canada shares a border. As the 1957 Fowler Report noted, "No other country is similarly helped and embarrassed by the close proximity of the United States." Maybe this American propinquity is the single most pervasive and influential fact for Canada. Professor Redekop suggests that whether we focus on geography or structures, on elites or culture, on economics or on history, the continental fact is preeminent.

Chapter 3 demonstrates the great influence of economics. The productive capacity of the economy, the giant corporations which themselves have power authoritatively to allocate "values" and manipulate consumption, the web of monetary and tax policies, the extensive labor-management regulation, the welfare state and the increasing governmental intervention in the free economy, all constitute part of a very complex relationship between economics and politics. But maybe it is not really a question of relationship. Could it be that Canadian politics is merely Canadian economics by another name? Professor McCready's analysis describes the close interrelationship.

In Chapter 4 Professor Hockin reminds us that Canada does not exist by itself but is greatly affected by interactions with other nations. Without understanding foreign affairs, we can never fully understand Canada itself.

Chapter 5 focuses on the past, stressing the importance of using chronology as both an ordering and an explanatory device. History is not only the main laboratory of political science but its basis. Perhaps Charles Beard was right: "Man speculates only in terms of the things he knows —things that have come out of the past." Professor McNaught explains why, without an assiduous study of the past, we cannot understand the present. Small wonder that many political scientists, not only in the area of theory, frequently write history though they may call it by another name.

1

Geography and Politics in Canada: Selected Aspects

C. F. J. Whebell*

The primary geographical fact about Canada is its enormous size. This alone underlies a whole family of political issues, historical and current. Only the U.S.S.R. and the People's Republic of China occupy larger territories, at least if one considers only coherent, single portions of the global surface. This leaves Canada as physically the largest polity with a democratic form of government—in the Western sense of the term. These two facts—great size and democratic traditions—make Canada unique and therefore of interest to students of politics, even if no other facts were relevant. But three other geographical facts distinguish Canada from almost all other national entities.

First of these is Canada's northerly position and the high latitudes to which it extends. Only the U.S.S.R. is comparable in this respect. Then there is the wide variety of landscapes in Canada, each of which provides a different basis for human settlements and life styles. Only a small fraction of the total area of Canada, however, has so far proved amenable to permanent settlement of much density and so the population of Canada is very scanty for its physical area and distributed in a very irregular manner. The third fact is Canada's global position, making it a very close —intimate is not too strong a term—neighbor of the most powerful democratic nation on earth, the United States, and a near neighbor, over the polar sea, of the presently most powerful socialist state, the U.S.S.R. With coastlines on three oceans, Canada is readily accessible for merchant shipping on both the Atlantic and the Pacific. In addition, all parts of the country now have quite good connections by air, some via the polar route, to Western Europe, which still has the greatest concentration of economic activity in the world.

*Associate Professor and Chairman, Department of Geography, University of Western Ontario.

A geographer approaching a study of the politics of Canada needs always to keep these facts in mind, indeed to begin with these facts as given. In general, geographers try to take realistic long-term views of the phenomena they study, and this is no less true of those who take a special interest in a study of political matters. The great geographical facts pertaining to any nation tend to have persistent effects on much of the political life of that nation or, to put it in more humanistic terms, these great facts provide perennial or recurring problems to be solved and challenges to be met in the survival or development of that nation. Politically, the responses lie chiefly in political institutions and policies.

On the whole, then, geographers studying the politics of Canada tend to start from the geographical facts and attempt to identify the influence they have on political events and on the political processes themselves. This can be done at several levels, from the local up to the global, from the geographical context of a single village to that of the entire nation in relation to the rest of the world (geopolitics). Certain parallel tendencies can often be seen between cases at different levels, and the challenge to the geographical investigator here is to devise appropriate conceptual tools to deal with a wide variety of cases with such parallels. In a federal nation such as Canada, a special set of problems arises from the way in which constitutional authority is shared; this often means that the challenge posed by a geographical fact is not dealt with as a single problem but has to be solved on various levels according to the constitutional structure. For example, in a major river or lake, the water as a resource is a provincial responsibility, but as a transport medium it is usually a federal matter, while the most immediate problems of water management may be most severely felt by some local authority on the waterway.

Three major concepts, or sets of concepts, are the foundation of a geographer's approach to the understanding of the complexities of Canadian politics, or, more precisely, to the identification of geographical realities of which the political system must always take account in some way. The first of these concepts is that of *resources*. Of the mineral, vegetable, and animal substances that occur in the world, those that are useful to man are considered resources; also included are certain physical or chemical processes such as the movement of water in streams and tides, the diffusion of heat from deep crustal sources (geothermal energy), and solar radiation and the emission of energy by radioactive elements. Not all natural substances and processes are necessarily considered to be resources at any one time. Muskrats are a resource (fur) but field mice are not, at least in themselves. Winds blowing near the ground are an energy resource, though not much used at present; but the vast energy of upper altitude winds such as the jet stream (*not* the trail of a jet plane) are not.

A notion of utility to mankind, either immediate or potential, is thus included in the concept of resources. What is considered a resource must, therefore, change according to its perceived utility. In turn, this perception varies with the state of technology as, for example, in the exploitation of petroleum deposits beneath the sea floor. This is now feasible but was almost unheard of a half-century ago. Even much more recently it was not considered practicable except in highly special circumstances. This one change alone has had profound effects on the concept of national sovereignty in the oceans and has led to much political stress even within Canada over which level of government, federal or provincial, has primary jurisdiction in this new domain of sovereign claims.

Distance, in addition to being itself a factor in the political events and processes, has a lot to do with how important a resource or potential resource is seen to be. For decades after the discovery of quality coal deposits in Alberta, very little of that coal could be mined profitably for shipment to Ontario, which consumed vast amounts for domestic and industrial purposes. Instead, the mines of Pennsylvania and West Virginia supplied the Ontario market. Only with political interference through massive subsidies could Alberta coal be transported for three thousand kilometres overland and still be available in the lower Great Lakes area at prices competitive with those from the much closer United States. The side effects of a high tariff charge, which in some respects is a subsidy, have made this tactic undesirable. Petroleum and natural gas are more easily transportable by pipeline, of course, but here political problems have arisen over the best routes, as there are a number of alternatives, each serving a somewhat different set of markets.

Some known substances and processes remain only potential resources because there is not yet an economically feasible method of transporting them great distances to the areas where they can be used to satisfy some demand. This category includes coal deposits in the Arctic archipelago.

This brings us to the second main concept that is part of the geographer's approach—the configuration of the population in relation to the territory; or, to put it somewhat more technically, the regional systems in which most of the important social and economic activity takes place and through which the political system is powered. Gold, as it is often said, is where you find it; but people are only where they have settled and made permanent homes. And it is a fact of life that people tend to cluster rather than to spread themselves evenly over the earth's surface. They cluster in hamlets, villages, towns, cities, metropolises, and certain linked sets of metropolitan urban complexes often called "megalopolises." Dependent on each grade of such clusters, in both social and economic terms, is a territory of appropriate extent—a few square kilometres for a hamlet, perhaps a half-million square kilometres for a metropolis. The dependent area of a metropolis includes, of course, sets of lesser clusters (cities, towns, etc.) with their own dependencies. One whole set of clusters plus dependencies forms a geographical entity termed a regional system, containing an urban hierarchy. The relationships between regional systems and among the clusters of different rank within one system are very much involved in many political issues, especially those we shall consider later under the concept of decentralization.

Each population cluster with its dependent territory comprises what may be called in political terms a core-periphery system: the cluster comprises the core and the rest of the area the periphery. A city may be a subsystem within the periphery of a metropolis, while a village may be a sub-system within that of the city. A geographically distinct set of these subsystems keyed to a metropolis or large city comprises a regional-level core-periphery system, although a complete and perfectly tidy nesting of the subsystems within the regional systems is not to be found in reality. The major aspect of the core-periphery concept that has relevance for the purpose of this book is that at each level the *core tends to provide the political leadership and local source of authority* for its dependent periphery. As a result, each such system or subsystem has tended historically to function as a political community and to become formally delimited by boundaries as a political territory under the authority of its respective core. A town or city would thus have become the core of a county or municipal district, a large city or metropolis that of a major section or province.

The political functions of larger cores are to some extent stacked; thus greater Halifax is both the major city forming the core of the province of Nova Scotia and also that of Halifax County. But the constitutional levels of authority are of course quite different and involve different institutions and buildings.

Two major ideas must be included in the concept of a geographical core-periphery system. First, the rapidly increasing concentration of population and economic activity in the core clusters, and especially those of metropolitan rank, has led in this century to an increasing disparity between them and their dependent peripheral areas (provinces or counties, at least). The cities get bigger and more powerful politically as legislative constituencies are redistributed to keep the representation-population ratio within accepted limits. The rural and small-town peripheral communities stagnate or even decline and so lose political strength.

The second idea is that the meaning of geographical facts such as distance, implying economic cost, is undergoing constant change. While the absolute physical distance between two towns, for example, remains the same, the social and economic meaning of that distance does not. The construction of a railway eases the communication difficulty and normally results in a greatly increased interchange of people, goods, and messages between the towns; the closing of a railway may, conversely, drastically reduce the level of intercommunication and so foster alienation. This is one of the single most important facts in Canadian history and politics. Innovations in the technology of transportation and communications, such as telegraphs, telephones, electronics, motor cars, airplanes, pipelines, containerization, and computerization, have all had far-reaching effects. But when a link in some newly developing transportation or communications network is established between a large city and a smaller place, the advantage generally lies with the former which can, with each set of innovations, administratively dominate and commercially compete with the subsystems in its dependent periphery. Hence, for example, we see the disappearance of country stores, one-room schools, or small industries such as cheese factories from rural and smaller urban places.

The great size of Canada with its immense distances and energy requirements for surface travel has meant that through historical settlement processes a number of distinct regional core-periphery systems have become established. The type of terrain and the pattern of land resources suitable for permanent agricultural settlement mean that some regional systems are large and some are small or fragmented. The northerly latitudes of Canada inhibit intensive settlement and so the major regional systems are in the south of the country, adjacent to the United States. Because none of the major regional systems of Canada is really immediately adjacent to shipping on either the Atlantic or the Pacific, the pull of the United States for commerce, migration, and information flow is relatively strong for inland regions of Canada. Paradoxically, the pull of the United States is also strong for the smaller regions on the two coasts, since the distances to major U.S. regional cores are much less than to any other country and the historic connections are well established through coastal shipping and kinship links resulting from migration. These geography-related north-south links have profound political significance.

The third main concept used by geographers studying political processes is that of the boundary. It is too frequently forgotten that a political boundary is an artifact, not formed by nature but by men, generally to resolve or prevent conflict between political communities. Where two such communities contend for territory lying between them, the conflict, which may even develop into armed encounters, is most often resolved by dividing the contentious zone and delimiting a formal boundary. When such a boundary is drawn through unsettled country it may be called an "antecedent" boundary. This type of boundary is very common in Canada at all levels of territorial unit, from the 49th Parallel, through the interprovincial level, such as the Ontario-Quebec boundary north of Lake Temiscaming, to the county and municipal district level where the phenomenon is common. Where rural townships are established, their boundaries are almost all highly arbitrary, though not usually formed to resolve local conflicts.

All antecendent boundaries lie across potential resources, dividing drainage basins, mineral-rich zones, forests, ecological habitats for fur-bearers and food fish, and so on into the jurisdictions of different polities. Though often unrecognized or ignored as resources at the time the boundary was delimited, these geographical phenomena become very important later on; the growth of society and technological changes all too often render the conflict-resolving boundary of long ago into a conflict-causing problem today. The current controversy involving the boundary between Labrador and Quebec is a classic example. More will be said about boundaries later.

In the light of the foregoing discussion, let us now examine the salient geographical patterns of Canada as shown on the accompanying maps. Map 1 shows the major physical divisions of Canada. The southern part of the Interior Plains and the Great Lakes-St. Lawrence lowlands are the best suited to commercial agriculture. Elsewhere such high-quality land is restricted to strips and isolated parcels in valleys and plateaux of the Cordillera and the Appalachians. Very little of the massive Canadian Shield can support effective agriculture, which can be undertaken only where

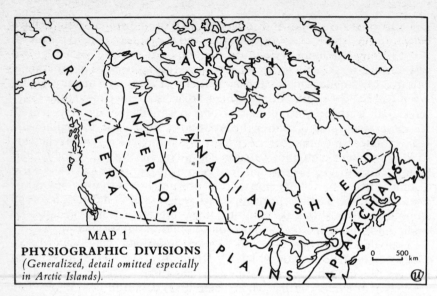

MAP 1
PHYSIOGRAPHIC DIVISIONS
*(Generalized, detail omitted especially
in Arctic Islands).*

overlying sand, gravel, or clay provide a base for cultivation. Canada's
northern position means that much of the Shield is not suitable for agricultural settlement, habitable areas being more northerly than the
Ontario-Quebec Clay Belt or the Lac St. Jean basin.

Other kinds of resources, of course, occur throughout the Shield and
in the Cordillera and the Appalachian mountains and plateaux. Mineral
deposits are the most notable, from the vast iron-ore deposits in the easternmost portion of the Shield to the gold in the valleys of the Yukon.
However huge an ore or fossil-fuel deposit, its size is finite and it will eventually be depleted; these are truly nonrenewable resources. Settlements
based only on a mining industry are therefore impermanent, as far as that
source of economic support is concerned. Sooner or later policies will
have to be formulated to provide for the people displaced by the closing of
the mines or quarries, the cause of many a ghost-town. Recent examples
are Rossland, B.C., Elliott Lake, Ontario, and Belle Island, Newfoundland, all in various stages of decline.

Many mineral deposits are remote from already well-settled districts,
and thus, as one-resource settlements, are entirely dependent on transported foodstuffs and very vulnerable to economic adversity. But mineral
and fossil-fuel resources, if discovered in agricultural regions, can give a
reinforcing impetus to the farming economy by increasing local markets.
The agriculture, on the other hand, can provide a second source of
economic support for the regional subsystems containing the nonrenewable resource. The only part of Canada in which both agriculture and
mineral resources (fossil fuels) occur together extensively is the south-
western part of the Central Plains, mostly in Alberta. Here a transportation innovation, pipelines, has altered the significance of distance and
made the minerals and fossil fuels accessible both to the adjacent United
States and increasingly to the more distant Great Lakes-St. Lawrence low-

lands. Any territorial unit with both agriculture and mineral resources obviously has a good hedge against possible economic distress; it also has a political bargaining edge, since in Canada resources per se are under provincial jurisdiction, though export arrangments are subject to federal control. The contention between Alberta and Ottawa over oil and gas exports and between Saskatchewan and Ottawa over potash quotas are cases in point.

Much of the southern part of the Shield, most of the Appalachians and the Cordillera (especially the Coast Range), and the northern portion of the Central Plains support another important resource—trees. Most of Canada's total area of commerical forest consists of smaller species of trees used for pulpwood, a large proportion of which is used in newsprint. On the West Coast there are huge trees suitable for saw logs; in the East there is also some commercial saw milling. This is a renewable resource and capable of providing for a permanently settled, if sparse, population as long as regrowth is properly managed. Here again the problems of resource management versus export trade involve an overlap between jurisdictions. The greater part of the forest-resource production of Canada is for export, since the domestic market is disproportionately small in relation to the total resources. Again there is federal-provincial contention over the division of revenues, optimal rates of resource depletion, management and reforestation practices, and pollution control.

Map 2 shows population patterns. The settlement concentration in the two regions mentioned earlier is quite apparent, as are the separate clusters of population in the East, the West, and on the Shield. There is not enough space in this chapter to go into historical explanations, but it will suffice to note that in the development of the political units in the East, first colonies and later provinces, the formal territorial units reflect the interests of some core of settlement and authority. For example, New

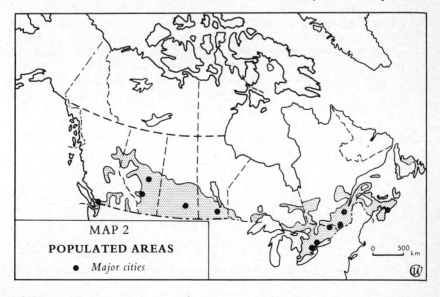

MAP 2

POPULATED AREAS

• *Major cities*

0   500 km

Brunswick is the dependency of the lower Saint John Valley, including Fredericton. In the Plains section, however, the territorial units were in part imposed by the federal government of the day as a matter of expediency, and the cores, except perhaps for Manitoba, have largely formed since 1905 within the antecedent boundaries. The division of the Great Lakes-St. Lawrence lowlands into two polities with no particular physical separation is a result of the well-known cultural differences between two incipient regional systems—anglophone Upper Canada (Ontario) and francophone Lower Canada (Quebec).

Because of the strong southerly bias of the populated cores, the vast bulk of Canada's territory forms a dependent periphery to these cores. Thus the Shield is largely administered by Quebec, Ontario, and Manitoba; the Appalachians by Quebec and New Brunswick, with an extension to Newfoundland; the Cordillera by British Columbia, and the nonagricultural Central Plains by Saskatchewan and Alberta. The North is largely administered federally. Both historically and at present this vast periphery has been seen as a zone of expansion, exploitation, and investment by the respective provincial cores. But in the case of a really major find or development in a provincial peripheral area, the capability of the appropriate core to develop it without help from elsewhere, including federal grants or underwritings from "eastern" banks, may be very doubtful; besides there is the usual problem of the export market which involves the federal government. A further complication occurs when the mineral body lies in two provinces.

All the foregoing discussion suggests some ways in which resources can involve political problems. The general supervision and control of mineral, fossil-fuel, and living resources always raises the question of the equity of the shared benefits. Should a province derive all the financial benefits from a major resource within its territory or should some revenues be distributed in some way to less fortunate provinces and, if so, how? The whole question of sharing off-shore mineral revenues comes to mind as an extreme example. In the multiple-use category of resources such as high-quality land on which farming, forestry, wildlife conservation, water management, and human recreation may all be in competition, ought the pattern and balance of uses be determined by one local jurisdiction or by a set, or stack, of jurisdictions balancing the interests of both local and more distant regional systems of population and their political surrogates? The answer must involve the creation of temporary or permanent institutions, such as committees, boards, or commissions, and the development of effective policies through the political process.

To explore this question a bit further, consider Map 3, showing principal river basins. It is immediately apparent that almost all major drainage systems in Canada are shared between jurisdictions. Some are shared with the United States, including Alaska, especially the Yukon, Columbia-Kootenay, the Red, the St. Lawrence and the St. John; the latter two are in part split down the middle by the international boundary as are four of the Great Lakes. As a natural substance, water is perhaps the most versatile commodity on earth. It is vital for life processes, essential

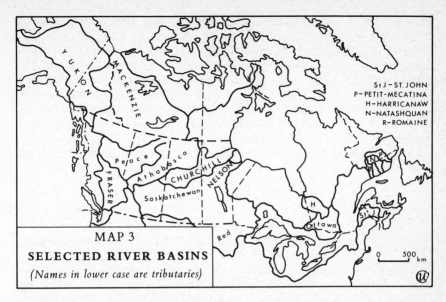

St J – ST. JOHN
P – PETIT-MECATINA
H – HARRICANAW
N – NATASHQUAN
R – ROMAINE

MAP 3

SELECTED RIVER BASINS

(Names in lower case are tributaries)

0   500 km

for domestic comfort and health, indispensable for industrial processes, significant for transportation, effective as an energy source, desirable for recreation, and aesthetically attractive in its natural settings. When this variety of characteristics—and it is not at all an exhaustive list—is set against the divided jurisdictions over the major water sources in Canada, it is not difficult to imagine the myriad conflicts and issues that involve water in some way or other. Long-term and complex problems associated with the St. Lawrence Seaway Authority, the Columbia River development, and the Garrison diversion project on the Red River all illustrate the point.

There are several problems involving water use that occur frequently. A user of river water, such as a factory or a city, may return raw effluent to the stream and impair the quality of the water for downstream users, such as farmers. This situation is further complicated if the offender is in one province and the affected area in another. A dam built for electrical energy may flood a tract of forest and cause great damage to hunting and other recreational activities. If a stream is to be tapped for irrigation, it has to be decided how the available water is to be apportioned upstream and downstream of the intakes. If an area is flooded because of the construction of a dam for canalization, power, irrigation, or any mix of these, it has to be decided whether compensation should be paid to those whose property is damaged and, if so, how damages should be assessed. These questions may seem to be legal issues, and they are, but only with respect to existing laws! The key questions are whether these laws should be changed and what criteria politicians should use in changing them.

When large-scale issues arise, as in the case of the Columbia River, individuals are not of central concern. The benefits of the dams, especially the Skagit Dam, accrue to large and distant clusters of people, chiefly in the United States; the immediate effects are borne by the small local population in British Columbia. The original agreement and its later versions involved state, provincial, and two federal governments. The same is true of the other international rivers, for example the Souris. The Canadian downstream part of this river may be adversely affected by a dam on the nearby Missouri River, which could perhaps divert too much water into the Souris for the well-being of Canadian farmers.

At a lower level, conflicts over the management of waterways within provinces have resulted in institutions such as the Conservation Authorities in Ontario which involve all municipal entities, rural and urban, that lie wholly or partially within the respective river catchments. The province has a strong presence on these institutions and rationalization of water management and related land uses has been furthered by such arrangements.

A special comment is required on the resources of Canada's oceans. The living resources are almost all mobile, fish and shellfish, whales and seals. To harvest these resources, it is necessary to employ essentially hunting procedures. Regulation, conservation, jurisdiction, and enforcement must therefore be based on principles other than simply designating a territorial area such as a timber berth or licensed trapline. Such waters are also used in Canada's foreign trade and exploited by fishermen, whalers, and sealers from distant countries. Finally, the Atlantic resources in particular are shared by five provinces. Potential political issues are therefore plentiful and highly complex.

Land, living, mineral, and water resources thus are rich sources of conflict and of issues that the political system at some level must try to resolve. In one aspect, such a problem may be an electoral issue, and become part of the campaign rhetoric of candidates. In another, the problem may be taken up by a bloc of legislators, or by a party, who want to resolve it by enacting laws, amendments, or orders-in-council. In still another, a class of resources may be important enough for a whole bureaucratic department to be assigned to oversee them and their exploitation. Thus many provincial and federal governments have or have had departments of mines, fisheries, forestry, wildlife, agriculture, water resources, electrical energy, conservation, irrigation, public parks, and so on. In recent years, however, greater public awareness of the interrelatedness of many natural phenomena has led to merging of these departments into departments of natural resources or of the environment. Outside the constitutional structure, there are, of course, pressure groups, such as farmers, sportsmen, and other associations who press their special viewpoints on the legislatures.

Because society is always changing, its views of resources are also going to change. Concern with pollution was not a popular issue a generation ago, nor was concern with the indirect effects of human activities on an ecosystem; for example, clear cutting of forests often had adverse effects on the water quality in streams because of greater sheet erosion of soil; or the use of persistent insecticides, such as DDT, on one pest had drastic long-term effects on major carnivores, such as salmon, at the top of food chains. Technology is constantly finding new ways to process and use natural resources and, conversely, technological innovation leads to constant reappraisal of resources and even to fresh ways of viewing or discovering unsuspected resources. The economy is constantly changing, mostly in the direction of imposing greater demands on the more easily available resources. With higher prices for given resources, the distance factor will be overcome and there will be greater pressure to exploit ever more remote areas of the Canadian interior and north, raising the probability of yet more conflicts and social issues. Prominent at this time are the questions of native land rights and the transportation of fossil fuels (oil and gas) from the shores of the Arctic Ocean along the Mackenzie River Valley. Land rights in the James Bay project of Quebec were settled by a monetary agreement. But has the last been heard of this problem?

Resources, then, will constantly provide new political issues for the geographer to study. There can be no final answers as the old Victorians, and maybe even their grandchildren, thought there could be. But there is another category of political issues that is best organized geographically by the core-periphery concept, and it is to this that we should now return.

It was noted earlier that the size, surface configuration, and northerly position of Canada have led to a number of regional core-periphery systems of disparate size and strength. Historically, this disparity was not very evident before the end of the nineteenth century, but the four original members of Confederation were certainly spatially distinct. Nova Scotia comprised a set of small settled zones around the margin of the peninsula, linked to Halifax; this is still true. New Brunswick comprised mainly a string of settlements along the Saint John Valley, together with a scattering of other settlements, mainly Acadian, along the Gulf shore; this is still mainly true, except for the relative rise of Saint John and Monction.

The Canadas were the other two charter members of the federation. Lower Canada (Quebec) extended down the St. Lawrence from just above its confluence with the Ottawa, but the settled area was not very deep and the main portion of the Shield and much of the Appalachian portion were unsettled and politically unorganized. Quebec City was the core and seat of authority. Since 1867 the population of Quebec has expanded into much of the Appalachians and some parts of the Shield, especially the Clay Belt and Lac St. Jean, though some of these settlements are not highly successful in economic terms.

Upper Canada (Ontario) was focused on the Lake Ontario plain and the peninsular wedge between Lake Erie and Lake Huron. It also has greatly expanded its population, particularly in a northerly direction onto the Shield as far as the Clay Belt with additional pockets on Lake Superior. Some of these colonization efforts have not been conspicuously successful either. Both Ontario and Quebec attained their present size when they were awarded vast tracts of Shield in 1912 to bring them to the water's edge of Hudson Bay.

In the Great Plains section of Canada the old focal point at Fort Garry, now greater Winnipeg, forms the core of Manitoba. This province also reached its present size in 1912 by extension to the shores of Hudson Bay.

But between Winnipeg and the Rocky Mountains the formation of the major urban clusters was less an outgrowth of agricultural colonization than of the railways built in the period 1885-1905. Since there were two main routes, the Canadian Pacific and the Grand Trunk Pacific, two main sets of towns were founded: Regina-Calgary and Saskatoon-Edmonton. When provincial status was granted in 1905 these sets were broken up by the boundary between Alberta and Saskatchewan, which was an official survey meridian or reference line. These two provinces therefore each began life with two potential major urban centers rather than one. However, even when they are considered as core regions (e.g. Regina and Saskatoon together with linking transport media) they still dominate only a small portion of the total territory they were awarded by fiat.

On the Pacific Coast, the colonial authority core at Victoria on Vancouver Island, reflecting the maritime character of the then British Empire, has been outstripped by the mainland port of Vancouver, reflecting the continental bias of Canadian federalism. Still, the institutions of authority remain at Victoria. It is therefore useful to refer to the pair, rather than to either one, as the core region of that province. Like Regina-Saskatoon, the transportation links between the mainland and the capital are included, though here they are ferry or airplane routes. The dependent periphery of British Columbia includes small pockets of agricultural settlement and mining activity in the interior valleys, as well as more extensive lumbering and ranching areas in the interior plateaux which are hard to reach from Vancouver by surface transport. By contrast, the intensive lumbering of the coast range and islands make effective use of water transport by sea to Vancouver.

The twentieth-century phenomenon of centralization has transformed the geographical patterns of Canada's regional systems and shows no signs of abating. The most obvious sign of this complex process is the explosive growth of the central core city or urban complex. This growth in part has resulted from immigration to Canada, most of which is destined for metropolitan centers. But there is also a very significant component from internal migration and this gives rise to a number of political issues.

Much internal migration to the large core cities is of young adults. As a result, the populations in the source areas of the periphery get gradually older on the average, with resulting high pressure on the social services, especially geriatric, of local municipal governments. This loss by migration of the employable part of the population both reflects the lack of local jobs and contributes toward the difficulty of inducing new economic investment in peripheral areas, many of which show numerous signs of economic distress. Many of the peripheral areas of the Canadian provinces, as has been shown, support only primary resource activities, often only one, such as fishing. When the resource is severely depleted, as in the case of the East Coast fisheries, or when lowered general price levels reduce production, as in the woodpulp industries of Quebec and Ontario, the economic distress of such peripheral areas can intrude upon the national political scene. Creation of special welfare programs such as family allowances, of special rehabilitation agencies such as PFRA (Prairie Farm

Rehabilitation Agency) which was created as a result of the dustbowl disaster in the Prairies, and DREE (Department of Regional Economic Expansion) represent the implementation of policies intended to effect a more equitable distribution of economic growth. DREE has been especially concerned with peripheral areas in various provinces which seem to have at least some natural potential for local growth; examples include fisheries on Lake Winnipeg, tourist development in northern Ontario, and wood-processing industries in Quebec and the Maritimes. The allocation of central funds to such projects and the designation of areas as eligible to receive funds are naturally matters for much political maneuvering, on a party or nonpartisan sectional basis, within federal and provincial parliaments.

A more direct consequence of the centralization process is the steady accumulation of political power by the core cities and metropolises, and the concomitant weakening of such power or influence by the peripheral areas. Ironically, this is done in the name of democracy—the "representation by population" principle. Each redistribution of constituencies, for example, tends to allocate more members of a parliament or legislature to growing cities, and fewer in total to the peripheral areas. In practice this means that many constituencies in peripheral regions get larger and larger. The legislature in Manitoba, for example, had sixteen members from Winnipeg metropolitan constituencies in 1951 and forty-one from the rest of the province; in 1974 the numbers were twenty-seven and thirty respectively. In the policy paper, *Design for Development,* published by the Ontario government in 1968, the two major objectives mentioned were the better equalization of economic growth throughout the province and an improved access to government by the people. In the latter case the objective is hardly achieved by the creation of constituencies as much as 160 km in length, and remote from the capital at that.

Overwhelmingly the single most striking geographical change in Canada since Confederation has been the growth of urbanization in the lower Great Lakes-St. Lawrence section: Ontario and Quebec. Each province has in general kept its regional structure of cities, towns, and villages, but the chief cities have grown to enormous size. Toronto still represents the core of Ontario, and comprises about a third of the province's population; but while Ontario has gained in overall population, the northern part of the province actually lost people between 1971 and 1976.

In Quebec, Montreal has outstripped its political superior and former economic peer, Quebec City. In fact, the Montreal-Ottawa combination must now be considered the core of the Canadian federation, though formed mostly after that fact, inasmuch as between them they include the chief political authority and a great deal of the commercial and financial leadership of the whole country. Thus at this level of conceptualization, the rest of Canada is politically dependent on this central core; numerous important political issues turn on the relationship between this core and the rest of the country.

The most important of these issues derives from geographical distance, and involves political integration. This may be defined as the general acceptance of the norms of national political life such as laws, legislative procedures, sources of authority, and so on. Communication is always essential to establish and maintain integration in a national territory, but clearly with Canada's huge size the problem facing the political leaders in Ottawa was and is a stupendous one. The historical solution was to weld together the colonies on two oceans by railways—the Intercolonial and the Canadian Pacific. In one form or another, however, this problem is still very much present, especially in view of the pulls to the south which are a feature of almost every region of Canada, and especially of the West Coast. In the present days of mass transportation and affluence it is easier for a Vancouverite to drive to Seattle than to Calgary; for a Winnipegger to visit Minneapolis than Toronto; for a Torontonian to take a trip to New York than to Halifax; and for a Montrealer to fly to New York or even to Paris than to Vancouver. In other words, the real cost of distance has become effectively less important, but not to the same extent in every region or in every direction.

One of the most salient consequences of the different shrinkages of distance has been the development, or at least the aggravation, of regional feelings of estrangement from or disaffection with the federal core at both the official or bureaucratic level and the commercial and popular one. This tendency obviously works against integration and in an extreme form may result in actual disintegration of the country through separatism. Some of this disaffection derives from resource management or revenue policies as explained earlier. The province owning the resource objects to the degree of federal interference in exploiting the resource through taxation, export arrangements, output quotas, production subsidies, and so on. Especially where the resource concerned is a primary foodstuff such as grain, livestock, dairy products, or fish, the producers presume the central federal authority does not appreciate their problems and their low income levels, which leads to particularist feelings. In extreme cases these feelings may lead to suggestions for a province such as Quebec or a set of provinces such as Western Canada to separate from the federation. Movements have also been proposed to separate part of a province to create a new one, such as in northern Ontario or Labrador.

Other forms of expressing disaffection have included the establishment of political parties of essentially regional origin and appeal. The primary producers of the plains region have organized several, two of which still exist: the CCF, an agrarian socialist party begun in Saskatchewan and now reconstituted as the NDP, and the Social Credit party, first prominent in Alberta. It is significant that attempts to transform both of these into national parties have been beset with difficulties; they have had to try to win members and establish a power base of voting strength in the populous lower Great Lakes-St. Lawrence region where interests and concerns are different. Reflecting the dominant views held in a primary-producing region, their party platforms have had to be restructured to appeal to more urbanized voters. Such attempts have met with only limited success. Perhaps an extreme example of this sort of problem has been the fate of the "national" Social Credit party, which decided to raise its sights to the federal level. In a matter of a few years the widespread though relatively low-level support across the nation shrank to a small area in the East where the francophone supporters gave the party their own title, Créditiste.

Conversely, the old, established national parties headquartered in the lower Great Lakes-St. Lawrence section have lost ground in various regional areas; the Liberals in the West and the Conservatives in Quebec, especially. The full reasons for this are of course complex and cannot be explored here. But two major factors are of great interest given a geographical orientation. First, the distance/cost between Ottawa and, say, Calgary inhibits close interchange of ideas and discussion of ideals, particularly on a mass basis; this is a special challenge for the integrationists. Second, there is little prospect that there will be established, or re-established, a national political party that can present one credible platform equally appealing to all sections of the nation, at least one with any chance of receiving a majority of votes in every section. Majorities, when they occur, will continue to amount to regional coalitions within a party, with all that this implies in terms of deals, trade-offs, compromises, and inconsistencies.

The political reaction of communities in the periphery to the accelerating accumulation of power by the core is also evident at the provincial level. Institutionally, the disaffection may be expressed by localized political parties such as the United Farmers of Ontario and Progressive parties in the 1920s and 1930s. It is also apparent in peripheral municipalities' complaints over what they perceive as exploitation by the core, especially in resource development. Though the local population may indeed be interested in some sort of growth and increased income and municipal revenue, they are often completely shocked by the rapidity and scale of such development when it arrives. Since the transportation links to a peripheral area are commonly rather poor, the sudden arrival of a new railway, a full-scale highway, or a landing strip makes the area suddenly accessible, and the resources there, whether timber, minerals, or energy sources, immediately change from potential to actual. Thus huge areas may be leased for pulpwood cutting, transforming comfortable small towns into roaring hives of economic activity and social stress, or startling somnolent villages into galvanic activity, to the discomfort and bewilderment of a population accustomed to a slower pace of life. Often the municipal councils are unable to cope with the pressures and ask for assistance from the province. Sometimes, as in the new Regional Municipality of Haldimand-Norfolk in Ontario, where a major industrial development occurred in an area of almost completely rural character, such assistance is thrust upon them without the asking—the British North America Act gives provinces total authority over municipal government. There are numerous other examples of such sudden resource developments across Canada.

A special case in point concerns recreation and tourism. Many small communities in the Canadian Shield and on the sea coasts and lakeshores had existed quietly for decades before the motor car explosion and road-building epidemic after World War I, and especially after World War II. As small remote communities suddenly became easily accessible there was wholesale development of summer cottages, hunting and fishing lodges, ski resorts, and hotels/motels, for example in the Muskoka Lakes area 160 km north of Toronto. With municipal voting rights dependent on real property, local voting power became dominated, at least potentially, by nonresidents. This was a windfall to the old population as long as the non-residents did not exercise these rights but could be assessed for taxes to defray essential local services such as schools. But two factors have changed all this. First, the cottagers and lodge owners came to demand higher levels of services, such as road maintenance, police and fire protection, and even water and sewerage, commensurate with the level of services in their city houses. Second, they began to make much more use of their properties on a year-round basis as better winter snow clearance on highways and all-terrain vehicles made areas accessible in winter. In a number of cases, the nonresidents' majority vote has elected a council that can legislate to the advantage of the cottagers and resort owners in opposition to the old permanent residents. Here is core-periphery conflict in a municipal microcosm: the core population controls the higher-order polity, the province, through its voting power at that level, while also controlling local elective councils in the periphery through their franchise as nonresident property owners. It is small wonder that the permanent residents of such outlying communities feel doubly threatened and sometimes find outlets for their anxieties by forming regional separatist or at least particularist movements.

The integration of Quebec into Canada and its converse require some special comment. The fact that it is a French-speaking regional system has meant that Quebec has remained distinct in two important ways. First, the life style (genre de vie) of the Québecois developed in substantial isolation from its parent country, France, and has therefore become highly distinctive, if not unique. Second, many essential elements of the Québecois life style were prevented from spreading into anglophone North America because of the language barrier. This condition did not, however, prevent many aspects of North American life, such as sports and the entire economic organization of society, from penetrating into Quebec. Quebec operates with a criminal code based on Britain's, the one that applies federally to all Canada, but has its own civil code based on the French model (the Code Napoléon).

The integration of Quebec into the Canadian federation has, however, so far been effected largely through anglophone links. This fact is, in turn, at the root of the development of Montreal-Ottawa as the federal core, with banks, insurance companies, and other major corporations in finance, communications, and manufacturing keeping their head offices in Montreal while operating nationally. Because of this, the functional language of higher business in Quebec has been English. Especially since the renaissance of the Québecois cultural identity in the early 1960s, this situation has seemed to many educated Québecois an unjust limitation on their upward social and economic mobility.

In a special sense, therefore, the rise of modern nationalism in Quebec and its expression in particularist and separatist political movements, either within existing parties or through new ones such as the Parti Québecois, is also an example of core-periphery antipathy. The core, though *within* Quebec, is not really *of* it, being properly a federal core. In distinction to this anglophone center of dominance, Quebec province is seen to be a disadvantaged periphery, which extends to the very foundations of the Sun Life Building and Place Ville Marie.

Quebec as a provincial territory has part of a federal-level core (Montreal) within it, as well as its historic provincial-level core (Quebec City). It also has an enormous territory (1.5 million square kilometres) as periphery, not very much of which is either purely francophone or particularly closely integrated with the provincial core. One such area is the Ottawa Valley, which has much better communications with Ontario than with Quebec City, and also has a large proportion of anglophone residents, especially in Pontiac County and near the federal capital city of Ottawa. The latter, designated by Quebec as the Outaouais Region for local government purposes, has been undergoing something of a development boom because of federal office building. A suggestion from the PQ government that the province would liberate Outaouais from federal dominance was met with a rebuff by the mayor of Hull. Clearly the economic self-interest of that city and region would seem to lie with the federal system. In an independent Quebec, Hull would be very much a provincial peripheral area rather than part of a higher-order federal core.

The northern portion, Nouveau Québec, which before transfer in 1912 was the Territory of Ungava, comprises nearly half of the present province, and lies entirely within the Canadian Shield. It is populated mainly by Inuit and Amerindians whose early contact with Europeans was through the Hudson's Bay Company. Their official language is, therefore, English and any connections they have with European-style institutions such as a church are British-derived rather than French-derived. The integration of this vast tract with the core of Quebec is an enormous challenge to the provincial (or national) government. That this will not be free from conflict has already been indicated by statements of Inuit leaders, particularly on French-language school instruction, for some of these statements hint at separation from Quebec. The mineral and energy resources of Nouveau Québec, however, are actually and potentially so valuable that integration policies are certain to be strongly and increasingly pursued. The development of the James Bay hydroelectric scheme is a clear indication of the provincial government's determination to keep control of this vast peripheral zone.

The far northern lands and waters of Canada also require some special comment. Though these immense tracts, well over a third of Canada's territory, are often referred to collectively as the North, they include different types of land in stark contrast to one another. The Yukon Territory, formed to provide an administrative framework during the Klondike gold rush, lies in the Cordilleran section. It is well forested and besides gold contains other metallic mineral resources. The Mackenzie District includes the northerly continuation of the Central Plains, drained by the Mackenzie River system and quite well wooded; the eastern half of this territory, however, is largely barren Canadian Shield country, but contains large mineral deposits such as those at Echo Bay (Port Radium) and Yellowknife. To the east of this district, which is bounded by the arbitrary line of the 102nd west meridian, is the District of Keewatin. Including parts of northern Manitoba and Ontario before 1912, the present territory is mostly composed of barren tract of Canadian Shield west of Hudson Bay. But, potentially of much more significance is the fact that Keewatin includes the whole of the bay itself, its islands, and the entire bed and subsoil of the bay. The boundary of this territory is at the water's edge of Hudson and James Bay where Manitoba, Ontario, and Quebec end (or begin). As elsewhere in the Shield, the metallic mineral resources are the principal known economic significance of this district. What may lie beneath the waters of Hudson Bay is open to speculation.

The final district, Franklin, is truly Arctic, consisting of all the islands north of Canada's mainland and Hudson Bay, together with the Melville Peninsula. These islands are not entirely in the Canadian Shield formation and so nonmineral resources such as fossil fuels occur. An exception is Baffin Island, which contains iron ore.

The whole northland is, of course, federally controlled. That is, it is a direct periphery of the federal core of Ottawa-Montreal. But the distances are so huge that integration is a problematical and enormously costly business. Resources, though known, are undeveloped because of the high costs of getting equipment in and material out. An exception may be allowed in the case of the District of Mackenzie, which is readily accessible from a main settled part of Canada, central Alberta, by road, rail, and pipeline linked with seasonal traffic on the Mackenzie waterway and, of course, by air. Even so, only the Mackenzie Valley section of the district is served very well by surface communications. Before the airplane and radio were available, integration was rudimentary indeed.

Two important points remain to be discussed on the North. First is its position between well-populated sections of North America and the Soviet Union. It thus stands as a defensive frontier, a killing ground, a warning zone in which distance means time—in tens of minutes—for countermeasures in the event of hostilities. The United States necessarily has a vital strategic interest in this vast area for its own national survival and has occupied a number of locations, under mutual defence agreements, for radar and other installations. Both Ottawa and Washington need to keep close control over this strategic area.

The second point bears on the distribution of population in the North. Nowhere is there much of a concentration of people; the entire population of the North totals less than 65 000, of which nearly half is in the Mackenzie District and mostly toward the southern part at that. In Franklin and Keewatin a very scanty population is scattered in extremely tiny clusters along the shorelines with very few inland settlements. In these two districts the people are mostly Inuit, but in Mackenzie there are some five or six tribal groups of Amerindians, who have recently formally termed themselves collectively the Dene nation.

The normal integration of these northern Territories into the Canadian polity is beset with severe difficulties. The most obvious of these, as has been mentioned, is distance. Another is social and arises from the growing sense of community among the Dene and the Inuit, and increasingly is expressed in the rhetoric of national feelings and aspirations. Almost certainly this trend occurs because formerly widely separated groups can now communicate closely with each other by aircraft and radio and so begin to establish a common outlook. This has reached the stage of legal opposition to the commercial groups in the developed provinces that, with federal government acquiescence, have undertaken major construction and exploitation of resources. Some talk has been reported of making a new province in the North, but this movement does not yet appear to be well institutionalized. Nevertheless, it is similar, on a larger scale, to the case of the Muskoka area cited earlier in that outsiders have had more power over local decisions than have local residents.

The major issue in the integration of the North concerns the sharing of the benefits of development. On the one hand, there are the rights of the original inhabitants, though these rights are not very precisely defined in law. On the other, are the needs of the south, the Canadian provinces and the United States, to develop the resources of the North for their cities and industries. On this side, there are two levels to consider, the federal and provincial. Constitutionally, the Territories are under federal jurisdiction. But if the federation is dominated by the two most populous provinces, Ontario and Quebec, then these necessarily have the most real influence on federal resource-development decisions; similarly, the firms undertaking exploration and exploitation and the corporations financing such activity are mostly headquartered in the East, in or near the federal core. The charge of colonialism seems hard to refute. Further, the materials coming out of the North en route to the major markets must cross at least one province, Alberta. Here also is a source of possible conflict about potential pollution, land expropriation, and royalty-sharing from transit.

There is also the complex issue of the location of the main processing plants for the raw materials, plants which create employment and revenue where they are built. Ought they to be in the North, which is almost impossible; in the nearest populated and well-organized area, such as Alberta for the Mackenzie District; in the main markets in eastern Canada; or outside Canada altogether? The answers to these questions do not depend entirely on the economics of location, as specific location costs can be greatly affected by political action in awarding production subsidies, tax holidays, special depreciation allowances, direct land grants, and transportation concessions such as freight-rate adjustments. The peripheral areas in provinces with substantial mining, pulpwood, and energy developments are, of course, subject to the same sorts of constraints. The North is different, however, in that the federal government is closely involved in a very direct sense, rather than mainly indirectly through its transportation and foreign trade responsibilities.

The last major concept for discussion here is that of territorial boundaries. Most of the internal and external land boundaries of Canada were settled well in advance of colonization and can thus be described as antecedent boundaries. Where these cut across terrain in a straight line, as the Saskatchewan-Alberta and northern Ontario-Quebec boundaries do, they traverse land of differing quality for settlement and transport development. In some areas along the boundary, such as swamps, rugged hills, or barren soil, communication is difficult, while in others it is more favorable. In the latter the real meaning of the boundary is most evident; it clearly divides two political systems with different laws, policies, social benefits, traditions, and even language. These areas are therefore most likely to be theaters of conflict should the policies of the adjacent provinces be divergent or even contrary to each other. If one province has a low charge on timber rights, while its neighbor has a higher one, the movement of timber across the provincial boundary (even surreptitiously) can be significant. Cross-boundary movement of other commodities such as wines and liquors is a well-known example of the same principle.

What is more important in this connection is the possibility that a part of one province may be more accessible to the core of another province than to its own core. In extreme cases this can result in a section of one province's periphery becoming socially and economically better integrated with the other province's core, though of course formal political control remains with its proper core. Such a condition exists in the Peace River section of British Columbia, the Kenora region of northwestern Ontario, the Clay Belt of northeastern Ontario although here it is more the social connections with Quebec that predominate, the middle Ottawa Valley portion of Quebec, easternmost Ontario near Montreal, the Madawaska section of the Upper Saint John River which was once termed "La République de Madawaska," and the south shore of the Gaspé, to name some outstanding examples. It would be an exaggeration to say that such conditions must necessarily lead to disaffection and separatism, but they certainly provide peculiarly interesting challenges to the respective provincial cores to devise and implement effective integrationist policies.

All the internal (interprovincial) boundaries in Canada are well-established and, discounting some very minor issues, agreed upon —except for one. The Labrador portion of Newfoundland had for centuries had an indeterminate inland limit. Since there was no pressing reason for Canada to exploit resources in that area, there was no urgency to formalize the boundary. An exception involved the coastal zone itself because of fisheries jurisdictions, especially over the tiny permanent and temporary settlements on the north shore of the Gulf of St. Lawrence. This boundary has lain just west of the Strait of Belle Isle since 1825. But the beginnings of timber exploitation into Labrador early in the twentieth century precipitated the issue of formal control between Canada, in right of Quebec, and Newfoundland, a separate British colony at the time.

Eventually the Labrador boundary question was arbitrated in 1927 by the Privy Council of the United Kingdom which made extensive use of the watershed in its delimitation of the Labrador section. This sort of boundary, like that between southeastern Quebec and the United States or that between southern British Columbia and Alberta, makes a great deal of sense in resolving issues over water or timber which has historically been exploited by means of waterways. But such a boundary may be conspicuously unsuccessful in terms of land and mineral resources, and of the ability of the political systems it separates to integrate effectively, through surface communications, their peripheral sections. The discovery and exploitation of the vast iron ore deposits in the geological structure known as the Labrador trough restarted the conflict, since the resource itself and the transport routes to exploit it cross the watershed defined as the boundary. The province of Quebec has never been happy with the 1927 arbitration, and maps published in that province have for decades carefully omitted any boundary line except for a hint of one just inland of the Atlantic coast. The agreement over the Churchill Falls power scheme between Quebec and Newfoundland points up this issue, since in effect Newfoundland agreed to share benefits with Quebec, including a guaranteed price for the electricity, without prejudice to the boundary issue as such. But it is obvious from a map that the Churchill Falls area is more easily integrated into the Quebec system than into that of Newfoundland proper, the capital core of which is just as far from Churchill Falls as is Quebec City, but much more difficult to reach.

A brief mention should be made of the new marine boundary issues. These are very complex and involve both the surface and waters of the sea, with the sea floor itself now a distinct aspect. Most of the issues are on the international level, such as the extension of territorial waters or control over pollution, sea-floor mining, or fisheries jurisdiction into oceanic waters. On these issues Canada confronts many foreign countries that have interests in the oceans around Canada. Internally these issues usually involve the provinces but at times also the federal government. For one thing, federal jurisdiction over navigable waters excludes provincial involvement; for another, the St. Lawrence is the only coastal zone where several provinces border on a body of salt water but are *not* jurisdictionally excluded from its use, as is the case around Hudson Bay.

Five provinces border the Gulf of St. Lawrence and extend into it. The advent of deep-sea mineral exploitation techniques such as drilling and dredging, has meant resources in the Gulf have had to be reappraised. Since the provinces have authority over natural resources, provincial authority was taken to extend over the sea floor and subsoil, as if it were submerged land. Since the early 1960s, the five Gulf provinces have agreed among themselves, without federal concurrence, to divide up the floor of the Gulf and have designated formal boundary lines to this effect. These are also antecedent boundaries, though of course in anticipation of mineral exploitation rather than settlement. Quebec obtained the greatest portion as it owned the tiny Magdalen Islands in the middle of the Gulf.

A special sort of federal-provincial conflict has occurred in the marine areas. When in 1966 the government of Canada proclaimed sovereign control over the sea floor and subsoil out to a depth of 200 metres of superjacent water in the first instance, this was taken to mean that the coastal provinces could simultaneously extend their jurisdiction over the minerals and potential revenues from this zone. The federal government challenged this position and does not recognize the eastern provinces' own partition of the Gulf floor, holding that such new territory accrued to Canada and not to a member province in the first instance. A Supreme Court decision upheld the federal claim in the Pacific, against the contention of British Columbia. But on the Atlantic Coast a political solution has been arrived at dividing up the potential revenues without actually settling the territorial claim; Newfoundland, however, is not a subscriber to the agreement. There is a true provincial-federal boundary in these coastal zones, because, unlike the situation in the Northwest Territories, there can never be a local self-governing council to represent a local settled (submerged?) population. Whether such a peculiar boundary is more likely to prevent or to promote conflict between provinces and federal government must remain an open question.

The discussion in this chapter about the geographical approach to Canadian politics has been highly selective. It has not dealt with external aspects, which involve foreign relations; it has not dealt with spatial patterns of voting, a subject commonly studied by geographers; nor has it dealt with *connectivity,* or the analysis of networks and flows, also a subject of geographical study, except very generally under the term "integration." Rather, the discussion has attempted to portray the broad realities of the physical and human patterns of Canada which must for a very long time be the theater and the basic stage on which our political drama is enacted. Some representative issues were included to show how important these basic geographical realities are in the scenarios of politics at federal, provincial, and local levels.

The geographer's approach does not, however, have much to say about who the actors on this stage, the political elite, shall be, nor does it deal with personalities, family background, ideological slant, or intellectual taste. All these human qualities are very important to the kinds of institutional structures and policies designed to cope with the nation's problems. The political elite is concerned with devising strategies and long-term social and ideological goals, and it is against these goals that the geographical realities and patterns must be re-evaluated and against which they take on new meanings from time to time.

Diefenbaker's "northern vision," Richard Rohmer's "mid-Canada corridor," Trudeau's "just society" are examples of imaginative concepts that give new meaning to already existing geographical patterns and prescribe the new priorities for programs to achieve these goals. Such policy orientations often change quickly as politicians rise to and fall from power and as newcomers look for new concepts or at least slogans to help their rise to power. The same real fact, for example, rural decline, may be of little interest to one set of politicians but of fundamental concern to another; which set may be dominant at any time depends among other things on the nongeographical principle of representation by population, on a driving need for political power in particular individuals, and on the leadership qualities of a few of them. None of these vital aspects of politics comes inevitably from the kind of reality geographers write about; but all have some connection with that reality in terms of an electoral power base, of the effective political expression of sectional interests, and of the careful balancing of sectional needs and aspirations to maintain an overarching concept of nation.

Almost every Canadian is at one and the same time subject to governance at local, provincial, and national levels. At each level geographical realities provide fundamental constraints on the policies in terms of the real costs of government, of resource development and management, and of integration. But if it is true that changing geographical realities can require adjustment of policies, of institutions, and even of constitutions, then it is also true that policies can transform geography. Macdonald's concept of a nation from sea to sea was ultimately expressed in Confederation, in integrating railway systems, and in totally altered regional patterns of population and production. It could happen again that an important idea, translated through policies and programs, would change the total geography of Canada in significant ways.

If we want to understand Canadian politics we cannot ignore Canadian geography. From pre-Confederation days right down to the present, questions relating to geography have always been immensely important. In a fundamental sense, whether we think of 1867, or railway building, or resource development, or defense policies, or core dominance, or regionalism, or separation, geography holds center stage in the drama of Canadian politics. In the end, the geography of Canada provides both obstacles and opportunities, but it is within the framework of the political system that these must be identified if the obstacles are to be overcome and the opportunities realized.

SELECTED REFERENCES

ATLASES AND MAPS

A map is above all a device for displaying large amounts of information for rapid visual retrieval, and permits simultaneous analysis, on a spatial basis, of numerous categories of data, for example, political areas vs. population vs. transport. Careful comparisons between differently constructed maps of the same area can yield a great deal of insight into the relations between various geographic factors and politics, whether in terms of issues and policies or electoral questions.

CANADA, DEPARTMENT OF ENERGY, MINES AND RESOURCES. *The National Atlas of Canada.* Toronto: Macmillan, 1974. A well-presented encyclopaedia of geographically displayed information about Canada as a whole and an essential source for data on population and resources.

CANADA, DEPARTMENT OF ENERGY, MINES AND RESOURCES, POLICY RESEARCH AND COORDINATION BRANCH. *Isodemographic Map of Canada.* Ottawa: Queen's Printer, 1971. A computer-transformed "map" that shows how the nation would look if mapped on the basis of units of population rather than units of land.

CANADA, DEPARTMENT OF MINES AND TECHNICAL SURVEYS. *Atlas of Canada.* Ottawa: Queen's Printer, 1957. An older edition of the national atlas. Comparisons with the newer one help to identify trends and processes.

CHAPMAN, JOHN, ed. *United States and Canada.* Toronto: Oxford University Press, 1967. This compact atlas illustrates Canada's position in comparison with the United States.

DEAN, W.G., ed. *Economic Atlas of Ontario.* Toronto: University of Toronto Press, 1969. For Ontario's economic and social patterns this atlas is very useful.

KERR, D.G.G. *A Historical Atlas of Canada.* Toronto: Thomas Nelson, 1961. The emergence of Canada's geography is depicted, along with numerous specific events such as battles, communications, and territorial evolution.

PLEVA, E.G., ed. *The Canadian Oxford School Atlas.* Toronto: Oxford University Press, 1957. Rev. ed., 1973. Though very selective, the thematic maps of Canadian geography are innovative and stimulating.

WEIR, T.R., ed. *Atlas of the Prairie Provinces.* Toronto: Oxford University Press, 1971. A good overview of the patterns of Canada's Great Plains, at scales larger than national atlases.

BOOKS

BERRY, B.J.L., E.C. CONKLING, AND D.M. RAY. *The Geography of Economic Systems.* Englewood Cliffs: Prentice-Hall, 1976. Especially Part 5, "Regional Economic Structure," and Chapter 15, "Canada: The Challenge of Growth and Change." The two chapters indicated comprise a good discussion of the basic geographical structure and processes of Canada.

CARTWRIGHT, D.G. *Language Zones in Canada.* A reference supplement to the Report of the Second Bilingual Districts Advisory Board. Ottawa: Queen's Printer, 1976. The question of federal language policies is given a geographical dimension in this monograph.

DOSMAN, E.J., ed. *The Arctic in Question.* Toronto: University of Toronto Press, 1976. The complex political significance of the Arctic is examined by a number of experts.

NICHOLSON, N.L. *The Boundaries of Canada, its Provinces and Territories.* Canada, Department of Mines and Technical Surveys, Geographical Branch, Memoir 2, 1954. Toronto: McClelland and Stewart, Carleton Library Series, 1977. This monograph is the standard work on the evolution of Canada's boundaries.

RAY, D.M. *Dimensions of Canadian Regionalism.* Canada, Department of Energy, Mines and Resources, Policy Research and Coordination Branch, Geographical Paper No. 49. Ottawa: Queen's Printer, 1971. A large number of social and economic variables are given detailed statistical and cartographic treatment.

SIMMONS, J. AND R. SIMMONS. *Urban Canada.* Toronto: Copp Clark, 1969. The phenomenon of Canadian urbanism is presented clearly and briefly. There are useful bibliographies after each chapter.

TROTIER, L., gen. ed. *Studies in Canadian Geography,* 6 Vols. 22nd International Geographical Congress. Toronto: University of Toronto Press, 1972. Robinson, J.L., ed. *British Columbia.* Grenier, F., ed. *Quebec.* Smith, P.J., ed. *The Prairie Provinces.* Macpherson, A.G., ed. *The Atlantic Provinces.* Gentilcore, R.L., ed, *Ontario.* Wonders, W.C., ed. *The North.* A series of short monographs which together comprise probably the most comprehensive introduction to Canadian geographical topics. Each volume has a short bibliography.

WARKENTIN, J., ed. *Canada: A Geographic Interpretation.* Toronto: Methuen, 1968. The standard interpretive work on the geography of Canada.

YEATES, M.H. *Main Street, Windsor to Quebec City.* Toronto: Macmillan, 1975. This work deals in considerable detail with the most intensely occupied area of Canada, including some comments on projections into the future.

2

Continentalism:
The Key to Canadian Politics

John H. Redekop[*]

Geography has made us neighbors;
history has made us friends;
economics has made us partners
and necessity has made us allies.
            President John F. Kennedy
            addressing Members of Parliament,
            Ottawa, May 17, 1961

INTRODUCTION

As used in this chapter, the term "continentalism" has two meanings: on the one hand it refers to North American continental activities involving both the United States and Canada as a single region; on the other hand it describes Canadian-American relations, specifically the overwhelming American impact on Canada, involving both governmental and private sectors. As will shortly be evident, this chapter deals mainly with activities associated with the second definition. Canadian politics is given a broad definition, including not only public policy, policy makers, and the structures within which they operate but also the phenomena associated with political socialization as well as the historical background.

My general hypothesis is that the overall American impact on Canada is the most important single fact for Canada and the main key to understanding Canada's emergence, development, and current situation. In other words, it is not only a matter of Canada's only neighbor, the most powerful country in the world, permeating and influencing almost every

*Professor and Chairman, Department of Political Science, Wilfrid Laurier University.

aspect of Canadian life, but a matter of the Canadian experience and Canada itself being a response to the United States and American developments, both governmental and private. Thus, while an understanding of the great gamut of Canadian-American relations is not in itself sufficient to explain Canadian politics it is absolutely necessary.

Given the magnitude and diversity of continentalist forces, J.M.S. Careless's observation seems appropriate: "To a large degree the American presence has shaped Canada. . . . One is tempted to conclude, in fact, that there could not be a Canada without the United States—and may not be a Canada with one."[1] In a similar vein, J.B. Brebner begins his last volume by asserting that "perhaps the most striking thing about Canada is that it is not part of the United States."[2] Sounding a more pessimistic note, Mel Watkins begins his introduction to Laxer's volume by stating that, "It has been our fate in this century to be absorbed increasingly into the American empire, to be dominated in virtually every aspect of our lives by giant American-based corporations."[3] Arguing that the American impact has already destroyed the basis of an independent Canada, the highly respected conservative philosopher, George Grant, expresses the most gloomy note of all: "Canada has ceased to be a nation, but its formal political existence will not end quickly."[4] Even as cautious a commentator as Mitchell Sharp, then Canada's Secretary of State for External Affairs, in his carefully considered statement on "Options for the Future,"[5] agreed that, "In a Canada undergoing profound and rapid changes . . . there has been a growing and widely felt concern about the extent of economic, military and cultural dependence on the United States."[6]

Why is it that such diverse observers, writing from various political perspectives, all stress a common theme? Let the evidence speak for itself. Given space limitations, I cannot describe the full scope and intricacies of North American continentalism with all its official and unofficial activities, but I shall present the most consequential aspects.

BOUNDARIES

Let us begin by considering Canada's formal boundaries. Since Canada has only one neighbor, all her boundary delineations, including the early ones negotiated by Great Britain, have involved only that neighbor. The Peace of Paris (1783) established the general line between the Atlantic and the western tip of Lake of the Woods with later adjustments spelled out in Jay's Treaty (1794) and the Webster-Ashburton Treaty in 1842.

The 1817 Rush-Bagot Convention for naval disarmament on the Great Lakes—the world's oldest disarmament treaty—stabilized relations in that region. Later the Treaty of London (1818) established the western border along the 49th parallel to the Rockies and the Oregon Treaty (1846), despite the Democratic Party's 1844 campaign slogan of "54°40' or fight" and President Polk's repeated threats extended the line to the West Coast and around the southern tip of Vancouver Island. The San Juan

Islands dispute was resolved in 1872 when the invited arbiter, the German Emperor, anxious to improve diplomatic and trade relations with the United States, awarded those islands to the United States. The last segment of Canada's boundary was fixed in 1903 when the American government, amidst shouts and threats, managed to win the bulk of its demands on the Alaskan frontier with Canada. President Teddy Roosevelt's "big stick" policy had once again paid off handsomely. With the ratification of the Boundary Waters Treaty in 1909 and the concomitant establishment of the International Joint Commission, Canada's boundary arrangements were complete. The country's demarcation thus became fixed and acceptable to the United States but for Canada the price was high; thousands upon thousands of square kilometres that once were part of British North America, from the Aroostook Valley to the Upper Mississippi to the Oregon Territory and to part of the Alaska panhandle, were permanently lost.

HISTORICAL DEVELOPMENTS

The gradual setting of boundaries, while politically significant in its own right, was quickly overshadowed by other political developments. The noted historian, A.R.M. Lower, asserts that "Canada, from the British Conquest on, had always been under the influence of the southern god. In every year of her history she has been 'Americanized.' "[7] American political designs on British North America were evident early. Already in the 1770s John Adams orated, "The Unanimous Voice of the Continent is Canada must be ours!"[8] A few decades later Thomas Jefferson, president from 1801 to 1809, declared the conquest of Canada "a mere matter of marching."[9]

With the outbreak of hostilities in 1812 the loosely associated Canadian provinces discovered a new sense of commonality—resistance to the United States—a recurring and frequent phenomenon ever since. Having frustrated the expansionist efforts of the bumptious southern giant, the emerging northern Dominion experienced its first clear sense of self-conscious nationhood. But Canadian anti-Americanism, triggered by the first colonial efforts at military conquest during the Revolutionary War and reinforced by the War of 1812, has always been tempered by widespread admiration, even envy. The attraction-rejection theme has been continuous. The positive sentiment was evident as early as 1837 when the militant Patriotes of Lower Canada included the actual words of the American Declaration of Independence in their own revolutionary resolutions: "In accordance with the example of the wise men and heroes of 1776, we hold as self-evident and repeat the following truths: That all men are created equal; that they are endowed by their Creator with certain inalienable rights; that among the number of these rights are life, liberty and the pursuit of happiness."[10] Canadian imitation of things American had an early start.

Canadian Confederation in 1867 was itself largely a response to the

American presence; as a defense strategy, as imitation, and as general alternative. When in 1866 the Americans ended the 1854 Reciprocity Treaty, the Canadian provinces found themselves in dire economic straits. To complicate matters, American commercial interests and settlers were rapidly encroaching on the western Prairies, American railroads were being extended into various Canadian regions, many Maritimers were looking enviously at the more prosperous New England states, and the victorious Northern Army stood poised for a possible march northwards. Granted, there were domestic French-English, economic, political, regional, and imperial factors that also played various roles but the truth remains that the major factors that brought about Canadian Confederation were American. "The fear of a slow death by absorption and a quick one by annexation hung over Canadian constitutional debates."[11]

The Fathers of Canadian Confederation were well aware of American notions of northern Manifest Destiny and of general American sensitivities. In order to avoid further irritation of the United States, the original name "The Kingdom of Canada" was changed to "The Dominion of Canada." But the Americans were not fully assuaged; when it became clear that Canadian Confederation was imminent, the U.S. House of Representatives adopted a resolution expressing displeasure with such action. As P.B. Waite observes, "the American purchase of Alaska one day after the British North America Act was signed on March 29, 1867—three months before it was proclaimed—was no mere coincidence."[12] Significantly, many U.S. maps of North America continued as late as 1888 to show Canada as a future addition to the great republic.[13]

Not surprisingly, the Fathers of Confederation saw much of value in the American political system. After due consideration they adopted the U.S. federal pattern—with slight modifications—as well as some constitutional guarantees, and a few years later established an American-style independent judiciary. Of course, I must hasten to add that these features were added to what remained, and evolved as, an essentially British parliamentary system.

Clearly the United States played a major and complex role in the whole Confederation phenomenon. Keeping in mind the events and pressures of 1867 and in view of the economic, defense, and cultural situation a century later, some Canadians understandably wonder whether the very agent that made the creation of Canada possible, the one that pushed Canada from "Colony to Nation" in one empire, has not in recent decades pulled it from "Nation to Colony" in its own.

Throughout the intervening century the United States has constantly loomed large in Canadian political and diplomatic affairs. The entry of British Columbia into Confederation on July 20, 1871 was closely related to American penetration and blandishments. The final vote in the B.C. legislature favoring union with Canada rather than with the United States was carried with only a slim majority. Predictably, Canada's first venture into diplomacy, albeit as part of the British team, involved the United States and took place at the Washington Conference of 1871. The extent to which Canada lost out in the ensuing treaty remains a significant question in its own right.

We have already noted the 1909 Boundary Waters Treaty which gave rise to the International Joint Commission with its wide range of judicial, administrative, investigative, and arbitral functions. This continuing and very useful agency has facilitated close cooperation between the two countries in resolving a host of problems and disputes from navigation and fisheries to pollution, water diversion, and hydroelectric power development.

A few years later, in 1911, a resurgence of anti-Americanism generated widespread rejection of the Reciprocity Treaty which the American Congress had reluctantly approved. Chanting the slogan, "No truck nor trade with the Yankees," the Canadian electorate soundly defeated Prime Minister Laurier's government and thus rebuffed their powerful southern neighbor. The election of 1911, it should be noted, was only one of many in which Canadian-American relations played a major part.

Other major events and developments that demonstrated the dominant role the United States played in the evolution of the Canadian polity included the Canadian-American Halibut Fisheries Treaty of 1923, the first Canadian treaty that was not countersigned by a British representative; the 1927 establishment of Canada's first permanent diplomatic mission to a foreign country when Vincent Massey was sent to Washington; and Canadian emulation of American isolationism, and even neutralism, during the 1930s.

Throughout these years the close and intense Canadian interaction with the United States was counterbalanced by equally close ties with the United Kingdom and the Empire. But with the granting of full Canadian autonomy in the Statute of Westminster, 1931, the situation began to change. By 1940, with the Ogdensburg Agreement between Prime Minister Mackenzie King and President Franklin Roosevelt, the traditional relationships had taken a new turn. In the words of Frank Underhill,

> All our Canadian experience since 1783 has depended upon our successful manipulation of our particular North Atlantic triangle—the triangle of Canada, Great Britain, and the United States. Until very recently our Canadian world has in effect consisted of this triangle. . . . We survive as a distinct individual Canadian entity by the feat of balancing ourselves in a triangle of forces in which Britain is at one corner and the United States at the other corner of the triangle. . . .
>
> This British century of our history was a happy century for us. We achieved independence without separation. . . .
>
> But now we have gone through the revolution of 1940. In that year we passed from the British century of our history to the American century. We became dependent upon the United States for our security. We have, therefore, no choice but to follow American leadership.[14]

The accuracy of Underhill's assessment was substantiated by subsequent events. Canada became caught up more and more in the American orbit. The 1956 House of Commons pipeline debate about an American-owned line drew attention to economic penetration. The Cuban crisis of 1962, the Bomarc missile crisis of 1963, the 1969 S.S. Manhattan voyage, and the long Canadian delay in recognizing Peking, which was caused partly by direct pressure from Washington but mainly by "Canadian uneasiness about provoking the wrath of the U.S. Congress,"[15] all illustrated the preponderant American role in Canadian foreign affairs and continental defense. Small wonder that many Canadians have been preoccupied with finding a counterbalance. John Diefenbaker, looking to the past, tried to revive Commonwealth ties but had little success. Although Pierre Trudeau later attempted to establish a counterbalance by broadening Canadian-European relations, with similar lack of success, his observations upon first entering federal politics are revealing. He commented that only about 30 percent of Canada's foreign policy was devised by the Department of External Affairs; the remaining 70 percent was "predetermined" by the Canadian-American relationship.[16]

Trudeau's concern was shared by others. The best-selling Canadian author, Farley Mowat, wrote about "the privileged position presently enjoyed by Canadians as 'most-favoured serfs',"[17] and even the sometimes continentalist head of the Canadian Institute of International Affairs, John Holmes, said that "The real nature of the alliance relationship is obscured by the rhetoric of 'free and equal partnership'. . . . We have bored the world too long with sermons about our unfortified frontier. In a nuclear age the unfortified frontier between a super-nuclear power and one which could not defend itself for five minutes is an irrelevant symbol."[18] The acute disparity between the political impact and military significance of the two countries could not and cannot be denied.

CONTINENTAL DEFENSE

The general thesis of this chapter, namely, that knowledge of Canadian-American relations holds the key to an understanding of Canadian politics, broadly defined, is nowhere better illustrated than in the area of defense policy. The rather surprising fact that the government's 1970 restatement of foreign and defense policy[19] contained no analysis of Canadian-American relations does not alter that situation. Six brochures were issued; none dealt with the one country that is truly important for Canada, the one that has greater impact on Canada than all the others combined. The explanation may lie in the fact that the complex relationship cannot be easily summarized or perhaps the Trudeau government does not consider continental affairs to be foreign affairs. After all, when Canada was intimately tied to, and subordinate to, the United Kingdom, Canadian-U.K. relations were not thought of as foreign affairs either.

In a fundamental sense, Canada has never been master of her own defense. "Actually, if the criterion is the ability to defend oneself without outside help, Canada has never been a sovereign state."[20] As early as 1823 the American Monroe Doctrine already extended a form of security to Canada, a fact acknowledged by Prime Minister Laurier at the turn of the century when he asserted that "the Monroe Doctrine protects us against enemy aggression."[21] In a more substantive form, continental defense arrangements were initiated in the late 1930s and are thus relatively recent. It was at Kingston, Ontario, in 1938, that President Roosevelt first gave explicit assurances that the United States, despite its general isolationist stance, stood ready to protect Canada from external aggression: "I give you assurance that the people of the United States will not stand idly by if domination of Canadian soil is threatened by any other Empire."

On August 18, 1940, at a dark period during the Second World War, the new policy was formally enunciated. Meeting at Ogdensburg, New York, Franklin Roosevelt and Mackenzie King met to discuss continental defense. The Ogdensburg Agreement created a Canadian-American alliance and established the Permanent Joint Board on Defense, an organization still functioning, to "consider in the broad sense the defense of the north half of the Western Hemisphere."[22] The PJBD, in turn, soon recommended the construction of the Alaska Highway, various new military airfields in Canada, and other defense projects. The Hyde Park Agreement of April, 1941, further intertwined Canadian and American military and economic war efforts by coordinating the mobilization of resources in both countries. In actual fact, as defense integration proceeded, Canada increasingly became only a junior partner. Assessing those developments, George F.G. Stanley has written that "at times Canada was treated as a satellite rather than a willing partner."[23]

In November, 1945, the American government requested Canada to extend the wartime alliance indefinitely; the Canadian government agreed. Shortly thereafter, in February, 1946, the Joint Military Cooperation Committee was established to formulate further joint defense plans. In late 1946 the long-standing Rush-Bagot Agreement was amended to allow for naval training ships to operate on the Great Lakes. Many arrangements were undertaken in Canada via orders-in-council. Finally, on February 12, 1947, Prime Minister Mackenzie King rose in the House of Commons and described the Declaration on Defense Cooperation, which was simultaneously announced in the United States. This agreement, proposed by the PJBD, committed Canada to the exchange of observers, exchange of military personnel, the establishment of common standards for arms, equipment, training methods, etc., reciprocity of "military, naval, and air facilities," and much more.

As a result of the Korean military action in 1950, Canada and the United States drew up a "New Hyde Park Agreement" in October of that year. The two countries agreed on detailed and close coordination involving military procurement, economic controls, use of raw materials, and industrial mobilization. Increasingly Canada functioned as a region within American continental defense planning. Not surprisingly, C. D. Howe, speaking for the Canadian government, announced in Washington that "Canada and the United States march side by side in time of war."[24]

A part of this dual march involved the building of radar installations across Canada to detect possible Soviet approaches across the Arctic and thus give advance warning to the bombers and interceptors of the American Strategic Air Command. They were of very little use to Canada. In 1951 the governments of Canada and the United States agreed to build the first line, the Pinetree Line, across southern Canada. About two thirds of the total cost of $450 million was borne by Washington; the rest by Canada. The second line, the Mid-Canada Line, was begun even before the first was completed, apparently because experts agreed that the first line was already inadequate if not obsolete; it had been built too far south. This second line, recommended by the PJBD, was entirely Canadian in equipment and financing, at a cost exceeding $170 million. Even before this second line was completed, the United States had already begun construction of a third line, the Distant Early Warning (or DEW) Line. The cost, about $450 million, was borne entirely by the United States. The line was completed in 1957.

Much controversy developed over alleged surrender of Canadian sovereignty in the Arctic. "The Americans ran the DEW line as if the Arctic were part of the United States. The Liberal M.P. for Mackenzie River, Mervyn Hardie, objected to the fact that when he wanted to visit his constituents at the stations he had to obtain a permit from the American head office in Paramus, New Jersey."[25]

The next stage in the development of total American hegemony in continental defense was the creation of the North American Air Defense (NORAD) in 1958. This new air defense arrangement bound the security of the two countries together as nothing before had done, except wartime emergencies during World War II. The American assumption was that the security needs of the two countries were basically synonymous. A few Canadians objected to the close security embrace[26] but most, including both the Conservative Diefenbaker government and the Liberal Pearson government, agreed to the proposals, perhaps fearing that failure to do so would provoke Washington to ask for something even more difficult.

In financial terms, NORAD could be seen as a bargain for Canada; the Americans agreed to foot more than 90 percent of the cost of providing as complete a security blanket as possible for the continent. But in political terms the cost was formidable. Theoretically the two countries have joint command but the arrangement was that the commander-in-chief would always be an American while the deputy-commander would always be a Canadian. NORAD headquarters was located in Colorado Springs, Colorado. The major innovation was that there was now a peacetime organization, having weapons, facilities and a command structure which could operate at the outset of hostilities in accordance with a single air defense plan approved in advance by the governments of Canada and the United States. The real clincher, of course, was that the commander, always an American, would always be operating under the direction of the President of the United States.

The degree to which the NORAD arrangements placed Canadian defense policy and security matters under American control became evident in the early 1960s. The Cuban missile crisis of October, 1962, was the acid test. As a result of President Kennedy's decision to challenge Soviet missile activity in Cuba, NORAD troops were alerted to be ready for immediate action. Prime Minister Diefenbaker was not consulted before the American decision. When he was eventually informed, he refused for forty-eight hours to sanction the alert but he was powerless to prevent it and against the explicit wishes of the Canadian prime minister, Canadian troops geared up for battle. The American authorities resented Diefenbaker's refusal to cooperate fully. Writing five years later, one of them observed that, "It wasn't as bad as it looked. This was because the Canadian forces went on full alert despite their government."[27]

The second crisis came the following year and may well have been related to the first. The Diefenbaker government, despite strong pressure from Washington, refused to arm its Bomarc missiles with nuclear warheads. Whether such a policy made military sense is still in dispute but in any event it was Canadian policy. The crisis escalated and in February, 1963 the minority Diefenbaker government was defeated in a House of Commons confidence vote. The Conservatives alleged American interference, especially in the ensuing election campaign which produced a Liberal government headed by Lester Pearson. The nuclear warheads were soon installed on the Bomarc missiles. A statement by Tom Kent, a senior official in the Liberal party who was later to become Prime Minister Pearson's executive assistant, gives some indication of Liberal party policy: "The first essential interest of Canada in the world today is the security of the United States; that takes overwhelming priority over everything else in Canada's external relations."[28]

The NORAD treaties were accompanied by certain economic arrangements, most notably the 1959 Defense Production Sharing Agreement. Continentalism in defense production had been agreed to as early as 1941 in the Hyde Park Agreement, but that had been during wartime; now an even more far-reaching arrangement was agreed to in peacetime. One reason why the Canadian government agreed to such a venture was that a large segment of its own fairly sophisticated defense industry collapsed in 1958-59 when production of the advanced, but costly, Arrow airplane had to be abandoned because the United States refused to purchase any of the planes. The Americans insisted on producing an acceptable alternative at home. Thereafter Canadian defense industries participated almost exclusively as subcontractors for the United States military-industrial complex, a relationship that persisted throughout the Indochina wars and continues today.

The key stipulation in the 1959 arrangement was that Canadian firms could henceforth bid on equal terms with American firms for U.S. defense contracts. The arrangement proved to be relatively lucrative for Canadian industry. In one year alone, 1965, Canadian arms exports to the United States amounted to $260 million or 30 percent of all Canadian in-edible end-product exports to the United States.[29] A corollary of these Canadian sales opportunities was that the Canadian government committed itself to purchase certain American war supplies for its own use. In

1966 such defense purchases in the United States amounted to $332.6 million.[30] The Canadian Minister of External Affairs could assert: "Think of the impossible position we would be in if the Defense Production Sharing Agreements were abrogated . . . to pull out would be to endanger our economy and safety."[31] However, the deal was at least as advantageous to the United States as to Canada.

Partly because of the booming trade in armaments and partly because of the resultant low defense costs for Canada—less than 14 percent of total national budget for Canada but well over 40 percent for the United States—subsequent Canadian governments have shown no reluctance in renewing the arrangements. Most recently, in 1975, the NORAD treaty was renewed by the Trudeau government for another five years. Of course, the NORAD treaty is only one part of a much larger whole; at present the total number of treaties between Canada and the United States exceeds 180, covering such diverse areas as "atomic energy, aviation, boundary waters, customs, defense, economics, extradition, finance, fisheries, health and sanitation, highways, maritime matters, migratory birds, military affairs, naval vessels, navigation, postal arrangements, hydroelectric power, tenure and disposition of property, smuggling, taxation, telecommunications, trade and commerce, and others. . . ."[32] Given such a context for formal defense treaties it is hardly surprising to have Canadian General Charles Foulkes assert that, "Canada has not always agreed with U.S. strategic policies, but it is usually frank enough to point out its views, and is staunch enough to support any challenge to our North American way of life."[33] The term "North American" is apt.

As Canada entered the last quarter of the twentieth century no one could seriously dispute the contention that Canadian security policies, Canadian defense production, perhaps even the bulk of overall Canadian foreign policy, can be understood only in the light of American hegemony in continental affairs.

CONTINENTAL ECONOMICS

We turn now to the second major area of American preeminence in the Canadian polity—the whole realm of economics. At the outset we need to emphasize two points; the awesome American economic influence on, and presence in, Canada, a sequel to historic British economic hegemony, has come almost entirely in response to Canadian desires, and, second, in large part the roots of this American economic penetration go back to Sir John A. Macdonald's 1879 tariff scheme, known as the National Policy. At first the National Policy seemed to be successful in that its aim of enticing foreign firms to establish branches in Canada was quickly realized. But in the longer term that kind of economic nationalism turned out to be self-defeating inasmuch as the Canadian government yielded up control over large segments of public policy. Accordingly, American corporations, and to a lesser extent American governments, came to play an ever larger role in Canada. Of course, part of that situation was simply the result of the naturally ominous impact of a massive economy on a relatively small neighboring one.

Let us briefly analyze the diverse ways in which American economic activity has influenced Canadian politics, especially in recent years. While focusing on current affairs we should keep in mind that throughout Canada's first century the American economic reality, from the tariff policies of the 1880s to the reciprocity question of 1911, to the Wall Street crash of 1929 and to wartime cooperation, was always a major question in Canada and frequently a central issue in election campaigns. Many of these American-related issues did not, and do not, pertain only to Canada, but their larger significance in no way decreased their importance for Canada.

Perhaps the most publicized aspect of the American economic impact involves investment, both direct and indirect. Direct investment refers to acquisition of minority or majority ownership in refineries, factories, warehouses, sales offices, natural resources, and so on. Such investment typically involves bringing in personnel, technology, machinery, brand names, and some measure of ownership and control. Much American money comes in as venture capital engaged in the discovery, refining, and merchandising of mineral resources, the development of certain agricultural commodities, the manufacture and distribution of consumer goods, and the operation of utilities and miscellaneous other activities.

Indirect or portfolio investments include bank loans and other credits given to foreigners, as well as the purchase of foreign bonds and debentures. The purchase of small amounts of Canadian noncontrolling equity stock by American residents would also fit into this category. The point to bear in mind is that indirect investment is basically a financial transaction that can be paid off while direct investment involves at least partial ownership and control. The difference between the two types of investment is, of course, crucial. In the case of indirect investment, control remains with the borrower; in the case of direct investment, it rests unequivocally with the lender and creates a liability that tends to be permanent and to grow.

As indicated in Figure 1, American investment has grown rapidly in recent decades, especially in the form of direct investment. By 1946 the U.S. share of Canada's total foreign liabilities had risen to 72 percent with direct investment liabilities accounting for about 40 percent of all Canada's foreign indebtedness. By 1952 the American component of the total had reached 77 percent and American direct investment had surpassed American portfolio investment. By 1964 approximately 80 percent of long-term foreign investment in Canada was American. The $12.9 billion that American firms had by that time invested in Canadian branch plants and subsidiaries accounted for 31 percent of all U.S. direct foreign investments; U.S. direct investment in the relatively small country of Canada was greater than the total of all U.S. direct investment in all of Europe or in all of Latin America. By the end of 1973, total long-term foreign investment was $51.415 billion of which 78 percent was American, 9.2 percent British, and 12.8 percent came from other countries.

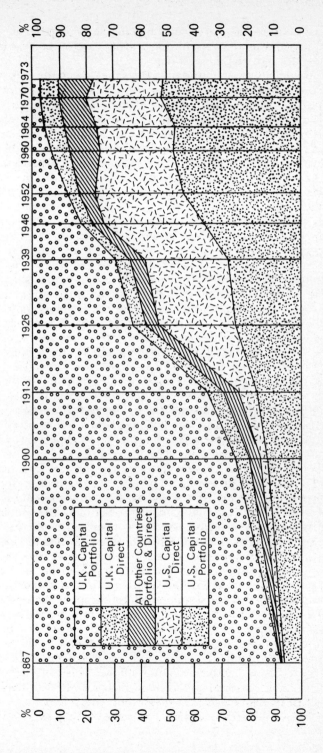

Figure 1
Foreign Investment in Canada

Sources: Statistics Canada, *Canada's Investment Position*, 1971-1973, pp. 42, 86, 87; and Kari Levitt, *Silent Surrender* (Toronto: Macmillan, 1970), p. 65.

American-controlled investment in Canadian companies, often wholly owned subsidiaries, had risen to $26.113 billion and constituted 79 percent of all foreign direct investment.

By the 1970s it was abundantly clear that, given the massive extent of American investment in Canada, the Canadian government was no longer in a position to spell out and enforce public economic policies on its own. Indeed numerous earlier task forces and royal commissions, most notably the 1957 Royal Commission on Canada's Economic Prospects, chaired by Walter Gordon, had already researched the dilemma. The Watkins Report in 1968 and the Wahn Report of 1970 had provided additional important information. In late 1971 the findings of the government review, *Foreign Direct Investment in Canada,* commonly referred to as the Gray Report, were released to the public. Most Canadians were surprised, some were shocked, and some were angry. The report opened with the statement: "The high and growing degree of foreign, and particularly U.S. control of Canadian business activity has led to a Canadian industrial structure which largely reflects the growth priorities of foreign corporations."[34] It continued, this has "led to the establishment of 'truncated' firms for which many important activities are performed abroad by the parent company, with the result that the development of Canadian capacities or activities in these areas is stultified."[35] Particularly significant, politically, was the further observation that "these developments have made it more difficult for the Government to control the domestic national economic environment. They have also influenced the development of the social, cultural and political environment in Canada."[36]

The foreign, mainly American, control of certain key sectors was indeed staggering: petroleum and coal products, 99.7 percent; rubber products, 93.1 percent; transportation equipment, 87 percent; chemicals and chemical products, 81.3 percent; machinery, 72.2 percent; and about 60 percent in all manufacturing. The list seemed endless. Partly because Canada had then and has now fewer restrictions on foreign investment than does any other major country in the world, and partly because of Canadian caution as well as American tax advantages, Americans had developed and continue to maintain a stranglehold on key segments of the Canadian economy: coal, gas, oil, iron, rubber, and some major metals, to name a few. Theoretically Canadian governments could, of course, nationalize all these foreign holdings but they have neither the capital nor the political support to undertake such a foolhardy task. Sir John A. Macdonald's National Policy had brought in infant industries but not infant firms. Over the years many of these infant industries had become giants and had squeezed out their host. Such was and remains the nature of the problem.

What had happened over the years was that the massive American branch-plant economy in Canada had acquired a dynamic vitality of its own. Its expansion had been financed almost entirely by retained Canadian profits and Canadian borrowing which was often available at preferred rates of interest because of the additional security provided by large parent firms. Indeed, Kari Levitt has demonstrated convincingly that in the 1960s Canadians actually were losers in the matter of investment flow. "In the period 1960-67 remitted profits of American subsidiaries in Canada ($5.9 billion) exceeded new capital inflows ($4.1 billion) by $1.8 billion."[37] The sum is substantially larger if license and management fees and royalties are included. Today, despite the activity of Canada's Foreign Investment Review Agency, forty of Canada's hundred largest firms are American-controlled and the extension of American ownership in most sectors continues virtually unchecked. Between 1960 and 1969, 606 Canadian corporations were taken over by foreigners, mostly Americans;[38] the rate has hardly changed since that time.

There are many ways, almost all of great political consequence, in which branch-plant activity influences Canada. As already suggested in part, the establishment and growth of American branch plants almost always means the importation of American technology, management, product development, advertising, market access, market control, and research activity or lack of activity. At a time when product specialization has become critical, especially for exports, the Canadian government is almost helpless in shaping or promoting branch-plant research and development. Easy access to U.S. technology and entrepreneurship discourages the development of domestic expertise in those areas. Also, given the common trading restrictions that parent firms place on foreign subsidiaries, Canadian governmental attempts to increase exports are seriously weakened. The case of the Ford Motor Company of Canada is a classic example. Its 1906 articles of incorporation give the Canadian firm market rights in all British Commonwealth countries (excluding the best, the United Kingdom), while the rest of the world is reserved for the U.S. parent firm or its other subsidiaries. Additionally, branch-plant purchases are often not subject to market forces but to parent-firm directions which often weaken Canadian government attempts to build up certain Canadian industries, to lessen regional unemployment, and so on. Significantly, 50 percent of all export sales of subsidiaries are made to parent firms and 70 percent of their imports are procured from parent companies, often despite the fact that materials can be bought at lower prices within Canada. There is also the problem of tax loss. Long before President Nixon's 1971 DISC (Domestic International Sales Corporation) policy, which provided a 50 percent tax benefit if export sales were made from within the United States rather than by foreign-based subsidiaries, hundreds of major branch plants in Canada were avoiding Canadian taxes by various transfer payments to their parent firms. Much to the consternation of Canadian governments, or at least of some ministers, these "corporations have mastered the techniques of manipulating our personal and social requirements in the interests of their private imperatives of survival,"[39] or expansion or control.

A further complication arises from the pervasive "miniature replica" phenomenon. Many American firms, with their huge domestic base, simply spill over into Canada where, without undertaking any research or product development and capitalizing on massive transborder advertising, they can easily make considerable profit on relatively small sales. The resulting market fragmentation with too many firms producing much too wide a range of products for the smaller Canadian economy results in high unit costs, inefficiency, less success in exporting, and instability in employment. Successive Canadian governments have found it increasingly difficult to develop public policies that can successfully control and redirect the activities of such a derivative and generally imitative Canadian industry. The Canadian government's frustrations in this regard have been complicated by the fact that most Canadians do not favor further governmental restriction on American investment in Canada if that would mean even a slight reduction in the Canadian standard of living.[40] The Canadian business community and the elite class generally are especially opposed to any further governmental intervention.[41]

In sum, the economic impact of burgeoning branch-plant activity, and there are now well over 8500 American-controlled factories in Canada, while very important is not necessarily advantageous. For example, between 1950 and 1960 the percentage of Canadian manufacturing output controlled by foreigners rose from 50 percent to over 60 percent but because of transfer payments to parent firms, inefficiency, and so on, the percentage of companies that lost money rose from 26 percent to 31 percent and the rate of profit after taxes fell from 9.5 percent to 4 percent.[42] Clearly, Canadian governments have a tailhold on a great monster.

Another aspect of economic continentalism is total industry integration. While several sectors are moving in this direction, the auto industry is the farthest advanced. The Automotive Agreement of 1965 created a single Canadian-American manufacturing and sales area, at the wholesale level, for virtually the entire automotive industry. However, given the fact that 95 percent of the Canadian automobile industry is American-owned, such integration did not change the Canadian segment very much. The two most important consequences were that the companies could rationalize production and thus increase their profits, and, second, with fewer lines produced in Canada but for the entire continental market, the Canadian industry could be very seriously disrupted by changes in American consumer preferences, American governmental policies dealing with gas consumption requirements, pollution standards, fuel prices, and a host of other matters. Without doubt, the Canadian automobile industry is now controlled far more from the boardrooms of Detroit and the legislative halls in Washington than by the Canadian Parliament. It is of note that "in 1968 the Canadian government gave up $80 million in customs duties to the industry and made no effort to recover any part of the sum for fear that the parent companies would break the pact."[43]

Another important element of continental economics and politics involves trade, especially following the 1935 re-establishment of general Canadian-American trade reciprocity. From earliest times Canadian prosperity has depended on trade. The old staples—fur, fish, timber, and wheat—given reasonable transportation systems could and did develop east-west commerce. But the new staples—nickel, iron ore, oil, newsprint, natural gas—generally destined for U.S. markets have tended to develop north-south trade patterns, thus contributing to "the economic and political balkanization of Canada."[44]

Increasingly Canada has become dependent on trade with the United States. This fact was already evident in 1929 when the American Wall Street crash hit Canada particularly hard. By 1932 Canadian exports to the United States amounted to only 47 percent of their 1929 peak. Other countries, also hit hard, turned to alternative markets but given geographical and distance factors, Canadian options were severely limited.

Since the Second World War the Canadian-American situation has become far and away the world's largest bilateral trading relationship. In recent years almost 70 percent of Canadian exports have gone to the United States and about 70 percent of Canadian imports have come from the United States. In actual figures, Canada's 1973 imports from the United States were valued at $16.484 billion and her exports at $17.07 billion. For the United States the figures, while proportionately less significant, were also high. In 1970 exports to Canada were 27.8 percent of total U.S. exports and imports from Canada were 21 percent of total U.S. imports.[45] This trade is critical for Canada. Between one quarter and one third of all goods produced in Canada are exported to the United States.[46] Canada must trade, and must trade with the United States, in order to remain economically viable; in Canada 24 percent of gross national product comes from exports while for the United States the corresponding figure is only 4 percent. Such extensive trading with only one country produces not only viability but also vulnerability.

However, the scope and magnitude of continental trade does not tell the whole story; we must also look at the pattern and specific aspects of the transactions. Foreign, especially American, controlled industries in Canada tend to export raw materials or only semiprocessed goods. For example, in a study of thirteen industrialized Western countries it was found that labor-intensive end products accounted for 60 percent of exports but for Canada the comparable figure, despite government efforts to develop more secondary industry in Canada, was only 19 percent.[47]

A further complication in continental economics pertains to extraterritoriality, a term that means the extension and application of American laws and policies into foreign countries, in this case Canada. When this happens, the political independence of the host country and its capacity to implement its own public policies are severely restricted. Space limitations do not permit detailed illustration of this phenomenon; suffice it to say that for many years such American ventures as the application of American antitrust legislation to subsidiaries in Canada, which prevents consolidation and rationalization of manufacturing in Canada, the application to Canadian subsidiaries of the U.S. Trading with the Enemy Act, which prohibits certain exports, and the 1965 application to Canadian subsidiaries of American "voluntary guidelines," which severely restricted economic freedom, all create major economic and political costs for Canada, especially when they are in direct conflict with Canadian trade policies. Interestingly, and very consequentially for Canada, the

United States is the only country that practises such extraterritorial application of law and public policy.[48] Of course, much of the importance of such extraterritoriality lies in subsidiary management's anticipation of affects and the desire to develop and retain good standing with the parent firm rather than in actual instances of blatant interference, thwarted exports, and so on.

There can be no doubt that continental economics weakens internal integration in Canada, strengthens the provinces vis-à-vis Ottawa, improves Canada's living standard but at a cost of decreased flexibility, and generally has transformed Canada into an industrialized country but one in a state of permanent economic adolescence with a branch-plant mentality resigned to perpetual reliance on external initiatives.

CONTINENTAL POLITICAL SOCIALIZATION

Political socialization plays a great role in any body politic; Canada is no exception. The key issue in this regard is the multifaceted and profound impact of the giant southern neighbor on Canada. Here again, as in the realm of economics, the bulk of the impact involves private rather than governmental activity and again the penetration is generally invited rather than imposed. Concerning expectations, mores, values, priorities, and life styles, the United States, despite persistent national differences about sense of destiny, greater social agitation and more dynamic liberalism, depth of patriotism, and a general world view, has become the most important shaper of Canadian social and political values. The extent of commonality and American influence has struck many people. More than two decades ago that astute British observer, Dennis Brogan, wrote, "I do not know of any real parallel to this situation, in which two countries have had so much in common. . . . It is not a question in Canada of imitating some American ways of doing things. Canada is part of the American culture in most aspects of daily life."[49] Canadians, generally unwilling to initiate corrective policies, have, however, not been blind to either the extent or significance of developments. As early as 1929 Archibald MacMechan observed that the danger "lies in gradual assimilation, in peaceful penetration, in a spiritual bondage—the subjection of the Canadian nation's mind and soul to the mind and soul of the United States."[50] In the late 1960s John Kenneth Galbraith observed, "If I were still a practising as distinct from an advisory Canadian, I would be much more concerned about maintaining the cultural integrity of the broadcasting system and with making sure Canada has an active, independent theatre, book-publishing industry, newspapers, magazines and schools of poets and painters. I wouldn't worry for a moment about the differences between Canadian or American corporations."[51] And two days before his retirement Prime Minister Lester Pearson declared: "The industrial and economic and financial penetration from the south worries me, but less than the penetration of American ideas, of the flow of information about all things American; American thought and entertainment; the American approach to everything."[52]

Canadian governments have not been unaware or unconcerned about these trends. Numerous royal commissions, task forces, special senate committees and other bodies have looked into the matter. In 1951 the Massey Report noted that, "Our use of American institutions or our lazy, even abject, imitation of them has caused an uncritical acceptance of ideas and assumptions that are alien to our tradition."[53] The 1957 Fowler Report re-emphasized the point: "Can we resist the tidal wave of American cultural activity? Can we retain a Canadian identity, art and culture—a Canadian nationhood?"[54] But diagnosis has proved to be easier than remedy. Canadian leaders and spokesmen, stressing the cultural mosaic, glorifying multiculturalism, and shaping a society seemingly having little more in common than a lowest common denominator of ambivalent anti-Americanism, constantly lost out. The Canada that these elites constructed could not easily be held together or integrated into something positive and dynamic. In brief, since early times Canadian society has been vulnerable and permeable. American culture has always had easy and usually welcome access. Indeed, as early as the 1920s a public opinion survey found that in every area of communications the mass of Canadians preferred American culture to their own.[55] For this reason, the long-time trends have not been reversed.

The whole matter of border crossings—vacation travel, brief excursions, employment commuting, and migration—has played an important part in the political socialization of Canadians, especially given the widespread Canadian border mentality derived from the fact that 80 percent of Canadians live within 160 km of the U.S. border and 90 percent within 320 km. Given the historical migration trends, it is not surprising that many Canadians see themselves as possible future Americans and have numerous relatives and friends "across the line." Between 1850-1950 some 7.2 million people migrated to Canada but some 6.6 million emigrated, almost all to the United States. In two years, 1882 and 1961, Canada lost as many people as came in.[56] For most years during the first three quarters of this century Canadian migration to the United States ranged between 30 000 and 100 000; only since 1966, because of new U.S. regulations, has it declined significantly. Generally American migration to Canada has been low, with the exception of a few years in the early part of this century and to some extent in recent years. Tourism keeps booming. In 1971 there were more than 35 000 000 Canadian visits to the United States and about 38 000 000 American visits to Canada. Unofficial figures for more recent years are even higher. All of this transborder movement is not without political and social consequence.

Hollywood and the entire American film industry constitutes another major shaper of Canadian ideas and values. Feature films are still the mainstay of the commercial cinemas and almost all the feature films shown in Canada are American. The establishment of the Canadian Film Board in 1939 and of the Canadian Film Development Corporation in

1968 have not changed things much. It has been impossible to beat American competition. In 1972 the CFDC helped to finance thirteen major films. Thereafter production declined rapidly. With the CFDC in mind, and considering also the shorter films and documentaries, one critic observed, "After seven years, 20 million tax dollars, and about 150 films, only about 6 percent of the Canadian theatregoing public were actually seeing any of the CFDC-backed films."[57]

The major problem has not been the quality of the Canadian productions but the stranglehold that certain American-controlled firms, such as Famous Players and Paramount, have on distribution and virtually all the big, money-making cinemas. In 1972, for example, fewer than 2 percent of the movies shown in Ontario were Canadian, in Quebec fewer than 5 percent. Most of the others, in all provinces, were American.[58] In 1975 Canada achieved the dubious distinction of becoming Hollywood's biggest customer, surpassing Italy. When compared to 1974, the total amount Canadians paid in 1975 to see American movies increased by 36 percent to reach $54.5 million. In that year the CFDC share of the box office revenue was about 4 percent or about $860 000.[59] In brief, Canadian films are not seen by many Canadians and for most Canadians are not even available.

Radio and television in Canada reflect similar trends; were it not for the Canadian Broadcasting Corporation which the Canadian government created in 1932, most of Canada might be only a region within the American networks' coverage area. As it is, even with massive governmental effort and expenditure, the current situation is certainly unique. Canadian nationalists would doubtless term it foreboding. As early as 1924 *Maclean's* magazine reported that "nine-tenths of the radio fans in the Dominion hear three to four times as many United States stations as Canadian."[60] The exposure to American programs was increased in 1936 when the CBC incorporated U.S. programs into its schedules. About the same time Canadian stations started using the American chart or "hit parade" system. This venture had a double impact. Aside from the general importation of musical fare it also meant that any Canadian artists who hoped to become known across Canada could succeed only if they achieved national acceptance in the United States. Hence it is little wonder that as late as 1973 only 2 percent of all the records sold in Canada were produced by Canadian firms.[61] Record production and distribution are almost entirely continental, which is to say American. As a result of recent Canadian Radio-television and Telecommunications Commission directives that figure has now reached 8 percent.[62]

But basic Canadian radio listening preferences have not changed. In early 1976 the CRTC ordered the FM cable systems in Canada to drop American stations and replace them with Canadian. The extent and depth of the angry response from the public shocked both the politicians and the bureaucrats and by fall, scarcely three months after the first phases of policy implementation, the CRTC was forced to cancel its FM Canadianization policy.

If radio and the record business are continental, television is even more so. Time after time the American norm becomes the Canadian norm. That axiom apparently held true even over the selection of a color television system. The technically better and cheaper SECAM III system was rejected in favor of the American NTSC system, mainly because of compatibility with American systems.[63]

The preferences for the U.S. offerings which persist in radio, are equally true for TV. The 1970 Davey Committee Report lamented the fact that English-speaking Canadians favor American to Canadian programs, 71 percent to 24 percent. CRTC regulations have increased Canadian content in recent years but with little impact on viewer habits. For one thing, such totally American spectacles as baseball's World Series and Hollywood's Academy Awards have been classified by the CRTC as Canadian for purposes of content regulation. Then, too, the Canadian networks carry a large number of American programs and, in addition, American TV stations reach about 55 percent of all Canadian homes. Rapid development of cable systems is raising that percentage. By 1974 it had climbed to about 80 percent and the more than four hundred cable systems are constantly expanding. The effect is profound; cable systems have indeed moved the American border 300 km north. The result is that probably two thirds to three quarters of Canadian viewers are watching American programs. A 1973 survey revealed that in Toronto Canadian programs attracted only 13 percent of evening viewers and only 9 percent in the prime time period from 8 to 10 pm.[64] Here, as elsewhere, trends are crucial, and the trends are clearly continentalist.

Some Canadians blame the Canadian television networks for the fact of foreign domination but from a strictly financial point of view and concerning viewer preferences and the all-important ratings, they are behaving quite rationally. For example, the CBC in 1975 paid only $2000 for each weekly episode of "All in the Family" for which it sold $24 000 in advertising. At the same time it paid out $65 000 a week to produce its own show, "The Beachcombers," which generated no more advertising revenue.[65] Little wonder that a generation of Canadians is growing up with basic political socialization derived from Sesame Street, Captain Kangaroo, Mary Tyler Moore, Archie Bunker, Walt Disney, Howard Cosell, and Walter Cronkite.

Official warnings about trends in the electronic media are also expressed over publications. In 1961 the Royal Commission on Publications observed that "communications are the thread which binds together the fibres of a nation. . . . The communications of a nation are as vital to its life as its defences, and should receive at least as great a measure of national protection."[66] The commission's fears were well-founded. In 1969, 95 percent of all the various magazines available in Canadian retail outlets were American imports. About 80 percent of all magazines read were American. For decades the two American giants *TIME* and *Reader's Digest* took about 40 percent of total magazine advertising in Canada. The 1974 figures were $18.8 million for the two and $39 million for all the members of the Magazine Association of Canada. The *Reader's Digest* had a circulation of 1 250 000 monthly and *TIME* 550 000.[67] In 1969 *Maclean's* switched to the size and format used by *TIME* so that ads appearing in the giant operation could be reproduced in *Maclean's* at no additional preparation cost. Even so, *Maclean's* was still at a great disadvantage because it had to provide its own editorial copy while *TIME* used its American copy. *Maclean's* rates, therefore, had to be much higher than those of *TIME*, just to recover cost. In 1970 the respective rates were $4 600 and $2 700 for full page ads. In February, 1976, the Canadian Parliament passed a bill whose requirements about Canadian content brought about the demise of the Canadian edition of *TIME*. But most Canadian *TIME* subscribers simply switched to the American edition and the basic problem remains unresolved. Illustrating the plight of Canadian magazines, the Davey Committee Report noted that "We spend more money buying American comic books than we do on seventeen leading Canadian-owned magazines."[68]

Largely because of continentalism Canadian authors and book publishers are also in dire straits. Throughout Canadian history the perennial Canadian theme of resistance to Americanization has been mirrored in actual fact; the parallel British influence has gradually weakened. Mark Twain, Hemingway, and a vast host of U.S. novels and novelists have become dominant. In 1969 two thirds of the value of all books bought in Canada was accounted for by imports, 80 percent of which came from the United States. Surprisingly, almost half of all American book exports go to Canada. Publishing in Canada, in 1969, was as follows: 59 percent by U.S. firms, 22 percent by British, and 19 percent by Canadian.[69] Of total Canadian bookstore purchases in 1973 apparently only 20 percent involved Canadian material.[70]

If we look at the big educational market the situation is even more lopsided. American publishers, at relatively low retail prices, flood the Canadian market with low-cost run-ons of their own domestic editions, often without any adaptation. In 1973 some 68 percent of all book purchases for Canadian classrooms were foreign books, mostly American, some with adaptation. An additional 29 percent were Canadian-authored but not published by Canadian firms and only 3 percent were Canadian-authored and Canadian-published.[71] The postsecondary situation was similar. A 1973 survey of 37 political science and sociology departments at Canadian universities showed that 55 percent of all prescribed texts were American-authored and American-published while only 13 percent were Canadian-authored and Canadian-published.[72] Wherever one looks the situation is the same. Only 7 percent of books sold through book clubs in Canada are Canadian and less than 2 percent of the 32 million paperbacks sold in Canada are Canadian-authored.[73] The figures are staggering. In 1970 Canada imported $245 million worth of printed material from the United States, more than the United States sold to all other countries combined. Canadian writers and publishers have come to understand the significance of a statement by Walter Wulff, a vice-president of McGraw-Hill International: "The prime objective of a foreign subsidiary is not its own publishing but the sale of the U.S. product."[74] Canada is the only country in the industrialized world whose total print medium is overwhelmingly dominated by foreigners, and by foreigners from only one country at that.

The spillover effect of such a situation into curriculum and general value formation is predictable. American concepts, problems, heroes, mythology, fads, and American mass culture (as contrasted with the more elitist earlier Canadiana) have become preeminent. Many Canadians seem to know more about the United States than about their own country. But what else should one expect when, for example, an adapted standard Grade 6 history text used in Winnipeg in 1975, *Canada—The New Nation*, has not one word on the Winnipeg General Strike but has two full chapters on Abraham Lincoln![75] Such instances are commonplace. A major 1968 study revealed that American magazines outnumbered Canadian magazines three to one in Canadian school libraries. One secondary school principal acknowledged that of a thousand books purchased for the new school library, not a single one was Canadian.[76]

Continentalism prevails at the university level also. Most Canadian universities use the Graduate Record Exam, a totally American-oriented test, to evaluate applicants for graduate school. In 1974 the University of Windsor rejected four of its own graduates who had A standings because their American GRE marks were not high enough. Often such behavior is justified on grounds of cosmopolitanism and internationalism, but for Canada these terms are almost synonymous with Americanism. Space limitations do not permit a description of the American emphasis in university curricula, or of the profound effect of American specialized and scholarly journals, or the numbers of Americans on university faculties, an issue that has been explored elsewhere.[77]

American dominance in the Canadian labor force constitutes another important phase of continentalism. As early as 1911 the so-called "internationals" controlled 90 percent of union members in Canada. By the mid-1950s the percentage had dropped somewhat to about 70 percent. In 1965 some 110 international, or American, unions had a total of 1 125 000 members in Canada while 52 Canadian unions had a total of 390 000 members or about 26 percent. In no other industrial country of similar size does one find a situation even remotely similar. Of course, the arrangement merely parallels the continental situation as far as entrepreneurship and management are concerned. For many spokesmen on both sides of the bargaining table, the international boundary might as well not exist.

Several other aspects of continental socialization deserve at least a brief comment. The Canadian sports culture, but especially professional sports, has become continental. The National Hockey League ownership and location of franchises have for half a century been more American than Canadian and the most important people associated with the government-protected Canadian Football League are the imported American players and coaches. Given the great commercialization of sports in Canada, Americanization is inevitable. But even at amateur levels the trends are the same. For example, most members of Canada's 1968 Olympic team trained at American universities. In fact, American college sports of all kinds have a much greater following in Canada than do Canadian college sports.

Although the two countries have different religious traditions, the

Americanization of Canadian religion is well-advanced. Most religious broadcasts on radio and TV are American, most religious books are American, and most of the dominant personalities are American. Billy Graham, Oral Roberts, Rex Humbard, Cardinal Cushing, the Mormons, and countless others have cut a very wide swath. Here, as elsewhere, the continental osmosis is almost entirely unilateral.

American service clubs from Rotary to Lions, youth organizations from 4H to Up With People, philanthropic foundations from Ford Foundation to Carnegie and Rockefeller, reformist organizations from the Women's Christian Temperance Union to ecology groups, quasi-political groups from the Non-Partisan League to women's liberation, and countless commercial ventures from Colonel Sanders Kentucky Fried Chicken to Amway have spread across Canada. The dimensions of absorption, not to mention emulation, defy measurement. Naturally, all these aspects must be seen in association with economic and defense aspects of continentalism; it is the cumulative effect that we are witnessing.

The policy problem for Canadian governments is awesome. American mass culture is enjoyed and sought after by the Canadian masses while a small minority, heavily subsidized by the Canadian government, attempts valiantly to retain or develop a culture uniquely Canadian. Its success is in doubt. In 1970 CRTC chairman Pierre Juneau concurred with the view that "Canada has one decade remaining in which its members have to make up their minds whether they want to remain a distinct political, cultural and geographical nationality."[78] Whether his pessimism or his time frame are in error remains to be seen.

CONTINENTALISM: SCOPE AND CONSEQUENCES

The limits of continentalism are very broad. More than 180 formal treaties link the two countries. Together they have undertaken numerous major ventures from the International Joint Commission's activities to the St. Lawrence Seaway Project to the Columbia River Treaty to reclamation of the Great Lakes to NORAD and much more. In scores of major policy areas, Canadian governments have emulated the Americans; sometimes, as with pollution controls, because there was no other option. The New Deal, the War on Poverty, civil rights legislation, ecology programs, prohibition, and electoral financing reforms are a few obvious examples. The Canadian public's emulation is equally diverse and extensive. Phenomena such as the Progressive movement, the civil rights movement, the antiwar movement, the Indian movement, and student activism in the 1960s all had mainly American roots. Indeed some movements, such as the New Left, petered out in Canada primarily because their roots and causes were alien.

The consequences of such extensive commonality can hardly be overstated. American influence on Canadian political practices and on the policies of the two major parties is great. Even greater is the impact on the life style, values and attitudes of the average Canadian. To a total stranger the overall trends must surely seem to be fixed and irreversible. Canada stands alone as the country that seems to be losing political, economic, and social autonomy as it becomes more urbanized, industrialized, educated, and affluent. Scores of national and provincial Canadian commissions have studied the relationship, or problem, but given the general and deep Canadian desire for things American, continentalism will probably continue to flourish and Canadian autonomy weaken.

In 1967 Blair Fraser wrote that, "Without at least a touch of anti-Americanism, Canada would have no reason to exist."[79] But the anti-Americanism that Fraser perceived has for decades been overshadowed by a more deeply rooted acknowledgement of dependence coupled with a mixture of envy and admiration. The complex love-hate relationship is more love than hate. True, in continental affairs Canada is a permanent minority but when agreement in preferences and policies, however such agreement is achieved, vastly overshadows basic differences, such a status is not entirely disagreeable. For many Canadians, closer ties to the United States are no threat. And, of course, whether or not Canada should join the United States is always an issue in Canada; the debate is real but it evokes little fear, a fact that is understandable since only 9 percent of Canadians believe that "Americans have a markedly different way of life."[80] For George Ball the picture is quite clear; Canadian resistance to Canadian-American union is pointless, "a rearguard action against the inevitable."[81]

CONCLUSION

Of course, continentalism cannot explain all aspects of Canadian politics. Such factors as the British and French roots, the current English-French controversy, the geographical setting, and the parliamentary system all play a part, but no other factor is as important as the proximity of and penetration by, the public and private sectors of the United States. For Canada, economics, culture, defense, and development are continental and the focal point of each continental system lies south of the border.[82]

In terms of the Eastonian systems approach we could describe the situation as follows: the Canadian sociopolitical environment includes the bulk of the American sociopolitical environment and the American political system, while the American environment includes virtually nothing of the Canadian. Similarly, American feedback plays a major role in Canadian inputs but Canadian feedback is virtually inconsequential for American inputs. Perhaps most importantly, as we have seen, a large percentage of Canadian demands and supports emanate from the American sector of the continental environment. That situation helps us to understand why many Canadians, and Canadian governments, look to American-dominated continental systems and subsystems for demand satisfaction and many other components of living in contemporary Canada.

In 1966 J. B. Brebner observed, "Any foreigner could tell them [Canadians] what they themselves felt compelled to deny—that the greatest force exerted on their development was the stimulating example of the people of the United States."[83] A few years later Prime Minister Trudeau made the same point more bluntly. During the 1968 national election campaign he stated that Canada is no more independent of the United States than is Poland of the Soviet Union; he then remarked that Canada has only 10 percent independence and can maneuver only within that degree of freedom.[84] In making that statement he both reflected and reinforced Canadian reality.

After the British conquest of Quebec in 1759, the bulk of settled North America flew one flag—until 1776. For Canada the intervening two centuries have been one long struggle for an autonomous destiny. Year by year the struggle becomes more complex and ominous; it is not yet clear whether the northern half of the continent has the capacity and will to exist independently or whether that early brief experience of "continental" unity under one flag will be reestablished but this time in a more encompassing and irreversible fashion.

ENDNOTES

1. J.M.S. Careless, "Hooray for the Scars and Gripes!" *The New Romans,* ed. Al Purdy (Edmonton: M.C. Hurtig, 1968), p. 134.
2. J.B. Brebner, *Canada* (Ann Arbor: University of Michigan Press, 1960).
3. James Laxer, *The Energy Poker Game* (Toronto: New Press, 1970), p. 1.
4. George Grant, *Lament for a Nation* (Toronto: McClelland and Stewart, 1965), p. 86.
5. Mitchell Sharp, "Canada-U.S. Relations: Options for the Future," *International Perspectives,* special issue, (Autumn, 1972).
6. John Sloan Dickey, *Canada and the American Presence* (New York: New York University Press, 1975), p. 66.
7. A.R.M. Lower, *Canadians in the Making* (Toronto: Longmans, Green and Company, 1958), p. 441.
8. Janet Morchain, ed., *Sharing a Continent* (Toronto: McGraw-Hill Ryerson, 1973), p. 69.
9. Morchain, *ibid.,* p. 70.
10. S.D. Clark, *Movements of Political Protest in Canada* (Toronto: University of Toronto Press, 1959), p. 302.
11. Morchain, *op. cit.,* p. 108.
12. See P.B. Waite, *The Life and Times of Confederation 1864-1867* (Toronto: University of Toronto Press, 1962), pp. 304-305.
13. See, for example, Morchain, *op. cit.,* p. 124.
14. F.H. Underhill, *In Search of Canadian Liberalism* (Toronto: Macmillan, 1961), pp. 256-260.
15. Dickey, *op. cit.,* p. 142.

16. Morchain, *op. cit.*, p. 50.

17. Farley Mowat, "Letter to My Son," in Al Purdy, *op. cit.*, pp. 3-5.

18. J.W. Holmes, "The Relationship in Alliance and World Affairs," *The United States and Canada,* ed. J.S. Dickey (Englewood Cliffs, N.J.: Prentice-Hall, 1964), pp. 100, 131.

19. Department of External Affairs, *Foreign Policy for Canadians* (Ottawa: Queen's Printer, 1970).

20. Morchain, *op. cit.*, p. 68.

21. Quoted in Brebner, *North Atlantic Triangle,* Carleton Library Edition (Toronto: McClelland and Stewart, 1966). p. 277.

22. Quoted in Roger Swanson, *Canadian-American Summit Diplomacy, 1923-1973* (Toronto: McClelland and Stewart, 1975), p. 71.

23. Quoted in John W. Warnock, *Partner to Behemoth* (Toronto: New Press, 1970), p. 105.

24. "Mr. Howe's History," *Saturday Night,* LXVI (November 7, 1950), p. 6.

25. John W. Warnock, *op. cit.*, p. 114.

26. See, for example, James M. Minifie, *Peacemaker or Powder-Monkey; Canada's Role in a Revolutionary World* (Toronto: McClelland and Stewart, 1960).

27. Quoted in *Financial Post,* March 25, 1967.

28. Tom Kent, "The Changing Place of Canada," *Foreign Affairs,* 35 (July, 1957), p. 581.

29. Kari Levitt, *Silent Surrender* (Toronto: Macmillan, 1970), p. 129.

30. Levitt, *ibid.*, p. 129.

31. *Ibid.*, p. 129.

32. Green H. Hackworth, "General Aspects of Canadian-United States Treaty Relations and Their Import for the Conduct of Relations between Nations on the Basis of Respect for Law and Mutual Interests," *Canada-United States Treaty Relations,* ed. David R. Deener (Durham, N.C.: Duke University Press, 1963), p. 125.

33. Charles Foulkes, "The Complications of Continental Defence," *Neighbors Taken for Granted,* ed. L. Merchant (New York: Praeger, 1966), p. 120.

34. *A Citizen's Guide to the Gray Report* (Toronto: New Press, 1971), p. 11.

35. *Ibid.*, p. 11.

36. *Ibid.*, pp. 11-12.

37. Levitt, *op. cit.*, p. 94.

38. Laxer, *op. cit.* p. 27.

39. Levitt, *op. cit.*, p. 29.

40. Morchain, *op. cit.*, p. 144.

41. Laxer, *op. cit.*, p. 45.

42. Levitt, *op. cit.*, p. 87.

43. C.W. Gonick, "Foreign Ownership and Political Decay," *Close the 49th Parallel, Etc.,* ed. Ian Lumsden (Toronto: University of Toronto Press, 1970), p. 65.

44. Laxer, *op. cit.*, p. 15.

45. Dickey, *op. cit.*, p. 22.

46. Gonick, *op. cit.*, p. 45.

47. Levitt, *op. cit.*, p. 127.

48. See Dave Godfrey and Mel Watkins, eds., *Gordon to Watkins to You* (Toronto; New Press, 1970), esp. pp. 204-219.

49. D.W. Brogan, "An Outsider Looking In," *Canada's Tomorrow*, ed. G.P. Gilmour (Toronto: Macmillan, 1954), pp. 271-273.

50. Archibald MacMechan, "Canada as a Vassal State," *Canadian Historical Review* (Toronto: University of Toronto Press, 1929), p. 347.

51. Quoted in the *Toronto Daily Star*, Sept. 14, 1968.

52. Quoted in the *Toronto Daily Star*, May 2, 1968.

53. Royal Commission on National Development in the Arts, Letters and Sciences, Vincent Massey, Chairman, *Report* (Ottawa: King's Printer, 1951), p. 15.

54. Royal Commission on Broadcasting, Keith Davey, Chairman, *Report* (Ottawa: King's Printer, 1957), Vol. I, p. 8.

55. Morchain, *op. cit.*, p. 190.

56. *Ibid.*, pp. 8, 138.

57. S.M. Crean, *Who's Afraid of Canadian Culture?* (Don Mills, Ontario: General Publishing, 1976). p. 72.

58. Crean, *op. cit.*, pp. 81-82.

59. *Ibid.*, p. 87.

60. Quoted in Crean, *op. cit.*, p. 29.

61. Crean, *op. cit.*, p. 17.

62. *Ibid.*, p. 54.

63. Lynn Trainor, "Science in Canada—American Style," in Lumsden, *op. cit.*, p. 247.

64. Dickey, *op. cit.*, p. 56.

65. Crean, *op. cit.*, p. 49.

66. Royal Commission on Publications, Grattan O'Leary, Chairman, *Report* (Ottawa: Queen's Printer, 1961), p. 4.

67. Crean, *op. cit.*, p. 224.

68. Special Senate Committee on the Mass Media, Keith Davey, Chairman, *Report* (Ottawa: Queen's Printer, 1970), Vol. I, p. 156.

69. Dickey, *op. cit.*, p. 51.

70. Crean, *op. cit.*, p. 182.

71. *Ibid.*, p. 189.

72. J.H. Redekop, "Authors and Publishers: An Analysis of Textbook Selection in Canadian Departments of Political Science and Sociology," *Canadian Journal of Political Science*, IX, No. 1 (March, 1976), p. 110.

73. Crean, *op. cit.*, pp. 208-9.

74. Quoted in S.M. Crean, *op. cit.*, p. 215.

75. Crean, *op. cit.*, p. 233.

76. *Ibid.*, p. 235.

77. See Robin Mathews and James Steele, eds., *The Struggle for Canadian Universities* (Toronto: New Press, 1969); and Wallace Gagne, ed., *Nationalism, Technology and the Future of Canada* (Toronto: Macmillan, 1976), esp. pp. 113-120.

78. Davey Committee, *Report, op. cit.*, p. 11.

79. Blair Fraser, *The Search for Identity: Canada, 1945-67* (Garden City: Doubleday, 1967), p. 301.

80. Morchain, *op. cit.*, p. 177.
81. George Ball, *The Discipline of Power* (Boston: Little, Brown, 1968), p. 113.
82. For a discussion of a systems interpretation of Canadian-American relations see J. H. Redekop, "A Reinterpretation of Canadian-American Relations," *Canadian Journal of Political Science,* IX, No. 2 (June, 1976), pp. 227-243.
83. Brebner, *North Atlantic Triangle, op. cit.*, p. 364.
84. See Lumsden, *op. cit.*, p. 71.

SELECTED REFERENCES

AXLINE, ANDREW, et. al., eds. *Continental Community? Independence and Integration in North America.* Toronto: McClelland and Stewart, 1974. The authors present a rigorous analysis of continentalism. Various aspects and components of North American integration are presented and important theoretical models discussed.

BOWLES, RICHARD P., et al. *Canada and the U.S.: Continental Partners or Wary Neighbors?* Toronto: Prentice-Hall, 1973. This introductory volume consists of scores of short articles, excerpts of all sorts, and discussion questions as well as connecting and interpretive sections. Topics covered include economics, cultural affairs, domestic politics, foreign affairs, historical developments, and prospects for the future.

BROSSARD, PHILIPPE J. *Sold American!* Toronto: Peter Martin, 1971. A closely reasoned monograph that argues that the primary cause of "the erosion of Canada's independence is not to be found in Washington, but rather in the boardrooms of the economic and financial elite of Canada."

CANADIAN-AMERICAN COMMITTEE. *The New Environment for Canadian-American Relations.* Montreal: Private Planning Association of Canada, 1972. A brief study by free enterprise spokesmen of the major problem areas in North American continentalism.

CARR, D.W. *Recovering Canada's Nationhood.* Ottawa: Canada Publishing Company, 1971. Written by a member of Canada's economic elite, this thoughtful book provides a frank examination of Canada's lack of national objectives, economic trends and policies, the inadequate performance of Canadian elites, and specific policy proposals.

CREAN, S.M. *Who's Afraid of Canadian Culture?* Don Mills, Ontario: General Publishing Co., 1976. A hard-hitting, lucid analysis of virtually all components of Canadian culture; special emphasis is given to recent American influences.

DICKEY, JOHN SLOAN. *Canada and the American Presence.* New York: New York University Press, 1975. Written by an American, this important book provides a balanced, yet penetrating account of all major aspects of the relationship.

FOX, ANNETTE BAKER, ALFRED O. HERO JR., AND JOSEPH S. NYE, JR. eds. "Canada and the United States: Transnational and Transgovernmental Relations." *International Organization* 28, No. 4 (Autumn, 1974). Special issue. The seventeen chapters in this advanced study present recent findings in many areas of a complex relationship and spell out various theories and explanations; a balanced and intensive study.

GAGNE, WALLACE, ed. *Nationalism, Technology and the Future of Canada.* Toronto: Macmillan, 1976. Consists of seven essays each dealing with broad areas of Canadian independence and its relationship to technological change.

GODFREY, DAVE AND MEL WATKINS, eds. *Gordon to Watkins to You; A Documentary: the Battle for Control of our Economy.* Toronto: New Press, 1970. A compilation of data, critical views, interpretive essays, and diverse excerpts set in a framework of socialist assumptions.

GRANT, GEORGE. *Lament for a Nation.* Toronto: McClelland and Stewart, 1965. This penetrating and pessimistic analysis of Canadian nationalsim and continentalism stands as a classic statement on the subject.

————. *Technology and Empire: Perspectives on North America.* Toronto: Anansi, 1969. An agonized and grandly argued book that criticizes America's march to world empire, especially as that march has affected Canada.

LAXER, JAMES. *The Energy Poker Game: The Politics of the Continental Resources Deal.* Toronto: New Press, 1970. A brief but powerful indictment reflecting a socialist orientation.

LAXER, ROBERT M., ed. *Canada Ltd., The Political Economy of Dependency.* Toronto: McClelland and Stewart, 1973. Written from a socialist perspective this volume analyzes various social and cultural aspects of dependency.

LEVITT, KARI. *Silent Surrender.* Toronto: Macmillan, 1970. A carefully researched economic study of the American impact on Canada with special emphasis on the multinational corporation.

LITVAK, I.A., C.J. MAULE, AND R.D. ROBINSON. *Dual Loyalty: Canadian-U.S. Business Arrangements.* Toronto: McGraw-Hill, 1971. This book describes the problems of continental business arrangements and Canadian policies adopted to deal with those problems. The bulk of the book consists of case studies.

LUMSDEN, IAN. ed. *Close the 49th Parallel Etc.: The Americanization of Canada.* Toronto: University of Toronto Press, 1970. The most wide-ranging survey of specific problem areas covering business, labor, media, resources, science, sports and much more; written, in the main, from a socialist perspective.

MATHEWS, ROBIN AND JAMES STEELE. eds. *The Struggle for Canadian Universities.* Toronto: New Press, 1969. A collection of letters, speeches, memoranda and articles dealing with the alleged Americanization of Canadian universities.

MERCHANT, LIVINGSTON T., ed. *Neighbors Taken for Granted; Canada and the United States.* New York: Praeger, 1966. A former American ambassador to Canada and various experts discuss developments that "threaten the American-Canadian friendship"; written mainly from a continentalist perspective.

MINIFIE, JAMES M. *Peacemaker or Powder-Monkey: Canada's Role in a Revolutionary World.* Toronto: McClelland and Stewart, 1960. This interesting and informative analysis makes a strong case for the view that Canada should adopt a neutralist stance in foreign affairs. Such a stance, the author argues, would be of great benefit to both Canada and the United States.

MOFFETT, SAMUEL E. *The Americanization of Canada.* Toronto: University of Toronto Press, 1972. When it first appeared in 1907 this study pioneered a new area of research. Many of Moffett's observations are still relevant. The introduction by Allan Smith adds substantially to the book's worth.

MORCHAIN, JANET. ed. *Sharing a Continent.* Toronto: McGraw-Hill Ryerson, 1973. The beginning student will find this panoramic survey of virtually the entire gamut of Canadian-American relations very useful. The scores of excerpts, the skillful introductions and general commentary and the fine bibliographies combine to make this book one of the most important in the field, even for those students already knowledgeable concerning North America.

POPE, w.h. *The Elephant and the Mouse.* Toronto: McClelland and Stewart, 1971. Presented as "A Handbook for Regaining Control of Canada's Economy," this slim volume provides the basic background for understanding the workings and consequences of foreign investment.

REDEKOP, JOHN H., ed. *The Star-Spangled Beaver; Twenty-four Canadians Look South.* Toronto: Peter Martin, 1971. A collection of diverse assessments of the American impact on Canada covering most of the major areas of transnational interaction.

ROTSTEIN, ABRAHAM AND GARY LAX, eds. *Getting It Back; A Program for Canadian Independence.* Toronto: Clarke, Irwin, 1974. Presented by the Committee for an Independent Canada, this compilation of interpretive essays and case studies covers most of the important aspects of Canadian economy and culture, both defined broadly.

SAFARIAN, A.E. *Foreign Ownership of Canadian Industry.* Toronto: University of Toronto Press, 1973. A sometimes sympathetic but still eminently thorough study of the behavior of branch-plant firms in Canada.

SWANSON, ROGER FRANK. ed. *Canadian-American Summit Diplomacy, 1923-1973: Selected Speeches and Documents.* Toronto: McClelland and Stewart, 1975. An excellent collection of major documents that convey a sense of immediacy. The introductory chapter and the summaries at the beginning of each chapter provide helpful interpretation.

SYKES, PHILIP. *Sellout: The Giveaway of Canada's Energy Resources.* Edmonton: Hurtig, 1973. Focusing mainly on petroleum policies, the author presents a hard-hitting examination of the big energy deals since 1950.

TUPPER, STANLEY R. AND DOUGLAS L. BAILEY. *One Continent—Two Voices: The Future of Canada-U.S. Relations.* Toronto: Clarke, Irwin, 1967. In this very useful introduction to the topic the authors argue that if Canadians wish to have Americans become more aware of them, they must resolve the continuing problem of Canadian identity and purpose.

WARNOCK, JOHN W. *Partner to Behemoth.* Toronto: New Press, 1970. This book presents a challenging, left-of-centre reinterpretation of Canadian military policy, especially with reference to Canadian-American relations since 1945.

3

Economics and Politics in Canada

Douglas J. McCready[*]

> The ideas of economists and political philosophies, both when
> they are right and when they are wrong, are more powerful than
> is commonly understood. Indeed the world is ruled by little else.
> Practical men, who believe themselves to be quite exempt from
> any intellectual influences are usually the slaves of some defunct
> economist.[1]

John Maynard Keynes, when he made this statement, was not referring to
Canadian politicians; he was referring to the influence economics and
economists have on our minds, our policies, and our wants. However, his
comment is directly relevant to our topic. This chapter examines the influence that economics has had on politics in Canada. The relationship is
extensive and of long duration. Canada's political structure evolved from
and reflects the pre-Confederation economy. Political parties and voting
behavior are both expressions of economic reality. Most public policies involve economic decisions and the possible restructuring of Confederation
also involves basic economic considerations. Throughout this chapter we
will see that economics has had a pervasive and profound influence on
Canadian politics; we will also see that a basic knowledge of the economics
of Canada is essential for a clear understanding of Canadian political affairs.

First, we must examine what economics is in order to understand its
role. Economics is the science of allocating resources.[2] Economists talk
about producing goods and services with labor, machines, raw materials,
and technology and then of allocating those goods among competing consumers. Most economists fix their sights on the market where consumers

*Associate Professor of Economics, Wilfrid Laurier University.

maximize their satisfactions, producers maximize their profits, and where prices, because of demand and supply, ensure that there are no excess inventories or unmet needs. This model allocates all resources. What these economists forget is that there are some goods that cannot be priced because they are not of the same genre. They also forget that production can be made easier or harder depending on how easy it it to get the raw materials. Finally, they forget that some people do not like the model because they do not feel that the market is fair or equitable to groups who cannot bring power to bear when they bargain. It is these last three points that give rise to a political system and that make it both possible and necessary for us to discuss the influences economics has on political components such as structures, policies, parties, and elections.

THE NEED FOR GOVERNMENT

Although in the popular press it may sound as if there are some economists who suggest that there should be no government, that is not the case. Even Adam Smith, the advocate of the basically unregulated marketplace, recognized the need for a government to provide some goods such as justice, defense, and lighthouses.[3] These goods are not provided in a marketplace because they differ somewhat from private goods. These so-called public goods are indivisible[4] or exhibit externalities, [5] or are so important yet so scarce that the community recognizes the need for collective allocation.

Secondly, government is needed to help exploit resources. Access to raw materials and access to markets can be hampered by lack of government. Thus, in Canada, the orderly development of a trading system required the establishment of a government and we shall see that the structure of the government was influenced by the way entrepreneurs wished the development to take place and in turn influenced further developments.

Thirdly, most people recognize that the initial misallocation of resources is often a circumstance over which there is little control and that in the absence of government the rich and powerful will get richer and more powerful, while the poorer and disadvantaged will find their lot in life deteriorating.

This chapter is not a defense of government but an examination of how economics influences the form that government takes, its policies, and the general political situation. We are, therefore, going to investigate the reasons for a federal form of government. We will examine the dissimilarities among the political parties as they have developed in various economic situations and note how advocacy of policy is related to the base from which the parties gain their strength. We will also see that there are fundamental reasons for the continuation of economic factors as key determinants of Canadian politics.

HISTORICAL REVIEW

In 1867, the economic stability and prosperity of the Maritime provinces through the interrelated fish, lumber, wooden shipbuilding, and carrying trades was very much in doubt. Although the Civil War in the United States had sustained exports in the early 1860s, in the long term the development of steel and steam were operating against the Maritimes. While in 1867 there was little obvious economic need, the Maritimes sought economic dominance by developing year-round trade ports for the Canadas.

In Upper and Lower Canada, manufacturing had grown and diversified after 1850. Large local supplies of raw materials and a natural protection arising from a lack of transportation facilities contributed to this growth of a manufacturing sector. However, the need for larger markets became evident and acted as a stimulus in the push of the two Canadas —now Ontario and Quebec—toward Confederation.

Confederation itself can thus be seen as an economic arrangement. The colonies were each looking for economic stability and growth. Ontario and Quebec, which had not prospered to the same extent as the Maritime colonies, were searching for ways to expand. This explains the initial decision on the part of Prince Edward Island and Newfoundland to remain outside Confederation and can also explain the bargaining power held by Nova Scotia and New Brunswick in the early days of Confederation.[6]

Note the use of the term "Confederation." If one were to form a new country from the original colonies for military purposes, a centralized form of government would have been preferable to a federation of the colonies. Indeed, the Fathers of Confederation did frame the British North America Act in centralist terms. The bulk of revenues and expenditures of the day along with residual powers were given to the central government.[7] This was, no doubt, influenced by the fact that the United States had just fought a civil war and was considered a military threat, particularly in the West.

The distribution of powers between the new federal government and the provinces entering the federation was mainly of an economic nature. Of the enumerated distribution of legislative powers in Sections 91 and 92 of the British North America Act, fifty-six percent can be classed as strictly of an economic nature and another twenty-six percent indirectly of an economic nature. Indeed, beginning in 1867 and continuing to the present, the provinces have jealously guarded their rights concerning the economic powers granted to them.

Since the major source of revenue in pre-federation days had been the tariff and since the major task of the federation was to form common tariff barriers with the outside world while breaking down the existing barriers between the provinces, it made the most sense to turn the tariff over to the central government. In return, the central government was to give the provinces per capita grants for their own operations. Further, other powers given to the central government in Section 91 of the British

North America Act included external relations and the costly area of defense, both of which were subject to Imperial control and assistance, and the ones most related to economic integration—trade and commerce, aspects of interprovincial transportation and communication, navigation and shipping, control of banking, currency, patents and copyrights, interest, bankruptcy, and so on. Two powers jointly shared were closely related to national economic development—agriculture and immigration—but in both instances, a clash was to be resolved in favor of the central government.

As additional evidence that Confederation was basically an economic arrangement, we note that it was explicitly stated in the British North America Act that a railway between Halifax and the St. Lawrence should be built. This was mutually agreeable for it made transportation of goods produced in Ontario and Quebec much easier and made the Maritime ports more important. There was also provision for the incorporation in Confederation of Hudson's Bay Company lands in the West, again a place for Ontario and Quebec manufacturers to go and a source of raw materials, including land. The 1867 agreement to form one country can thus be seen as essentially an economic agreement; economics can be found throughout the document.

Contrast the emphasis on economic matters with the minor attention given to language and culture, reference to which can be found only in Section 133 of the BNA Act.

To listen to Trudeau or Lévesque in 1977, one would think that matters have changed, that after 110 years an emphasis on language and culture has become very important. Yet, a careful examination of public opinion polls as well as the campaign leading to the PQ victory in Quebec in November, 1976 leads one to believe that other issues such as high rates of unemployment, strikes, and scandal were more important than language or culture or even separatism itself.[8]

Before we leave history, it may be instructive to examine the political history of relevant issues in the late nineteenth century. Three stand out as well-known and important. Clearly, the building of the transcontinental railway was an issue in the first change of government in Canada. The execution of Louis Riel in 1885 stands out as important to the future of Canadian politics. Finally, there was the issue of Canada's first National Policy. All three were largely economic in nature.

The building of the railway can be seen as a result of the expansion to include British Columbia and Manitoba in Confederation (the usual explanation) or it can be seen as a result of economic pressures for the development of natural resources by interests in Ontario and Quebec and the desire of settlers in British Columbia to have trade routes for fur and later gold with the eastern colonies, including a desire to provide better access for settlers.[9] The ensuing political difficulties which came to be known as the Pacific Scandal were very much economic in nature. The Pacific Scandal arose from competition between the Canadian Pacific Railway and the Grand Trunk Railway, the fact that the government of Sir John A. Macdonald wanted to keep taxes low and insisted on private enterprise constructing the railway, and the involvement of American versus British funds.[10] In August, 1873, a royal commission was appointed to look into the financing problems of the Canadian Pacific Railway Company and on the opening of Parliament on October 23 of that year, the commission presented the evidence. After a two-week debate Sir John A. Macdonald resigned on November 5, 1873.

Obviously, the development of the CPR was an economic and technological achievement with great political significance. It is clear that business interests pressed hard for the building of that railway. In the financing, the question of multinational as opposed to purely national enterprise was a major issue and here we see the start of an historical trend in Canada of strong connections between businessmen and politicians.

The Louis Riel rebellions are tied up with some of the same economic issues as was the building of the Canadian Pacific Railway. After the Canadian government purchased Hudson's Bay Company lands in the Red River Valley, the Métis led by Riel protested the potential loss of their own lands to new settlers. Riel fled to the United States but returned to Saskatchewan in 1885 to protest again the loss of lands to new settlers. This time Riel was convicted and hanged for treason, an event that led to racial divisions in Ontario and Quebec and had long term consequences. Since 1885, the fortunes of the Conservative party in Quebec, largely because of Riel's execution, have not been promising.[11]

Finally, Macdonald's National Policy, built squarely on a high tariff, was purely economic. Early in the history of the new Dominion, tariffs were raised, mainly to provide an adequate revenue for the new government to function. Later, tariffs were used as the key instrument in a deliberate attempt to foster industrial development in Canada. Originally, Macdonald had advocated reciprocity with the United States but a policy of tariff protection became a second-best solution to Canada's trade problems. To this day, the Conservative party is represented as the party that stands for high tariffs and a strong link with Britain.[12]

Each of the three policies has manifested itself in Canadian political life for nearly a century. Perhaps we can find some common thread in these early issues that could be instructive today. First, they all arose because of a push by some interests for expansion of trade and for economic growth. Second, each can be seen as involving a dichotomy of interests between big business and the small businessman, consumer, and voter. The Canadian Pacific scandal arose because government was allowing one company to get larger with the aid of United States financiers and another company, the Grand Trunk, and the voters were not willing to permit that to happen. The Riel rebellions can be seen as a Métis backlash to the government's promotion of fast development of the West in the interests of Ontario businessmen. The message getting through to Quebec voters, who themselves had only minor business interests, was that Ontario business interests were favored by the Conservative party. The National Policy can be seen as a tool to achieve future reciprocity in tariff policy but it can also be seen as an attempt by government to establish the growth of the business sector rather than the farm sector. The cost of goods and services imported for consumption would rise, thereby permitting domestic firms to charge more and also encouraging foreign interests to jump the tariff barrier and invest directly in Canada.

ELECTIONS

Since the late nineteenth century many elections have focused on economic issues. Obvious examples are the 1911 election in which reciprocity was a most important issue, the 1962 election in which the value of the Canadian dollar became an issue, and the election of 1974 in which wage and price controls were at stake. There is some suspicion that the election of 1930 was thrown by Mackenzie King so that he would not be prime minister when the economy was weak.[13] The election result of 1935 was obviously associated with the lack of improvement in the economy. Thus, elections have often centered on economic problems of the time.

Economic factors were important even in those elections which were ostensibly fought on other issues. Thus, for example, Diefenbaker's National Dream can be viewed in economic terms. What Diefenbaker did was to capitalize on a certain amount of humdrum economic existence in which people saw themselves as having jobs, paying taxes, and gaining steadily but slowly in a standard of living, but not in an exciting way. He transformed that existence into a dream of rapid economic growth in which we all shared the growing pie. Instead of government budget surpluses, he promised to be daring in investing in the future and, more importantly, to start with additional payments to the disadvantaged old-age pensioners and the residents in the Atlantic Provinces. Thus, while some may classify the 1957 and 1958 elections as having been fought on closure and the implied loss of touch of the Liberal party, the real issue was probably an economic dream.

In the same way, the Trudeau era dawned with the coining of the phrase "a just society" in which the Diefenbaker dream of an enlarging economic pie to be shared by all was reawakened. The 1968 election can be seen almost purely in these terms although the personalities of the leaders doubtless had some effect.

One must ask about the election of a separatist party in Quebec in November, 1976. Was there anything economic in that event? Clearly, the answer is yes. Lévesque won the election because of an economic backlash against the Liberals, not because of separatism.[14] Significantly, in a recent survey carried out for the *Toronto Star* by Goldfarb Consultants Ltd. it was found that "jobs, not language, are the issue in Quebec."[15] There had been strikes, taxes were increasing, unemployment was high and the Liberals could apparently only offer more of the same. Lévesque, besides being a separatist, was also associated with Quebec growth in the early sixties; he himself seemed to promise hope for a better economic future.

Significantly, much of the debate about separatism involves economics; "To all but the most romantic economic separatists, we can demonstrate that it makes better economic sense to change arrangements within the country than to set up a separate shop."[16] As Quebec prepares for a referendum on separatism, more will be heard about the economic deal that Quebec has had in Confederation. Already, Jacques Parizeau, Quebec's finance minister, has released data that purport to show that Quebec has paid more for federation with Canada than the province has received. While the inclusions and exclusions in such a cost-benefit study are hotly debated by politicians in Ottawa, Quebec City, and Toronto, there is no doubt that much of the referendum vote will depend on whatever beliefs the voters have about the economic benefits resulting from being part of Canada. Thus separatism, ostensibly a cultural phenomenon, seems to be increasingly presented in economic terms.

The *Toronto Star* study previously cited showed that 96 percent of the people in Quebec believe the province to be wealthy and 49 percent believe Quebec to have put more into Confederation than it takes out. As one respondent replied, "They're trying to scare us into changing our minds but it won't work. Our minds are made up."[17] Here, it is not so much fact as belief about an economic issue that will be crucial.

Obviously, unemployment causes disenchantment among the electors even when the opposition does not use it specifically as an issue. Thus, given all other things equal, the prime minister who chooses an election date will typically wish to wait until the unemployment figures are low. It has been argued that the number of elections called for June, September, or October are linked to Canadian weather conditions, but it could also be argued that elections held in those months are held when the unemployment figures on an unadjusted basis are likely to be lowest.[18] An election held in the winter catches many people seasonally unemployed and, therefore, much more likely to be disenchanted with the government.

Moreover, the economy can be artificially or temporarily stimulated prior to an election by tax cuts and spending increases even if in the longer run these policies lead to inflation. In the events of 1972 to 1975 there is some evidence to support this notion. At the time of the 1972 election, unemployment was very much an issue with the result that the Liberal party gained a smaller percentage of the popular vote than in 1968 in every province except Newfoundland.[19] After the 1972 election there were many policies introduced that either increased spending or decreased taxes and we know that the 1974 election reestablished the Liberal majority.[20] Those policies of 1972-74 have not been without cost, however. Inflation in Canada rose steadily after the 1974 general election so that on October 13, 1975 Prime Minister Trudeau reluctantly announced that wage and price controls would be effective as of midnight that night. While it may be, as Trudeau explained, that some of our inflation was imported from abroad, the introduction of wage and price controls domestically was an admission that a large part of inflation was domestic and some part of that can be traced back to government action between 1972-1974. To some extent the government bought its own reelection in 1974 and made the voters pay for it after the election with wage and price controls.

There are further reflections that economists have on elections; these emanate from the theory underlying choice. Economists see all decisions in terms of their effect on resource allocation. Some decisions are made by individuals through a price system but we have already demonstrated that not all goods are subject to that mechanism for allocation. In fact, the government frequently makes the decisions for the individuals. But how does the government know how much defense or how many lighthouses to provide? To a large extent it relies on the voting system in deciding on what and how much to provide.[21]

There are many problems associated with this phenomenon. Economists have for many years been interested in the degree to which different voting systems accomplish the task of telling politicians how to allocate public funds.[22] There are logical criteria to be met but for this chapter it is sufficient to indicate that majority voting as practised in Canada does not meet these criteria.

Economists, then, do not justify majority voting on the basis that it meets strict theoretical criteria for making decisions on collective preferences. Rather, economists impute a motive to the government just like the profit motive or the motive attributed to consumers (maximizing satisfactions). The motive attributed to government is the motive to maximize their chances of reelection.[23]

Thus, a government will try to put together a program or combination of policies to satisfy the largest group of voters. In introducing any specific measure, it is aware that there are costs associated with compensating those who are against the measure. Those costs may be paid by direct monetary reimbursement or the government may implement a measure specifically desired by the group that has been hurt and thus pay the costs indirectly. Resource allocation, then, is taking place without an election and there is some reason to believe that the result is that wished by a majority of voters, otherwise the voters, at the next opportunity, would presumably turn against the government and choose the alternative party which they felt would better reflect their individual preferences.[24]

POLITICAL PARTIES

In the last section, when we discussed the effect of the "unseen hand" on elections, we said that governments would attempt to put together policies that would maximize their chances of reelection. Of course, opposition parties will attempt to do the same thing, to formulate policies that maximize their chances of forming the next government.

In this model, which is similar to Adam Smith's "unseen hand," political parties are supposed to act as mediators between competing interest groups in the political arena. When examined carefully, the mediation has tended to be between economic interests and the parties tend to be identified with particular economic classes.[25]

Chi, in his analysis of class cleavage, dealt with the identification of union members and blue-collar workers with the four major Canadian parties. He found that the NDP and Social Credit party have strong identification with blue collar workers (54 percent of NDP voters and 47 percent of Social Credit voters are blue-collar workers). Even more important is the influence that direct union membership has in the party structure of the NDP for this represents a preference, at least in the eyes of some voters, for strong labor organization as a counterbalance to business.[26] The Social Credit party, on the other hand, may represent working-class voters but in a very different context. The working-class support for the Social Credit party is unorganized to a much greater extent than the NDP support (65 percent as opposed to 55 percent for the NDP).

Social Credit is conventionally portrayed as right wing, which is consistent with its support from blue-collar workers who are less organized than those who support the NDP. The Social Credit solution to the economic disadvantages faced by its supporters is to advocate an economy in which free enterprise is dominant, in which large corporations are not powerful, and in which the individual has the power to become part of the economic elite. However, once in power provincially in Alberta and British Columbia, the Social Credit party has been pragmatic and has accommodated big business.

The NDP, which is portrayed as socialist, favors control of big business, including nationalizing some firms, and balancing big business by big unions and big government as its solution to the economic ills suffered by society. This orientation befits the large percentage of its supporters who have a union background. However, again, the NDP's rise to power in certain provinces has blunted its stated intentions to counterbalance big business with big unions, as can be seen during 1974 in British Columbia, even though the rhetoric of big government has not been thwarted to the same extent.[27]

The identification of union members and blue-collar workers with the NDP or the Social Credit party is not surprising since both parties started as protest movements. Both parties were founded during the 1930s depression as a response to economic dislocations that were particularly severe in the Prairie Provinces.

One aspect of class cleavage or economic scission that has not been dealt with by Chi or others is the voting behavior of professional, managerial, or white-collar classes. Both the Conservative and the Liberal parties receive approximately 60 percent of their votes from white-collar workers, and about one fifth from union members. The remaining votes come from other blue-collar workers. Thus, the two parties share similar voter profiles. However, they advocate different policies. It is hypothesized here that these different policies develop from the differences in the type of white-collar worker who votes for one party versus the other.

Meisel, in his book, *Working Papers on Canadian Politics*, provides some figures about the 1968 election.[28] One election cannot be proof that occupational groups act in a specific manner, although it seems likely that there is stability in the voting behavior of the various occupational groups.[29] Unfortunately, Meisel's data do not permit us to determine how business executives or professionals of large firms differ from those connected with small firms. We have other evidence, however, that the Liberal party is favored by those in big business, while those who favor the PCs tend to come from the small business or independent business sector.[30]

Figure 1 is developed from Meisel's statistics on the 1968 election. Here one can see that the Liberal and Conservative parties do have the largest number of voters from those within the professional class and other white-collar groups such as people in sales and clerical occupations. It will also be noted that the Progressive Conservative party garnered a large percentage of farmers' votes and although western farms are big business operations insofar as farming is concerned, they are not big in terms of businesses. They have a much greater affinity for the independent business sector.

Figure 1

1968 Vote by Occupation by Party

(In Percentages)

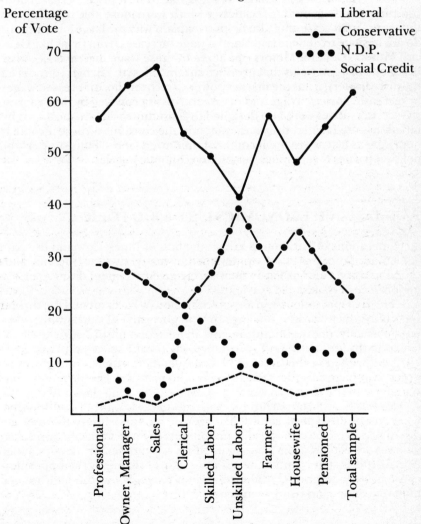

Source: Calculated from Meisel, special computer run of 1968 crosstabulation.

At this point it may be useful to clarify what the implications of support by various economic groups are for particular political parties. The mediation of economic questions undertaken by the Liberal party and the NDP is more in terms of bigness. The model will be very much business versus labor and the government is seen as being a big balancing force. On the other hand, the Progressive Conservative or Social Credit parties are more inclined to smallness, from which a number of policies will naturally follow. Thus, the Progressive Conservative Party and Social Credit have tended to advocate policies to assist small businesses and individuals. A natural outflow was the original proposal to index taxes—a Conservative proposal designed with the individual in mind. Even the wage and price advocacy of the PC party in 1974 can be seen in terms of support for the less powerful businesses which were less able to shift price increases onto consumers and against big businesses which were more able to shift price increases. Such reasoning also helps to explain why the large labor unions do not hesitate to demand substantial wage increases from firms like General Motors. General Motors can agree to those wage increases because, being one of a few firms that produce automobiles (the firm is considered the price leader), it has the market power to recover those increased wages by increasing prices. Wage and price controls as proposed by the Progressive Conservatives were also designed to assist those who are most hurt by inflation—the farmer, the pensioner, and the consumer whose income is not rising as fast as are the incomes of unionized labor. Thus support for political parties is very much related to economic policies.

PARLIAMENT: ECONOMICS IS THE BIG TOPIC

The operations of Parliament are, at the best of times, slow and the parliamentary process is poorly understood by many. Even so, the time allocation and the rules of Parliament surely give us some indication of the importance of issues.

The first major debate in any given session of Parliament is the throne speech in which broad guidelines for the government's program are set out. Normally, many announcements about economic measures are contained in throne speeches. For instance, the throne speech on January 4, 1973, as printed in the *House of Commons Journals,* runs to four pages of which two pages are devoted to economic matters. The debate on the speech from the throne is continued over eight sitting days and opposition leaders have an opportunity to move motions of want-of-confidence.

Motions of want-of-confidence provide an opportunity for areas of dissatisfaction to be publicized. The contents of these want-of-confidence motions are usually economic. Again, if we refer to the throne speech debate of the first session of the twenty-ninth Parliament, the opposition chose in their want-of-confidence motion to single out the high rate of unemployment and rising living costs.[31]

Other opportunities for discussing the economy come in the debate on the budget speech when the same procedures apply as during the throne speech. Here, economic policy is *the* issue. In the budget speech, there is a review of the state of the economy along with a statement about the general principles being applied to government spending and taxation. There are usually specific proposals for tax changes as was evidenced by the tabling of four ways-and-means motions at the conclusion of the budget presented in February, 1973.[32] Again, the want-of-confidence motion on the budget itself referred to high unemployment, spiraling cost of living, and lack of incentive for Canadian business enterprise and development.[33]

In January of each year the government tables a document in the House of Commons, known as the Estimates. Since 1968, all estimates are referred to functional standing committees of the House of Commons for deliberation. Thus, for example, the Standing Committee on Transport and Communications examines the estimates of the Ministry of Transport. The standing committees are given three months (March, April, and May) to complete their examination while the House of Commons is given twenty-five days in which the opposition chooses to debate whatever it wishes. At the end of each time period allocated to opposition debate (five days in the fall, seven days before March 31, and thirteen days before the end of June), the House of Commons votes supply and appropriation (that is, gives authority to departments to spend) without further discussion.[34]

Following a fiscal year, it is the duty of the auditor-general to conduct a post-audit of financial transactions and to report his findings to the House of Commons. The auditor-general is to report misuse of funds, overexpenditure of appropriations, expenditures not authorized by Parliament, fraud, and inefficiency in departmental operations. The Public Accounts Committee, a standing committee of the House of Commons, is charged with examining the report and calling on departmental officials to explain mismanagement. Over time, the auditor-general's Report has revealed such gross irregularities as horses on the government payroll on Sable Island, the *Bonaventure* fiasco, in which an aircraft carrier was refitted for double the $8 million estimated but scrapped three years later, and the fact that many hundreds of thousands of square metres of government office space were unused. In the 1976 auditor-general's Report there is a poignant discussion about how to control government spending; the auditor general claims that currently there is no effective control.

A great deal of time in the House of Commons and the standing committees is devoted to the Estimates and the auditor-general's Report. The Public Accounts Committee is so important in our political system that since 1958 the opposition has been allowed to designate the chairman; the current chairman is Allan Lawrence of the Progressive Conservatives. The 1976 auditor-general's Report indicates that control of government spending may become an even more important political issue.

Question period, sometimes seen as the heart of parliamentary interaction, is an occasion for the opposition parties to raise issues of national significance. Obviously, the questions are often designed to gain information and/or to make the government party appear incompetent. However, very many of these questions deal with the economy.[35]

No research, to the author's knowledge, has been carried out on the time allocation in the House of Commons and its committees. There is a strong probability, however, that such research would show that more than half of all parliamentary time is spent on economic matters.

A further indication that economics is closely related to politics is that a government defeated on a money bill is considered defeated on a non-confidence motion. As well, parliamentary rules preclude initiation of money bills from any other source than the government. In fact, the governing party is sometimes referred to as occupying the "treasury benches." Thus, functions that deal with the economy are obviously very important to Parliament.

THE CIVIL SERVICE

Canadian economic historians have suggested that growth and development have been heavily dependent on the changing fortunes of staple products. The thesis goes that the public service emerged to assist in the development process. Thus, at the outset, canal and railway construction was primary. A long-term geological survey became the next important function. Gradually, the public service assumed a protective function and eventually a promotional function. Four of the original departments, all still important, were tied to Canada's staples and Hodgetts has suggested that today the responsibilities of five departments are primarily staple-oriented.[36] Moreover, many of the Crown corporations and government boards deal with economic matters; for example, the setting of service rates to be charged by private companies, the establishment of interest rates, the regulation of natural resource development, and the marketing of various commodities.

Since the civil service is oriented toward serving the government of the day, it might be argued that its influence on decisions is not important and that policies adopted by government are established by the politicians. However, the civil service has an appreciable influence over policy and it has a certain structure built into it so that it must be examined apart from party and policy.

The civil service is a well-educated group of individuals working both to assist in the planning and actualization of the hopes and wishes of the community. More and more the public service, with its experience and expertise, advises and influences the politician. The civil servant is revered as being highly knowledgeable. Thus, the advice he gives cannot easily be rejected.

Because the civil service is highly educated and operates so that political firings are virtually impossible at the middle and lower levels, it does not matter much which party is in power. Nor does it matter very much what promises have been made to the electorate, for the implementation and ultimately the success of any policy hinges on the civil service's cooperation in the planning and execution of that policy. Once in power, all parties, whether provincially or federally, have tended to adopt similar policies, which doubtless bears some relation to the fact that the public service, at least at the decision-making level, is of one economic class and has a great deal of influence over policy.

Canada owns many economic enterprises either because the government believes that the undertaking is best handled as a monopoly or because the government wishes to exercise a certain control over the economy. After financial difficulties were faced by a number of small individual railways shortly after the beginning of this century, the government acted by buying those railways and consolidating them into Canadian National Railways. In the economic turmoil of the 1930s, the Bank of Canada was formed to institute and control monetary measures in the economy. There are now 366 Crown Corporations[37] with undertakings varying from eleven different harbor commissions which facilitate infrastructure to subsidiaries of the Canada Development Corporation such as POP Shoppes of Canada. The latter is rarely thought of as being government-owned.

The Financial Administration Branch of the Treasury Board has divided the list into eight groups, but for our purposes they may be thought of as being in one of three categories. Departmental corporations are responsible for administrative, supervisory, or regulatory services and their transactions are included in budgetary revenues and expenditure. An example is the Agricultural Stabilization Board. Agency corporations, responsible for trading and service operations, report through a minister and get parliamentary appropriations but their budgets are separate from the government accounts. The Canadian Mint is an example. Proprietary corporations, such as Air Canada and the Canadian Broadcasting Corporation enjoy a great deal of autonomy and carry on as any normal business would. Crown corporations can thus be viewed as regulatory bodies, supply bodies, or operating corporations, but each is used by the government to affect the economy.

It is the departmental corporations that attract a goodly amount of political attention. The Unemployment Insurance Commission, for example, became an important issue in the 1972 election campaign and although it is a Crown corporation it must be viewed as an arm of government about which the electorate will express strong opinions. Similarly, the Canadian Wheat Board in 1974 was accused of making final payments to farmers on the previous year's crops just prior to voting. Obviously, then, these Crown corporations can, through their effect on the economy, influence voters to be in favor of or opposed to the governing party and collectively are very significant in Canadian politics.

ARE REGIONAL CLEAVAGES ECONOMIC?

There is a theory that holds that Canadian politics can be explained as attempts to balance regional cleavages.[38] These regional cleavages are based on the idea that Ontario and Quebec represent the core whereas the remainder of Canada is seen as the periphery. The core is dominant in the number of corporations registered in those two provinces (in 1973, 91 percent of corporations federally incorporated were in Ontario and Quebec) and in corporate taxes collected (in 1969, 67.9 percent of corporate taxes were collected in Ontario and Quebec). The political consequences of the core-periphery model are many. It has been suggested that the periphery will show its alienation in ideological polarization. In Canada, significantly, much of the support, and indeed the spawning, of the Social Credit and New Democratic parties involves the periphery.

Perhaps it would be best to examine some specific issues to determine whether regional cleavages are economic. It is sometimes difficult to understand what makes an Albertan join a separatist party. Really, he is saying that Ontario (he mentions Toronto) has controlled the economy to his detriment and he intends to redress that by making Ontario suffer. Indeed, he argues Alberta has succeeded financially despite Ontario. He believes that national policies have been imposed over the years to keep markets secure for Ontario-manufactured products at the cost of making the West dependent on natural resources, which he quite correctly asserts will not last. The end result, he fears, will be an Alberta without diversification and without a resource.

Such economic attitudes are widespread. In 1973 Prime Minister Trudeau, several cabinet colleagues, and some top civil servants met with a number of Prairie and B.C. civil servants and politicians at what was called a "western summit." Almost all the demands presented at that time were economic in nature and arose from economic alienation. The demands of the Western Provinces included provincial control over monetary policy, equalization payments, and greater support of grain farmers.

Of course, virtually all federal-provincial matters are part of the rubric of both economists and political scientists. Economists tend to stress the equalization formula, the benefits and costs of conditional, unconditional, and tax-sharing schemes whereas political scientists stress the effect of party on grants received by a province, and the effects of travel distance, language, and ideology on political decision making.[39] Even an ideal federal constitution can be drawn up in terms of the degree of indivisibility of public goods (or the externalities of public goods) as Breton has done.[40] Economists are deeply concerned about the division of powers between the central authority and lower-level authorities in a constitutional setting. The stress that economists put on this question may differ from the stress of political scientists but is nevertheless just as revealing about our political system. In trying to determine who should provide what, economists learn a great deal about political realities. Knowing that conditional grants are more expensive than unconditional grants for the same level of provincial satisfaction is an important piece of information in our understanding of Canadian politics. The theoretical model on which one can base such statements requires a specific decision on whether one wishes to maximize provincial satisfaction or whether federal preferences are to dominate.

In Canada there has been very little overt differentiation in programs between provinces. However, in subtle ways there has been differentiation by federal officials. Fishing grants are not naturally oriented to the Prairie Provinces nor do they receive any major sum. Urban-renewal grants are more oriented toward provinces with larger urban populations in cities settled many years ago and they usually benefit most. In this way, grant programs do vary according to the degree to which the grants are directed at regional-specific programs.

Federal-provincial relations involve a redistribution of incomes, on a provincial rather than individual level. The usual suggestion by market economists is that people should move to the area where their own preferences for taxes and public goods coincide with those of the government. However, when the federal government gives matching conditional grants there is much less difference between the public goods provided by the provinces. Thus, individuals find it more difficult to attain their own preferences by moving.

NATIONALISM: ECONOMIC FORCES AT WORK?

Nationalism is not consistent with economic development. We do not find our politicians opting for a freer flow of goods into or out of Canada; we do not find our politicians opting for a freer flow of foreign funds into Canada; we do not see our politicians opting for greater immigration so that Canadians can capture more economies of scale. Most economists, however, would opt for freer trade, a greater flow of foreign investment funds, and greater immigration. Most economists would opt for less nationalism, while most politicians and substantial segments of the public are extremely nationalistic.

Nationalism is the only reason for the adoption of the maple leaf flag in 1965, for Expo in 1967, and for the great rise in Liberal popularity in public opinion polls in March, 1977, after a year of lagging behind in those polls. Nationalism is not big business versus the little man; it involves everybody and involves general sentiment. That is why politicians find it an attractive political vehicle, particularly when economic times are rough.

Nationalism, then, is a diversion from economic reality and those politicians who are able to take people's attention away from the economic reality of Canada are often rewarded by getting high ratings in the public opinion polls and by winning at election time.

At this point we might ask how nationalism has affected Canada. Certainly, the very existence of Canada is the result of nationalistic influences. Prior to Confederation, the United Empire Loyalists had settled in parts of Ontario, New Brunswick, and Nova Scotia and had brought with them a strong allegiance to the British Crown. They were not anxious to develop strong links with the United States and thus there was a need for rail lines and economic expansion to the West. While in this chapter we have tended to see the development of Canada as economic, it must be recognized that nationalism and a desire to establish alternatives to the natural north-south trade patterns were also important factors.

Tariffs, which we mentioned earlier as part of the National Policy, resulted in a large amount of foreign investment. Initially, the foreign investment was encouraged as a means of establishing manufacturing but later the Canadian government was keen to invite exploitation of raw materials. Even though foreign direct investment may have been a result of Canadian policies, foreign control becomes the cause of further problems because, once established, these firms become a dominant force affecting the economic environment in major ways. For example, our educational system, our research efforts, our industrial structure, and our balance between exports and imports all become less changeable because of the number of branch plants that have developed.

Traditional economics does not admit a problem of dependency. Each party, whether it be individuals or firms, tries to accrue a greater benefit to himself at the expense of the other. However, both enter into the market of their own free will, and because there are alternative buyers and sellers, an even-handed relationship between the traders is assumed. Thus, no theoretical recognition of a dependency problem is possible in traditional economics.

It is when Canadians begin to examine some of the intertwined political problems, many of them of an economic nature, that concern arises. It is recognized that Canadian exports dependent on components and technical data from the United States are subject to the Export Control Act of 1949, an act that emanates from the United States government. Further, the United States Trading with the Enemy Act, Foreign Assets Control Regulations, and the Cuban Assets Control Regulations apply to exports of affiliates and subsidiaries of United States firms, even when they make no use of U.S. components. Finally, the United States Department of Justice has jurisdiction under the Sherman Act and the Clayton Act to scrutinize and prosecute when Canadian subsidiaries of U.S. firms combine or are taken over.

Large multinational firms are bound to exert a political influence. Typically, those firms recognize the importance of being politically active. Taxes and regulations, export and import controls, and pricing policies are all of direct interest to these firms. Also, highly placed corporate individuals have moved into politics; for instance, the former vice-president of Imperial Oil moved to a policy and research post in the office of the leader of the opposition.

There are, therefore, two types of consequences that arise from foreign direct investment. The first consequence is one that can be measured. A calculation can be made of the economic costs of exports foregone, the costs of American control over Canadian industrial structure, and the amount of our gross national product that flows out of the country to pay for projects of firms' owners in other countries. There has been some debate about the net costs to the Canadian economy on these matters.[41]

Far more subtle and, in the long run, more consequential is the participation by branch operations in Canadian political life, particularly concerning the Liberal party. Contributions to party coffers, advertising assistance, and ultimately a connection on a personal level between cabinet members and some of the directors of these foreign subsidiaries constitute a threat in many eyes to political sovereignty.

There can be little doubt that Canadian policy is dictated to some extent by direct foreign investment. Certainly, the fact that Canadians have not seemed inclined to make risk capital available privately in competition with foreign firms has caused the federal government to look more favorably at expansion of the government sector. Examples are quite numerous; the latest one is the Canada Development Corporation. The Canada Development Corporation has as one of its directors the Deputy Minister of Industry, Trade, and Commerce, but has issued shares to the public through a massive campaign to get Canadians involved.[42]

Also, the government has created a Foreign Investment Review Agency (FIRA) to control the further erosion of Canadian ownership. As a regulatory body FIRA was initially quite strict, but recently there have been fewer attempts to stop foreign takeovers.[43]

What we have, then, is a political life largely shaped by an economy, shaped in turn by past political decisions which, when examined, turn out to have been mainly economic decisions. It is a very basic cycle. Once the option is taken to interfere in the marketplace, other decisions follow. Thus, the controversy over multinational corporations and nationalism itself is largely shaped by economic decisions made long ago.

IS POLITICS REALLY ECONOMICS BY ANOTHER NAME?

The approach of economics assumes self-interest on the part of the voter and on the part of the policy maker. Certainly, many voters and policy makers fit this rational model but the world is not composed exclusively of rational human beings. It would be dull if it were.

The economic approach is only one of many. Moreover, it overlaps with the continental approach and the geographical approach as well as with others. However, as we have seen, the economic approach to Canadian politics makes a great deal of Canadian political activity comprehensible though it does not explain everything.

There is no doubt that economics does not explain our hesitance to accept more foreign (American) ownership of our firms. Rather, we have a fear that foreign ownership will lead us to an ultimate loss of nationhood. While we would not lose our jobs, we would lose our pride, our nationalism, and that is not a strictly economic matter—certainly it is not measurable in dollars and cents. It is this nationalism, rather than economics, that best explains the adoption of a flag in 1965, the whole concept of bilingualism, and the great excitement over Expo '67 and the Montreal Olympics.

Another phenomenon that seems to lie beyond the realm of economic explanation is charisma. Trudeau has used charisma to his advantage since 1968 but it will be noted that it is most effective when the economic issues are perplexing; least effective and least needed when, economically, times are good. The rise of the Liberal party in the public opinion polls early in 1977, after a year of being below the Progressive Conservatives, demonstrates the diversion from economic issues that can be achieved. Pierre Trudeau, at about the same time as the rise in the polls, began to focus on the issue of national unity and in particular carried that message to the U.S. Congress where he made a widely televised speech. By implication, he let it be known that he was the only one who could keep Canada together. Thus, the heaviest unemployment since the Second World War and severe inflationary pressures no longer constituted the primary issue. Public attention was thus largely diverted from economic areas in which Trudeau and his government had done very badly and which had been the cause for the continually unfavorable polls during 1976.

CONCLUSION

It is no accident that the old name for economics was political economy. All the classical economists called it by that name. . . . Indeed, at the present time there is some question as to whether the two sciences are not showing signs of amalgamating again, perhaps into economic politics rather than into political economy.[44]

In writing these lines, Kenneth Boulding confirms what we have noted in this chapter, namely, that one cannot separate an understanding of Canadian political reality from an understanding of economic problems. Though the situation is somewhat modified during wartime, politics has been, and will continue to be, tied to various economic factors.

Thus, economics can explain much in Canadian politics; to a large extent it can account for regional voting patterns; it can help explain why sons follow their parents in voting behavior (social class tends to be transferred to the next generation). Many elections, many feelings develop directly or indirectly from economic problems or issues.

To understand why we have a federal system of government; to understand why Canadians rely on government ownership of public enterprise; to understand why the political parties adopt the positions they do (particularly on issues such as foreign ownership, protection, and support for small business and farmers); and, to understand why governments in

Canada tend to last for rather lengthy terms, it is necessary to have a knowledge of economics.

It would be foolish to assert that nothing matters in politics but the economy. Yet, it would be equally foolish to argue that the economy is not central to the political system both historically and currently. Thus, the study of politics cannot, and should not, be divorced from the study of economics.

ENDNOTES

1. John Maynard Keynes quoted by C.R. McConnell, *Economics,* 6th ed. (New York: McGraw-Hill, 1975), p. 2.

2. Resources here refer to more than natural gas, coal, iron ore, etc. There are human resources and physical products as well as natural resources which must be allocated.

3. Adam Smith, *The Wealth of Nations* (London: Routledge, 1913), Book V, pp. 541-644.

4. An indivisible good is one that an individual cannot be excluded from consuming simply because he does not pay for it. An example is national defense. If there is a missile in northern Canada and it is fired to detonate an enemy's projectile, all people in southern Canada benefit whether they have paid or not. No private company will provide missiles in optimum quantity since they would have no way to force people to pay for these goods.

5. An externality arises when one or more economic units derives an economic gain or loss from an economic action initiated by another economic unit. For instance, a new technological process to produce pulp and paper is introduced by firm A. The effluent from this process does not affect firm A but rather firm B, a fishing enterprise. Since firm A does not derive any loss from the effluent, there will be no pollution control unless forced by collective action.

6. Although Section 118 of the British North America Act spoke of the subsidies as a "final settlement," the federal government offset a determined bid for separation by Nova Scotia by increasing its subsidies. New Brunswick held out for a more favorable bargain upon surrendering its export duties which it did not do until 1873. See J.A. Maxwell, *Federal Subsidies to the Provincial Governments in Canada* (Cambridge: Harvard University Press, 1937).

7. See *Report of the Royal Commission on Dominion-Provincial Relations* (Ottawa: Queen's Printer, 1940), Book I.

8. René Lévesque, himself, avoided making separatism an issue. He spoke repeatedly about economic issues.

9. See H.A. Innis, *Political Economy in the Modern State* (Toronto: Ryerson, 1946), pp. 251-256, and *A History of the Canadian Pacific Railway* (Toronto: University of Toronto Press, 1923).

10. Innis, *A History of the Canadian Pacific Railway, op. cit.,* pp. 78-84.

11. In only two elections since have the Conservative party fortunes been good in that province. In 1930, with a depression having started under the Liberals, the Conservatives received 44.7 percent of the Quebec vote. In 1958, when

the rest of the country was clearly voting for Diefenbaker, Quebec voted 49.6 percent in favor of the Conservatives.

12. For a contrary and well-documented view see John Weir, "Trade and Resource Policies," *Political Parties in Canada,* ed. C. Winn and J. McMenemy (Toronto: McGraw-Hill Ryerson, 1976), pp. 228-249.

13. There is no doubt the economic situation played a role in the campaign. As well King confided to his diary on learning the results of the election, "I shall be glad to throw on to Bennett's shoulders the formation of a government and finding a solution for unemployment and other problems." See H.B. Neatby, *William Lyon Mackenzie King* (Toronto: University of Toronto Press, 1963), pp. 327-42.

14. At least 20 percent of the votes garnered by the PQ must have come from nonseparatists. "Question Period," a CTV production aired February 27, 1977.

15. *Toronto Star,* May 14, 1977, p. 1.

16. Joe Clark, MP, "Notes for Remarks to the German-Canadian Business and Professional Association," February 4, 1977, Toronto.

17. *Toronto Star,* May 14, 1977, p. 1.

18. Canadian elections have been held between June and the first week of November on twenty-two occasions. Since there have only been thirty elections, 73 percent of all elections have taken place in those months. July and August are not favored because of the number of people on holidays during those months.

19. In 1972, the percentage who voted for the Liberal party by province, changed from 1968 in the following manner: Newfoundland, +2.4; N.S., −4.1; N.B., −1.2; P.E.I., −4.4; Quebec, −4.0; Ontario, −8.2; Manitoba, −10.5; Sask., −1.8; Alta., −10.7; and B.C., −12.8. Calculation made from Report of the Chief Electoral Officer.

20. In 1974, the Liberal party increased its seats in the House of Commons from 109 to 140. Policies introduced between 1972 and 1974 include: indexing personal taxes, old-age pensions, family allowances, and civil service pensions. Also in this period family allowances were increased by more than 100 percent, new horizon grants were started, LIP and OYP grants were fully utilized and parliamentary salaries were increased—all to gain parliamentary and electoral support.

21. A voting system implies that the government continuously interprets public opinion polls and the views of pressure groups, the media, and political advisors.

22. See Kenneth Arrow, *Social Choice and Individual Value* (New York: Wiley, 1951); and Clifford Hildreth, "Alternative Conditions for Social Orderings," *Econometrica* (January, 1953), 81-94.

23. Albert Breton, *The Economic Theory of Representative Government* (Chicago: Aldine, 1974).

24. For a full description of this topic, see Roland McKean, *Public Spending* (New York: McGraw-Hill, 1968), pp. 10-30.

25. N.H. Chi, "Class Cleavage," *Political Parties in Canada, op. cit.* Chi concludes that "there are class differences in access to income, but also there are class differences in party support."

26. The United Auto Workers and the Steel Workers have been central to the NDP's financial survival.

27. One only need refer to the nationalization of potash in Saskatchewan, car insurance in British Columbia, Saskatchewan, and Manitoba, and the original medical care bill in Saskatchewan for proof of this statement.

28. John Meisel, *Working Papers on Canadian Politics* (Montreal: McGill-Queen's University Press, 1975), p. 291.

29. Mildred Schwartz, *Politics and Territory* (Montreal: McGill-Queen's University Press, 1974). Schwartz makes reference to the stability of voting behavior on p. xii.

30. The evidence is mainly circumstantial. Previous cabinet members from the Liberal party have been favored with large numbers of board of directorship appointments on their retirement from politics. The movement in the opposite direction has been significant as well. Note the directorships currently held by Sinclair (Margaret Trudeau's father who was a former cabinet minister), Turner, etc. or the directorships held in the past by Harris, Sharp, or Winters. All are with large corporations—some multinational. Previous PC cabinet people have been less favored. Even those who were considered to be good administrators have not moved freely between politics and big business, for example, Churchill, Alvin Hamilton, Fairclough, or Bill Hamilton.

31. Government of Canada, *House of Commons Journals,* January 15, 1973, p. 36.

32. Government of Canada, *House of Commons Journals,* February 19, 1973, p. 126.

33. Government of Canada, *House of Commons Journals,* February 22, 1973, p. 138.

34. Donald S. MacDonald, "Changes in the House of Commons—New Rules," *Canadian Public Administration,* 13, No. 1 (Spring, 1970), 33-34.

35. A count of the questions asked between April 28 and May 5, 1977 shows that 26 percent were of an economic nature. Issues depend on the timing of the release of statistics, reports, etc. and during that week no unemployment or price change statistics were released.

36. J.E. Hodgetts, *The Canadian Public Service: A Physiology of Government, 1867-1970* (Toronto: University of Toronto Press, 1973), p. 21.

37. Clive Baxter, "What's at Stake in Canada's 366 Crown Corporations," *Financial Post,* May 14, 1977, p. 5.

38. See Douglas McCready and Conrad Winn, "Geographical Cleavage: Core vs. Periphery," in C. Winn and J. McMenemy, *op. cit.,* pp. 71-88.

39. See Richard Simeon, *Federal-Provincial Diplomacy* (Toronto: University of Toronto Press, 1973); and Simon McInnes, "Federal Systems and Centre-Periphery Analysis: The Canadian Case," paper presented at the XLVIth Meeting of the Canadian Political Science Association, Toronto, June, 1974.

40. See Albert Breton, "A Theory of Government Grants," *Canadian Journal of Economics and Political Science,* XXXI (1965), pp. 175-187.

41. See Kari Levitt, *Silent Surrender* (Toronto: Macmillan, 1970); *Eleventh Report of the Standing Committee on External Affairs and National Defence Respecting Canada-U.S. Relations,* Ian Wahn, Chairman (Ottawa: Queen's Printer, 1970); *Foreign Ownership and the Structures of Industry,* M. Watkins, Chairman (Ottawa: Queen's Printer, 1968); Abraham Rotstein, "Development and Dependence: The Canadian Problem," *Economics: Contemporary Issues in Canada,* ed. D.A.L. Auld (Toronto: Holt, Rinehart and Winston, 1972); and Grant L. Reuber, "Foreign Investment in Canada: A Review," in D.A.L. Auld, *op. cit.*

42. The 1976 Annual Report of the Canada Development Corporation shows

17 127 shareholders, 74.8 percent of whom own less than fifty shares. When originally offered to the public in August, 1975, an installment purchase plan was established, thereby permitting many who otherwise would not buy shares to do so.

43. In one recent month, all applications submitted to FIRA were approved.

44. Kenneth E. Boulding, *Economics as a Science* (New York: McGraw-Hill, 1970), p. 77.

SELECTED REFERENCES

AULD, D.A.L., ed. *Economics: Contemporary Issues in Canada.* Toronto: Holt, Rinehart and Winston, 1972. A collection of articles, which can be read without economic training, dealing with such topics as foreign investment, pollution, inflation and unemployment, poverty, and Quebec separatism. Although the book was written for beginning economists, it was designed to draw their attention to some political issues that can be dealt with in economic terms.

BARTLETT, RANDALL. *Economic Foundations of Political Power.* New York: The Free Press, 1973. This book deals with three questions. First, how government decisions are made; second, how this allocation process affects the allocation of resources in the economy; and third, whether there are relationships between economic and political power. The book has a theme found in this chapter —the actions of government influence the economy, including the distribution of wealth, and that in turn influences the actions of government.

BRETON, ALBERT. *The Economic Theory of Representative Government.* Chicago: Aldine Publishing Company, 1974. This short, theoretical work uses standard economic theory of supply and demand to analyze public spending. However, Breton, in his analysis of the market behavior that underlies public-spending decisions, makes some very perceptive comments on the institutional framework. It is here he suggests that governments try to maximize their own probability of reelection—a special view of the unseen hand.

BOULDING, KENNETH E. *Economics as a Science.* New York: McGraw-Hill, 1970. Boulding treats economics as part of a broader analysis in which the background of the discipline is most important. He treats economics as a social science, a behavioral science, a political science, and so on. If one reads the chapter on economics as a political science, one is struck by the fact that political science can be viewed as an economic science as well.

BUCHANAN, JAMES M. AND RICHARD E. WAGNER. *Democracy in Deficit: The Political Legacy of Lord Keynes.* New York: Academic Press, 1977. A recent book in which two economists trace the impact of Keynesian economic theories on our political institutions, and the effects that these institutional changes have wrought on economic policy decisions. An excellent, although somewhat advanced, example of how economics creates political bias which in turn effects economic choices.

CARRIGAN, D. OWEN. *Canadian Party Platforms: 1867 - 1968.* Toronto: Copp Clark, 1968. This book is a summary of each party platform in each of the twenty-eight elections between 1867 and 1968. A reading of this volume will impress the reader with the importance of the economy in party policy in Canada.

ENGELMANN, FREDERICK C. AND MILDRED A. SCHWARTZ. *Political Parties and the Canadian Social Structure.* Toronto: Prentice-Hall, 1967. In this book political parties can be seen from numerous perspectives. The roots of political parties are particularly relevant to the reader who wishes to examine the economic ramifications.

HODGETTS, J.E. *The Canadian Public Service: A Physiology of Government, 1867 - 1970.* Toronto: University of Toronto Press, 1973. This book, sponsored by the Social Science Research Council of Canada to examine one aspect of the setting of decision making in Canada, is a thorough analysis of the origins and sociology of the Canadian public service. The reader gets a feeling for the importance of the civil service as well as why decision-making has economic bias.

INNIS, H.A. *Political Economy in the Modern State.* Toronto: Ryerson, 1946. Harold Innis was an internationally known Canadian economist whose stress on political economy was extremely significant. Innis's view of the CPR and some of the other historical developments are referred to in this chapter.

LA FOREST, GERARD V. *The Allocation of Taxing Power under the Canadian Constitution.* Toronto: Canadian Tax Foundation, 1967. This study is a more recent and fairly readable account of the division of economic powers between the central government and the provinces. The first chapter on history is particularly important.

LEVITT, KARI. *Silent Surrender.* Toronto: Macmillan, 1970. This book has had an influential impact on the nationalism of the early 1970s. It deals with the influences of multinational corporations—a "slide into a position of economic, political and cultural dependence on the United States." Kari Levitt has written a plain and forceful book which shows how Canada's dependence has come about and opens avenues for those interested in changing that dependence.

MCKEAN, ROLAND N. *Public Spending.* New York: McGraw-Hill, 1968. Already a classic in the field of public spending, this book develops the concept of the unseen hand in the decision-making process. Most of the book is relevant to policy-making in any country but there is a section on public debt in the United States that the reader may wish to skip.

MEISEL, JOHN. *Working Papers on Canadian Politics.* 2nd ed. Montreal: McGill-Queen's University Press, 1975. In this volume, Meisel examines voting behavior in the 1968 election as it relates to a number of personal attributes. Here the reader can begin to understand the importance of class cleavage in Canadian political life and particularly the importance of economic background in voting perception and behavior.

ROYAL COMMISSION ON DOMINION-PROVINCIAL RELATIONS, *Report.* 1 vol. Ottawa: Queen's Printer, 1954. Commonly known as the report of the Rowell-Sirois Commission, the original document was published in May, 1940. The fact that it had to be reprinted attests to its importance as a document on Canadian federalism. In the *Report* and the studies commissioned by the investigators, a great deal of the history of Canada can be garnered, particularly as it relates to the economy and the influences that it has had on Canadian political life.

SIMEON, RICHARD. *Federal-Provincial Diplomacy: The Making of Recent Policy in Canada.* Toronto: University of Toronto Press, 1972. This book was sponsored by the Social Science Research Council of Canada as part of a series on "Studies in the Structure of Power." Simeon examines three federal-provincial issues of the 1960s, the Canada Pension Plan, finances, and the constitution, from the point of view of the participants. Because the focus is on decision-making, Simeon plays down the fact that all three issues were to a greater or lesser extent economic in nature.

SMITH, ADAM. *An Inquiry into the Nature and Causes of the Wealth of Nations.* New York: The Modern Library, 1937. Adam Smith, a philosopher, is considered by many to have been the father of economics. Certainly, he was a strong advocate of a marketplace economy in which supply and demand determine the allocation of goods and services. Yet, in this book (Book V, Chapter 1), Smith acknowledges that certain types of goods must be administered by the government.

WINN, C. AND J. MCMENEMY, eds. *Political Parties in Canada*. Toronto: McGraw-Hill Ryerson, 1976. Although ostensibly about political parties, this book has much useful information on other topics as well. Some of the chapters deal with the economy directly or indirectly. For our purposes, the chapters on Geographical Cleavage, Class Cleavage, Redistributive Policy, and Trade and Resource Policies are particularly useful.

4

Foreign Affairs:
Canada Abroad as a Measure
of Canada at Home

Thomas A. Hockin*

INTRODUCTION

The prism through which Canadians look at the world is colored and
shaped by the domestic experience of Canada. There are distinctive features about Canada's domestic experience, and it is the premise of this article that these features plus the habits of mind of Canada's policy elite
affect the way Canadians look at the world. One can ascertain much about
Canada and its political ideas by observing what it says and does internationally.

By focusing on foreign policy and external relations one cannot understand everything about Canadian politics. However, by focusing on
some of the unmistakable tendencies in our foreign behavior and in our
statements about world problems one can glimpse some important
realities about the way we think things ought to be done or are done at
home politically. In fact, a student cannot gain a secure grasp of vital beliefs and characteristics that affect domestic political activity without looking outside the domestic arena to examine the external by-products. A
good detective in search of causes will examine the imprints and residue
of a bullet shot as well as the bullet itself.

Equally important, key characteristics of domestic political life can be
overlooked because they are so familiar. These emerge more forcibly
when revealed by external activity and rhetoric. Foreign affairs, therefore, amount to a cornucopia of activity yielding insight into domestic activity. Just as the activity of a father in his job may indicate something of
how he acts at home, so also the way a nation approaches multilateral organizations reveals something about how federal or intergovernmental
relations are handled at home. Even allowing for a generous amount of

*Professor of Political Science, York University.

natural human hypocrisy, the way a social worker tells others to act will tell us something about how he acts at home. Similarly, recurrent Canadian prescriptions for international amelioration should tell us something about dominant notions for improving domestic political well-being. Also, foreign policy can be especially helpful in identifying that most elusive phenomenon, the national ideology. It was Edmund Burke who once said that you can identify the dominant beliefs of an age by recognizing the questions that are never raised, let alone answered, by dominant opinion. So, too, with Canadian ideology. It remains difficult to identify what the Canadian ideology is by searching for it directly. Its contours can be drawn, however, by ascertaining what is never taken seriously or even considered. Prescriptions for international peace or progress that are seldom, if ever, uttered, let alone considered, by the Canadian foreign policy elite give us a sense of the domestically unthinkable. Focusing on these generally unsaid prescriptions can be a useful first step in identifying what lies within the realm of the respectable at home.

In short, every major manifestation of a nation's foreign affairs can yield insight into the nation itself. All the manifestations—aid programs, alliances, diplomatic machinations, or economic and commercial relations—can be useful material for the student in search of domestic political reality.

Nor is this all. Unlike direct observations of Canadian domestic political debate and Canadian political structures, foreign relations remind us that no nation is isolated from the outside world. An over-long observation of domestic political activity can engender myopia; a study of a nation's foreign policy and foreign relations can be a useful antidote to this disability. For example, there are few nations in the world so heavily influenced by one of its neighbors as is Canada. Canada's relations with the United States are well worth studying by every student of Canadian politics. These relations are a continual reminder that Canadian politics do not and cannot function in a vacuum on this continent.

Let us be frank, however, about the limitations of the approach in this article. Not everything about Canadian government and politics can be understood by looking to foreign relations. For example, foreign policy pronouncements by political parties at election time are a particularly unreliable guide to actual behavior. Moreover, almost all voting behavior studies confirm that the foreign policy planks of Canada's federal political parties do not count for much at election time. Bread-and-butter issues or personalities seem to matter more. Similarly, activity at the more arcane levels of diplomacy, such as in votes in various UN agencies or in obscure multilateral subcommittees, are quite divorced in most instances from popular political pressure. No one should look to the latest Canadian sub-amendment to a motion in a UNESCO subcommittee for a reliable indicator of popular Canadian perception on anything. Much of what the Department of External Affairs or the Department of National Defense do every day is profoundly elitist. Policy is often decided by specialists in comparative isolation. Nothing can be assumed about Canadian opinion or Canadian political institutions from the vast bulk of minutiae churned out by these organizations. In domestic public policy almost every shift is hedged and circumscribed by a multitude of interest groups clamoring for consideration; not so with all the day-to-day shifts in foreign activity. Canada's policy to the Maldive Islands or to Luxemburg is singularly free of much domestic attention or concern.

Yet these qualifications are really a reminder of the importance of a profound study of foreign policy and foreign relations to a proper understanding of Canadian political structures and attitudes. Elections come and go. One-time Canadian Prime Minister Louis St. Laurent once said that electoral platforms are all "cream puff " anyway. Similarly, many of the details of what Canada doés internationally are of no consequence domestically. However, attention to trends and shifts in foreign policy of intensive and extensive domestic concern can be ignored only by those who wish to remain stubbornly myopic.

This article is an attempt to focus on some foreign policy matters of signficant breadth and depth in the hope that they will give a few preliminary intimations of domestic reality.

CHARACTERISTICS OF CANADA'S EXTERNAL POLICIES

Not all of Canadian external policy can be discussed here; accordingly, this article will center on certain key characteristics of Canada's external policies. It will be argued that a not inconsiderable change in Canadian policies is evident in recent decades. From an emphasis on considerable voluntarism, a particular type of internationalism, and a fair dose of altruism lasting from at least 1945 to the late 1960s, Canada has moved to an emphasis on less voluntarism, less altruism, less continentalism, and to a different type of internationalism. All this may reflect changing domestic political reality, yet the exact content of the domestic change is not explored here. It is up to the reader after examining other chapters in this book and other readings to do that.

Arnold Wolfers reminds us that, compared to continental Europe, English and American thought and history led to a distinct philosophy of international relations in the twentieth century.[1] Although Canada is not explicitly included in his analysis, at least one fundamental premise at one time relevant to the United States and Britain is still applicable to Canada. The experience of all three nations stands in vivid contrast to Europe's experience. Geographical separation from the Continent—for Britain, the Channel, for the United States and Canada, 4000 km of Atlantic Ocean—led to what can best be called a "voluntarist" tradition in each country. This is the tradition that gave impetus to the search for moral opportunity in international politics. On the continent of Europe, the propinquity of nations as well as centuries of suspicion have made survival the major goal of diplomatic activity. Canadians, looking from afar at

European nations, tend to be impatient with their Hobbesian dilemmas and have been more attracted by the opportunities to forge moral principles into international relations and to try to elevate the whole nature of these relations above the unsavory business of balance-of-power politics. Before this voluntarist period, of course, the isolation of North America led to isolationism in foreign affairs, as prescribed in George Washington's farewell address and sympathized with by Sir John A. Macdonald. But what interests us here is the rationale behind, and the content of, the Canadian search for moral opportunity in the world when it did finally emerge.

It has been suggested, and I think rightly so, that one distinguishing characteristic of Canada is its unmilitary ethos.[2] The content of Canadian voluntarism, however, is based on something deeper than a kind of axiomatic antimilitarism. For if Canada is so firmly antimilitaristic, why did it play a major role in initiating the establishment of NATO in 1947 and 1948? Why did Arthur Meighen signal "ready, aye, ready," to assist in British military adventures in the 1920s? Were the Canadian protagonists in these cases exceptions to the rule? Actually, an analysis of these instances may lead us to a deeper and more significant source of Canadian voluntarism.

Compared to other nations since the turn of the century, Canada has had considerable success in economic growth and the establishment of peace, order, and good government. Also Canada has not started any wars; other nations have. It was not and is not unnatural for Canadians to suspect that the usual cause of international conflict is that other unruly nations simply transpose their own internal ways of doing things—their internal tyranny, violence, revolutionary upheaval—to the international arena. The Canadian antidote then is clear: the world is in need of peace, order, and more material prosperity. The rules of the international game must be changed to elicit more salutary modes of international behavior. Given this outlook, the Canadian may often be inclined to see in military force a tool of the foreign disease, a manifestation of the barren and sorry condition of balance-of-power politics. In entering into negotiations for the establishment of NATO in 1948, Louis St. Laurent regretfully acknowledged that communist "aggression" could be deterred only by brute military force. The most interesting element about Canada's initiative, however, was its concomitant insistence, through Article 2, that NATO should be "no mere military alliance" but an economic and holy alliance.[3] It is clear that since World War I Canada has never believed that a Hobbesian balance of military power is the only possible international system.

The above paragraphs, however, do not tell the whole story; the Canadian thrust in world affairs is actually twofold. On matters of economics, laws of the sea, and above all on Canadian-American questions, Canada's intention seems to be the exploitation of the Hobbesian system for national advantage. Yet at the same time, on political and military problems in many other international constellations outside of North

America, Canada's foreign policy from 1945 to approximately 1969 was distinguished by its continual, remarkably patient, voluntarist plodding for something to supplement, even transform, balance-of-power politics in the United Nations, in disarmament meetings, in trade and aid commissions, in peace-keeping activities, in the International Control Commission, in the Commonwealth, and even in NATO.

Of course, to be tough about problems close at hand and voluntarist about others is to hold a bifurcated view of world affairs. Even so, one must not overlook this voluntarist streak, for it seems to be the foundation of most of what has been creative in Canadian foreign policy. It was based on a tremendous faith in the possible results of sensitivity, goodwill, good intentions, and hard work. If there was a Canadian prescription for the international system, then it seemed to be to inculcate each participant in the system with a similar faith. This has been a part of the Canadian attitude, to international affairs at least, since the end of the First World War. This attitude can be dismissed as illusory, naive, or hypocritical and its exposition as trite. To dismiss it may be equally disingenuous. Exponents for this are found in the Liberal, Conservative and New Democratic parties, and it has survived a great number of shocks and disillusionments.

This insistence on transforming the international system may have begun with the first hopes of a League of Nations. Sir George Foster, Minister of Trade and Commerce in the Meighen administration, extolled the League of Nations to the Commons in 1921, replete with Woodrow Wilsonian references on how the League should transform the international system:

> Then there comes an article with reference to the registration of Treaties which, though simple in itself, is of paramount importance. It means that every Treaty be registered and ultimately be published. What does that mean? It cuts straight across the customs of thousands of years when secret treaties were made between powers which aroused the suspicion and massed the resources of one set of powers against others, and not only led to suspicion but to lack of faith and confidence and ultimately to broils and to war. This marks the era of open diplomacy.[4]

The search for a better international order is not, of course, confined to one party. The CCF and the NDP have been perhaps the most outspoken advocates of the moral elevation of international politics. In 1935 J.S. Woodsworth stressed armaments as the fundamental cause of enmity and distrust:

> We have seen the German nation through Hitler absolutely repudiate the Versailles treaty, and of course we are all indignant over that. But let me point out that Germany is correct in her contention that she was not the first to repudiate the Versailles treaty, that the Allies failed to live up to their obligations under it. When Germany laid down her arms, she laid them down on the express

condition that the other nations would proceed to disarm. That the Allies have not done.[5]

The search for moral opportunity has also been directed to alliances, and was perhaps best expressed by L.B. Pearson in the House in February, 1949, when he analyzed the proposed NATO:

> We should also make sure that the Atlantic pact does not become merely a screen for narrow nationalist suspicions and fears; it must make a collective contribution to the social and economic betterment of the peoples of its member states. . . . In the past, alliances and leagues have always been formed to meet emergencies and have dissolved as the emergencies vanished. It must not be so this time. . . . The Canadian government, therefore, attaches great importance to the part which the pact may play in the encouragement of peacetime co-operation between the signatories in the economic, social and cultural fields.[6]

A further touching outburst of the Canadian voluntarist faith issued from Howard Green when he was Secretary of External Affairs in the Diefenbaker government:

> What is Canada's role in this world? I suggest, Mr. Speaker, that there must be no escapism in Canada. As a people we have traditions of courage, of common sense and of religious faith. Our nation was not founded by people who were in the habit of wringing their hands, giving up and refusing to face facts no matter how unpleasant they might be.
>   This is not the character of the Canadian people. We must take our part in world affairs and do it with a spirit of optimism. This is no day for a pessimist in world affairs. . . . I feel that Canadians should face the world with optimism and also idealism, and this our people have been doing. . . . How else can you explain the fact that there has been practically unanimous endorsation of the large programmes of aid to the less fortunate peoples of the world?[7]

Paul Martin expressed another ingredient of the Canadian voluntarist faith, the impatience with cold-war rivalries that do not accommodate themselves to orderly change:

> Surely it should be possible, even with the competing political systems, to find the minimum of agreement required to deal with some vital matters of international business. Surely the international community should be able to help in situations involving bloodshed or hunger without regard to the final choice of a political system by the peoples concerned. Can we not agree that the only sane policy or diplomacy is one of peace, since the alternative is nuclear suicide?[8]

The Canadian voluntarist world view is no less distinctive and compelling because its expression sounds like a parade of cliches, or because its substance sounds hopelessly naive. It emanates, no doubt, from Canadian national experience and its emphasis on stability, order, material prosperity, and goodwill. Canada projects to the international arena the mental habits learned from domestic experience; Canadian foreign policy becomes a kind of rationalization of the Canadian experience. The Canadian philosophy reads like an antidote to the ills and suspicions of European history and to Hobbesian (all against all) international systems. Equally interesting, this philosophy is unlike the American in that it is less messianic, less impatient, more sensitive to national differences, and places more emphasis on maintaining order.[9]

In addition to transferring domestic habits of mind to international politics, Canada's contemporary attitude toward Europe has been based in a large measure on Canada's experiences with Europe since 1914. Canada's vivid impressions of Europe in this century cannot be confined only to the two wars. They are related to political developments after each war as well.

The first such experience produced an attitude remarkably similar to, but not quite as messianic as, the American attitude. Hans Morgenthau,[10] Henry Kissinger,[11] Stanley Hoffman, and others write of the United States' self-conscious idealism in plunging into the First World War, not so much to defend a father or brother but to redeem Europe from power politics and Machiavellian intrigues and corruption. This idealism was most clearly expressed in Woodrow Wilson's vision of the reign of law and the end of balance-of-power politics, expressed in his apocalyptic conception, the League of Nations. As the League crumbled, the Treaty of Versailles collapsed and Europe returned to power politics as usual. The legacy of World War I and its aftermath in Canada and the United States was one of distrust and moral censure.

"It was European policy, European statesmanship, European ambition that drenched this world with blood," complained the Canadian delegate to the First Assembly of the League of Nations.[12] Prime Minister Arthur Meighen congratulated his delegate for stating so frankly "the price the world has paid for the European diplomacy of the last hundred years."[13] James Eayrs has shown how Canada, from 1920 through the 1930s, tried, usually with success, to keep free of the intricacies of European politics. The Canadian attitude toward Europe was typically voluntarist. Canada was a new nation, as yet uncorrupted by European diplomacy and power politics. Removed from the European cauldron by 4000 km of ocean, living in a fireproof house, Canada found it natural both to condemn and to sympathize with European exigencies and difficulties; Canadians were conditioned to think that actions in foreign affairs were more matters of volition than of necessity, and wars more the result of bad faith and greed than the fault of the precarious arrangements of the international system. Canada could share, therefore, Herbert Hoover's or Warren Harding's impatience with Europe.[14] To the voluntarist, success and peace in foreign affairs seemed to be more a matter of good intentions and goodwill than of power and balance. Canada and the United States shared this attitude.

There was, however, an additional admixture in the English-

Canadian attitude that prevented Canada from turning its back completely on Europe. If it was American idealism that involved the United States in the reconstruction of Europe after World War I, it was Canada's membership in the British Empire, later the Commonwealth, which, despite annoyance at British condescension to Canada, prevented Canada from thoroughly immunizing itself against Europe. Also, Britain was perceived as somewhat disinterestedly poised outside Europe and therefore semidetached from the Continent's specific quarrels.[15] This mixture of insularity and involvement seemed to give Britain a kind of superiority of judgment similar to North America's. This similar attitude of superiority and of voluntarism, combined with Canadian membership in Empire and Commonwealth, inextricably involved the English-Canadian imagination and resolve when Britain became threatened by developments on the European continent. The English-Canadian concern, however, was more likely to be triggered by Britain's plight in Europe than by France's (as French-Canadians could not fail to notice) or by Europe's plight in general.

This voluntarist, yet not entirely detached, experience so shaped Canada's attitude to Europe that it was both continued and transformed when Canada played an active, even an initiating, role in the creation of the North Atlantic Treaty Organization from late 1947 to March of 1949. Superficially, this sudden and self-willed immersion in European balance-of-power politics might appear as confirmation of the end of the fireproof-house attitude, the end of the voluntarist syndrome in Canadian foreign policy. In fact, the Canadian attitude to the alliance was even more voluntarist than that of the United States. During the preliminaries of the treaty negotiations, Canada seemed to act as if it were the only nation anxious to concentrate on the "ought" of a better world order instead of solely on the existing unhappy conditions of power balance in Europe. The Canadian government invented, and worked steadfastly for, the inclusion of Article 2 into the treaty organization's Charter. This article, commonly called the "Canadian Article," expressed the intentions of the signatory nations to develop relations not only in military but also in economic and cultural fields. Canada's heavy participation in peace-keeping ventures and unstinting effort in disarmament negotiations since the early 1950s have no doubt flowed from this voluntarist outlook as well.

By 1960, however, the world did not seem to be accommodating itself to anyone's projects of voluntarism, let alone Canada's. Progress through peace-keeping, the UN, NATO, and disarmament negotiations was slow, almost imperceptible. As early as 1963, John Holmes, Director General of the Canadian Institute of Internal Affairs, could write of the need for Canada to search for a function in the world in order to allow Canada "to feel responsible, to fulfil a mission, limited though this may be."[16] Another observer, reviewing the Diefenbaker years and the prospects for the 1960s under a Liberal government, called for a clear identification of Canada's role in the world.[17] True voluntarism in the international system was hampered by rigidities and lack of maneuverability, and this resulted in considerable introspection in Canada about what Canada's world role ought to be.

Canada did not reject voluntarism and internationalism in the 1960s, but the impulse was redirected and more limited. To command more domestic support, Canada emphasized its role and influence in holding multilateral organizations together, such as the UN, NATO, and the Commonwealth, as well as its contributions to international police actions and calls to come to the conference table. It may not be far fetched to describe this as Canada's "federalist" approach to world politics, because the "organization-maintenance" and brokerage tactics that the Pearson government found essential within Canada from 1963-1968 could be comprehensibly transposed to the international system.[18] By 1967 this tendency to put the viability of organizations before the purposes of organizations, to present ambiguous schemes for peace-keeping, and the insistence on the curative powers of negotiating tables began to be attacked by spokesmen in all major political parties. By the time the new Trudeau government had to decide on the renewal of NATO membership in April, 1969, it was clear that the Atlantic Alliance had proved to be an expensive and profitless arena for the proponents of voluntarist action. Also, the organization-maintenance arguments for heavy Canadian contributions to NATO were wearing thin. Canada's influence in the alliance was either chimerical, or, if real, it could be destroyed if Canada boasted of it in public.[19] All this experience in the military arena combined nicely with a new emphasis of the Trudeau government. This emphasis dismissed the "helpful-fixer" role of the 1950s and 1960s as inadequate as a basis for policy on its own terms, and useful only if it could be clearly linked to national interests. As a result, the Trudeau government found Canada's NATO commitments too expensive in relation to the country's other national interests in foreign policy, and therefore Canada's military contribution to NATO was halved.

THE EXPERIENCE IN THE SEVENTIES

What remains in the 1970s of these predispositions to internationalism, altruism, and voluntarism? Some suggestions based on the images of top foreign policy makers are worth examining.

A study of the Canadian external policy elite (CEPE)[20] reveals several of the instincts of voluntarism. First, there is still a willingness to involve Canada in disputes between other countries if it is felt necessary. Senior officials in the Department of External Affairs are the most insistent that Canada need not be "more careful not to be drawn into disputes between other countries." The most skeptical group of departmental officials on this question, the top policy makers in the Department of Industry, Trade and Commerce, also seem to be more in favor of the voluntaristic side than of its opposite. Also, a somewhat altruistic stance on foreign aid is evident. Of all of the reasons for giving aid, the elite most favors giving help to those countries that "most need help." When asked if an important objective of Canadian aid policy ought to be to "assist those recipient countries whose need is greatest," an almost overwhelming agreement from the CEPE was forthcoming. This inclination to help the most needy outranked the other ten motivations for giving aid. Dramatically discredited as a motivation for giving aid was using it as a device "to resist the spread of communism." To this proposition only 61 out of 303 respondents agreed and only four strongly agreed.

A tighter, more moralistic, test lay in the question: "Canada should restrict its relations with countries that deny human rights." Only the academics in the elite group were divided on this question. Generally there was more of a disinclination to make such restrictions, with the key policy makers in the Department of Industry, Trade and Commerce being the most disinclined. Another rather tight moralistic test is one that carries with it clear and speedy shifts in the status quo away from home industry to developing countries. Asked if Canada should "speedily remove all tariffs on imports from less-developed countries" the CEPE, (similar no doubt to most other national foreign policy elites), expressed more disagreement than agreement. The ITC group seemed the most hostile to this, academics the least hostile.

Since the early 1970s world events have put Canadian altruism and internationalism to further tests. The possibility of a northwest passage for American and Soviet icebreakers through our Arctic region is one example. Nor can the possibility of nickel and manganese extraction from the sea bed of international waters arouse enthusiasm among the Canadian external policy elite. In Law of the Sea Conferences, Canada, a major world producer of nickel, has taken a "national interest" position quite distant from one of altruistic internationalism. Canada wishes to retain a policy in which coastal states retain control over the continental shelf's sea bed. Other developments dealing with law of the sea and territorial integrity make it appear as if the old emphasis on voluntarist action and internationalism has contracted somewhat and Canada has become a bit more like the old Europeans in its emphasis on the protection of national sovereignty and integrity. Canada's unilateral declaration of a 320 km offshore fishing zone as of January 1, 1977, is perhaps another example of a highly protective position on the law of the sea.

The Trudeau government's idea of the "continental defense of North America" also appears to be less continentalist and alliance-oriented than ten years earlier. In fact there is something false in trying to describe Canada's current North American military activity as an exercise in continental defense. This is to phrase it in a way more attuned to the perceptions of Canadians in the 1950s than in the 1970s. A majority of Canadians may now be as worried about defense of their territorial sovereignty against *all* comers, not simply Russians or Chinese. In all three major federal political parties, the rise of anticontinentalist movements and the concern for pollution controls, sovereignty, and fishing rights combine to put a whole new perspective on the old meaning of the "defense of North America." In fact, the 1971 White Paper on Defense ranks "the defence of North America in cooperation with U.S. forces" as a second priority. The first priority is "the surveillance of our own territory and coastlines, that is, the protection of our sovereignty."

In fact, it is possible now, for the first time, to glimpse the beginnings of a strategy for Canadian military activity. The deployment of forces is now more closely tied to domestic nonmilitary activity compared to specifically military assignments. Since 1968 Canadian defense ministers have envisaged an active role for Canadian long-range surveillance aircraft in the North, both for adequate antisubmarine capability and for research and control over the Canadian sea bed. The Canadian government, therefore, will be choosing what the government has called a "long-range aircraft of substantial size, with a capacity to operate electronic systems" for surveillance. This activity would not simply be confined to "looking for hostile submarines, but to exercising surveillance over foreign fishing fleets which may be invading Canadian territorial waters, as well as exercising surveillance of possible attempts to exploit the continental shelf without our permission, and possible incursions by land and by sea in our territory in the north."[21] Judging by the way in which these equipment problems have been posed by the government it appears that a mixture of civilian as well as military objectives will determine decisions on equipment. This shift appears to be in line with missions envisaged for other maritime forces also.

When asked to judge the importance of various roles, the CEPE generally ranked the "defense of Canadian sovereignty" and "surveillance of coastal waters" of very high or high importance. "Participation in peace keeping operations" received similarly strong support. Not far behind came "fulfilling of alliance commitments" and "sharing in the defense of North America." Moderate to low importance dominated responses to the idea that the Canadian Armed Forces are to be used to "symbolize Canada's international status," to "help counter the Soviet threat," and "to gain diplomatic influence with allies."[22]

Events of the late sixties and early seventies may also point to a similar perceptible shift in the character and motive of Canadian external policy on questions other than defense. This shift may have been both obscured and exaggerated, however, by some critics who have portrayed it as a movement away from an internationalist emphasis to isolationism. In fact the Trudeau government, if anything, has broadened the geographical scope of Canadian attention. It has attempted to move beyond the old Atlantic triangle, Commonwealth, and UN cornerstones of Canadian external policy through its increased emphasis on more contacts with China and the Soviet Union and in its increased emphasis on aid to francophone Africa, Latin America, and non-Commonwealth Africa as well as its emphasis on increasing trade with countries on the Pacific Rim and in Latin America. Canadian expenditures abroad on international development are now over 0.5 percent of the GNP and exceed $1 billion annually. Also, in the mid to late 1970s a greater proportion of aid allocations has in fact been given as grants than was the case in the late 1960s and early 1970s. It is not internationalism that has diminished as a feature of Canadian external policy, it is the old voluntarist component of Canada's internationalism that appears to have diminished somewhat. We are now hearing less about acts of faith and moral responsibility. We have seen that Canada's defense priorities have shifted to an emphasis on independence and protection of sovereignty. The residual value of its NATO commitment seems to be symbolic (that is, Canada continues to support Western Europe in a clear case of a Soviet attack) and it is diplomatically useful in that membership allows Canada to keep itself informed. The Trudeau government has not ruled out peace-keeping roles for Canada but Lester Pearson's voluntarist readiness to contribute to peace keeping is clearly de-emphasized in both the recent Defense White Paper and the 1970 Foreign Policy White Paper of the Trudeau government. Canada's disillusionment with the results of good intentions in its peace keeping in Cyprus, the Middle East, and Southeast Asia (through the International Control Commission) has contributed to uneasiness in Canada about these ventures.

In addition, Canada now requires that a great deal of its aid be reciprocated by expenditure on Canadian goods and services. This tying of aid somewhat blurs the old altruistic image. For example, it was revealed in the House Standing Committee on External Affairs and Defense on May 18, 1976 that Canada's bilateral aid to the ten main receiving countries in 1974-75, with a total population of 937.4 million, was $300 million. Of this, 60 percent ($198 million) was spent on Canadian goods and services through tied-aid provisions. In fact, in 1975 Canada had a trade surplus with these same ten countries of $368 million.[23] These figures suggest that Canada is a greater beneficiary in its economic relations with these countries than are the developing countries themselves.

The mixed character of Canada's aid performance is obvious in the CIDA head's further testimony before the House of Commons Committee on External Affairs and Defense, February 4, 1971:

> A third concern I have, when studying the local impact of our assistance, is that the apparent Canadian interest has often been our preoccupation, to the clear disadvantage of the low-income country. The tying of much of our aid to procurement in Canada is without doubt a burden and a restriction upon these countries. We have been unable, except in special circumstances, to undertake projects that had a high local cost component; and this has been a serious obstacle to development in some cases. Several ministers of agriculture in African countries will testify to that. Some hard questions need to be asked for our own self-interest. In any case, are Canadian interests and local interests often—or indeed ever—irreconcilable? If development is seen in a long enough perspective, they surely are not. . . .
>
> Under the guidelines of the foreign policy review, we now tie about 50 percent of our bilateral assistance to procurement in

Canada. Meanwhile, we have recently been receiving back in the value of the contracts made by CIDA borrowers the equivalent of about 50 percent of the funds we contribute on untied terms to that pool. CIDA and Industry, Trade and Commerce are making a special effort to improve Canadian suppliers to win a fair share of the contracts awarded by multilateral institutions. Bread thrown on the waters does return to you, and not necessarily after many days. This is surely evidence that, even in considering the short term, Canadian interests and local interests are not irreconcilable.

Canada's membership in the Commonwealth remains intact but here, also, the approach has changed. The voluntarist emphasis on moral action in this organization, so evident in both Lester Pearson's and John Diefenbaker's actions over Rhodesia and South Africa respectively, has disappeared. Perhaps the clearest example of this new attitude is Prime Minister Trudeau's view of the Commonwealth which he expressed in a press conference before leaving for the Singapore Commonwealth Conference on January 5, 1971. He emphasized two themes: first, that he could not and would not attempt to "pull off any miracles" by helping to reach a compromise on the issue of British arms sales to South Africa; and, second, he spoke at length about using the conference to discuss "techniques of improving, shall we say, the parliamentary democratic system. This to me is very fundamental: it is as important as any other issue."[24]

Compared with the past image of active mediator cultivated by Pearson and Diefenbaker, the shift in emphasis is dramatic. While attending this and later conferences, the prime minister argued further against "the helpful fixer" role for Canada and the Commonwealth by suggesting, as in 1971, that the Commonwealth in the future ought to concentrate less on "immediate problems" and spend "two or three days in a general discussion of the world political situation and world economic situation." Somewhat ironically, however, Mr. Trudeau ended up, against his will it appears, accepting a role on a committee to study the volatile issue of selling arms to South Africa.

Perhaps the Trudeau approach to foreign policy cannot be called isolationist, simply less voluntarist than much of postwar Canadian foreign policy. If the latter is correct, then the sentiments of those who argue that internationalism is impossible without voluntarism become relevant. Yet a totally voluntarist foreign policy would be so ignorant of empirical restraints as to relegate Canada to the endless role of a Sisyphus or a Don Quixote. Surely the Canadian task in international affairs is one that balances the appropriate degree of voluntarism with self-interest. Carleton University Professor Peyton Lyon perhaps expresses best the tone and attitude such a balance would produce:

> Certainly Canada would be foolish to boast about its crisis-solving capacity, to thrust its way uninvited into the disputes of others, to commit a large proportion of its resources to be ready for calls

that may never come, to accept assignments on impossible terms, to break off valuable relationships in an attempt, probably vain, to enhance Canada's eligibility as an intermediary, or to make mediation and peace keeping the sum total of foreign policy. But, so long as we steer clear of such obvious follies, why shun the blessed function of peacemaker? Why not recognize that Canada is a nation with some diplomatic, technical, and military strength, and a reasonable reputation for objectivity and inoffensiveness? And that, because of these characteristics, it may from time to time be invited to participate in international action to prevent or contain violence? Why not let the United Nations secretariat and other governments know, without fanfare, that Canada will continue to entertain such requests sympathetically?[25]

I have suggested above that the Canadian voluntaristic tendency may have stemmed from a Canadian desire to do good works in order to help elevate, in some small way at least, the style and content of international relations. I have surmised, not dissimilarly to Arnold Wolfers' views of the Anglo-American tradition in world affairs, that this tendency may stem from our luxury of being isolated geographically from the rough Machiavellian world of European statecraft. As we have seen, this voluntarism, if not extinct, is now more muted. When asked in the mid-1970s if "international politics is basically amoral," it appears that more in the CEPE tended to see the world in these cool terms than not. Defense officials were most prone as a group to see international politics this way. ITC as a group came close to being divided on this image. Another test of this image was a further proposition put to the elite. It read: "In international relations, the gain of one country is usually at the expense of another." More than twice as many of the elite disagreed rather than agreed with this zero-sum view of the fruits of international relations. Perhaps a large part of the elite has moved to the following assessment of international relationships: that the system may be amoral but gains in the system are not widely seen as implying denials to others!

IMAGES OF INTERNATIONAL POLITICS, WORLD PEACE, AND CONTINENTALISM

Canada's approach to the world is not defined solely by its self-regard but also by its image of the international system. Relevant here, but notoriously difficult to identify with certainty, is the metaphorical image an elite member has for coherently ordering, in his or her mind, the phenomena of international relations. There is so much to international relations, so much to international politics, that one is driven to crude ordering devices or metaphors to grasp it. After considering various indirect questions to get at this, the Canadian International Image Study eventually decided to present some summary phrases of some well-known ordering devices and to allow the respondents to choose.* No one metaphor or ordering device came close to being preponderant with any part of the elite, let alone the elite as a whole. Thirty-seven percent of ITC elite preferred the image of international relations as a "complex of transactions across borders"; "projection abroad of domestic policies" was their second favorite. Except for the National Defense elite which, as a group, picked it as their second metaphor, the idea of international relations as an arena for "maximization of power" scored very low. Another metaphor also found to be almost entirely unacceptable is the quasi-Marxian view of the world as an arena primarily of "economic exploitation."

Of the thirty-three respondents from External Affairs, twelve chose "global and regional systems with differentiated national roles"; nine chose "complex of transactions across borders." Of the nineteen Department of National Defense elite who answered, the "global and regional systems" ranked first, with "the maximization of power" image second. Of the twenty-eight academics who responded, ten chose the "transactional" image, six the "global and regional systems" image, and five the "search for equilibrium." When asked for the least acceptable metaphors, the academic elite (thirty answering) marked "economic exploitation" and "competition among value systems" the least acceptable.

One would be foolish to hazard any generalization from this information on the general mind-set or metaphorical coloring that the elite gives to international relations. Clearly the marxian "economic exploitation" image is nowhere very influential nor is the Gaullist "national definition" nor the heavily ideological "competition among value systems." The prisms through which the Canadian foreign policy elite views the world seem to reflect more the refractions of the transactional and systems views of international relations than anything else. A fair number of the elite did not choose any of these images; in which case, perhaps, another amalgam of the above metaphors, or of other metaphors altogether, may be more compelling.

The elite's normative or prescriptive nostrums for world peace are no

* The question read as follows:
17. a) Writers have used different metaphors in organizing their views of international relations. Which of the following do you think is the most accurate representation?
    ____a) Arena for national definition and presence
    ____b) Competition of value systems
    ____c) Complex of transactions across borders
    ____d) Economic exploitation
    ____e) Global and regional systems with differentiated national roles
    ____f) Projection abroad of domestic policies
    ____g) Search for equilibrium
    ____h) Maximization of power
  b) Which do you think is the least accurate representation?
    a___b___c___d___e___f___g___h___

doubt varied and detailed. The CIIS study took the three causes of war outlined by Kenneth Waltz in his *Man, the State and War*, and tested various propositions.* The philosophers of international politics examined by Waltz trace the causes of war either to the inadequacies of individuals, or to national domestic imperfections, or to the inherent instability of international relations.

Here, too, generalization is risky but when asked to assess different factors as "necessary factors for world peace" the CEPE as a whole thought least of the extreme rightist view, which holds that "the predominance of the free world" is a necessary condition, and the Rousseauistic view that "human nature must be changed" to ensure world peace. Surprisingly, significant distrust in "disarmament" as a necessary condition was also evident. In Waltz's terms, "international system" prescriptions and "domestic configuration" prescriptions seem to be most prevalent (see items 3, 5, 6, 7, and 9). Less emphasis seems to be given to prescriptions that call for improvement of individuals acting in the system. All of this amounts to a quite remarkable shift from the nostrums of Howard Green, J.S. Woodsworth, and George Foster in earlier decades.

The Canadian external policy elite indicates a high degree of dissensus about the future. Gradual change is expected but not necessarily harmonious change. However, there are more optimists than pessimists, based on the criteria adopted in a study by D. Leyton-Brown, R. Byers, and P.V. Lyon.[26] It found slightly more agreement than disagreement among senior officials and M.P.s who were reputed to be influential on foreign policy on the propositions that "international law would gain in respect by the year 2000," and the proposition that "resort to military force would be less in the year 2000." On three separate propositions that, by the year 2000: nuclear proliferation would be inevitable; the world's

*The question read as follows:
We would now like your assessment of eleven different factors related to global security. A necessary condition for world peace is:
  1. The predominance of the "free world"...................................._____
  2. Changing human nature..._____
  3. Narrowing the gap between the rich and
     the poor countries..._____
  4. Leaders of high moral conviction.._____
  5. A military balance of power ...._____
  6. Restraint of nationalism ...._____
  7. Effective civilian control over the military ...._____
  8. Good personal relations among world leaders........................._____
  9. Collaboration between the United States and
     the Soviet Union ...._____
 10. Disarmament.._____
 11. Changing social attitudes ...._____
 12. A further spread of nuclear weapons is inevitable................._____
 13. Significant progress has been made toward
     detente between the United States and the
     Soviet Union ...._____

wealth would be more equitable; and nuclear war would be less a threat, the elite on balance was more pessimistic than optimistic.

Propositions used to test the elite's views on questions that were pretested to reveal continentalistic or nationalist tendencies are also of importance since so much of Canadian international action is in relation to the United States. It is no doubt fair to say that there was considerable sentiment in the first ten years after World War II for strong and close relationships with the United States. Now a more cautious approach appears to be emerging.[27] Approximately twice as many members of the CEPE disagree or strongly disagree, as agree or strongly agree with the propositions that Canada and the United States should adopt a "formal continental energy policy" and that free trade between Canada and the United States would be desirable. ITC is almost split on the former proposition, however. The CEPE appears split on the proposition that "increased domestic ownership of Canadian industry would promote Canadian economic well-being," although there is slightly more agreement. There is also division on the proposition that "American capital should be permitted a major share in the development of Canadian natural resources," although here there is slightly more disagreement than agreement. On the umbrella nationalistic contention that the "costs to Canada of economic interdependence with the United States outweigh the benefits," twice as much disagreement as agreement was registered with a rather surprising amount of similarity among the policy elite in External Affairs, ITC, and the academics. Could one suggest, then, that the CEPE is mildly nationalist when it comes to impending changes in the American-Canadian economic relationship but is not nationalist in its reading of the present status of Canadian-American economic interdependence?

CONCLUSION

In conclusion, it appears that certain attitudes, such as the voluntarism, continentalism, and even internationalism, of Canadian external policy makers may have changed in the postwar period. This paper has not assessed how much. More important, this paper has tried to show that the images and policy outputs of the Canadian external policy elite do reveal some predispositions or biases that help to identify Canada's role in the world and to reveal something of their views of the international system. Further analysis is necessary to identify with certainty the content and contours of all of this. Meanwhile it is no doubt safe to say that considerable caution now exists in the policy elite about the extent to which the national interest should be sacrificed for international good. This reserve is rooted, no doubt, in the elite's somewhat cool perceptions of the international system. It may also rest in the growing complexity inherent in identifying modes of Canadian economic, cultural and political survival in an increasingly competitive and interrelated world.

As suggested at the outset of this chapter, the prism through which

Canadians, and especially policy elites, look at the world is colored and shaped by the domestic experience of Canada. We can ascertain much about Canada and its political ideas by observing what it says and does internationally. Domestic and foreign affairs are both part of the larger phenomenon we call Canadian politics. Even though there are important limitations to the approach which focuses on external relations it warrants extensive attention. Without a doubt, if we ignore the perspective of international affairs, our knowledge of Canadian politics will surely be both distorted and incomplete.

ENDNOTES

1. See Arnold Wolfers and Lawrence Martin, eds., *The Anglo-American Tradition in Foreign Affairs* (New Haven: Yale University Press, 1956).

2. James Eayrs, *Northern Approaches* (Toronto: Macmillan, 1961), Ch. 3.

3. Canada, *House of Commons Debates*, March 28, 1949, p. 2062.

4. *Ibid.*, 1921, p. 51.

5. *Ibid.*, 1935, p. 1872.

6. *Ibid.*, 1949, p. 239.

7. *Ibid.*, 1961, p. 4020.

8. Paul Martin, *Paul Martin Speaks for Canada* (Toronto: McClelland and Stewart, 1967), p. 25.

9. Compare Canada for example to Stanley Hoffman's description of the United States in his *Gulliver's Troubles* (New York: McGraw-Hill, 1968), especially Ch. 5.

10. Hans J. Morgenthau, *Politics Among Nations* (New York: Knopf, 1972), Ch. 1.

11. Henry A. Kissinger, *The Troubled Partnership* (New York: McGraw-Hill, 1965), Ch. 2, 8.

12. James Eayrs, *In Defence of Canada*, Vol. 1 (Toronto: University of Toronto Press, 1964), p. 3.

13. *Ibid.*, pp. 1-11. This contains a vivid description of the Canadian distrust and impatience with the "war drunk lunatics . . . of Europe."

14. *Ibid.*, pp. 5-6.

15. *Ibid.*, p. 5. The Canadian high commissioner in London wrote in 1926 of the abyss of European politics: ". . . the miserable little struggles for petty personal triumphs and, except on the part of the British, the lack of ideals. I don't wonder the United States keeps out of this European menagerie."

16. John Holmes, "Canada in Search of its Role," *Foreign Affairs*, (July, 1963), p. 663.

17. Peyton Lyon, *The Policy Question* (Toronto: McClelland and Stewart, 1963).

18. This interpretation of the Pearson years is developed at length in T. Hockin, "The Federalist Style in Canadian Foreign Policy," *An Independent Foreign Policy for Canada?* ed. S. Clarkson (Toronto: McClelland and Stewart, 1968).

19. See L. Hertzman, J. Warnock, and T. Hockin, *Alliances and Illusions* (Edmonton: Hurtig, 1969), Part III.

20. The Canadian International Image Study (CIIS) is presently being conducted by R. Byer, D. Leyton-Brown, and P. Lyon. This study, with which this author was originally involved, is an attempt to ascertain the images of the

Canadian external policy-making elite on Canada's role in, and the structure of, the international system. The three elite groups comprising the CEPE in the Canadian International Image Study were chosen to assure coverage of the entire elite, not a presumably representative sample. The governmental elite consists of both senior officials and elected politicians. The 179 senior officials were selected on a positional basis. All officials in policy positions at the rank of Head of Division and above were selected in the Departments of External Affairs, Industry, Trade and Commerce, and National Defense, and in the Canadian International Development Agency. In addition, individuals of similar ranks, occupying positions with significant foreign policy responsibilities, were interviewed in all other departments and agencies. This "other departments" group was aggregated to preserve anonymity, except for the Department of the Environment where enough officials were interviewed for separate departmental mention. Elected politicians were selected by a mixture of positional and reputational criteria. Ten serving cabinet ministers were interviewed, and twenty-six other members of Parliament were selected by a panel of judges as being active and influential in the foreign policy process. There is no claim that these MPs are representative of all parliamentarians.

The only nongovernmental elite group interviewed were academics. While it could be argued that businessmen, union leaders, or spokesmen for special interest groups are also influential in the Canadian foreign policy process, it was felt that only academics as a group demonstrate interest and influence across the full range of foreign policy issues. The academics were selected on a reputational basis by a panel of judges from a comprehensive list of Canadian academics with a significant number of publications on Canadian foreign policy. The interviews were substantially conducted during the period May to August, 1975.

21. *Globe and Mail*, February 1, 1971, p. 7.

22. An article drawing extensively on the CIIS's findings on elite images of defense policy will appear shortly, authored by R. Byers, P. Lyon, and D. Leyton-Brown. The arguments in this paragraph may or may not reflect the wider analysis to be found in their forthcoming article.

23. Standing Committee on External Affairs and Defense, *Report* (Ottawa: Queen's Printer, 1976), p. 44.

24. Press release, Prime Minister's Office, January 5, 1971.

25. Peyton Lyon, "The Trudeau Doctrine," *International Affairs* (Winter, 1970-71), p. 26.

26. D. Leyton-Brown, R. Byers, and P.V. Lyon, "Images of the Future: Consensus and Dissensus within the Canadian Foreign Policy Elite," *Canada's Foreign Policy: Analysis and Trends*, ed. Brian Tomlin (Toronto: Methuen, 1977).

27. This subject is explored by P. Lyon, R. Byers and D. Leyton-Brown in an article based on CIIS data, to appear in 1977 in the *International Journal*. My comments above are not meant to reflect in any way what may be presented in that article.

SELECTED REFERENCES

AXLINE, A., et al. *Continental Community?: Independence and Integration in North America.* Toronto: McClelland and Stewart, 1974. This is a good collection of essays on various dimensions of the Canadian-American relationship.

CLARKSON, S. *An Independent Foreign Policy for Canada?* Toronto: McClelland and Stewart, 1968. This is a collection of lively essays on the independence question. If this volume, written ten years ago, is compared to others such as Kari Levitt's *Silent Surrender* or A. Rotstein's *Precarious Homestead,* it also gives the reader an idea of how the concerns on this topic have changed.

EAYRS, J. *In Defence of Canada.* Toronto: University of Toronto Press, 1964. Eayrs's three volumes of historical studies on defense are definitive, readable, and essential for an understanding of past Canadian defense policy and its effect on foreign policy.

GRAY, C. *Canadian Defence Priorities: A Question of Relevance.* Toronto: Clarke Irwin, 1972. Gray's book is rapidly becoming out of date but it is the best introduction available to the issues of the 1950-1970 period.

HOCKIN, T., et al. *Canadian Condominium.* Toronto: McClelland and Stewart, 1972. This slender volume examines many of the domestic influences on Canadian external policy at the beginning of the 1970s. It gives special attention to Canadian-American issues.

HOLMES, J. *Canada: A Middle-Aged Power.* Toronto: McClelland and Stewart, 1976. A one-time top official in External Affairs, a past Director General of the Canadian Institute of External Affairs, now doing research and teaching, John Holmes writes with great balance, insight, and clarity on Canada in the world. This is the second edition of his essays.

THOMSON, D., AND C. SWANSON. *Canadian Foreign Policy: Options and Perspectives.* Toronto: McGraw-Hill, 1971. No comprehensive brief book on Canadian foreign policy will please everyone. This book at least discusses most of the major foreign policy issues that have emerged in the early Trudeau years.

TOMLIN, B. *Canada's Foreign Policy: Analysis and Trends.* Toronto: Methuen, 1977. A good compendium of new approaches to the study of Canadian foreign policy.

5

History and the Perception of Politics

Kenneth McNaught*

Lord Bolingbroke once remarked that history is "philosophy teaching by examples."[1] The "examples," of course, are all important for they are of necessity selective, yet universality is always claimed by those who make the selection. From the patriotic-narrative history of Thucydides and Herodotus, through the more analytical history of Vico to the extraordinary expansion of Clio's claims in the twentieth century, history has consistently embraced the totality of human experience. Clio has reached out promiscuously to artists of pen and brush, to princes and politicians, to theologians, merchants, and scholars, and even to the unpredictable progeny of the computer. Enriched by the methods and findings of the social sciences, the historical craft has remained the essential integrator of every study relating to man. Without knowledge of the details and patterns of the past a student of politics is like a man without a memory. He is the merest existentialist groping amongst the chimerical experiences of the present, which is, in any case, no longer existent. He will see warfare in Vietnam, terrorism in Quebec, anglophone response to bilingualism in Calgary or Vancouver or to unilingualism in Quebec, with about the same degree of understanding as the man who cuts off his finger to prove to himself that he is alive. The pain is present, the loss acute, but comprehension is absent. And already the loss is in the past.

If all the facts that the political analyst-theorist has to consider lie in the past, even if he is only a pollster, a futurist, or utopian, in what way is he not a historian? The answer is that he is a historian whether he accepts the tag or not. And this being the case, it is to his advantage to know and become involved with the kaleidoscopic problems of writing, interpreting, and using history. The very table of contents of this book underlines the indissoluble marriage of politics, or the understanding of politics, and the historical process. This fact is evident whether by history we mean what has actually happened or whether we mean the evolution of a

*Professor of History, University of Toronto.

discipline by which we may enhance our comprehension of the past. Environment, values, structures, processes, the exercise of power: historians and social scientists alike aspire to define, describe, and assess the role of such "forces."

Increasingly it seems as if some supra-academic prism has been trained upon all this diligent endeavor. Amoebalike splintering has always been an intellectual passion and the advent of counting has served, ironically, to inflame a proclivity to focus on ever smaller segments of any discipline. Historians have not been immune to this pervasive trend. Statistics, for long thought to be the means by which scholars might bring the facts of ever more complex social evolution under control and at the same time enrich and support their description of past politics, has exploded to include not only tax rolls and other state-kept records, but every conceivable collection of facts to be culled from church basements and newspaper files to trade unions and chambers of commerce membership records. We learn about voting patterns in and out of legislatures, about mobility and other social patterns (poor people have tended to take in more roomers and to move less frequently than rich people), about incidents of violence carefully categorized by class, region, and decade. Patterns emerge and we discover that a lot of women have moved into the "work force," have been paid less than men, and have found the routes to the top somewhat tortuous. Even ideas are now counted, assigned numbers, and forced into computer-card holes. Their significance will then depend on how many holes catch the attention of the machine.

Aside from controversies about the value of mechanized quantification, the peculiar evolution through which historians have both broadened and narrowed their interests has enriched the historical process immensely. Yet no matter how specialized, methodical, or even present-minded the historian becomes, his *essential* role is that of integrator. Sooner or later the "story" part of his function has to predominate; even Whig history is narrative. The detail and the analytical basis of fact may be endlessly enriched but sooner or later the historian has to put it all together, with or without a conclusion.

Those historians, such as A.J. Toynbee, who have minimized the importance of time in their comparative history become, in fact, social scientists. That is, like all scientists, they search for laws, or even *a* law, which is all explaining. I recall an evening spent several years ago with the American political scientist Louis Hartz and four Canadian historians. Only one of the historians agreed with Hartz that the purpose of historical research was to discover and define a law that could explain the development of new nations—particularly Canada and the United States. I was surprised on two counts: first, because we all assumed that Hartz knew something about history as such,[2] and second, because the historian who supported him is best known for well-crafted descriptive-analytical writing based solidly on primary sources. His history is concerned at least as much with personality and the discreet event as with determining forces, either ideological or physical. In short, while this pro-Hartzian academic is fascinated by patterns of thought, action, and community he cannot help testing them in the white water of people and accidents. The fact that Macdonald was a dipsomaniac and, while bedded down in a bilious bout of recovery, could make remarkably vulgar suggestions to an emissary from Rideau Hall as to what the governor-general could do with his vice-regal request for an immediate audience, is an angular datum that such a historian finds difficult to fit into an explanatory law.[3] Similar problems arise over Mitchell Hepburn maintaining a vibrant residence-cum-hospitality suite in Toronto's King Edward Hotel, the premature death of Sir G.E. Cartier, Count Frontenac's personal financial problems and vainglorious personality, or Mackenzie King's impenetrable foibles.

In Canada the relationship between social scientists and historians has been peculiarly close. The political economist, H.A. Innis, for example, emerges as historian par excellence in a recent book on Canadian historians;[4] Carl Berger depicts Innis's *The Fur Trade in Canada* as "one of the few books in Canadian historical literature that truly deserves to be described as seminal." Berger's almost hyperbolic assessment flows from the growing tendency of historians to ransack the evidence in search of patterns, laws, or explanatory principles; that is, to use the conceptual approach of the sciences. This tendency can be seen not only in the new breed of quantifying historians[5] but also in social and intellectual historians who do not use the computer. Ideologies, Marxism or liberalism for example, become single-cause explanations of global evolution.[6] Yet history is not likely to fall completely prey to law making any more than good scientists are likely to ignore the past. The interrelationship of the two approaches is, indeed, the mainspring of any university, a point made recently by a Canadian physical scientist. "The university is false to its calling if it does not declare that it is first concerned with the understanding through history of man and his imaginings, of life, of matter and materials and only consequentially with the instrumentalities, methodologies and techniques that arise out of this endeavour."[7]

The perception of politics must always originate with an attempt to understand "man and his imaginings" through history. But history is not only what has happened and the people or circumstances that made it happen. It is also the "instrumentalities, methodologies and techniques" employed by historians to delineate and analyze the past. I take it as a priori that a political scientist must be more or less aware of the origins and evolution of any institutions, behavior-belief patterns, or customs that he cares to study. Thus a noted British historian, who is putting what he preaches into practice as Dean of the School of Humanities and Social Science at the Massachusetts Institute of Technology, can refer to ". . . the distinctive contribution that history brings to the social sciences, because of its roots in the humanities. It is one of the tasks of historians to explain to their fellow social scientists that they must refresh their store of ideas by resort to history, literature, music and philosophy."[8] Cultural characteristics, along with social science concepts of class, economic systems, popular or working-class culture, social control, and other "one dimensional devices used to explain how societies hold themselves together" must be integrated by history.[9]

Let us examine a few concerns of Canadian political science in order to test the applicability of the foregoing general remarks: the nature of our constitution, our party system, our regionalism-federalism, and the economic and social bases of our political ideas.

I suppose the most common error to be found in undergraduate essays and examination answers is the assumption that our constitution is the British North America Act. This is not surprising when one considers the popular usage in the media and even among our political leaders. The classic example of this is the reverberating demand that we must "repatriate our constitution." Apart from courtesy copies of the British statute, the BNA Act has never been "in Canada" (and there is no verb "to patriate"), and it is not our constitution. The pervasiveness of this error, and it is not confined to students alone, is similar to other total misconceptions that could be multiplied many times. The Proclamation "Act" was, almost without fail, "issued" in 1763—unless it was 1760 or 1774. That great charter of French-Canadian rights and the "fifth cause" of the American Revolution, the Quebec Act, was "passed" by George III in 1774—or thereabouts. Laurier lost the election of 1911 because of the Reciprocity "Treaty," the Progressive "party" won sixty-five seats in the 1921 federal election and Pierre Trudeau "issued" the War Measures Act in 1970. The list is endless and many items will seem irrelevant or even pedantic to issue-oriented students. Yet pedantry, or precision, is the sine qua non of genuine political *or* historical understanding.

It is the historian who will insist most quickly on a sequential reading and understanding of the basic documents, including the primary evidence from which alone we may understand the significance of continuity. Thus, to the historian, the preamble to the BNA Act, which declares that Canada shall have "a constitution similar in principle to that of the United Kingdom" is probably the most revealing part of the Act. He will not only emphasize the failure of the Act to describe the powers of the executive, legislative, and judicial branches of the various governments established and provided for by the Act, but also the consequent need to know the whole of British and colonial history in order to understand what the Act says. Throughout the Act continuity is of the essence: existing laws, powers, and procedures all continue as before and until they are altered by the new governments. To understand the Act requires a thorough knowledge not only of pre-existing practices and laws but also of what was in the minds of the people who framed it. Look, for example, at Sections 58-68 which purport to describe the "provincial constitutions": the "Executive Council of Ontario and Quebec shall be composed of such persons as the Lieutenant-Governor from time to time thinks fit," and in Nova Scotia and New Brunswick the "Executive Authority" (why the different phraseology?) shall "continue as it exists at the Union, until altered under authority of this Act." The entire operation is *déja vu* with the exception of the division of powers and revenues and within specifically political passages, such as the future acquisition of the North-West and the building of the Intercolonial Railroad, which were, as Macdonald noted, the consequences of a very political union.

These whimsical reflections on history and our "constitution" lead directly into the question of historical evidence and the perception of politics. Let us take a few specific subdivisions of this question to illustrate the general problem: the party system, political culture, and regionalism. It is generally conceded that the achievement of responsible government in Canada was a function of the party system. But as that party system evolved through the spasms of confederation, expansion, schools, language crises, war, and urbanization-industrialization, it took on deep-grained, specifically Canadian characteristics. These characteristics are the very ones most likely to be minimized, or even unknown, by law-making, model-oriented social scientists.

In early writing on the party system the model was usually British: parliamentary supremacy, a two-party structure based on a majority party and a loyal opposition, with Section 18 of the BNA Act endorsing the Westminister model. In the 1930s, 1940s, and 1950s a different, but equally law-making, model found favor and was thought to break fresh ground by anyone who had not read Goldwin Smith or Lord Bryce. Canada was a North American, continent-wide federal state. Therefore the political party requirements described by F.J. Turner, Charles Beard, and Pendleton Herring in their analyses of the American political experience must also apply to Canada. Because of geography, extent, federalism, and isolation from Europe, Canadian politics must be, and must have been, a brokerage mechanism, eschewing ideology. Like the American, the Canadian could only be a two-party system with each party offering a department store variety of goodies to regions, classes, and interest groups. Thus, as prescribed by the American model, third or minor parties had as their principal function the preservation of the two-party system. They could force particularist issues upon the attention of one or another of the major parties but having thus "stung," as Richard Hofstadter summed it up, they must die. Their essential function was that of a safety valve to let off steam which might otherwise explode the great North American two-party system.

Well, it is the role of history to examine and, if necessary, explode just such myths or laws. In Canada the historical record demonstrates pretty conclusively that our federalism, our immigration patterns, our parliamentary rather than presidential-congressional constitution, our deeply rooted regional identities, our personal proclivities, our isothermal lines, our east-west waterways, and our other peculiarities have sustained something other than a two-party system. From the day of the "loose fish" who flip-flopped from vote to vote in the nascent stage of political parties through W.S. Fielding's Nova Scotian secessionist reformers, Mercier's Parti National, Ontario's Patrons, the Progressives, the CCF-NDP, Social Credit, and the Parti Québecois it is clear that those periods in which we have had a two-party system are indistinct and at best an exception rather than a rule. Even in the classic period of 1896-1917 the rumblings of labor, farmers, and Henri Bourassa enter many codicils to a two-party model.

Although most political scientists now concede that since at least 1921 it is virtually impossible to descry a genuine two-party system in Canada, it is the historically oriented scholar who is most likely to identify and stress the flaws in the penumbra of that lingering model. He will be less inclined to view our increasing propensity for minority government as an aberration, or the disturbing tendency of minor parties to survive (even through metamorphosis) as something that has to be explained by reference to deviations from a North American norm. The Lipset-Hartz-Hofstadter parlor game of "whatever happened to populism and socialism" is historically irrelevant to the Canadian condition. Congealed liberalism and separation of powers no doubt explain something about American politics, but the steady withering of American social-democratic minor parties from the peak 1912 presidential vote of slightly more than 6 percent is not to be understood by reference to a law established in the 1770s or at any other time. In the perception of Canadian politics an acquaintance with history helps to avert surprise as we note that Lester Pearson never had a majority during his tenure as prime minister, that Edward Schreyer presided over a creative minority government for four years, and that Pierre Trudeau, after arriving in a similar position in 1972, remarked with wry intellectual honesty: "we are more forced to listen . . . probably as a result of that some of our legislation will be better . . . we'll have to compromise." No doubt William Davis will be able to add some revealing comments when he finds time to pen his reflections.

The interaction in Canada of an increasingly flexible federal structure with regional identities and a sense of continuity that has been sustained and enhanced by monarchy, empire, commonwealth, and special relationships with the francophone world, one which never suffered the constrictions of a unifying and centralizing civil war, or of cumulative apprehension, has produced a unique sense of ideas, structure, and custom that defies the model maker. The whole point is the uniqueness, and this can *only* be understood by the attitudinal moraines deposited by history. The largely unwritten customs of our constitution are clearly not to be understood by simplistic reference to a Westminster model or a Turner-Beard-Hofstadter model. Those customs, and therefore our whole political life, are to be understood by reading the lives, letters, speeches, and actions of the people who established them. The liberal British aristocrats who goaded, guided, and responded to our political evolution; the land-grabbers, railway promoters, grain speculators, timber and other merchants; the defenders of religion, language, and schools; the anticonscriptionists, strikers, and protesters of all sorts—without knowing something about all this glorious melange and the people who tried to articulate Canadian beliefs and aspirations, the contemporary analyst will be about as secure as a goose on shell ice.

A few examples will illustrate the above argument; they may seem idiosyncratic but that is the nature of history. How can the political scientist explain the persistence of a monarchical structure in Canadian law and politics without reference to history? According to opinion polls, most Canadians today are unaware of the fact that we live in a monarchy, let alone that Queen Elizabeth is the Queen of Canada. Yet there is clearly resident in Canada a deep understanding of the continuities represented by monarchy and all its forms. Talk to any of the thousands of lawyers who are admitted every year to the various Canadian bars and you will find no perplexity in distinguishing between federal and provincial Crowns; but you may find some difficulty in comprehending the apparent ease with which these young men and women accept and work within an "illogical" structure. Again, why did the *rouge*, Wilfrid Laurier, think it wise to leave the power to disallow Canadian legislation in London? Why did the radical republican Mackenzie recant completely and return happily under amnesty to a colony of the British Crown? Why does the Lévesque government, heir to generations of francophone condemnation of the Manitoba Schools Act, justify its own school legislation with the argument that it will do for Quebec what the earlier law did for Manitoba? Why did massive majorities, French- and English-speaking, endorse the proclamation of the War Measures Act in 1970? Why did Laurier accept a knighthood and Trudeau exhibit a functional and even leadership interest in the Commonwealth?

Facile answers to such thorny questions are many. The domination of the charter groups that man our power elites, the pervasive legacy of John Locke, the co-optative power of continentalism, our colonial complex, the class relations inherent in capitalism, geographic and natural resource determinants—any and all of these facts give clues to the meaning of the story. But it is the task of the historian, while taking account of all of these facts and their implied methodologies, to try to weave them into a balanced account. Since historians are no more likely than other scholars to achieve objectivity, whatever that may be, the balance will vary from pen to pen, but if there is no balance the product will not be history. It is the special responsibility of the historian to stir into his mix the accidents, the vagaries of personality, and the concurrence of propitious or disadvantageous circumstances. He must deal pertinaciously with the "ifs" of the past and present. *Would* there have been two western rebellions if Louis Riel had not been born, or if he had been "sane"? Would there have been the monumental shift of Quebec from the Conservatives to the Liberals if Macdonald had not decided to let Riel hang, though every dog in Quebec might bark in his favor? What would have been the fate of democratic socialism had Woodsworth not been the product of his background—a Canadian Savonarola; or if the Lewis family had not possessed or developed its special blend of social conscience and political shrewdness? And need one recount the staggering array of "improbabilities" that bedeck the life and diaries of Mackenzie King?

In the midst of all the "ifs" and idiosyncrasies of the historian's selective process he will endeavor to derive patterns from his research. Yet even if he decides that Rome fell because of the triumph of Christianity and barbarism or that Canada is defined by the dominance of metropolitanism, he must put in the shading of personality, doubt, and cumulative loyalties. The historian or political analyst who omits these real, if amorphous, forces from consideration will be unduly surprised by the present, and ill-prepared to discuss policy for the future. This implies a utilitarian role for history, and not by accident. If history must deal in particularities and probabilities rather than in laws, it nevertheless is "philosophy teaching by examples." Thus a historian who knows something about the continuities of political attitudes and customs will not be surprised by the reassertion in every kind of social crisis of the belief that order underlies liberty; that apparently authoritarian measures can be justified in defense of this principle as long as their application is followed by lenience and compromise. This is not a Canadian law, but it is a general pattern of sorts and justifies certain assumptions when policy has to be made.

Lack of attention to historical continuities often leads even the most perceptive contemporary observers into surprisingly ahistorical positions. One example is the editorial campaign of the *Toronto Star* to turn Canada into an American-style republic. Despite diligent use of market research techniques, the *Star* is unlikely to win its war against Canadian history, even with the aid of painfully obvious slanting of its coverage of the royal family. Another example is supplied by the courageous, libertarian editor of *Le Devoir*. Claude Ryan is probably the most sophisticated political editor in the country, yet his response to the Quebec election of 1970 and the federal election of 1972 betrayed a startling disregard for the validity and vitality of certain kinds of *collectivités* which he usually stresses. The underrepresentation of the Parti Québecois, which was widely assumed to be one reason for the October Crisis of 1970 in Quebec, and the minority government "mess" in Ottawa, led Ryan to conclude that we should abandon our single-member constituencies and adopt proportional representation and formal coalition governments as is done in much of Western Europe.[10] He seemed to ignore several historical forces. One is that minor parties support proportional representation only as long as they are not within sight of governmental or official opposition status. One hears little of proportional representation from Péquistes or NDPers today. Another factor is our cumulative suspicion of coalitions; the flexibility of our evolving parliamentary-party system is not something that any of our parties is likely to give up lightly, as has been demonstrated most recently in Ontario. Finally, most Canadians do not agree that an injustice is suffered when a particular party fails to get a number of seats in a legislature directly proportional to its share of the popular vote. The historical evolution of constituencies as collective identities and the electing of legislators to represent them are even more important than academic adjustments of the popular vote across the country or across individual provinces. A West German model or a Scandinavian model may be intellectually gratifying, but it does not conform to Canadian history. As Mackenzie King said of Earl Grey, who tried to promote proportional representation in 1909, the governor-general was a "faddist."

When all is said and done, it remains the job of the historian to prevent faddism. While making use of the methods and findings of the social sciences he will remain essentially a conservative within the academic fold. It is never wise to ignore a conservative—especially in Canada.

ENDNOTES

1. Henry St. John, Viscount Bolingbroke, *On the Study and Use of History, Letter 2.*

2. L. Hartz, *The Liberal Tradition in America* (New York: Anchor Press/Doubleday and Co., 1955) is in many respects elaboration of a thesis advanced by H.G. Wells in *The Future in America* (New York: Anchor Press/Doubleday and Co. 1906) and either ignores or dismisses evidence that does not support the thesis, such as the political history of the South. See further my exchange with Hartz in J.M. Laslett and S.M. Lipset, eds., *Failure of a Dream* (New York: Anchor Press/Doubleday and Co. 1974), pp. 397-424.

3. The relationship between the existence of a members' bar in the House of Commons and the caliber of speakers in the chamber has been previously noticed by an astute observer of Canadian politics who, like all effective political scientists, is three quarters historian. See Norman Ward, "The Formative Years of the House of Commons, 1867-91," *Canadian Journal of Economics and Political Science*. Vol. XVIII. 1952.

4. Carl Berger, *The Writing of Canadian History* (Toronto: Oxford University Press, 1976).

5. Canadian examples would include J.P. Wallot (on early nineteenth century French Canada), E.L. Shorter (on social patterns in Western Europe), Michael Katz (on nineteenth century urban classes in Ontario), and J.M. Beattie (on crime in eighteenth century England).

6. See, for example, Gad Horowitz (like his mentor, Louis Hartz, historian-by-courtesy) *Canadian Labour in Politics* (Toronto: University of Toronto Press, 1968) Ch. 1; or S.B. Ryerson, *Unequal Union; Confederation and the Roots of Conflict in the Canadas, 1815-73* (Toronto: Progress Books, 1968).

7. Dean James Ham, School of Graduate Studies, University of Toronto, Convocation address, December 3, 1976.

8. H.J. Hanham, review of *Perspectives on the Social Sciences in Canada, Canadian Historical Review*, LVIII, No. 1 (March, 1977): 86.

9. See R. Twomey's perceptive article, "Capitalism, Society and the Rule of Law," *Bulletin of the Committee on Canadian Labour History*, 3 (Spring, 1977): 10-19.

10. *Le Devoir*, November 25, 1972.

SELECTED REFERENCES

BERGER, CARL. *The Writing of Canadian History: Aspects of English-Canadian Historical Writing: 1900-1970*. Toronto: Oxford University Press, 1976. A pioneer work of historiography and intellectual history.

GRANATSTEIN, J.L., AND PAUL STEVENS, eds. *Canada Since 1867: A Bibliographical Guide*. Toronto: A.M. Hakkert, 1974. This is the best concise critical bibliography for post-Confederation trends in historical literature.

MCNAUGHT, KENNETH. "The Multi-Party System in Canada," *Essays on the Left*, eds. L. LaPierre et al. Toronto: McClelland and Stewart, 1971. An attempt to explain the historical reasons for rejecting an American (or any other) model.

————. "Political Trials and the Canadian Political Tradition," *Courts and Trials,* ed. M. Friedland. Toronto: University of Toronto Press, 1975. A discussion of historical patterns as opposed to laws.

MILLBURN, GEOFFREY. *Teaching History in Canada.* Toronto: McGraw-Hill, Ryerson, 1972. A stimulating collection of commentaries on the nature of history, including the interpretation of Canadian history.

SILVER, A.I. "Some Quebec attitudes in an Age of Imperialism and Ideological Conflict." *Canadian Historical Review,* LVII, No. 4 (December, 1976). One of the best examples of the significance of careful intellectual history for understanding the political present.

TRUDEAU, PIERRE ELLIOTT. "The Practice and Theory of Federalism," *Social Purpose for Canada,* ed. M. Oliver. Toronto: University of Toronto Press, 1961. Still one of the most interesting applications of a historical perspective by a practising politician.

Part Two:

Values Form the Foundation of Canadian Politics

The two chapters in this section argue that unless we have some knowledge of Canada's dominant belief systems and how they have developed, we have not really understood Canadian politics. These systems are important not only for knowledge of the general political climate but for decision making in various political arenas.

In the first chapter, Professor Christian demonstrates the extent to which ideology has been and continues to be important in Canadian politics. Since ideologies are simultaneously descriptive and normative, their significance is sure to continue. Moreover, since belief systems influence behavior, we can only answer the most basic questions about Canadian politics by studying those belief systems, even though they may be vague and not easily stated.

The second chapter tells us much about political socialization and political culture. Culture denotes learned behavior patterns shared by groups of people. What is our mode of thinking, acting, feeling, our way of life? How do we acquire it? How do we express it politically? Without answering these questions, or at least understanding them, we are unable to comprehend the ideological basis of our entire political system. Professor Whittington spells out clearly the significance of political values and attitudes for political behavior.

Both chapters remind us that politics is largely the expression of ideas and that in a healthy, vibrant society there must be no minimization of thought about thought, especially thought about political thought.

6

Ideology and Canadian Politics

William Christian*

Writers in the past have struggled very hard to settle on a definite meaning for a word we use quite regularly with little difficulty in everyday speech; and that word is politics. Politics, some have said, concerns the authoritative allocation of values; others, more simply, have claimed that it determines who gets what, where, why and how, or who dominates over whom. Mao told the world that political power grew out of the barrel of a gun, but more recently we have learned that politics is really about people. It is certainly not my desire to add yet another definition to an already lengthy list. Rather I want to point to a feature of politics which is obliquely revealed by the very confusion to which I have just pointed; that is, politics is first and foremost a dispute by means of words, and a dispute about words. The most noteworthy feature about politicians is that they talk. Indeed, when impatient soldiers seize power and put an end to electoral and parliamentary activities, they ofen brag that they have "closed down the talk shop." But then they proceed to talk themselves: they make pronouncements, issue manifestos and decrees, and give commands to their troops.

   The central importance of political words was highlighted with typical brilliance in the seventeenth century by Thomas Hobbes. The eighteenth century Scottish writer, David Hume, also placed this element at the center of his understanding of political life. He drew attention to the "empire of opinion" as the single most important factor in securing the obedience of the mass of the populace to their political regime. Even if the soldiers who follow their commanders in a military takeover can subjugate the majority of the citizenry through terror or the threat of terror, they themselves obey their commanders for some reason other than fear

*Associate Professor of Political Science, Mount Allison University.

of punishment. Usually they believe in the rightness of the actions taken by their leaders and give voluntary, and often enthusiastic, assent.

Almost every adult has at least some opinions about politics. These may not be particularly profound or coherent and may consist of a series of beliefs, such as "we pay too much tax" or "the government cannot be trusted." Such beliefs might be quite fragmentary and indeed even inconsistent: for example, a man might oppose strikes in the public sector, but favor a particular strike by policemen, firemen, or nurses, without ever thinking that he might be inconsistent.

This simplest kind of opinion about politics can be of two kinds. It can either refer to beliefs about what is, or about what ought to be. For example, Mr. Trudeau ran into considerable criticism when he mused after the imposition of wage and price controls in 1975 that the free-enterprise system no longer existed in Canada. The prime minister appears to have taken it for granted that his observation was not controversial. But the reaction from the Canadian business community was swift and vigorous. Not only did businessmen deny that the free-enterprise system was dead, they also vigorously repudiated the suggestion they took to be implicit in the prime minister's remarks; namely, that it was not a bad thing that it was.

It is these kinds of opinion that the eighteenth-century Anglo-Irish political writer, Edmund Burke, called prejudice, and which he characterized as the wisdom of unlettered men. He thought that it represented an important aspect of political life and one that every serious student of politics would want to take into account. But this simple kind of opinion or prejudice has two grave limitations. First, it is not systematic. Traditions arise at various times and reflect the concerns of diverse ages. Canadians are quite capable of responding to appeals for vigorous leadership, while at the same time lamenting the erosion of the independence of the private member of the House of Commons. Second, prejudice is not comprehensive. It touches political life only here and there. It may, for instance, yield a strong response in favor of or against continued Canadian contribution to NATO, but not about the James Bay hydroelectric project.

The search for a simple but complete description and explanation of political life has taken on an increased urgency since the period of the French Revolution in the late eighteenth century. Here the increasing democratization of politics has been decisive. As politics has become less and less the concern of a small and relatively homogeneous elite, and has more and more come to involve millions of men and women, there has developed a pressing need for a way to explain and justify political actions in terms that are intelligible to, or at least acceptable to, an electorate that has often been told that theirs is the only opinion about political affairs that matters. Hence we have witnessed since the 1820s and 1830s the development of various explanatory and justifying theories that we now recognize easily by the suffix "-ism": liberalism, conservatism, anarchism, Marxism, Leninism, Stalinism, Maoism, nationalism, fascism, national socialism, and many, many more. Even the word ideology itself was coined fairly recently, at least in historical terms, during the French Revolution. With these dogmas, political leaders offer their followers relatively systematic insights into the nature of political life, present, past, and future.

"The philosophers have only interpreted the world in various ways. The point however is to change it." This maxim of Marx's adorns his tomb in London's Highgate Cemetery. It captures the essence of what ideologies seek to do: they all try to move men to action. The ideologist is always a rhetorician, an artist with words. But unlike the novelist, poet, or playwright, whose words aim at amusement or insight, the ideologist always selects his words carefully with a view to urging his listeners or readers to act, and not merely to believe. The conservative wants to preserve the state; the revolutionary wants to destroy it and create another. The anarchist proclaims a pox on all states, and wants to destroy all organized power so that the free creative individual can flourish. All share the common hope that their followers will heed their words and will act in an appropriate way.

Although the ideologist appeals to truth, he generally treats it in a cavalier fashion: not for him the quiet sifting of evidence, or the calm reflection about principles. These, for the most part, are not preconditions to actions, but hindrances. Men of action have long been hostile to the disinterested inquirer after truth. Lenin, for instance, was rudely impatient with mere theorists; and in the first book of *The Republic,* Plato describes Thrasymachus's vehement verbal attack on Socrates.

The philosopher, the lover of wisdom for its own sake, is not the immediate ally and friend of the ideologist or the rhetorician. To the extent that the philosopher seeks understanding, his conclusions may or may not lend support to the ideologist. But he will always be an uncertain and unreliable friend, since he will not accept the primacy of the ideologist's values and goals without question or without comment. The more militantly ideological governments see the danger of the philosopher clearly and quickly, and generally take such steps as appear necessary to restrain free inquiry.

The nature of the modern state renders impossible the Platonic dream of a philosopher-king. Priests, soldiers, politicians, all who hope to move large masses of men to concerted action, have need of ideology. Depending on their needs and contexts, these ideologies can be either jealous and exclusive, or moderate and tolerant. Even similar ideologies can appear under different guises. For example, the harsh and austere Marxism in the Soviet Union tolerates little opposition. At the same time the leaders of the communist parties in France and Italy are taking great pains to affirm their commitment to the liberal democratic political systems of those countries and participate in open electoral contests that they claim would continue, even under a communist government. Even within a single country an ideology can take on a variety of hues. In the United States, liberalism has been put to the service of the blacks and of the poor, while at other times it has displayed an oppressive and persecuting aspect as it did in the early 1950s when Senator Joseph McCarthy launched his crusades against alleged communist infiltration into all walks of American life.

Consider now the relationship between those who develop or use an ideology and those who listen to it or follow it. How do political leaders make use of words to move citizens and voters in a democracy to action, especially the action of casting a vote for a particular political candidate or, in the context of most modern Western democracies, on behalf of a particular political party, or even for a particular political leader? It is obvious that the political slogans and arguments a politician can use come from a relatively limited range of ideologies. Liberals, conservatives and social democrats can secure a hearing in a country such as Canada and can turn that hearing into votes. But communists and fascists have never commanded an attentive audience in this country, or succeeded in securing widespread popular support. At times doctrines like Social Credit have gained a limited popular following, generally regionally concentrated. For the most part, however, Canadians have preferred to choose their political candidates from parties whose leaders have espoused one of the three ideologies mentioned above. Why is this the case?

There are two important lines of explanation. One is that offered by Professor Louis Hartz and his collaborators in *The Founding of New Societies* (1964), later modified by Gad Horowitz in *Canadian Labour in Politics* (1968). The second follows the general argument of George Grant, especially in *Lament for a Nation* (1965).

For Hartz the decisive factor about North and South America, South Africa, Australia, and New Zealand was that they were "fragment" societies. By this Hartz meant that the emigrants from Europe had not represented all elements of the society they left. By the time this emigration began in earnest, the old European societies had broken with their feudal past and had generated liberal or bourgeois strains. The feudal period had been noteworthy for its emphasis on hierarchy and on organic unity, or collective solidarity as it might also be called. A number of factors had shattered the unity of the old society and had brought forth the bourgeois man, the independent individual, seeking to make his own way in the world and trying to discard the fetters of the old society. Although ultimately victorious, the bourgeois did not eliminate all the old feudal strains. These coexisted into the nineteenth century when some of the limitations of the liberal vision became apparent. Then a new force, socialism, emerged from a synthesis of the previous two movements in European history. The socialist shared with the feudal or tory strain the longing for social or communal solidarity but accepted the liberal's notion of the importance of freedom. The socialist, then, advanced the ideal of collective freedom and combined this with a value that was implicit but subordinate in the liberal's vision, namely, equality. In Europe all three traditions survived, though the latter two, liberalism and socialism, became pre-eminent.

In North America, to concentrate on the aspect of Hartz's analysis that is of special importance for us, the situation was different. As fragment communities, the American colonies, New France, and later

Canada, did not receive the full measure of their European inheritance. The immigrants to North America tended to be preselected. Those who went to the American colonies were predominantly liberal, whereas those who went to New France came from France before the liberal spirit had yet penetrated with force; they represented a more feudal strain. The "process of contagion" that was at work in Europe by which "ideologies give birth to one another over time" did not occur in the New World.[1] Having lost close contact with the jostling ideologies in Europe, the ideologies in the New World lost some of their original richness. In the United States the liberalism of John Locke became the prevailing ideology, whereas in New France a kind of feudal catholicism prevailed. These monolithic ideologies reacted to rivals by trying to assimilate or expel them.

What about the English-speaking settlers on the lands that eventually became Canada? Hartz argues, and his collaborator Kenneth McRae follows him in this argument, that Canada was, in McRae's words, "almost a classic instance of a two-fragment society."[2] In the English colonies, McRae observes: "As the central figure of the English-Canadian tradition we encounter once again the American liberal."[3] It is the brunt of the Hartz-McRae thesis that English Canada is a liberal fragment, very much like the American. There are differences but these are subtle and minor.[4] The implications of this analysis are clear. Because English-speaking Canada is a liberal fragment, it does not contain the necessary feudal element to generate its own variant of socialism, and because the liberal ideology congealed before the development of socialism in Europe, it did not receive this part of the inheritance. Australia, on the other hand, is a unique example of a radical fragment because the significant migration to Australia took place in the middle to late nineteenth century and was constituted by people profoundly affected by the radical movements in English life such as Chartism.

Gad Horowitz rejects this mildly pan-North American approach of Hartz and McRae. Although he finds the general thesis a compelling one he thinks that too much is lost by emphasizing the similarities between Canada and the United States. The strain, Horowitz contends, was sufficiently strong to prevent liberalism from having an open field. As a consequence Canadian liberalism was not able to develop the ideological intolerance of its American counterpart, and when British immigrants in the late nineteenth and early twentieth centuries came to Canada with socialist or laborite ideas they were not treated as aliens or foreigners. The time of congealment occurred later than Hartz and McRae were willing to admit, and the consequence of this later congealment was that Canada possessed a socialist movement of British rather than continental-Marxist inspiration which, if not the decisive force that it was in Europe, at least seems to be having an enduring presence in Canadian political life.

In *Political Parties and Ideologies in Canada* (1974), Colin Campbell and I took this argument a stage further. We agreed with Horowitz that the presence of an electorally successful Canadian socialist movement was a key difference between the United States and Canada; and we also agreed with Horowitz that Canadian Liberalism, Canadian Conservatism, and Canadian Socialism differed from those ideologies with similar names to the south. As we saw it, the Hartz-Horowitz notion of congealment was the major stumbling block in analysis. The process of ideological development we had studied convinced us that the Canadian pattern was much closer to the European than it was to the American, or to fragment communities in general. Although we recognized that there has been a considerable debate about the ideological nature of the United Empire Loyalists, it struck us that it could be generally admitted that the tory strains among the loyalists shifted the ideological images of the two North American English-speaking settlements in such a way as to affect subsequent settlement, with the more liberally inclined choosing the United States and the more conservative immigrants preferring to retain contact with the mother country. Subsequent cultural, economic, and political links with the United Kingdom reinforced the strength of the tory segment in Canada and gave it a substantial, but by no means dominant, presence.

Thus the stage was set for the later reception of British socialist ideas because Canada already contained the seeds out of which socialism could be generated. Just as Liberalism and Conservatism had adapted themselves to their new environment, Canadian Socialism grew out of indigenous forces. With the transformation of the Canadian party system in the aftermath of the First World War, the stage was set for the creation of an electorally successful socialist party during the Great Depression. Although this process took place a good deal later than in Europe, it was more analogous to the pattern there than to the ideological developments, or lack of them, in the United States. The Canadian ideological system, therefore, did not congeal, but developed into the open-ended process of mutual exchange and influence that leaves the way open for future modifications.

In *Lament for a Nation* (1965), George Grant argued that the most likely future development would be, ironically, the destruction of just those tory and socialist aspects of the Canadian political conversation that differentiated it from the ideological structure of the United States. Although fundamentally at odds one with the other, socialism and toryism did share this one important belief: that there were public goals of more importance than the satisfaction of private desires. In itself this may not sound like a striking assertion, but it was Grant's claim that the liberalism that was unchallenged in the United States and was becoming increasingly dominant in Canada denied just that point, and held the satisfaction of private desires to be the highest and indeed the only valid social goal. This aim was inherent in the notion of maximizing individual freedom, the keystone of liberalism. It was possible for the first time in the history of the world because modern science in harmony with modern technology held open the possibility of a total conquest of nature, both non-human and human, and hence held out the dream of man the unlimited creator, of Prometheus unbound. It was for this reason that Grant lamented the defeat of Canadian nationalism. He reiterated the same position in his collection of essays, *Technology and Empire* (1969); namely, that the triumph of Canadian liberalism entails the destruction of an independent Canadian state.

Grant's argument and the earlier thesis by Hartz share this in common: they both agree that the ideology known as liberalism is widely diffused and strongly held by the preponderant majority of English-speaking North Americans. This forms what some political scientists call the ideological environment; others refer to it as the political culture. I prefer to describe it as the political tradition. It might, of course, be possible in principle to test these hypotheses through public opinion polls, which are often adequate guides to the state of popular prejudice at any given time. However, they would not be reliable tests of the almost ineluctable progress toward ubiquitous liberalism that Grant fears, or the dialectical interchanges that Hartz admires.

Be that as it may, it is not expected that the ordinary citizen has a comprehensive and conscious view of politics that he could readily articulate. As a child he will learn something about politics from his parents, from his parents' friends, from his school, and from his playmates. It is not at all uncommon to hear eight-, nine-, and ten-year-olds discussing contemporary political issues with great vehemence and even great certainty. As a child grows into adolescence, school becomes a more important source of his ideas. He also begins to absorb ideas from other sources, such as the news media; even popular radio stations usually devote a small portion of each hour's broadcasting to spot news reports. This latter impact continues on through life and often creates political attitudes in quite subtle and unintended ways.[5] Work, marriage, and the aging process will modify these attitudes, but probably not in any fundamental way. The child is father to the man.

For most people active involvement in politics is limited. Most vote in federal or provincial general elections, though far fewer in municipal elections, and note with varying degrees of pleasure or dismay news reports of parliamentary and governmental activities. A few make personal contributions of money, services, or time at elections, and even fewer display an enduring or abiding willingness to be active in political life. Most are anxious to get on with the business of living and are content to leave politics to others.

These others are the politicians. We in Canada have been among the few nations to have inherited and then successfully adapted the British model of representative parliamentary government. For the most part this method of government proved unsuited to the needs, desires, or capacities of the nations in Africa and Asia to which it was exported, but it did thrive in New Zealand, Australia, and Canada. For our purposes, its salient features are as follows: relatively frequent elections based on universal suffrage; a reasonably fair system of representation by population; secret ballots; news media with considerable liberty to support or condemn particular policies, parties, and men; and political parties with designated leaders.

It is these institutions and practices that allow our representative system to operate in a satisfactory manner. They allow a coherence to develop between the latent ideological presuppositions of the governed and the more explicit positions of the political parties. When politicians talk they do not always say what they mean, and this feature of their discourse has given them the altogether undeserved reputation of always being liars and cheats. This condemnation totally misunderstands the politician's role. It is his responsibility to move men to action or to persuade them that actions taken by others are desirable. To do this he has to consider not the line of reasoning that led him to the particular conclusions he has reached, however persuasive he might find it personally, but rather the line of argument that will convince others. If this is wicked, then it is a singularly common vice. The salesman tells his customer about the advantages of buying a particular good, not the profits that will accrue to the manufacturer or the commission to the salesman. A bachelor will approach a lady, not with suggestions that he needs company, but instead by suggesting that it might interest her to accompany him to a concert or a dinner. This is not hypocrisy—that involves feigning virtues one does not possess; rather it shows an awareness that others are not necessarily moved by the same considerations that touch us.

What distinguishes the politician is that he must always be concerned with the effect that his words will have on others. A high American government official has recently been forced to resign his office as a consequence of a few chance remarks made in private. We still remember certain striking phrases from past debates and campaigns: The Old Man, the Old Flag, the Old Party; King or Chaos; Meighen's "Ready, Aye Ready"; Bennett's "Blast a way into the markets"; and more recently, John Diefenbaker's "Unhyphenated Canadianism" and Pierre Trudeau's "Just Society." As a consequence the politician has to be chary of the striking phrase, since it may return for many years to haunt him. In the same way, the expression of a merely personal opinion may be costly, a lesson that Prime Minister Trudeau has had many occasions to learn.

All this is not meant to suggest that there is no connection between what a politician says and what he believes. Quite the contrary. Rare indeed is the politician with the skills of consummate duplicity who can build a career by professing doctrines he does not hold. Even rarer is the man who would wish to do so. The politician grows from the same political tradition as the voter to whom he appeals. He is subject to the dreams, illusions, and myths of the civilization whose values he shares. But he also plays a role in the unfolding and developing of ideological principles by deepening them here, broadening them there, and, most important of all, applying them to the shifting maze of changing circumstances. It is the completeness and coherence of his ideological vision, as well as his skill in inducing others to act in accordance with its imperatives, that is the true mark of the statesman.

Were it true that Canadian politicians from the time of Confederation and beyond have engaged in an endless series of brokerage transactions, reconciling the conflicting interests of manufacturer, farmer, and merchant; Protestant and Catholic; French and English; East and West;

center and periphery; men and women; rich and poor, then one would expect the history of ideological development in Canada to present the aspect of "a tale told by an idiot, full of sound and fury, signifying nothing." Yet nothing could be further from the truth. The history of the leading Canadian political parties has a consistency that can best be understood by recourse to an explanation that assumes that voters, parties, and leaders guide their activities by reference to ideas and principles that they inherit from their political tradition.

Before sketching this development it is useful to summarize the argument. Man is a social animal; he is also an animal who thinks. Men therefore have ideas about the nature of the political community in which they live and, more important, often have strong opinions about the way that their community ought to be reordered to make it better. For the most part, however, Canadians have not been a particularly reflective people, and indeed Sir John A. Macdonald once expressed with curious enthusiasm his view that he thought it improper to "waste the time of the legislature and the money of the people in fruitless discussions on abstract and theoretical questions of government." Nonetheless, as Gad Horowitz's modification of Louis Hartz's theory suggests, Canadians have inherited and subsequently developed a number of ideological perspectives.

There is a good deal to be learned about Canadian politics by carefully examining the ideas that have been central to its political tradition. In the first place we can clearly see that there is a sharp distinction between the character of political debate in the United States and this country. Whereas in the United States Lockean liberalism and the eighteenth-century Whig inheritance, powerful and noble as they have been, constitute the salient features of that tradition, in Canada Lockean liberalism has never had the same freedom from competition. In the United States, to make a broad and rough distinction, men are called conservatives if they find that Lockean vision most attractive in the form it took in the late nineteenth and early twentieth centuries, before Franklin Roosevelt's New Deal in the 1930s. The men who are called liberals accept the value of the transformation of American thought and practice that Roosevelt consciously and unconsciously wrought. The conflict is one of different strains within a tradition, but is not any the less bitter because of that. A civil war is often the most savage kind of dispute. In Canada Conservatism refers to the principles of the Progressive Conservative party, Liberalism to the ideals of the Liberal party and Socialism to the doctrines of the New Democratic party and before it, the Cooperative Commonwealth Federation (the CCF). Although these parties have been strongly influenced at times by events in the United States, their development for the most part has been quite distinct and independent.

In the second place, by understanding the nature of ideological development in Canada we can see more clearly some of the dynamics of political debate both between and within parties. We can note, for example, that there are certain stable principles underlying each of the major national political parties that guide, but also limit, their capacity to respond to changing national problems. It is time to look at these principles and their embodiment in the concrete realities of political life.

Liberalism is the first candidate for examination. The Liberal party has been the preeminent feature of electoral and parliamentary life in the twentieth century: Laurier was prime minister from 1896 to 1911; King from 1921 to 1930, with a brief break in 1926, and again from 1935 to 1948; St. Laurent from 1948 to 1957; Pearson from 1963 to 1968; and Trudeau from 1968 to the present. In all the Liberal party has formed the government for about fifty-seven of the first seventy-eight years of this century.

As Canada's electorally most successful political party the Canadian Liberals have stood for an appropriately wide range of policies, many of which have shown little apparent relationship to the central tenets of Liberalism. But on issues that were to have a decisive effect on the nature of the Canadian polity I think that it can be shown they have revealed a remarkable consistency. Their salient concerns have been twofold. In the first place, they have taken as their major concern the condition of the individual. Put so starkly, this may seem like an odd principle, indeed one that was hardly likely to be opposed. But it must be remembered that organized society often puts forward claims on behavior and belief that seem oppressive. And subordinate groups, be they corporations or trade unions, often behave in an aggressive way to members and nonmembers alike. It is against the claims of social groups, including the nation, that Liberalism elevates the individual. Recent reforms of the laws governing abortion and divorce bear the imprint of this principle.

Secondly, they have been concerned with enhancing freedom. Modern science allied with modern technology has opened up possibilities that are still being dreamed of. The politician, of course, paints on a circumscribed canvas, but there can be little doubt that Canadian Liberalism has accepted in principle that more freedom is intrinsically desirable.

Within Canadian Liberalism, there have developed two conceptually distinct strands. Both share the fundamental concern for individual freedom, but they differ on how best to realize it. The first of these strains I shall call business liberalism because it is a doctrine that historically and at present has a strong appeal among businessmen and those who support business interests. This doctrine takes the view, so eloquently enunciated in the nineteenth century by writers such as John Stuart Mill, that the state is the institution most likely to restrict individual freedom. Although businessmen are most interested in avoiding restrictions on their own economic affairs, they also tend to be most suspicious of government initiatives generally.

The rival strain I call welfare liberalism. This traces its intellectual roots to the nineteenth-century English writer, T.H. Green, and took its original political inspiration from the British chancellor of the exchequer and subsequent prime minister, the Liberal Lloyd George, and also from the rhetoric and practice of the American President, Franklin Roosevelt, especially in his New Deal measures intended to combat the ravages of the Great Depression of the 1930s. Rather than fearing the state, welfare liberals look to it as the most effective social institution available to free citizens from other forms of restrictions, including those imposed by large business organizations. Both business and welfare liberals talk the language of freedom, with its corollary, the language of rights. Their debate, though at times spirited, may sometimes become a dull and lifeless thing, because it is a debate within an ideology, not between ideologies. It involves men who are in fundamental agreement over basic values, and in disagreement only over the most appropriate means to achieve those ends.

These two strains came out clearly in the Liberal party platform of 1957: "The Liberal party believes in the minimum of interference and control by the state . . . and is opposed to any scheme of overall control of the economy; but it is in favour of intervention by the government when required to meet the needs of the people."[6] The welfare liberal element made its first major inroads into official Liberalism in the convention of 1919 that chose Mackenzie King as Sir Wilfrid Laurier's successor. It was here that the Liberal party pledged itself "in so far as may be practicable," and "having regard for Canada's financial position" to introduce "an adequate system of insurance against unemployment, sickness, dependence in old age, and other disability, which would include old age pensions, widows' pensions, and maternity benefits."[7] King himself had realized that there might appear to be some superficial resemblance between the ideas he was pressing and socialism, and was therefore especially anxious to indicate that both the pedigree and the aspirations of his program were securely in the liberal tradition. He recognized that intervention by the state might necessitate "some interference with individual liberty" but he urged that "where wisely applied and enforced, it is an immediate restriction, that a wider liberty in the end may be secured."[8] In regard to the regulation of industrial concerns, he put the difference between a liberal approach and socialism as follows: "It is the business of the state to play the same part in the supervision of industry as is played by the Umpire in sports to see that the mean man does not profit in virtue of his meanness, and on the other hand that nothing should be done which will destroy individual effort and skill. Some may term this legislation Socialism, but to my mind it is individualism."[9]

As we shall see, this apparent similarity between some of the measures favored by welfare liberalism, and those advocated by socialists and social democrats, added a major degree of flexibility to Canadian party policies. It meant that King could introduce old-age pension legislation in the 1920s in response to the urgings of J.S. Woodsworth and, more significantly, that he could persuade the Liberal party to adopt a wide-ranging collection of social welfare measures during 1943 and 1944 when the CCF was posing its most serious electoral threat. It should be clear from the preceding discussion that King was not adopting socialist measures because of supposed political expediency, but instead was responding to a deep strain of humanitarian liberalism. King himself was neither insensitive to the arguments of business liberalism nor unaware of the strength of the business liberal element within his party. But hesitation in the face of conflicting ideological pressures within the party, and concern for the popular reception of proposed policies, does not deny a fundamental ideological concern. Rather, King's obsession with the timing of the introduction of his measures reflects an acute perception of the extent to which the politician's understanding of the implications of an ideological position can be out of step with the electorate's. King's unfolding of the implication of Canadian Liberalism had to await subsequent ideological development in the electorate; King was a Liberal, but he was manifestly not in a hurry. His refusal to be publicly out of harmony with either his party or the voters was rewarded by phenomenal political success.

To show that King's dominance over Canadian Liberalism from 1919 to 1948 was not repudiated by his successors, we can quickly note a couple of subsequent reiterations of what I have identified as the hallmarks of Canadian Liberalism. In 1948, the convention that chose Louis St. Laurent as Liberal leader affirmed that: "Liberal policies are those which protect, sustain and enlarge the freedom of the individual. The Liberal . . . believes in freedom because he believes the resources of human personality and endeavour to be rich and varied beyond calculation or prediction."[10] And later Lester Pearson wrote in his Introduction to Jack Pickersgill's pamphlet on the Liberal party that: "The fundamental principle of Liberalism . . . is belief in the dignity and worth of the individual . . . the first purpose of government [is] to legislate for the liberation . . . of human personality."[11] Not surprisingly we see similar principles advocated by Pierre Trudeau: "The first visible effect of freedom is change. A free man exercises his freedom by altering himself and—inevitably— his surroundings. It follows that no liberal can be other than receptive to change and highly positive and active in his response to it, for change is the very expression of freedom."[12]

Canadian Liberalism has, as we have seen, held to these central understandings and values throughout most of its history. Can we conclude that Canadian Conservatism as manifested in the Progressive Conservative party (and its predecessors under several different names) and Canadian Socialism as manifested in the New Democratic party and prior to that in the Cooperative Commonwealth Federation, were similarly unalloyed? Did these parties present voters with stark and clear alternatives? For the most part they did not. That is no great problem to understand since a certain amount of ideological overlap is not only convenient, but is probably a necessary condition for stable democratic politics. It might be superficially appealing to see political parties contesting for power and presenting voters with striking alternatives, but to the extent that these rival views represent fundamentally incompatible modes of community life, the omnipresent danger would be that the party in power might not relinquish office peacefully after an electoral defeat if it anticipated that all its good work would be undone by its rival. Jurisdictions where ideological disputes are deep present a sad panorama for supporters of parliamentary and representative government; Northern Ireland, South Africa, Lebanon, Pakistan, Chile, and Argentina are only a few recent examples of many spectacular failures.

Canadian Conservatives and Canadian Socialists have offered up an ideological menu of considerably greater variety than Canadian Liberals. Let us look first at the older of the two, Canadian Conservatism.

There are four elements that we can identify as making major contributions to Canadian Conservatism. These are toryism, nostalgia, hostility to rapid change, and business liberalism. This is obviously a bit of a mixed bag, but each separate element is important. Consider toryism first. George Grant and others have told us that one of the distinguishing features of Canada is that it was founded by men who were committed to an orderly, stable, hierarchical, and nondemocratic society. It was not by accident that they held these views, and not merely through contemplation of the society to the south, though the horror with which they reacted to developments there to a large extent sharpened their determination not to repeat the same mistakes. The British North America Act speaks, so this argument runs, in terms of "Peace, Order and Good Government" not "Life, Liberty and the Pursuit of Happiness." Although representation by population was introduced for the lower house, this democratic notion did not run to universal or even to manhood suffrage; and, moreover, an undemocratic Senate, with members appointed for life to insulate them from electoral pressure, was created and endowed with powers virtually equal to those of the House of Commons. Significantly, Canada was to remain a constitutional monarchy; it was the British, not Macdonald, who opposed the name, Kingdom of Canada.

This toryism had dual roots in Canada. In Quebec the Catholic Church had preserved the feudal inheritance from France against the dangerous liberal ideas of the English-speaking traders and merchants. In English Canada, as we have seen, a number of factors were at work. Immigration to British North America, especially after the American Revolution, was not charged with the same ideological character as was immigration to the United States. The United Empire Loyalists, although not a homogeneous social or ideological group, had known a society in ferment and transition and did not wish to experience it again in their new-found home. The proximity of the United States reinforced their tory tendencies and these gained support from some of the later immigrants. This is not to suggest that English-speaking Canada was ever monolithically tory. Quite the contrary! Opponents of the Horowitz thesis think that they can discredit the whole argument by demonstrating that the Loyalists, instead of being pure tories, were contaminated by Whig or Liberal ideas. But this tory touch is exactly what the Horowitz thesis requires, since nobody doubts that liberalism forms the central core of the Canadian political traditions. What this argument establishes is that there was at least a strong tory element in Canada from the beginning, and that this element has not been destroyed by subsequent developments.

The second element of the Conservative ideological mix was nostalgia. Clearly this longing for the past is not the exclusive property of any political party, or even of politics itself. It is a universal human emotion, but it does not strike all with the same intensity or frequency. At times, however, it comes to be predominant in certain men and certain situations. Arthur Meighen was certainly subject to it in his views on both social and imperial relations. More recently, John Diefenbaker made nostalgia into a potent political weapon, one which had, for a time, a significant electoral appeal.

Nostalgia is closely associated with the third Conservative element, a disposition to be hostile to rapid change. Again, this is a well-nigh universal attitude, though it is more powerful in some than in others. It is my contention that the tory strain in Canadian Conservatism has made this party throughout its history the most attractive choice for those whose character or situation leads them to find nostalgia or caution appealing.

From its inception, however, the Progressive Conservative party, or Liberal-Conservative party as it was known for the greater part of its history, has espoused business liberalism as well. This combination of toryism and business liberalism is not at all strange, though these two doctrines are logically incompatible. Like welfare liberalism and socialism, they can serve as useful allies. The business liberal can concede the maintenance of social hierarchy to toryism, and in return can expect that tory collectivism's view of the national interest will be strongly colored by the needs and interests of the business community. Indeed no political thinker in the middle of the nineteenth century in Canada could have hoped to gain the electoral support of the property-owning electors without adopting liberalism in some guise. It was Macdonald's insight that tory and business liberals could both be brought into alliance around the National Policy, with its program of the acquisition of the West, the building of a transcontinental railway, and the protective tariff, that stands as the greatest tribute to the breadth of his ideological vision.

It was the Liberal, Laurier, more than anyone else, who set the tone for the future ideological development of Canadian Conservatism. His brilliant success in undermining the Conservative party's support in Quebec slowly isolated the tory element in English Canada from the collectivism and hierarchism of the *bleu* tradition in French-Canadian society. Combined with Macdonald's fateful decision to allow the execution of Louis Riel, the stamp was increasingly set on the Conservatives as the party of English business liberalism. They were cut off from precisely that segment of Canadian society, the rural Catholics of Quebec, for whom toryism was a powerfully compelling ideology. Under Borden and Meighen the liberal aspect of Canadian Conservatism became increasingly powerful.

Nonetheless there remained within Canadian Conservatism an element that manifested itself in the form of a belief in the primacy of politics over economics, the view that it was the responsibility of the government to ensure that the interests of the nation were considered as paramount, superseding all others, including those of the business community. It was this aspect of Canadian Conservatism to which George Grant drew attention when he wrote that Socialism and Conservatism in Canada both protect "the public good against private freedom."[13] It would be wrong to exaggerate this element in Canadian Conservatism, but it would be even worse to ignore it.

R.B. Bennett's unsuccessful New Deal legislation of 1935 is a case in point, and no one who reads the texts of Bennett's radio addresses can fail to notice the subordination of private interests to the national need in a time of grave crisis. Nevertheless, by 1935 this older tradition had become recessive. In the 1920s, 1930s and early 1950s Canadian Conservatism relied increasingly on business liberalism for its public appeal. The tory element in the party served as a check on the transformation of the party's doctrine into welfare liberalism, while giving it a residual element of ideological flexibility it was loathe either to lose or use.

It was left to John Diefenbaker to revive and attempt to transform the ailing Conservative party. He brought to the leadership not only a personality and eloquence rarely seen in Canadian political life, but also an understanding of the party that was quite uncongenial to the Montreal and Toronto business interests that had come to dominate it. The liberalism to which he had been exposed in his youth was the welfare liberalism of the Progressive movement. But the potential radicalism that led many other Prairie liberals toward socialism, or at least social democracy, was restrained in Diefenbaker by a nostalgic toryism. Diefenbaker's toryism gave him just the element he needed to reconcile and reassure, at least temporarily, the business liberal element within the party. In his campaigns of 1957 and 1958 he offered the voters a skilful amalgam of policies reflecting business liberalism (fiscal responsibility), welfare liberalism (increased pensions), and toryism (loyalty to Crown and Commonwealth). This combination was especially powerful in the mid-1950s. Canadian Liberalism had substantially narrowed the scope of its ideological vision during the leadership of Louis St. Laurent, especially under the influence of his senior cabinet minister, C.D. Howe, who looked unfavorably on the welfare liberal aspects of his party's ideology. This ideological restriction gave Diefenbaker's Conservatism much room.

Under Diefenbaker, however, Canadian Conservatism was a welter of contradictions that could not withstand close analysis and that disintegrated when called on to guide a government. Diefenbaker's failure demonstrates quite clearly the need for political leaders to have relatively coherent ideologies. His failure to forge a new alliance between toryism and liberalism allowed Lester Pearson to regain a precarious hold on power by bringing the welfare and business aspects of Liberalism into balance once again.

It was Diefenbaker's successor, Robert Stanfield, who articulated the needs of the new toryism with wisdom, if not eloquence. In a memorandum to caucus dated November 14, 1974, he summarized the principles for which he thought Canadian Conservatism stood. There he acknowledged the role the old toryism had played in the party: "Resistance to changes and the support of privilege has [sic] been a part of the behaviour of Conservatives from time to time, but neither is nor ought to be Conservative principle."[14] He went on to outline what he thought the Conservative party should stand for:

> Conservatism recognized the responsibility of government to restrain or influence individual action where this was in the in-

terests of society. Whether a government should or should not intervene was always a question of judgment, of course, but the Conservative tradition recognized the role of government as the regulator of individual conduct in the interests of society. . . .

The emphasis on the nation as a whole, on order, in the Conservative tradition that I have described, was surely seldom more relevant than it is today. . . . This is a period when true Conservative principles of order and stability should be most appealing. . . . Again I emphasize that these kind of bedrock principles are national in scope and reflect an overriding concern for society at large. Enterprise and initiative are obviously important; but will emphasis upon individual rights solve the great problems of the day; I mean the maintenance of acceptable stability, acceptable employment, and an acceptable distribution of income. Would we achieve these goals today by a simple reliance on the free market, if we could achieve a free market?

It would certainly be appropriate for a Conservative to suggest that we must achieve some kind of order if we are to avoid chaos; an order which is stable, but not static; and order therefore which is reasonably acceptable and which among other things provides a framework in which enterprise can flourish. That would be in the Conservative tradition.[15]

I have reproduced this statement at some length because I think it represents a genuine contribution to the Canadian political conversation, the kind of deepening and broadening of an ideological tradition for which a country ought to be grateful to its leaders.

Not long ago it would have been thought nonsense to talk about Canadian Conservatism in ideological terms; yet by the time of the Conservative leadership convention in 1976 even journalists were attempting an ideological analysis of the positions of the various candidates. The candidates themselves took these matters seriously, and the single most dramatic event of the candidates' speeches occurred when the former Liberal minister, Paul Hellyer, attacked the "red tories" in the party. The convention revealed with brilliant clarity the extent to which the Progressive Conservative party still exists as a coalition of disparate ideological groups. As Jim Gillies put it in a newsletter to delegates: "Red Tory. Blue Tory. Nobody has to tell you about these divisions. They're real. And they've hurt us at the polls. And in part, this leadership contest is a contest for control of the party being waged between different groups."[16] It remains to be seen whether the new leader, Joe Clark, can succeed in welding these disparate groups into a new ideological synthesis.

If it used to be disputed whether or not there was much of an ideological difference between the Liberals and the Conservatives, at least there was never much disagreement that the Cooperative Commonwealth Federation and the New Democratic Party represented a distinctive and radical alternative. Two features stand out in connection with the electoral success of Canadian Socialism. First, and unlike most socialists in the United States, Canadian Socialists have for the most part been flexible rather than dogmatic and doctrinaire. They have looked for inspiration to the British Labour party and to the Social Democrats in Sweden, rather than to German Marxists. Second, and in this they also differ from American socialists, they have usually sought to make an electoral impact in alliance with welfare liberalism, rather than as a pure ideology.

We have seen in the analysis of the political traditions in the United States and Canada, that the former country lacks the presence of a distinct feudal or tory strain from which a socialist response could emerge. In contrast, Canadian toryism made collectivist modes of thought acceptable, and toryism's defense of privilege gave socialists a real ideological target. How much harder it must have been in the United States where the public philosophy held that all men were created equal! These egalitarian protests against privilege could, in Canada, take on a collectivist hue, and hence produce, in the combination of collectivism and egalitarianism, an indigenous Socialism. Woodsworth put the case clearly in an attempt to steady the direction of the newly formed CCF:

> Undoubtedly we should profit by the experience of other nations and other times, but personally I believe that we in Canada must work out our own salvation in our own way. Socialism has so many variations that we hesitate to use the class name. Utopian Socialism and Christian Socialism, Marxian Socialism and Fabianism, the Latin type, the German type, the Russian type —why not a Canadian type?[17]

In addition to the indigenous ideological material which existed in Canada, and from which Socialism could be generated, it is appropriate to mention three other sources that made important contributions. First there was the inspiration of the Social Gospel movement. Especially in the West, there were Christian ministers, generally of evangelical inclination, who rejected the notion that they should restrict their attention to the care of the souls in their pastoral charge, and preferred instead to devote their energies to social transformation. The first leader of the CCF, J.S. Woodsworth, came from this background. When faced with the problem of the immigrants in Winnipeg, Woodsworth cried out that they posed "a challenge to the church" and demanded that it no longer "merely preach to the people." In future it ought to "educate them and to improve the entire social conditions."[18] Woodsworth's *My Neighbour* indicated even more clearly the change from a concern for eternal, to one for secular, salvation. "*Someone* is responsible! Every unjustly treated man, every defenceless woman, every neglected child has a neighbour somewhere. Am I that neighbour?"[19]

Second, there was the continuing immigration from the United Kingdom. We noted earlier that the ideological structure of Canada had not congealed in the same way as that in the United States, and as a consequence immigrants from Great Britain, who arrived bearing socialist ideas that had developed in their native land in the century and a half since the American Revolution, were not rejected out of hand as strange and alien. Although some brought with them a more extreme kind of socialism, the failure of the One Big Union and the Winnipeg General Strike of 1919 to create a serious revolutionary movement persuaded most Canadian Socialists to stay with the British Labour tradition, with its emphasis on reform through electoral and parliamentary means.

Finally, and this factor was very significant, by about 1900 the Canadian trade union movement had been converted to Gomperism. This doctrine, named after the American trade union leader Samuel Gompers, emphasized the principle of bread-and-butter unionism, stressing that unions should use their strength to obtain better wages and working conditions for their members through direct bargaining with employers rather than through legislation. Politically, the trade union movement was to work within the framework of the established political system, supporting friends of labor within either of the major parties, wherever they were to be found. Indeed, Wilfrid Laurier achieved a notable success in weaning the trade unionists away from the Conservatives, and in establishing the Liberal party as the chief beneficiary of their support. In this he was aided by the young Mackenzie King who in 1909 became Minister of Labor. This victory of Gomperism meant that for the most part the Canadian trade union movement, representing the most politically active and conscious part of the working class, tended in a Liberal rather than Socialist direction. The attempt to forge close ties with the trade union movement was perhaps even more significant than the search for electoral success, in imbuing Canadian Socialism with a strong liberal element.

It is impossible here to trace the ebb and flow of the doctrinal compromises that mark the history of both the CCF and the NDP. It is enough to note Walter Young's observation about the CCF, which applies equally well to the NDP: their "liberalism kept them from becoming communists while their socialism prevented them from becoming liberals."[20]

Canadian Socialism had to wait until 1961 to consummate its formal alliance with the trade union movement. A growing number of unions felt that Gomperism was unsatisfactory in a parliamentary system with as strong a tradition of party discipline as Canada's; individual members of parliament, however sympathetic to labor they might be, were unlikely to defy the party whip in order to support labor's cause against the policies of their party. As a consequence it was thought necessary for the labor movement to ally with a political party dedicated to advancing its cause. This alliance involved the infusion of a heady dose of the welfare liberalism favored by the trade union movement into the ideology of the New Democratic Party. This new balance has not lacked critics.

In 1971 the leadership convention that met in Ottawa to choose the successor to T.C. Douglas was faced with an intense and dramatic challenge from a socialist faction within the party; known as the "Waffle," they chose the relatively obscure James Laxer as their candidate. The strength of his showing (he ran second to the heir-apparent David Lewis who enjoyed the confidence and support of the vast majority of trade union delegates), indicated the depth of dissatisfaction with the liberal-socialist ideological mixture within the party. Lewis's success was followed by the isolation and destruction of the Waffle movement as a challenge to the party's ideological compromise, but the NDP convention that met in 1975 to choose David Lewis's successor was also split ideologically.

This time there were two candidates from the parliamentary caucus, Ed Broadbent, the eventual winner and Lorne Nystrom, as well as three candidates from outside the caucus who presented challenges in various ways to the more moderate parliamentarians. Douglas Campbell, a perennial contender for NDP leaderships at various levels, represented an extreme and almost revolutionary brand of Socialism which the NDP has strongly and consistently combatted. His appeal, of which the following is a representative sample, fell on deaf ears and he was quickly eliminated from the race.

> Cuba, Portugal and Vietnam have shown us how to stand up to the last bastion of decaying capitalism—the U.S.A. and its colonies—Canada, Britain, etc. We must unite with our progressive sisters and brothers of this planet and break the chains of capitalism.
>
> We have nothing to lose but our chains.[21]

John Harney, a former member of the NDP federal caucus, also offered a more distinctive socialist appeal, though he eschewed Campbell's Marxist rhetoric.

> Should I be chosen by you to be leader, I promise you nothing but renewed effort and hard work, a total dedication to the socialist, democratic and egalitarian principles which move and guide us all, and a burning hope that someday this Party, during or after my leadership, will be chosen to shape the destiny of this nation to the kind of greatness we socialists all desire.[22]

Rosemary Brown from British Columbia made the attack on the party's ideological moderation that struck the most responsive chord among the delegates. She offered the following pledge:

> That I will never forget that our party has its roots in the prairie soil, where it grew in spite of the dust and depression, fed by sweat and tears and the passionate hatred of injustice:
>
> that I will never forget that we are the party of the working people, and that our task and our duty is to bring them legal and moral justice in the face of attacks from power and privilege:
>
> that I will be unbending in my stand against every form of oppression which deforms and crushes people and prevents them from the fulfillment of their lives: and that as leader of our New Democratic Party, I will be answerable to the members of this party as we go forward to become the government that will build a truly socialist, truly humane society—here in Canada.[23]

Ed Broadbent couched his eventually successful appeal in much less radical terms, directing it both to moderate socialists and, more important, to welfare liberals within the party.

Our democratic socialist objectives will be outlined clearly and honestly. We will challenge the supremacy of corporate power and private decision-making. . . . I am confident that, united together, we in the New Democratic Party can accomplish in the days ahead a record of economic change every bit as profound as the great transformation in social legislation that stands as our proud record in the past. We can build a nation with a sense of compassion, a sense of community and above all a sense of equality.[24]

Thus it can be seen that the Liberals, the Progressive Conservatives and the New Democrats have each put forward rival visions of the central values that ought to shape the Canadian nation. By taking these differences seriously, and by looking at them carefully and in detail, we can see more clearly what Canada is, and what it is likely to become.

There are, naturally enough, limitations to this approach. I do not want to be taken as suggesting that it explains every aspect of Canadian politics. I shall mention a few areas where it fails. First, it is not a comprehensive explanation of decision making, especially in regard to day-to-day decisions. Politicians may misunderstand the nature of the situation they face, and because of this mistake, may respond in a way totally out of harmony with what ideology would suggest. The application of principles to situations is never an easy task, and even two Liberals who understand a particular situation in roughly similar ways may want to respond to it by emphasizing different aspects of their ideology.

Secondly, matters of modern government are often technically difficult, and all governments rely heavily on advice from civil servants. As a consequence, ministers may be subtly guided in unintended directions on complex issues. John Diefenbaker, for example, never trusted the senior civil servants who had been appointed by, and who, Diefenbaker thought, had become unwarrantedly accustomed to associating with, a Liberal government. He suspected them of offering him advice on possible policies that reflected their, rather than his, preferences. This kind of dispute came to the fore in the conflict with James Coyne, governor of the Bank of Canada, and eventually led to Coyne's resignation.

Finally, all political parties are associated with powerful interest groups whose concerns and perspectives are limited to their own needs and aspirations. To them, national problems or ideological considerations stand in the way of achieving their own goals. Western farmers want their wheat sold at high prices; Maritime fishermen want protection against foreign overfishing; oil companies want what they consider a reasonable return on their investment in exploration and development. Pressure from such groups may induce a government to compromise its ideological principles.

What, then, are the important advantages to be gained from approaching Canadian politics through the study of the ideologies of its political parties? (It should not be forgotten that there are many political parties in Canada, especially at the provincial level, the study of which would repay attention.) Perhaps the chief advantage is that it allows us to understand, better than any other approach, that there are important questions to be decided about the kind of country Canada will become. Although these may be obscured in the details of day-to-day parliamentary debate, or in the drama of a leadership convention, or the excitement of an election campaign, they remain at the heart of civilized political life. Any country that fails to deal with them honestly and directly runs the continual danger of drifting into consequences that a little foresight might have averted.

Almost as important, by understanding that there are differences of principle separating the major political parties, we can compensate for the excessive concentration on images that newspaper and television reporters and editors find so fascinating. Much, of course, does depend on individuals, on their personalities, and even more on their capacities. But preoccupation with such matters might lead us to throw out the baby with the bath water; perhaps it might be better to have a boring, ugly, stuttering, and lame prime minister who would try to create the kind of Canada in which we would want to live than an eloquent and charismatic leader who has no attractive political ideals.

It is also valuable to pay attention to the nature of the Canadian ideological conversation so that we do not forget that we are not Americans. It is no doubt important to us what goes on in the United States and we cannot help at times being saturated by the debates that take place there. We may even, at times, listen to them and benefit from them, as we could also profit from greater attention to the discussions in the United Kingdom, France, Germany, Japan, and other of our friends and even enemies. But eavesdropping on a conversation should not make us a party to it. We do not want to spend all our time listening to others, lest we forget how to talk and to think ourselves.

ENDNOTES

1. Louis Hartz, ed., *The Founding of New Societies* (New York: Harcourt Brace, 1964), p. 6.

2. Kenneth McRae, "The Structure of Canadian History," in Hartz, *op. cit.*, p. 219.

3. *Ibid.*, p. 234.

4. *Ibid.*, p. 339.

5. See H.A. Innis, "The Bias of Communication," and "A Plea for Time," in *The Bias of Communication* (Toronto: University of Toronto Press, 1951).

6. National Liberal Federation, *The Liberal Party of Canada* (Ottawa: Liberal Party of Canada, 1957), p. 15. Quoted in G. Horowitz, *Canadian Labour in Politics* (Toronto: University of Toronto Press, 1968), p. 34.

7. D.O. Carrigan, ed., *Canadian Party Platforms* (Toronto: Copp Clark, 1968), p. 82.

8. W.L.M. King, *Industry and Humanity* (New York: Houghton Mifflin, 1918), p. 336.

9. Quoted in H.B. Neatby, "The Political Ideas of William Lyon Mackenzie King," in *The Political Ideas of the Prime Ministers of Canada*, ed. H.B. Neatby (Ottawa: University of Ottawa Press, 1968), p. 125.

10. "Resolution Adopted by the Third National Liberal Convention," (Ottawa, 1948). Quoted in Carrigan, *op. cit.*, p. 181.

11. Lester Pearson, "Introduction," J.W. Pickersgill, *The Liberal Party* (Toronto: McClelland and Stewart, 1962), p. ix.

12. Pierre Trudeau, *Conversations with Canadians* (Toronto: University of Toronto Press, 1972), p. 86.

13. George Grant, *Lament for a Nation* (Toronto: McClelland and Stewart, 1965), p. 71.

14. Robert Stanfield, "Memorandum to Caucus," November 14, 1974, p. 13.

15. *Ibid.*, pp. 13-14.

16. Jim Gillies, "Letter to Delegates," Progressive Conservative Leadership Convention, February 1976, p. 4.

17. Quoted in Grace MacInnis, *J.S. Woodsworth: A Man to Remember* (Toronto: Macmillan, 1953), p. 274.

18. J.S. Woodsworth, *Strangers within our Gates* (Toronto: Missionary Society of the Methodist Church, 1909. Reprinted 1972 by the University of Toronto Press), p. 311.

19. J.S. Woodsworth, *My Neighbour* (Toronto: Methodist Book Room, 1911. Reprinted 1972 by the University of Toronto Press), p. 20.

20. Walter Young, *Anatomy of a Party* (Toronto: University of Toronto Press, 1969), p. 137.

21. Douglas Campbell, "Nomination Speech of Douglas K. Campbell, NDP Leadership Candidate," Winnipeg, July 6, 1975.

22. John Harney, "Notes for an Address by John Harney," Winnipeg, July 6, 1975.

23. Rosemary Brown, "Rosemary Brown for NDP Leader," Winnipeg, July 6, 1975.

24. Ed Broadbent, "The text of a Speech by Ed Broadbent given at the Eighth Biennial Convention of the New Democratic Party," Winnipeg, July 6, 1975.

SELECTED REFERENCES

GENERAL

It is a pity to report that Canadians have not been particularly well served by the historians of their intellectual heritage. No student, however, should ignore the contributions of Louis Hartz, Kenneth McRae and Gad Horowitz.

HARTZ, LOUIS, ed. *The Founding of New Societies*. New York: Harcourt Brace, 1964. Particularly recommended are the articles by Hartz and McRae.

HOROWITZ, GAD. *Canadian Labour in Politics*. Toronto: University of Toronto Press, 1968. Horowitz's study of the Canadian intellectual heritage appears as the first chapter of this book; the rest of his work is devoted to a study of the relationship between the Canadian labor movement, and the CCF and the NDP, and would be of interest to anyone concerned with the trade union influence on Canadian socialism.

CHRISTIAN, WILLIAM AND COLIN CAMPBELL. *Political Parties and Ideologies in Canada.* Toronto: McGraw-Hill Ryerson, 1974. Attempts to look at the Hartz-Horowitz thesis in some detail, examines the history of Canadian ideologies and attempts to present a coherent framework for analysis.

GRANT, GEORGE. *Lament for a Nation.* Toronto: McClelland and Stewart, 1965. A classic analysis of liberalism and its effect on other Canadian ideologies.

————. *Technology and Empire.* Toronto: House of Anansi, 1969. Those interested in Grant's analysis can follow it up in this collection of essays.

WINN, CONRAD AND JOHN MCMENEMY, eds. *Political Parties in Canada.* Toronto: McGraw-Hill Ryerson, 1976. A critique of this general approach can be found in this collection of essays.

DOCUMENTS

CARRIGAN, D. OWEN, ed. *Canadian Party Platforms.* Toronto: Copp Clark, 1968.

CRAIG, G.M., ed. *Lord Durham's Report.* Toronto: McClelland and Stewart, 1963.

WAITE, P.B., ed. *Confederation Debates in the Province of Canada.* Toronto: McClelland and Stewart, 1963.

CANADIAN LIBERALISM

KING, W. L. MACKENZIE. *Industry and Humanity.* New York: Houghton Mifflin, 1918. A somewhat turgid work, but required reading for students of Canadian Liberalism.

PICKERSGILL, J. *The Liberal Party.* Toronto: McClelland and Stewart, 1962. A flaccid polemic with which students must eventually come to terms.

SMITH, GOLDWIN. *Canada and the Canadian Question.* Toronto: University of Toronto Press, 1971. A reprint of Smith's nineteenth century tract.

TRUDEAU, PIERRE ELLIOTT. *Federalism and the French Canadians.* Toronto: Macmillan, 1968. Along with Smith, Trudeau is a more exciting and controversial liberal.

CANADIAN CONSERVATISM

CREIGHTON, DONALD. *Sir John A. Macdonald*, 2 vols. Toronto: Macmillan, 1952, 1955. A classic biography of Sir John A. Macdonald.

GRAHAM, ROGER. *Arthur Meighen*, 3 vols. Toronto: Clarke, Irwin, 1960, 1963, 1965. Biography.

MEIGHEN, ARTHUR. *Unrevised and Unrepented.* Toronto: Clarke, Irwin, 1949. Meighen's own collection of speeches is a good introduction to one of the most intelligent and articulate Canadians.

WILBUR, J.R.H., ed. *The Bennett New Deal.* Toronto: Copp Clark, 1968. Wilbur's collection of documents and commentary is a useful introduction to Bennett's controversial attempt to reconstruct Canadian conservatism.

Report of the Round Table on Canadian Policy. Port Hope Conference, 1942. This report was the Conservatives' attempt to recreate a policy alternative to the Liberals in the early 1940s.

CANADIAN SOCIALISM

CCF. *Regina Manifesto.* Regina: CCF, 1933.

CCF. *Winnipeg Declaration of Principles.* Montreal: CCF, 1956. Both of these works are essential reading and are part of the considerable treasurehouse available concerning socialist thought in Canada, not least because of the Canadian academic community's close ties with the CCF and the NDP.

LAPIERRE, LAURIER et al., eds. *Essays on the Left.* Toronto: McClelland and Stewart, 1970. A good representative sample of current modern Canadian socialism and welfare liberalism.

LEAGUE FOR SOCIAL RECONSTRUCTION. *Social Planning for Canada.* Toronto: Thos. Nelson and Sons, 1935. Also an essential work.

WOODSWORTH, J.S. *My Neighbour.* Toronto: Methodist Book Room, 1911. Repr., Toronto: University of Toronto Press, 1972. Shows particularly well the Social Gospel inspiration of the early Canadian socialists.

YOUNG, WALTER. *The Anatomy of a Party: The National CCF, 1932-1961.* Toronto: University of Toronto Press, 1969.

There is a longer selected bibliography covering all the forementioned areas in:

CHRISTIAN, WILLIAM AND COLIN CAMPBELL. *Political Parties and Ideologies in Canada.* Toronto: McGraw-Hill Ryerson, 1974.

7

Political Culture:
The Attitudinal Matrix of
Politics

Michael S. Whittington*

That individual values and attitudes have an impact on individual be-havior is a universally accepted assumption in the social sciences and is the basic assumption of this chapter. If we move from the individual as a focus of analysis to societies as a whole, it is logical to make a secondary assump-tion, that of a necessary causal link between societal values and attitudes and the patterns of behavior that characterize that society. The dominant set of values and attitudes in any social system is referred to as its "culture,"[1] and it is the study of culture that has been the dominant con-cern of anthropologists, sociologists, and even social psychologists up to the present. As political scientists, however, we are concerned with ex-plaining the specifically political patterns of human interaction in society. We believe that because there are patterns of behavior we can identify as political, there are also specialized political attitudes and values shared by members of society. We assume therefore that if we could understand political attitudes we might be better able to explain political behavior. When we focus on the set of political values and attitudes that are domin-ant in a society we are focusing on what is referred to as the "political cul-ture" of that society, and the political culture approach to the study of politics is one that assumes causal links between the political culture and patterns of political behavior.

*Associate Professor of Political Science, Carleton University.

THE CONCEPT OF POLITICAL CULTURE

While the term political culture is of fairly recent coinage, the concept it-self dates back at least to Plato who recognized better than many who followed him that certain public attitudes had to be fostered to achieve the ideal political order. This theme has remained current and appears continually in the writings of political philosophers up to the present day.[2] More recently, theories of national character have been developed by anthropologists and psychologists in an attempt to explain the persistent "misbehavior" of certain countries in the international community and the consistent "sweetness" of others. However, it was the development of techniques such as survey research that opened the door to the study of political culture as we know it today in political science. By combining the analytical insights of earlier anthropologists and social psychologists with the methodological tools of behavioral research, it was possible for people such as Gabriel Almond, G. Bingham Powell, Lucien Pye, and Sidney Verba to flesh out the concept of political culture and to formulate some empirical generalizations about actual political cultures in the modern world.

Before considering the utility of the concept of political culture in the study of Canadian politics, it is necessary to clarify some of the ambiguities which are implicit in the term. In the first place, the "stuff" of the political culture is *attitudes* and *values*, which are "phenomena of the mind." While the *behavior* of people in political life may provide us with clues as to what attitudes probably underlie their behavior, and while attitudes are significant to social scientists precisely because of the potential impact they have on behavior, we must always remember that political culture is an attitudinal and not a behavioral category. A second implication of defining political culture in terms of attitudes is that attitudes exist in individual minds. Thus, when we aggregate individual attitudes to make generalizations about political culture, it is important to recognize that the result is an artificially generated variable. Political culture is no more and no less than the sum of the attitudes of many separate individuals.

Our definition of political culture also presumes that it is possible to distinguish between political and nonpolitical attitudes. It is assumed that all things in the real world can be classified as political or nonpolitical *objects,* and that attitudes toward or about specifically political objects are the relevant ones to a student of political culture. Thus, the general problem of political science, that of defining the boundary between the political and the nonpolitical, is of specific concern to the student of political culture. All that can be said is that some real world phenomena such as political leaders, governmental institutions, and regime-related symbols are clearly in the political category and others such as sun spots, microorganisms, and pebbles on the beach are clearly not. There remains a large grey area of social objects such as labor unions, religious groups, and bureaucratic agencies that are hard to categorize.

A factor that further complicates the boundary problem is that political culture is in some ways only a subset of the general culture of a society.

In other words, we must recognize that our political attitudes are probably affected by our nonpolitical attitudes. The best example of this is the apparent relationship between how we perceive ourselves generally, as intelligent, adaptable, competent, and so on, and how we perceive ourselves in political roles, as able to have an impact on government, competent to make political judgments, or politically aware.[3] Therefore, while we must recognize the difficulty in drawing the line between political and nonpolitical attitudes, having drawn it we must also keep in mind that political and nonpolitical attitudes may well be interrelated.

To this point we have established that political culture is made up of political attitudes, and while we have considered some of the implications of this sort of definition nothing has been said about whose attitudes count. On the one hand, from the perspective of policy analysis, it would be fairly easy to conclude that it is the attitudes of the policy-making elite that are significant; but on the other hand, if we are interested in predicting the outcomes of elections, it is perhaps the attitudes of the mass public that are more significant. The political culture approach, however, makes no distinction between mass and elite attitudes and values, but merely states that the political culture of a nation is the overall distribution of attitudes in a society. We must conclude from this, and from the fact that most studies of political culture have in fact focused on mass attitudes, that elite attitudes need not be viewed as anything unique or special in terms of defining political culture. Such a view may be a weakness in the approach and will be examined later.

THE UTILITY OF THE CONCEPT

The original intention in developing the concept of political culture was to foster cross-national comparison of political systems. Thus, when it is used to analyze Canadian politics, we can compare the Canadian system with others in the international community. It tells us how we are different from other systems and possibly helps us to identify the political characteristics that make us unique. At another level of analysis, however, the political culture approach can be used to explain regional and provincial differences in political life within Canada. It has long been recognized that in Canada the style of politics varies from province to province and from region to region even though the basic institutions of government may be virtually identical. For instance, it has been argued that Canada has at least three political cultures if we focus on levels of political development. John Wilson describes the Atlantic Provinces as underdeveloped, Ontario, Quebec, Manitoba, and British Columbia as transitional, and Alberta and Saskatchewan as developed according to the type of party system operating in the provinces. From another perspective, Simeon and Elkins demonstrate the generally high levels of trust and efficacy in Ontario, B.C. and Manitoba by contrast with the Atlantic Provinces, which are characterized by "a pervasive disaffection from the political process." French-speaking Quebecers fall more closely in line with the Atlantic Provinces, while English-speaking Quebecers seem to reflect more closely the positive attitude of Ontario.[4] By focusing on regional or provincial cultures we may be better able to understand the underlying divisive forces within our confederation.

From a very pragmatic point of view, the political culture approach is useful in the study of Canadian politics because it can be studied from many angles. The most obvious and perhaps the most reliable technique for analyzing basic political attitudes and values is survey research; one simply finds out what attitudes prevail in a society by asking a scientifically selected sample of individuals a set of carefully structured questions which basically answer the question, "What are your values?" However, we may also uncover dimensions of the political culture by simply observing the behavior of individuals in political circumstances. Because we know that people's behavior is affected by what they believe, it is often possible to guess what attitudes underlie certain behavior patterns. For example, if we observe a high voter turnout at elections it is logical to suppose that there is a generally favorable attitude to taking part in elections, although it is not possible to make very sophisticated deductions about what kinds of positive attitudes. Finally, at the most macroscopic level, we can discover something about the long-run value preferences of a society by investigating the legal and institutional framework within which politics occurs. For instance, the very existence of parliamentary institutions probably reflects a deep-seated commitment to representative democracy in Canadian society. While this might seem obvious, we have to make the assumption that the values in the political institutions of a society are congurent with the dominant values of the society. Any great discrepancy would probably not last very long, for if the institutions are nondemocratic and societal values are democratic, there would be considerable pressure for change and even for revolutionary change. Thus we can say that the most elementary values of a system will normally be embedded in its political structures and may, in a limited way, reflect the political culture of a society.[5]

Finally, while there have not been a large number of studies of political culture per se in Canada, the attitudes that are the "stuff" of political culture have been studied from two broad perspectives. The most established of the two perspectives looks at attitudes and values as independent variables which have a causal impact on political behavior. In this regard we have studied attitudes such as partisanship or political interest not as entities in themselves but as factors that can help us to explain behavior. The most recent of the two perspectives looks at attitudes as dependent variables, which are themselves caused by the process of learning known as political socialization. Again the interest of the researcher is not in the substance of the attitudes and values but rather in how and in what circumstances individuals acquire them. Thus we would look at party identification among children to discover the relative roles of the family, school, or peer groups in teaching us about politics. In sum, although there is a paucity of data that focus primarily on political culture, there are a great many studies that provide us with information which is secondarily useful in building up a generalized picture of the Canadian political culture.

THE CANADIAN POLITICAL CULTURE

Canadian Political Values

Values are perhaps the most fundamental and complex of all human mental phenomena. They not only provide the ultimate parameters for our behavior, but they also set the mental context within which we develop our attitudes or orientations to specific objects in the real world. In our political values, those values which define for us the appropriate goals for government and the legitimate means to be used to achieve those goals, we have the ultimate foundation of our political culture; all other political attitudes must fall within the boundaries established by our basic political values. The problem with values is that they are often so fundamental that we do not recognize them as such and if we are aware of them we may have difficulty articulating them. Accordingly it is difficult to study values through survey techniques. In the case of political values we are perhaps a bit more fortunate in that we can assume that to a large extent, our institutions reflect the values that currently prevail in our society and simply use the institutionalized values as a reflection of our political values. In fact, many studies of Canadian political values have employed precisely this basic technique.

Perhaps the fundamental political value in Canada is popular sovereignty, for it is the principle that goes the farthest toward operationalizing the basic goal of democracy, the common good or the common interest. Athenian democracy, where all citizens participated equally in the policy decisions of the state, represents a sort of ideal of popular sovereignty but because modern societies are too large and complex for everyone to participate directly in the policy process, we have evolved a system whereby citizens choose their policy makers through periodic elections. A system of representation by popular elections presumes a secondary value, that of political equality. This value is institutionalized through the principle of "one man (or woman) one vote" and the guarantee of political freedoms such as freedom of assembly, association, conscience, and expression. These political freedoms are necessary to ensure that we have real alternatives from which to choose when we exercise our franchise.

Another value that can often conflict with the value of political equality is majority rule, a principle aimed at ensuring that the many and not the few are the ones whose interests are served first. The problem here is that majorities can become oppressive vis-à-vis minorities, even to the extent of denying them their political freedoms. While Canadians seem fairly much in agreement that there must be a balance between the rights of the minority and the rights of the majority, people differ considerably on where the balance should be.[6] For instance, while all Canadians would agree with the principle of freedom of expression, not all would agree that political movements advocating the overthrow of the regime should be permitted to publish their views freely. Similarly, while all would agree with the principle of freedom of the press, many would like to see censorship of various kinds to ensure that what is published is not greatly at odds with the dominant values and morality of our society. In fact, once we move beyond a discussion of a few of the most fundamental political values it becomes increasingly difficult to generalize about the whole of Canadian society; the best we can hope to do in such a situation is to describe the "value mix" typical of Canada to make cross-national comparisons. Where the value mix varies among regions or provinces within Canada, we can use the resultant generalizations to attempt internal comparisons.

The conflict between liberal and nonliberal values is a central aspect of Canadian political life, and in fact our unique mix of these values helps to set us apart from those societies closest to us in political values, the United States and the United Kingdom.[7] In the extreme, liberalism includes a commitment to individualism, to individual as opposed to collective or group rights, to the principles of privately owned property, and to economic free enterprise and capitalism. Socialism, by contrast, is committed to collectivism, economic equality, social and economic planning, and in general to a larger role for government in the social and economic affairs of the citizenry. According to Horowitz and McRae, Canada tends to be more conservative than either liberal or socialist in its value mix. This sets us apart from the United States which is seen as far more liberal than either Canada or the United Kingdom, and from the United Kingdom in that we are more liberal and less conservative than they are. Our conservatism is manifested in a higher commitment to political order than to political freedom. As one author has put it:

> Canadian political society has thus stressed order, loyalty and deference to government more than popular assent. Rather than "life, liberty and the pursuit of happiness", the need has been peace, order and good government. Social equality is desired but with less fervour than in America. Hierarchy in all spheres of life is taken for granted.[8]

Canadians, by and large, have a collectivist view of the social order but this view differs from the collectivism of socialism in that it is rooted in the "noblesse oblige" style of lord-serf relationship characterized by feudalism. The nobility must provide welfare for their serfs because they are only serfs and cannot look after themselves, not because the serfs have any right to it. Because of this view, the policy orientations of the Conservative and the NDP are very similar in areas such as social welfare. The differences exist in the justification for welfare policy: the Tories support it for paternalistic reasons—because "we must look after those who cannot look after themselves"—and the NDP support it for egalitarian reasons—because every Canadian has a right to a certain standard of living.

A further political value that is difficult to link with any particular ideology, but has been ascribed to Canadians, is that of corporatism. Corporatism assumes basically that it is groups of people, not the state at one extreme or the individual at the other, that are the sources of political legitimacy. Robert Presthus, in an attempt to explain Canadian politics in terms of the interaction among the elites of various interest groups and government, best elaborates this feature of the Canadian political culture.[9] McRae and Horowitz explain its presence here as a result of importing feudal values into pre-Confederation Quebec and Tory values through the Loyalist immigration after the American Revolution. However, while these arguments based on historical analysis and speculation are very convincing, they do not tell us much about the actual distribution of corporatist values throughout Canada. All we can safely conclude is that there is a flavor of corporatism to our political culture, one that may vary from region to region, class to class, and cultural group to cultural group within Canada.

To conclude this section we should emphasize that the evidence concerning our political values is based primarily on impressions. We can be fairly sure about some of our value differences vis-à-vis non-Western societies, and we can even feel fairly confident, although only at a high level of generalization, about some of the differences and similarities between our national political culture and that of the United States and United Kingdom. However, what the usual historical and institutional approaches to defining our political values fail to do is to explain adequately the distribution of political values among the subcultural groups that make up our society. Such explanation will only come about through extensive and systematic research designed specifically to discover the political value mix of Canadian society.

Canadian Political Attitudes

Whereas political values define the goals of government in Canada as well as the scope of legitimate means for achieving these goals, political attitudes are very specific orientations to things in the real world. The most primitive of our political attitudes involves simple awareness or knowledge of political objects which is usually referred to as "political cognition." These cognitive orientations to political objects, for instance, knowledge of the prime minister or knowledge about the role of Parliament, form the attitudinal "ground zero" on which all our more sophisticated attitudes are built. In the absence of these cognitive political attitudes there can be no political culture at all. However, having made the point that cognition is the attitudinal basis for all other kinds of political attitudes, we must add that such political knowledge is seldom untainted by our values and our emotional preferences. For instance, if we become aware of an actor in the political system called Pierre Trudeau through comments about him from parents or friends we will soon acquire a general perception of him as somebody we like or do not like. This is an "affective attitude." The sum of our affective attitudes consists of the positive and negative feelings we have about objects in the real world. We tend to acquire political likes and dislikes at the same time as we first become aware of an object. Similarly, as we become more sophisticated we develop evaluative attitudes which are judgments about the goodness and badness of political things based on how they measure up to our basic political values. Examples of this might be an assessment that the wiretap legislation is bad because it has provisions that compromise the right of privacy, or a judgment that televising parliamentary debates is good because it will make MPs more sensitive to public opinion. Obviously there is a spillover effect here for few people can totally separate their emotional preferences from their value judgments, and often we will selectively perceive the real world in such a way that it conforms to our preconceived notions about it. Thus if we believe all Liberals are in favor of bilingualism and we meet a Liberal who speaks out against that policy, we will try a number of interpretations of his behavior before changing our general perception of Liberals. We can entirely overlook the statement he has made; we can dismiss his statement as a lie designed to fool us; we can simply view him as an exception; or we can argue that he never was a Liberal in the first place! In sum, while it is possible to separate cognitive, affective, and evaluative attitudes analytically, they are usually mutually interrelated in reality. In other words, our values and emotions color our perception of the real world; our feelings may depend upon what we perceive and our values themselves may only be rationalizations of what we feel.

One of the first attempts to classify political cultures was made by Gabriel Almond and Sidney Verba.[10] Their three categories—parochial, subject, and participant—have since been used by many political scientists. A parochial political culture exists where there is a low awareness of the political system as a generalized object, where there is virtually no cognitive awareness of specific political structures, and where the individual does not see himself in any way as an actor or participant in the political process. The best examples of parochial cultures are the bushmen of southern Africa, the remote tribes of the Amazon basin, and some primitive peoples in New Guinea. The subject political culture exists where there is a high awareness of the system as a generalized object, and a high awareness of the output structures of the system, but a relatively low awareness of input structures. The individual sees himself as affected by the activities and outputs of the system, but does not see himself as a participant in the process. The Spain of Franco or the Portugal of Salazar might be taken as examples of a subject political culture, although in neither case are these pure subject societies. The most highly developed type is the participant political culture where the individual is aware of both the input and output structures of the system and perceives himself as an active participant in the political process. The participant accepts the system as something that influences his life, but, unlike the subject, he sees himself as having the potential to influence the system as well. The Western liberal democracies are hailed as participant political cultures, with the United States as the paragon of this type. It must be noted here that these three categories are ideal types and that political cultures are all heterogeneous in varying degrees. Societies with predominantly participant attitudes to the political system will always include some individuals who are basically subjects and even some who are parochials. In Canada, for instance, a country that has normally been viewed as having a predominantly participant type of political culture, rural Quebec has often been styled a "subject fragment" and some of the native peoples, particularly in the far North, have until very recently been seen as parochials. A further caveat that must be entered here is that the parochial-subject-participant classification is developmental with the more developed or participant orientations superimposed on the earlier subject and parochial ones. Thus the empirical differences among modern democratic systems, most of which are predominantly participant, can be seen in the way parochial and subject attitudes are blended into the dominant participant culture. For example, it is possible that the greater emphasis on liberal values in the United States and on conservative values in Canada is related to a better integration of subject orientations in Canada. In other words, the often violent and disruptive nature of political dissent in America may be a result of lower levels of subject orientation to political authority. By contrast, Canadians' more ordered and acquiescent attitudes to political authority may be a result of subject orientation modifying the basically participant attitude toward government.

A final qualification or caution, essential if we are to use the political culture approach effectively in the study of Canadian politics, is related to the concept of a blend of parochial, subject, and participant attitudes. A political culture is a blend in two senses; on the one hand a society will contain individuals whose attitudes are predominantly parochial, subject, or participant, in the manner described above; on the other hand, however, we must remember that the individuals will themselves display a mix of attitudes. Each of us, in the process of political socialization, goes through several stages of development. The very young child will start his or her political development as a parochial, will evolve to a subject orientation to politics, and, finally, in a system such as ours, will probably acquire a set of participant orientations. The way in which the more sophisticated attitudes are grafted onto the already developed ones will obviously have a profound impact on the way we come to relate to politics as adults. Thus extreme deference to authority in our youth may lead us to only passive forms of political activity, such as voting, when we achieve adulthood. Or conversely, it might be argued that some deferential adolescents may rebel against their subject orientation and turn to more active forms of political participation, such as demonstrations, in adulthood.

We have discussed two aspects of the attitudes that make up a political culture: the mental processes of the individual, that is, cognitive, affective, and evaluative attitudes; and the general orientation to various political objects, that is parochial, subject, and participant orientations. However, we have said little about the objects in the real world toward which our attitudes are directed. For instance, what are our attitudes toward Parliament, the prime minister, political parties, the issues of the day, and the legislative outputs of the system? Up to this point, we have referred to these objects in the real world as "political objects"; now it is necessary to say specifically what we mean.

Political objects initially can be classified as either *system-related* or *self-related*.[11] The system-related objects can in turn be categorized according to the level of the political system to which they belong. To borrow David Easton's taxonomy, system-related political objects can be "political community-related," "regime-related," or "authorities-related." Political community-related objects include the following: structural features such as the geography of Canada, physical boundaries, internal barriers, and the land itself; symbols of Canada as a nation, such as the flag, maple leaf, the beaver, historical traditions, and national heroes; and, finally, conceptual or ideational entities such as the concept of a discrete nationality, the Canadian identity, or the Canadian way of life. It can perhaps be argued that the Canadian political culture is lacking in strong affective and evaluative orientations vis-à-vis the political community, particularly but not exclusively, in Quebec where allegiance to the province may be stronger than allegiance to Canada. This situation may be the result of a paucity of widely accepted symbols and concepts that could give us a focus for nationalism, or it might be that we have never been able to develop such symbols precisely because there has never been a real consensus about the legitimacy or even the pragmatic desirability of the political community as we know it. Certainly the fate of Canada as a unified nation may in the near future rest upon the strength and durability of whatever positive political community-related attitudes we do share.

Regime-related objects include the structures of government, such as Parliament, the judicial system, the public service; the symbols of our system of government such as the Crown, the Bill of Rights, or the opening of Parliament; and the principles or concepts that underlie the system such as responsible government, supremacy of Parliament, and the rule of law. Attitudes toward regime-related political objects in Canada seem to reflect a greater national consensus than attitudes to the political community. Even in Quebec, where there is a definite sentiment for separation from the Canadian political community, there appears to be a commitment to achieving that goal democratically and, if at all possible, within the existing legal structures. Even to the extent that there is an ideological split between the left and the right in Canada, that split is more concerned with the results of government, such as a better distribution of wealth, than with the system itself. Thus, as far as basic political values are concerned, Canadians probably have positive attitudes to the principles of popular sovereignty and parliamentary democracy and there is even a general agreement at the present time in most of the provinces that some form of federalism is the best method of parceling out the revenues and responsibilities of government.

Authorities-related objects include the incumbents of specific political roles, such as Trudeau, Clark, and Broadbent; the symbols of the authorities such as the political parties; and the issues of the day such as inflation, capital punishment, or health care. Because it is a feature of our regime that we are expected periodically to dismiss our political office holders through elections, the attitudes of Canadians to authorities-related objects will be unstable over time. The exception here may be attitudes toward political parties since studies have shown that the patterns of affective and evaluative orientations toward specific parties may remain fairly consistent over time. Later on we will return to the question of partisanship, the stability of party identification, and the implications of this situation for the Canadian political culture.

While system-related political objects seem to make up the great bulk of the potential objects of our attitudes, it is these attitudes that have been studied the least. There have been a few studies of partisanship and some relevant questions in national election surveys and Canadian Institute of Public Opinion surveys, as well as some papers on children's attitudes, but the research has been piecemeal. More often than not the data on Canadians' attitudes to system-related objects have been incidentally in the process of studying something else entirely. Certainly if we are better to understand the Canadian political culture we will have to embark on larger-scale research projects on our attitudes to the various aspects of our political system.

In contrast to the system-related attitudes, the self-related attitudes have been studied fairly frequently in Canada. Self-related attitudes are those involving the individual's perception of himself in relation to the political system. While these attitudes are obviously influenced by perceptions of system-related objects, they are also affected by perceptions of self [as an object]. The reason why more research has focused on these self-related attitudes is that political scientists have tended to be more interested in the developed democracies than in other countries. These political systems tend to have political cultures ranging from subject-participant to participant, and as a result it is attitudes toward participation that best define the cross-national variations. Therefore most self-avowed studies of political culture are in fact studies of a small set of self-related attitudes such as efficacy, cynicism, trust, involvement, apathy, alienation, or deference, all of which are seen as influencing the individual's propensity to participate. While such studies give us only a partial picture, they at least permit us to make some generalizations about the Canadian political culture in terms of Almond and Verba's very broad categories.

Richard Van Loon has described the Canadian political culture as generally spectator-participant.[12] Because Canada has a very high level of political involvement in comparison with other countries, it is fairly obvious that at the broadest level of generalization our national political culture can be said to be participant. There are wide variations in the levels of participation within Canada, and significant regional, ethnic, class, and educational differences do exist. However, if we look at Canada as a whole, compared to other systems, there is no question that we are political participants. We have high voter turnout, high awareness of politics, and a high level of interest in political events. However, what is unique to Canada, by comparison with other generally participant political cultures such as the United States, is the apparent psychological motivation for our political activity. While Canadians feel they have a considerable effect on politics, this does not seem to be as significant a motivating factor as their general interest in politics as a sort of game. Thus, as Van Loon has put it, we are interested and involved spectators in the game of politics. We are often very excited about the outcome of an election, but there seems to be a general feeling that little in the way of major policy shifts is likely if our side does not win. This spectator orientation to politics is related to the nonideological nature of our political parties, which is in turn related to the lower (relative to the U.S.) levels of partisan identification in Canada. One interpretation of this phenomenon, which Van Loon has dubbed "apolitical" politics and which Kornberg[13] has called a "generally less politicized" society, in that it is in the interest of Canadian elites to avoid the real gut issues that should concern Canadians. Therefore they foster a politics that is uncreative and conceals the real issues in order to maintain the status quo.[14] Another interpretation might be that the parties reflect a genuine and fairly widespread satisfaction with the status quo among the vast majority of Canadians. Whatever the reasons, Van Loon's description of our political culture as spectator-participant seems fairly apt at the national level of generalization.

In the past few years there has been a new spate of material that emphasizes regionalism as a critical factor in determining political events in Canada. These writers argue convincingly that there are very wide attitudinal differences from one part of Canada to another, and that therefore it is misleading to speak of a Canadian political culture.[15] They argue that we have two, several, or many, political cultures depending on which political community one chooses to study. No one would disagree that there are wide attitudinal variations in Canada, variations that reflect regional as well as cultural, economic, and demographic cleavages. Furthermore, who can disagree with the assertion that these attitudinal variations are critical in determining political behavioral differences? However, by accepting this point of view, we need not denigrate attempts to generalize about the political culture at the national level. As we have already pointed out, a political culture, be it national, regional, provincial, or even local, is still simply an aggregation of the attitudes of individuals who are members of the relevant social matrix. The larger the aggregation, the more difficult is the task of generalizing, but the task must be carried on at all levels if we are fully to understand the value and attitudinal foundations of Canadian politics. The attitudes we have in common, even if very few, are as important as our attitudinal differences in determining the nature of Canadian political life.

THE POLITICAL CULTURE APPROACH: SCOPE AND LIMITATIONS

The political culture approach is perhaps the most inclusive of the approaches considered in this collection. In fact none of the other approaches to Canadian politics described in the other chapters are so incompatible with the concept of political culture that they could not be plugged into the model we have just described. The first five chapters look at aspects of the environment of the Canadian political system. These are some of the most significant independent variables which, through the process of political socialization, come to color the values and attitudes that make up our political culture. In other words, one of the ways in which these variables shape Canadian politics is by shaping our political culture.

The third section of this volume focuses on the structures of the Canadian political system. From the political culture perspective, these are some of the political objects toward which we acquire attitudes. Conversely, however, the political structures must reflect the dominant values of our political culture if they are to be effective. If political structures serve to enshrine political values that are not congruent with the values of Canadian society, then either the people's attitudes must change to conform to the institutionalized values, or the institutions must change to reflect societal values better. One way or the other, the analysis of political structures is an essential and integral companion to the political culture approach.

The section dealing with processes is also completely compatible with the political culture approach. The processes of Canadian politics are to a large extent the product of our political culture and in an immediate sense the motivation for studying political culture has been to gain a better understanding of parties, elections, ethnic conflict, the broad directions of public policy, and so on.

In the fifth section of this book the two chapters focusing on political elites are compatible with the political culture approach in a unique way. We have already pointed out that the political culture of a society is composed of the attitudes of all its members, not only the attitudes of the politically powerful or influential. It may be a limitation of the political culture approach that its proponents are very willing to accept the assumption that mass values and attitudes are significant even in elite-dominated processes such as policy making. It is clear that the decision making that porduces public policy is influenced by the values and attitudes of the policy-making elites. Therefore, in the short run, it is possible that the policy makers could implement policies that are not in the interest of the mass public and are even incompatible with the general political culture. However, because Canada has a system of representative democracy, the authorities or political elites of our system must periodically face a critical electorate; and hence if the values of our political elites are incompatible with the values of the mass, then the elites will ultimately face electoral defeat.

A second factor to be considered in attempting to integrate elite approaches and the political culture approach, and one that is perhaps more important, concerns the role that the elites play in the socialization process. It seems likely that the political elites in Canada are influence leaders who help to stimulate change in the public's political values and attitudes that constitute the political culture. In this sense the political elites stimulate the attitudinal change that enables our political culture to develop.

While there is no reason to assume that elite values will necessarily be incongruent with mass values, a Marxist approach to Canadian politics assumes that major incongruities do exist. The basic assumption here is that there is a primal and unresolvable conflict of interest between the ruling class and the working class, and that to a large extent the working class is not conscious of the conflict. In this sense, through the socializing agencies of the system, political culture is manipulated by the elites, or the ruling class, to maintain a set of political values that will perpetuate the status quo. The problem of Canadian politics from a Marxist perspective is to alter the political culture so that the working classes become conscious of their economic and psychological enslavement and work together to overthrow the dominant capitalist minority. While many Marxists would dismiss the political culture approach as one that has a status quo bias, it can be countered that, because the attitudinal status quo must be overturned to foster true class consciousness, the political culture approach can help people to understand more precisely what it is they are attacking. Thus, it might well be argued that the Marxist and political culture approaches are completely compatible and mutually helpful if their proponents will assume a broader intellectual perspective.

The major analytical limitation of the political culture approach, ironically, is a result of the inclusiveness that gives it such a broad analytical scope and utility. In some ways the political culture approach is so inclusive that it is impossible to study it empirically. The de facto paucity of comprehensive research focusing on Canadian political culture is a reflection of the difficulty in operationalizing conceptually manageable research projects that are also tight enough to be readily fundable. Despite these very real limitations and even if we are unable to do the kind of systematic and comprehensive research that would give us a full picture of the Canadian political culture, we should continue to use the approach macroscopically, for it is an analytical tool that gives us the conceptual perspective to integrate all the partial and piecemeal research flowing from the other approaches to Canadian politics.

ENDNOTES

1. The uses of the term culture in psychology, sociology, and anthropology are many and varied. The one used here is the least elaborate as well as the least ambiguous.
2. Rousseau is perhaps the most outspoken advocate of using the educational system to mold public attitudes to foster better government. Dicey analyzes

English constitutional government in terms of attitudes that make it possible; more recently Lasswell has written on the personality traits that best contribute to democracy. Finally Louis Hartz and his followers such as Gad Horowitz and Ken McRae have tried to explain differences in political systems in terms of the dominant ideological commitments of their citizenry.

3. See J.H. Pammett and M.S. Whittington, "Political Culture and Political Socialization," in *Foundations of Political Culture*, eds. J.H. Pammett and M.S. Whittington (Toronto: Macmillan, 1976), pp. 5-10.

4. See R. Simeon and D.J. Elkins, "Regional Political Cultures," and John Wilson, "The Canadian Political Cultures," in *Canadian Journal of Political Science* (September, 1974). See also Allen Gregg and M.S. Whittington, "Regional Variation in Children's Political Attitudes," in *The Provincial Political Systems*, eds. D. Bellamy, J.H. Pammett, and D. Rowat (Toronto: Methuen, 1976).

5. See Gabriel Almond and A. Verba, *The Civic Culture* (Toronto: Little Brown, 1965), pp. 20-21.

6. For a more detailed discussion of this point see R. Manzer, *Canada: A Socio-Political Report* (Toronto: McGraw-Hill Ryerson, 1974), pp. 265-298. See also W.B. Devall, "Support for Civil Liberties Among English Speaking Canadian University Students," *Canadian Journal of Political Science* (September, 1970), p. 437.

7. Louis Hartz, ed., *The Founding of New Societies* (New York: Harcourt-Brace, 1964), Chs. 4 and 7. See also Gad Horowitz, "Conservatism, Liberalism and Socialism in Canada," *Canadian Journal of Economics and Political Science* (May, 1966), pp. 144-171.

8. See K. Naegele, "Canadian Society: Some Reflections," in *Canadian Society*, ed. Blishen et al. (Toronto: Macmillan, 1961), pp. 27-29.

9. R. Presthus, *Elite Accommodation in Canadian Politics* (Toronto: Macmillan, 1973), p. 39.

10. Almond and Verba, *op. cit.*

11. Most of this section is drawn from Pammett and Whittington, *op. cit.*, and R. Van Loon and M.S. Whittington, *The Canadian Political System* (Toronto: McGraw-Hill Ryerson, 1976), Chs. 3-4.

12. R. Van Loon, "Political Participation in Canada," *Canadian Journal of Political Science* (September, 1970), p. 385. See also, Van Loon and Whittington, *op. cit.*, Ch. 4.

13. A. Kornberg, I. Smith, and D. Bromley, "Some Differences in the Political Socialization Pattern of Canadian and American Party Officials," *Canadian Journal of Political Science* (March, 1969), p. 73.

14. John Porter, *The Vertical Mosaic* (Toronto: University of Toronto Press, 1965).

15. Simeon and Elkins, and Wilson, *op. cit.*

SELECTED REFERENCES

ALMOND, GABRIEL, AND SIDNEY VERBA. *The Civic Culture*. Boston: Little, Brown, 1965. This is the classic work on political culture. It defines the basic concepts and provides the basic typologies that are for the most part still being used. The book does not deal with Canada so the substance is not as important to us here as is the theoretical material in the first chapter.

HARGROVE, ERWIN. "Popular Leadership in Anglo-American Democracies," *Popular Leadership in Industrialized Societies,* ed. L. Edinger. New York: Wiley, 1966.

———. "Note on Canadian and American Political Culture." *Canadian Journal of Economics and Political Science,* (February, 1967). While somewhat outdated, these two pieces give a fairly enlightened overview. Based on historical rather than survey material the pieces provide impressionistic comparisons of Canadian and American political values.

HOROWITZ, GAD, "Conservatism, Liberalism and Socialism in Canada." *Canadian Journal of Economics and Political Science,* (May, 1966). In part a criticism of the Hartz-McRae interpretation, this article has been very influential in Canada. It is based on historical analysis and explains the ideological mix of Canadian politics in terms of importation of values in successive waves of immigration.

LIPSET, S.M. *The First New Nation.* New York: Basic Books, 1963. While the book focuses on the United States, Lipset contrasts United States political values to those of Canada and offers explanations for the differences through the use of census data.

MANZER, R. *Canada: A Sociopolitical Report.* Toronto: McGraw-Hill Ryerson, 1974. Not strictly speaking a book about political culture but chock full of data relevant to political culture. The framework of this book is also significant because it provides a model of the basic values of Canadian society.

MCRAE, K.D., "The Structure of Canadian History," *The Founding of New Societies,* ed. L. Hartz. New York: Harcourt Brace, 1964. Must be read in conjunction with Horowitz. It is an interpretation that uses much the same approach but comes to slightly different conclusions.

PAMMETT, J., AND M.S. WHITTINGTON, eds. *The Foundations of Political Culture: Political Socialization in Canada.* Toronto: Macmillan, 1976. A collection of original articles focusing on political attitudes as dependent variables.

PRESTHUS, ROBERT. *Elite Accommodation in Canadian Politics.* Toronto: Macmillan, 1973. The first chapter is a very perceptive overview of the basic political values of Canadians.

SIMEON, R., AND DAVID ELKINS. "Regional Political Cultures in Canada." *Canadian Journal of Political Science,* (September, 1974). Excellent article based on survey data which looks at attitudinal differences across the regions of Canada. Limitation of the article is that it looks only at efficacy, trust, and involvement as dependent variables.

VAN LOON, R. "Political Participation in Canada." *Canadian Journal of Political Science,* (September, 1970).

———, and M.S. Whittington. *The Canadian Political System.* Toronto: McGraw-Hill, 1976, chs. 3-4. This material develops the theory of a spectator-participant political culture at the national level in Canada.

WILSON, J. "The Canadian Political Cultures." *Canadian Journal of Political Science,* (September, 1974). Excellent article based on survey data which reject the existence of a national political culture because the regions are at different stages of political development.

ZUREIK, E. AND ROBERT PIKE. *Socialization and Values in Canadian Society,* Vol. 1. Toronto: McClelland and Stewart, 1975. A collection of original articles dealing with political socialization. The introductory article is particularly interesting for it is a critique of existing approaches to political socialization from a Marxist perspective.

Part Three:
Structures are Central in Canadian Politics

Structures and institutions are probably the most permanent elements of Canadian politics. The first chapter in this section deals with structures in general; the second examines the nature and far-reaching consequences of Canada's federal arrangement.

Institutions can be thought of as agencies and offices arranged in a hierarchy with each agency or office having designated functions and authority. Individuals holding these offices and exercising these functions possess status and carry out roles. A broader definition of institutions refers to stable patterns of group behavior. In either case we can think of institutions as the result of specific kinds of political socialization but also as central agents of such socialization.

As you read the first chapter you will come to understand that political institutions such as Parliament, cabinet, courts, or political parties, no matter how important and powerful they may be, reflect human characteristics and thus are not totally rational, efficient, consistent, or ideal. Among other things Professor Redekop argues that the institutional approach draws our attention to our political heritage and helps us to understand legitimacy, liberty, and responsibility, three important elements in Canadian politics. As you proceed through the second chapter you will see why federal structures have been central in Canadian politics and, quite appropriately, in writings about Canadian politics. Professor Meekison has amply demonstrated that almost all important issues in Canadian politics are either directly or indirectly related to federal-provincial relations.

8

Canadian Political Institutions

John H. Redekop*

INTRODUCTION

In recent decades much has been written about new ways of looking at Canadian politics. A tendency to minimize the role of formal structures has won considerable popularity. Analyses that explain how political affairs operate within institutional patterns and according to constitutional arrangements are sometimes rejected as being too traditional. But surely the important question is not whether a perspective is traditional but whether it helps us to get an accurate picture of political reality and thus to understand the complexities and dynamics of Canadian politics. In this chapter we shall see how important it is that we understand Canada's institutional and constitutional arrangements, both formal and informal, as they function in our parliamentary democracy.

Naturally, no one approach to so large a subject can tell us everything that we should know, and therefore students would do well to familiarize themselves with other interpretations. Writers who draw attention to powerful groups in Canadian society, to elites, important individuals, economics, geography, the impact of the United States, French-English interaction, and to much else, help us to broaden our understanding. However, what many writers seem to overlook is the very important fact that whatever the source of political pressures, whatever the reason for political demands, and whatever the vehicles for their expression or satisfaction, Canada's integrating political institutions constitute the arena in which competing assertions and claims are adjudicated. Having a general knowledge of the actual workings of the Canadian political system will provide us with the overall framework; explanations of various aspects of Canadian politics can then be fitted into place.

Having stressed the importance of focusing our attention on political

*Professor and Chairman, Department of Political Science, Wilfrid Laurier University.

structures, I must hasten to emphasize that even in a stable parliamentary democracy these are constantly evolving. Pressures for adaptation and reform seem to be unending. At any given time many individuals and groups, as well as political jurisdictions such as cities and provinces, are pressing hard for changes. That in itself indicates how important the formal and informal political institutions actually are.

This chapter will not concentrate on making a case for the institutional interpretation, although it will do that in part; it will mainly describe and assess that approach. The central hypothesis is straightforward: whether we define political science as the study of the state, the study of government, the study of power, the study of the authoritative allocation of values, the study of political behavior, the measurement of verifiable political facts, or, indeed, almost any other way, we must have a sound knowledge of political institutions if we wish to understand Canadian politics.

At the outset we need to clarify our terms. I define political science as the study of the institutions and processes of government, as well as the study of the organization, behavior, policies, beliefs, and doctrines of individual people and groups of people associated with government, for the purpose of making explanations and generalizations of political phenomena. Government, in turn, is defined as the office holders in certain institutions who, by whatever means, have come to be recognized as the bearers of ultimate power within a polity and whose main role is the authoritative allocation of resources and values in that polity. Politics, then, refers to all activity whose main purpose is to reshape or influence governmental processes; to influence or replace governmental office holders; to influence the formation of public policies; to influence the implementation of public policies; to generate public awareness of, and response to, governmental institutions, processes, personnel, and policies; or to gain a place of influence or power within government. Clearly, institutions are very important in such a view of political reality.

Let me further clarify my perspective. When I speak of the institutions of government I am referring to the recognized and accepted arrangement of ultimate power in a country. Thus government institutions consist of those structures whose incumbents actually or potentially regulate all other power centers or institutions within that country. Normally this set of institutions consists of the executive, legislative, judicial, bureaucratic, policing, and military branches. Political parties and, to a lesser extent in Canada, educational institutions, organized religion, economic structures, the media, and other interest groups overlap with the institutions of government defined more narrowly. The boundary problem can be a thorny one but if we keep our central focus on those institutions whose members or incumbents claim collectively to be maintaining general control over the whole political jurisdiction and whose authority is generally accepted, though not necessarily respected, then we can probably avoid some of the problems of definition. In any event, our main concern is not to delineate precisely the limits of government but to evaluate the importance of those institutions or structures that lie at the heart of government.

In most countries, formal institutions of government are clearly spelled out in the constitution; however, the actual arrangement rarely conforms to the formal prescription or description. Canada is a prime example of such a situation; the cabinet, for example, is not even mentioned in the British North America Act, yet it ranks as probably the most important of all Canadian political institutions. Similarly, the prime minister remains unrecognized in our constitutional documents though in actual fact he wields more power than any other individual. These examples, and others that could be cited, tell us that, while written constitutions and official descriptions may provide useful information about government institutions, they tend not to be accurate or adequate. In Canada, and even more so in Britain, New Zealand, and certain other countries, an adequate description of government institutions can be gained only by studying the actual power arrangements and structures produced by tradition and convention.

Sometimes the institutions of government are viewed mainly as arenas of conflict or as "rules of the game of politics"; other times they are seen in terms of people in action. Doern and Aucoin, for example, define structures as "regular patterns of behavior that exist between policy actors and organizational units."[1] Such a view helps us to understand the importance of what political actors do but seems to minimize the legitimizing significance of the continuing power arrangements themselves. Small wonder, then, that many writers look beyond the incumbents and place much emphasis specifically on the institutional units. One such writer, Milliband, identifies the following as the key institutions that, in a functional sense, together comprise the state system: the executive government, the ministerial departments, the public corporations, the central banks and regulatory commissions, the military, the judiciary, and the legislative assemblies.[2] Whatever our inclination, we do well to avoid a mechanistic, an organismic, or an overly idealistic view of government institutions. As far as Canadian politics is concerned, preoccupation with any one of these emphases probably takes us away from a clear understanding of political reality. Canadian politics, I suggest, consists of a great diversity of sometimes haphazard activity, arising from an amorphous array of ideas and ideologies. This activity is undertaken by thousands of people who constitute the mammoth governmental establishment or are significantly associated with it. The general unity, legitimacy, and continuity of their activity derives logically and obviously from the more or less official institutions of which they are a part and through which their activities are expressed.

SPECIFIC INSTITUTIONS

Of all Canadian political institutions Parliament is probably the most consequential. Our whole parliamentary tradition, going back to the establishment of parliamentary supremacy in the British Isles, proceeding to the establishment of a representative assembly in Nova Scotia in 1758 and subsequently in all the other British colonies in North America, through to the winning of responsible government in the colony of Nova Scotia in 1847 and in the Province of Canada in 1849, and the creation of the Dominion of Canada in 1867, all involved verbal and sometimes even physical battles over how various institutions should relate to one another. Should the monarch be subordinate to Parliament? Should the executive be responsible to the elected members of Parliament? Should Parliament be bicameral and, if so, how should the two houses relate to one another? What powers should be exercised by the governor-general and the lieutenant-governors? How should the provinces be officially represented in Parliament? To what extent should the Canadian Parliament be subordinate to the British Parliament or to the British judiciary? These and many additional questions obviously focus specifically on institutions and the debates and controversies involving these institutional relations were not inconsequential niceties or formalities undertaken while the real stuff of politics was conducted elsewhere. These problems and their resolution *were* the real stuff of politics! The sometimes heated confrontations at Charlottetown, Quebec, and London were first and foremost debates over institutional accommodations and arrangements.

Institutional powers and relationships continued to be matters of much importance in later years. In 1896 the governor-general, Lord Aberdeen, challenged the cabinet's power by refusing to agree to appointments made by a defeated government. The entire King-Byng crisis of 1926 was essentially a battle for institutional supremacy rather than a personality conflict or a partisan ploy. Prime Minister King's response to the Chanak Crisis in 1922 together with the Balfour Declaration of 1926 and the vitally important Statute of Westminster in 1931 expressed and, in the last instance, legitimized the full autonomy of Canada and the institutional supremacy of the Canadian Parliament in external as well as internal affairs. More recently, a 1949 amendment to the British North America Act which gave Parliament the power to amend that Act except for areas involving provincial matters, certain education guarantees, certain language guarantees, and parliamentary sessions and terms, constitutes another important stage in the development of the Canadian Parliament as an institution.

In our own day Parliament, as an institution, still looms large. Politicians can make promises on the hustings or agree to deals in smoke-filled rooms but no statutes can be enacted or amended, no taxes legally imposed and no funds legally appropriated unless formally approved by Parliament. Of course, Parliament may delegate certain powers to others and, on occasion, will allow governments to collect and spend monies before the legislation is finally approved, but as an institution it always has the right to intervene and to call a halt to any executive action. It did exactly that on February 19, 1968 when the House of Commons rejected a tax measure the cabinet had assumed would pass and some of whose provisions the cabinet had already implemented.

Perhaps the most important role of the House of Commons as a formal institution involves the matter of expressing official confidence or nonconfidence in the cabinet. After an election it is the official party representation in the House of Commons and not any behavior of elites, classes, groups, or individuals that determines what party will form the government and whether it will have majority or minority status. Whatever the result, any government of the day must resign or call an election as soon as the House of Commons by a majority vote expresses nonconfidence in it. Admittedly, in February, 1968 the Liberal government maneuvered the House, more particularly Opposition Leader Robert Stanfield, into a second vote which reversed the original decision but such a reversal does not indicate any kind of weakening of Parliament's power; rather, it illustrates once again that the life of Canada's national government depends on the collective decision of the House of Commons.

When we look to the Senate we see an institution whose power, while formally substantial, has in fact been largely eroded. However, during the Coyne affair in 1961, and on numerous other occasions when the Senate has amended, criticized, or held up government legislation it has shown that governments still do well to reckon with it. The relatively weak position of the Senate illustrates the fact that an institution's actual powers are often quite different from its official powers. It also tells us that institutions are dynamic entities that can gain or lose political power.

The institution we know as the cabinet lies at the center of our political system. Its great power derives not from the personal qualities of its members, though these qualities do have some significance, but from the political power that has devolved upon that institution over the centuries. The incumbents decide how that power is to be used, they may even extend or reduce it, but it exists quite apart from who they are because it rests in the institution itself. Individual ministers, even all of them collectively, might wish to see a death sentence commuted, new tariff rates proclaimed, support for the U.N. terminated, or increased government subsidies given to deep-sea fishermen but their wishes are of little consequence until, as cabinet, via orders-in-council, they transform these wishes into public policy. Not surprisingly, Doern and Wilson assert that "no understanding of the political policy processes in Canada can be fully and intellectually complete until one examines (or attempts to mentally simulate) policy-making from the vantage point of the collective cabinet."[3]

The prime minister, similarly, cannot be seen only as a powerful individual or the epitome of the elite. He must be seen for what he is in our system; the top leader in the country who derives his power because of the office he holds in formal institutions: party, cabinet, and Parliament. His personal traits—eloquence, intelligence, leadership skills, general charisma, or whatever—may be very important in helping him to achieve his office and may greatly influence what he does while in office but they are not the source of his power. As an individual he may wish to appoint a new senator or judge, to establish a royal commission, to invoke the War Measures Act, or to call a general election but his wishes in themselves will achieve nothing until he acts as prime minister in an official capacity. Quite accurately his position has been termed the *Apex of Power*.[4]

Though as a person he may not change one iota, he holds that power only so long as he retains his parliamentary seat and he and his cabinet enjoy the support of a majority in the House of Commons. It is this institutional support that gives him his political legitimacy and political clout. Prime Minister Trudeau once stated that when backbenchers leave the parliamentary chambers they are "nobodies." When he ceases to be prime minister he may still be popular and even influential but in terms of wielding official power he becomes a nobody himself for he has then lost his institutional base.

Space limitations do not permit us to describe in any detail the importance of all our other national political institutions and structures. We could discuss at length the institution of the monarch; the office of the governor-general; the special, joint and standing committees of the House of Commons; the various committees of the cabinet but especially the Treasury Board; the ministers who head departments; the speaker; the auditor-general; the commissioner of official languages; and the chief electoral officer. In each instance the power exercised arises not from the person as person but from the person as office holder, as bearer of the powers of an institution. The Treasury Board, for example, does not consist merely of a half dozen prominent and powerful Canadians who have taken it upon themselves to decide to negotiate with postal employees about working conditions or to apportion the country's budget to various governmental departments and agencies; rather, the Treasury Board functions as an official institution charged with official duties. As in the case of the House of Commons and the cabinet, so also here, the whole is more than the sum of its parts and, in the long run, the fact that the official responsibilities of that institution are properly carried out is much more important than who the individuals happen to be who are currently entrusted with doing what needs to be done.

In addition to all the institutions already mentioned we have a large number of regulatory commissions, Crown agencies and corporations, and the whole gamut of the federal bureaucracy comprising part of our governmental structures. It is one thing to know that a certain prominent Canadian is opposed to the building of any Mackenzie Valley pipeline, that five big-name Canadians oppose all wage and price rollbacks, that ten influential Canadians favor governmental subsidization of Canadian television, that twelve wish to terminate all government grants for medical research done outside Canada, or that fifteen favor the nationalization of the CPR; but it is something quite different to know that the prominent Canadian is Commissioner Thomas Berger, that the five big-name Canadians constitute the Anti-Inflation Board, that the ten comprise the Canadian Radio-Television and Telecommunications Commission, that the twelve make up the Medical Research Council, and that the fifteen serve as the Canadian Transport Commission. By and large, as far as politics is concerned, people's opinions and wishes have far-reaching and continuing importance only if associated with some recognized institution or structure. Of course, what we have surveyed at the national level exists also at provincial and local levels, albeit sometimes in modified forms.

As we survey the political scene, it quickly becomes evident that institutions are still proliferating and, on balance, still growing in significance and power. Nationally, we are witnessing the development of various new agencies, most notably the very important political institution known as the Federal-Provincial Conference of First Ministers with its continuing secretariat and its official location in Ottawa's refurbished Union Station. Provincially, we see increasing power emanating from workmen's compensation boards, pollution control agencies, and the burgeoning ombudsman offices, to name some obvious instances. Canadian political institutions are still very much alive and thriving. To attempt to understand Canadian politics without becoming generally familiar with Canada's constitutional arrangements is like trying to find one's way in Peking without a map, without a guide, and without any knowledge whatsoever of the Chinese language.

INSTITUTIONALISM AND OTHER PERSPECTIVES

We have seen that it is impossible to understand Canadian politics without substantial knowledge about the structural arrangements; now we want to see how the institutional interpretation fits in with all the other orientations set forth in this book.

If we attempt to explain Canadian politics from a geographical point of view it quickly becomes evident that institutions cannot be overlooked. The original fixing of boundaries—national, provincial, or municipal—and the establishment of governments in those jurisdictions illustrate the inseparable connection. But that is only the beginning. Subsequent jurisdictional disputes and cooperation involving resource ownership and development, transportation and communication policies, pollution control, commodity marketing regulations, industrial development grants, recreational and parks policies, and the establishment of regional governments and district boards of all sorts, all involve continuing institutional decisions. A geographical orientation draws our attention to the physical environment and the people in it, but unless we add the dimension of institutions we cannot really talk of politics other than the "politics" of anarchy.

Turning to the continentalist interpretation we find a similar situation. The overwhelming impact of various American institutions on Canada, from the Federal Reserve System to the Department of Agriculture and from the Pentagon to the Immigration and Naturalization Service, is common knowledge. Then, too, quite apart from the effect of all the specifically American structures we have the very wide range of effects arising from such joint structures as NORAD, the St. Lawrence Seaway Authority, the International Joint Commission, and the dozens of other Canadian-American institutions.

Economics, our next orientation, may well be defined as the science of the production, distribution, and consumption of wealth but such activity cannot be carried on without a clearly recognized and relatively stable institutional arrangement. The traditional discipline of political economy reflected well the existing and continuing close interrelationship of economic activity and formal governmental structures. Especially in our day, when governments are becoming very much involved in regulatory, welfare, and proprietory activity in the economy, a re-emphasis of that relationship is timely. Virtually every organization of government influences the Canadian economy, is influenced by it, or both. To attempt to explain Canadian politics from an economic vantage point without giving a large place to cabinet decisions, to the Department of National Revenue, to the Treasury Board, to the Canadian Transport Commission, to the Tariff Commission, to the Anti-Inflation Board, and the whole host of relevant provincial agencies from marketing boards to tourist bureaus is to attempt the impossible.

An approach focusing on international relations also requires a knowledge of institutions. Without doubt, interests and ideologies, power and personalities, traditions and ambitions all play a part, but the whole range of activities from trade to extradition, from warfare to peace making, involves institutional cooperation or confrontation. How could states ever negotiate trade agreements, arms-control pacts, peace treaties, or anything else without mutual recognition of institutions? Moreover, such international or supranational phenomena as the Organization of Petroleum Exporting Countries, the European Economic Community, the Commonwealth of Nations, the Organization of American States, and the U.N. with all its specialized agencies function as noteworthy or even formidable institutions in their own right.

The historical approach to Canadian politics, the next on our list, relies particularly on structural relationships and evolution. How can we possibly understand the nature of Crown powers in Canada, the dynamics of responsible government, or the extent of personal rights and liberties if we are not prepared to learn about the evolution of the constitutional monarchy, about cabinet precedents, or about the British court system and common law? Many of the critical points in our history, such as the passage of the Quebec Act of 1774, of the Constitutional Act of 1791, of the Act of Union in 1840, of the British North America Act in 1867, and of the Statute of Westminster in 1931, to name only the most obvious ones, either established new institutions or gave greater legitimacy to those already existing. Of course, Canadian history involves leaders and movements and ideologies and resources but it involves institutions in a profound way. Any attempt to explain Canadian politics from a historical perspective must address itself to the development of our institutions.

We turn now to approaches that focus particularly on values and ask ourselves how institutions fit into ideological or value-oriented interpretations of Canadian politics. Not surprisingly, much attention is given to institutions. Discussions about conservative or liberal or socialist or social credit ideologies boil down largely to questions about what should or should not be done by various governmental institutions. The conservatives revere traditional institutions such as the monarchy and the Empire-Commonwealth; they tend to see contemporary institutions as the product of centuries of community experience and they are generally reluctant to change anything very much or very quickly. The liberals are more ready to alter institutions and to work through them to enhance personal liberty and general welfare. The socialists, of course, want to strengthen governmental institutions to further the welfare state and to bring about greater public ownership of the major sectors of production and distribution; while social credit apologists have as their main idea the notion that state institutions should control credit and the whole financial sector much more than they do now. Thus we see that, in explaining Canadian politics, writers who emphasize ideology must deal with institutions to show how the important ideologies have developed and what their supporters advocate.

Next, we consider political culture. Let Michael Whittington state his observation as given elsewhere in this volume:

> The political structures must reflect the dominant values of our political culture if they are to be effective. If political structures serve to enshrine political values that are not congruent with the values of Canadian society, then either the people's attitudes must change to conform to the institutionalized values, or the institutions must change to reflect social values better.

There we have it, stated unequivocally. Other writers in that area agree with Whittington that institutions are important. That is not surprising, for institutions do have a great impact on our political culture, responses to them are part of our political culture, and in their operation they must be in fundamental alignment with the central values in our political culture.

Looking at the federalist analysis of Canadian politics we see that here, too, institutional arrangements are basic. Confederation itself can be defined as institutional accommodation and evolution. Such later developments as decisions by the Judicial Committee of the Privy Council, the establishment of shared-cost programs, national disallowance of provincial legislation, the drawing up of taxation agreements, several important amendments to the BNA Act, and the continuing discussions about constitutional "patriation" and an acceptable amendment formula all involve the question of institutional jurisdiction. One of the great studies of Canadian politics, the 1940 Rowell-Sirois Royal Commission report, dealt largely with institutional responsibilities and resources in our federal arrangement. Almost by definition, a federalist interpretation of Canadian politics, obviously relevant and important, makes sense only if we think in terms of constitutions and institutions.

As Richard Simeon has pointed out, "Federalism is not only a response to regionalism, but also ensures that it will continue."[5] It does so in several ways. In the first place, the federal framework leads many politicians, pundits, academics, and opinion leaders to assume, even assert, a provincial perspective which, in turn, filters down to the electorate and the general population. Also, it provides "an institutional focus for loyalty and identity" and as "a political cleavage laid over other cleavages in the society . . . it tends to force other cleavages into the same mold."[6] If we analyze the operations of various kinds of pressure groups, of political parties, and of governments themselves, we can see that federalism as an institution tends to highlight "those cleavages which reinforce the territorial division" while other cleavages "will either be defined in such a way that they do conform to the pattern, or they will tend to be ignored."[7] To the extent, which is considerable, that the formal federal structures fragment social forces, blunt social cleavages, and in general inhibit the development of national pressures and sentiments, they not only perpetuate regional and provincial differences but greatly influence Canadian politics as a whole. Noting that when Alberta and Saskatchewan were created in 1905 from a single undifferentiated area, they "rapidly developed into two quite distinct political systems,"[8] Simeon writes as follows:

> This suggests that institutions are not simply the outgrowth or products of the environment and that they are not just dependent variables in the political system. They can also be seen as independent forces, which have some effects of their own: once established they themselves come to shape and influence the environment. . . . There must be some congruence between institutions and the underlying social system, but it is equally evident that the effect is two-way.[9]

We turn our attention now to political processes and the exercise of power. Let us deal first with processes. Many political scientists today are much attracted to studying the dynamic, integrative, aggregative, and redistributive aspects of political processes. Such an emphasis is well taken but processes do not take place in a vacuum. We have earlier noted that government itself can be defined, at least in part, in terms of authoritative allocation of values, but what makes such allocation authoritative? I suggest that it is mainly the institutional setting, that is, the formal offices held and the official powers exercised. Let us assess the validity of such a view as we scan the next four approaches.

To talk about political parties is to talk about organizations whose leaders seek to control state institutions. In a functional sense, of course, the party structures themselves, while technically not part of the governmental machinery, form part of the total complex of political institutions. And when we talk about political elections we are not describing the selection of leaders in the sense that a Rotary Club chooses its executives, but we are describing the selection of leaders for external, or at least overarching, institutional positions.

Many students of Canadian political parties have described the importance of institutions.[10] Even Winn and McMenemy, while striving to move beyond the traditional institutional descriptions, acknowledge that an adequate analysis must give a large place to structures. Quite appropriately, they study "the place of parties in the larger political system and in the ongoing political process."[11] Their input-throughout-output model helps us understand Canadian politics only if we apply it to actual institutions. Where there are no structures, there can be no flow; without governmental institutions, no party platforms or cross-pressure compromises ever become governmental policies. Whatever else political parties may be, they are fundamentally important because they are political institutions that express and accommodate the interests of various regions, classes, and groups.

If parties, as institutions, play a major role in politicizing certain societal cleavages, the electoral system, as an important institution in its own right, has a major effect on political behavior and electoral results. As Alan Cairns has demonstrated,[12] Canada's electoral system operates in a way that greatly exaggerates regional differences and that, by and large, results in underrepresentation for those parties whose support is more evenly distributed throughout the country. Consequently, and quite logically, party leaders tend to adopt policies and programs that have the greatest appeal in regions where they are already strong. Thus the Conservatives under Diefenbaker and the Liberals under Trudeau, while vociferously espousing the virtues of unhyphenated Canadianism and national unity, actually adopted policies with specific regional appeals which would, presumably, produce the best possible electoral results.

Moving on to the perspective that stresses dualism, we find that English-French cooperation and conflict in Canada often involves governmental institutions. Constitutional provisions set much of the framework but they did not resolve the probelms. The question of "adequate" French-Canadian representation in the military, the regulatory agencies, the bureaucracy, the Crown corporations, the courts, and the cabinet remains a matter of contention. The Royal Commission on Bilingualism and Biculturalism, the Canadian Radio-television and Telecommunications Commission, the Public Service Commission, the commissioner of official languages, and other institutional centers have dealt with various aspects of this deep division, but if the 1976 election of a separatist government in Quebec reflects public opinion even in a limited way, then the division persists. And, of course, separatism itself involves a quarrel over institutional relations. If the institutional dimension were of no great consequence, then the champions of the French-Canadian culture would surely ignore it and attend to the business of protecting and building their "nation." But they know that the institutional situation is not peripheral; they know that it is central and that is why they have made institutional autonomy a first priority. A separatist movement may have a great political program but unless institutions are altered such a program comes to nothing.

Public policy, as suggested earlier, cannot be divorced from governmental structures either. It differs from the policies of private organizations primarily in its scope and in the coercive institutional power that lies behind it. Introducing their important study of public policy, Doern and Aucoin point out that "the emphasis on the plurality of structures is an important feature of the book."[13] Lamenting the fact that the "structuring of those policy roles" has not been studied intensively and asserting that "part of the problem was the dominance of constitutional studies,"[14] their balanced analysis nonetheless gives full recognition to the formal or institutional relationships among the several components of the policy process. The titles of seven of their nine chapters include names of formal government institutions.

Most obviously, the development of public policy involves extensive and complex bargaining among structured pressure groups and distinct units of government. As far as the competing and cooperating governments are concerned, relative institutional autonomy is an ongoing concern and not only in Quebec. Accordingly, attempts to deal with poverty in Canada tend to be transformed into problems of regional and provincial disparities; transportation debates focus on such problems as in which province a service facility will be located rather than on meeting social needs; and issues such as medical insurance, funding postsecondary education, and the operation of pension plans are debated in terms of governmental jurisdictions rather than how the public can best be served. Similarly, the language question becomes an Ottawa-Quebec problem and oil export policies degenerate into an Alberta-Ottawa controversy or confrontation rather than a discussion of what is, in the long run, in the best interest of Canadians.

The foregoing discussion clearly demonstrates that any attempt to explain Canadian politics from a policy perspective cannot avoid an emphasis on institutions since our statutes from the Criminal Code to the War Measures Act are the products of institutional interaction; they are enacted by governmental institutions and then are applied by governmental institutions of one kind or another.

We have seen how important institutions are for the approaches that emphasize environment, values, structures, and processes; now we ask ourselves what significance institutions have for the approaches that focus on political power and behavior. Admittedly, all institutions are made by men but they are the products of many generations and, once established, seem to have a character and momentum of their own, a character that greatly influences the behavior of incumbents. Even mass movements and social classes tend to develop as responses to certain arrangements of authority.

If we consider the role of individual leaders we see a mixed situation. An explanation of Canadian politics emphasizing key people tells us that to a large extent people such as John A. Macdonald, Wilfrid Laurier, J.S. Woodsworth, Mackenzie King, John Diefenbaker, Pierre Trudeau, René Lévesque, William Aberhart, or Maurice Duplessis probably shaped political institutions as much as they were shaped by them. But that does not detract from my central thesis, which simply asserts that institutions are important. The issue is not some kind of institutional determinism or even institutional preeminence, it is only a question of institutional significance. I suggest that, by and large, the men and women whose ideas and actions dominated or now dominate Canadian politics operated mainly as office holders in, or shapers of, governmental institutions.

The place of institutions in an elitist interpretation of Canadian politics is similar to that described in the previous approach; elites influence governmental institutions but they also work through them. Of course, not all elites, or all members of elite groups, are necessarily political. What, we may ask, transforms certain elites into political elites? The answer is simple; they have either maneuvered themselves into positions of power in governmental institutions or have found ways of influencing other people who fill those positions. C. Wright Mills, perhaps the foremost advocate of the elitist approach, agrees. "No one . . . can be truly powerful unless he has access to the command of major institutions, for it is over these institutional means of power that the truly powerful are, in the first instance, powerful."[15]

Moving on to the "group theory" view of Canadian politics, we quickly come to realize that a major, if not *the* major, reason for the formation of pressure groups is the goal of putting pressure on office holders in governmental institutions. In our parliamentary system this means focusing mainly on the cabinet rather than on backbenchers. Group leaders and lobbyists tend not to be interested in just any people who happen to be eloquent or charismatic or who possess gifts of leadership. Quite understandably, they give their attention to people who possess institutional power. From 1963 till 1968 pressure group spokesmen took their message to Lester Pearson. Then sudenly they seemed to forget about him altogether and zeroed in on Pierre Trudeau. Pearson had not changed as a person but he had given up his institutional position and the group spokesmen fully realized that that basic fact made all the difference. Not only do Canadian pressure groups strive to influence institutions such as the cabinet, the Canadian Transport Commission, the Anti-Inflation Board, or the House of Commons Standing Committee on Veterans' Affairs, but in our pluralist society they themselves function as important institutions.

Experts in the area agree on the close association between pressure groups and governmental institutions. David Truman states: "The power such groups dispose is involved at every point in the institutions of government, and the efforts of these formations are in various ways aided by, restricted by, and identified with institutionalized government."[16] A. Paul Pross, in commenting on the authors who contributed to his volume, notes that "They have turned their attention to the impact major institutions—particularly Parliament and the civil service—have had on pressure groups, and they have noted the way in which such groups have adapted to the requirements of the constitution."[17]

The last approach in this general category, at least as presented in this book, is the Marxist class analysis of Canadian politics. How important are

governmental institutions from a leftist vantage point? Even a brief glance
at Resnick's chapter in this volume, or a survey of almost any other Marxist study indicates that institutions are given a prominent place. Stanley
Ryerson has described in detail how the bourgeois class gained control of
governmental institutions in the nineteenth century.[18] Resnick echoes
similar views. Social classes always play major roles but the really important aspect is that the dominant class exercises its power through governmental structures. The main purpose of politicizing the proletariat, it appears, is to enable it to gain control of government institutions and then
reform or maybe abolish them, depending on which Marxists are speaking. Consider some of Resnick's statements: "the analysis of the state
should be at the very heart of political science"; "Marxist theory would
argue that state intervention becomes necessary as capitalism fails to function"; "the state has been involved in fostering capitalist accumulation for
centuries"; "labor relations boards, labor codes, and the like can be important carrots in winning labor support"; and, "the capitalist state exercises
very effective behind-the-scenes control over such institutions as the
CBC." Clearly, a Marxist analysis has much to say about political institutions. Marxist critics are sometimes inclined to reject the so-called institutional approach as sterile but in fact they use many of the same institutional categories. Perhaps most of them would even agree that formal
political institutions such as federalism and Parliament have played an
important role in inhibiting the development of a national, class-based
politics in Canada.

Where does this necessarily brief survey leave us? Well, it leaves me
with the distinct impression that consideration of political institutions has
an important place in every interpretation of Canadian politics presented
in this book. Many approaches, of course, go far beyond institutional considerations but none can, or in fact does, ignore them. But these fifteen
approaches do not exhaust all possibilities and presumably some readers
might believe that there are other approaches and methodologies in
which institutions play no part. Naturally, I cannot deal with all possible
ways of looking at Canadian politics but let us touch briefly on three general methodologies that have thus far not been considered specifically:
structural-functional analysis, behavioralism, and systems theory.

Discussing the first of these three, Oran Young asserts that the "conceptual framework of the structural-functional approach centers around
the question, What structures fulfill what basic functions and under what
conditions in any given system?"[19] Marion J. Levy, Jr. reminds us that the
first basic step in structural-functional analysis involves definition of "the
unit to be discussed."[20] The units, it turns out, are mainly political institutions. Philippa Strum and Michael Shmidman add the following observations: "Functionalism concentrates on the political functions performed
by people and institutions."[21] "In the final analysis, the functionalist will
take the basic, formal structure of government and attempt to discover
who within it actually has power, how much, and how it is used."[22] Func-
tionalists, they conclude, "ask what political functions are performed in all
societies, and then they are able to move to a consideration of the institu-

tions or structures that perform them."[23] Institutions, clearly, are very important for structural-functional analysts.

Arguing, as they do, that one cannot understand the workings of political institutions without first examining the behavior of the individuals who comprise them, behavioralists have often paid little explicit attention to institutions. However, as Robert Murphy points out, when they talk about voting behavior, political participation, the psychological characteristics of political man, and the rest of their quantifiable or non-quantifiable data and concepts, the institutions of the political system form the integrating framework.[24] Without such an integration, voting statistics, the results of multivariate analysis, or data on leaders remain unrelated if not meaningless facts.

As its name suggests, systems theory, which can be seen either as an area within behavioralism or as a separate methodology in its own right, focuses on the relationship of political institutions to one another and to other phenomena. The conceptual structures that Easton and others have developed bear a striking resemblance to actual institutions.[25] That makes sense since all the systems theory emphasis on demands, supports, transformation, feedback, and so on becomes credible only if one postulates an actual set of political institutions. The whole approach correctly assumes that processes are important but that, at least in politics, processes do not exist without institutions.

SOME GENERAL PROPOSITIONS

While the main thrust of the institutionalist perspective is that in any polity, be it Soviet, South African, or Canadian, institutions play a major role and deserve serious study, there is also a second, more ideological thrust that contends that certain kinds of institutions are especially important because they play a vital role in the development and functioning of free democracies. The following propositions will serve to illustrate this second thrust.

1. The institutional approach, following in the Enlightenment tradition, gives a large place to continual refurbishing, modification, and reform. It rejects the Platonic or Marxist views that political problems can be resolved once and for all. For most institutionalists politics is, or at least should be, open and social conflict converted into peaceful, continuing competition. Institutions of government, especially representative assemblies, are seen as arenas in which, over time, proximate solutions are worked out for society's political problems.

2. The institutionalist interpretation of politics acknowledges that power is the basis of politics and asserts that while establishing institutional safeguards is not a sufficient condition for an orderly exercise of power, it is a necessary one. Given the fact that the "great problem of history has been to turn absolute power to democratic uses," the development in Canada of a set of institutions through which political

power is exercised as an efficient, controllable, and largely predictable force is a major achievement.

3. Most institutionalists hold to the view that rationality can be applied to the realm of politics and that it can modify or even replace continuity and traditional practices as the basis of authority. In Canada, political changes involving, for example, Crown powers and the head of state incorporate this phenomenon. Political institutions are thus important inasmuch as they exemplify the highest achievement of the enlightened, rational mind.

4. By and large, institutionalists agree that those institutions that check authority, balance power, and generally promote limited government are most important. In Canada the federal arrangement, the electoral system, cabinet accountability, the independent judiciary, the functioning of official opposition parties, parliamentary supremacy, and the whole body of British common law serve to protect a substantial sphere of private life and to reinforce freedoms.

5. Institutionalists generally have great respect for a society's political constitution, whether it is formally spelled out as the American was intended to be, whether it is largely unwritten as the British is, or whether it is a blend of largely inherited conventions and formal legislative enactment as the Canadian constitution has come to be. Any country's basic law is important because it establishes both the organizational framework and a fundamental philosophical orientation. In addition, it assigns responsibilities, describes basic processes, sets forth the conditions and terms of office holding, and usually spells out formal amending procedures.

6. Competition, as an operating principle, is a central notion for most institutionalists. The basic argument is that individual as well as collective competition produces substantial freedom and progress, and that institutions of government play a vital, conducive role in achieving those ends. The problem, as institutionalists see it, is to prevent competition from degenerating into oppression by any single segment of society. The way to prevent such oppression, it is argued, is to establish constitutional limits on governments and to have periodic and uncoerced elections. In such an arrangement, individual and group competition operates to produce collective benefits. Those institutionalists with a socialist inclination do not object to a relatively great concentration of power, provided it is held by the government, but they, too, believe that such a concentration of power, indeed, the whole question of socialism itself, should be decided by a free electoral vote.

CONCLUSION

In light of all that has been said so far we can say that, all things considered, an emphasis on governmental institutions is an important perspective on Canadian politics in its own right and that institutions cannot be ignored by any of the fifteen not explicitly institutional orientations presented in this book. Accordingly, we should perhaps see the institutional approach as a common denominator for all approaches, for surely, despite all the protestations to the contrary, its terms are the common language of the discipline and the standard reference points. Admittedly, in a sense the institutional approach may be elementary but that makes it no less important. Only a thorough knowledge of the basics enables us to probe more deeply.

There are additional limitations inherent in the institutional approach. In itself it tends to see politics as too static; arrangements are sometimes presented as too fixed. That is why we do well to consider other perspectives. As in the study of the human body, so also in political science, a thorough knowledge of anatomy is essential, though not sufficient, for an understanding of the processes.
politic.

This approach also tends to neglect foreign affairs and international politics. Perhaps this shortcoming arises from the fact that, as there were no really important world institutions for a long time and even now there is no form of world government, there seems to be nothing of substance in this area to talk about. Let us not overlook international institutions that may be less than governmental in authority.

Similarly, a narrow conception of the institutional approach may lead us to overlook the importance of the individual, be he prime minister, lobbyist, newspaper columnist, or voter. There is a danger that we separate institutions from people and thus lose touch with reality.

Finally, a narrowly delineated institutional approach may well underestimate the significance of violence in politics, even in Canadian politics. Without doubt, violence, the threat of violence, and the whole phenomenon of unanticipated disruption of normal affairs is becoming more important. Preparation for defense, planning for the possibility of insurrection, and the fear of war are very real preoccupations of Canadians and Canadian governments. A straightforward institutional emphasis on agencies and offices often overlooks such matters but that inadequacy can surely be corrected.

The importance of structures and institutions is attested to by the degree of attention devoted to them by major authors writing textbooks about Canadian politics. Here are the numbers of institution-oriented chapters in some common texts: Van Loon and Whittington, nine out of seventeen;[26] Ward's revision of Dawson's major text, eighteen out of twenty-three;[27] Ward's revision of the abbreviated text by Dawson and Dawson, fourteen out of fifteen;[28] Fox's third edition of collected articles, ten out of nineteen;[29] Khan, MacKown, and McNiven, six out of twenty-two;[30] Kruhlak, Schultz, and Pobihushchy, twelve out of twenty-three;[31] Vaughan, Kyba, and Dwivedi, twenty out of twenty-five;[32] Mallory, ten out of ten;[33] and White, Wagenberg, and Nelson, seven out of eleven.[34]

It may currently be popular in some circles to reject any institutional emphasis but such rejection, as we have seen, is not warranted. Moreover, some of it seems to rest on a false assumption, namely, that some of us believe that once we have described all our institutions, nothing more remains to be said. But those of us who give institutional studies a significant place make no such claim. What we emphasize, unabashedly, is that political institutions, simultaneously the reservoir and culmination of our collective experience, are of considerable importance. We believe that a good case can be made for the view that they constitute an integrating framework, both theoretically and actually, and that any interpretation that ignores institutions is incomplete.

ENDNOTES

1. G. Bruce Doern and Peter Aucoin, *The Structure of Policy-Making in Canada* (Toronto: Macmillan, 1971), p. 4.

2. Ralph Milliband, *The State in Capitalist Society* (London: Weidenfeld and Nicholson, 1969), pp. 53-54.

3. G. Bruce Doern and V. Seymour Wilson, eds., *Issues in Canadian Public Policy* (Toronto: Macmillan, 1974), p. 1.

4. Thomas A. Hockin, ed., *Apex of Power* (Scarborough, Ontario: Prentice-Hall, 1971).

5. Richard Simeon, "Regionalism and Canadian Political Institutions", *Queen's Quarterly*, 82, (Winter, 1975), p. 508.

6. Simeon, *ibid.*, p. 508.

7. *Ibid.*

8. *Ibid.*, p. 504.

9. *Ibid.*

10. See, for example, Frederick Engelmann and Mildred Schwartz, *Canadian Political Parties: Origin, Character, Impact* (Scarborough, Ontario: Prentice-Hall, 1975).

11. Conrad Winn and John McMenemy, eds., *Political Parties in Canada* (Toronto: McGraw-Hill Ryerson, 1976), p. 1.

12. Alan C. Cairns, "The Electoral System and the Party System in Canada, 1921-1965," *Canadian Journal of Political Science*, 1, No. 1 (March, 1968), pp. 55-80.

13. Doern and Aucoin, *op. cit.*, p. 1.

14. *Ibid.*, p. 7.

15. C. Wright Mills, *The Power Elite* (New York. Oxford University Press, 1956), pp. 3-4.

16. David B. Truman, *The Governmental Process* (New York: Alfred A. Knopf, 1960), p. 7.

17. A. Paul Pross, *Pressure Group Behaviour in Canadian Politics* (Toronto: McGraw-Hill Ryerson, 1975), pp. 1-2.

18. Stanley Ryerson, *Unequal Union; Confederation and the Roots of Conflict in the Canadas, 1815-1873* (Toronto: Progress Books, 1968).

19. Oran R. Young, *Systems of Political Science* (Englewood Cliffs, N.J.: Prentice-Hall, 1968), p. 28.

20. Marion J. Levy, Jr., "Some Aspects of 'Structural-Functional' Analysis and Political Science," *Approaches to the Study of Politics*, ed. Roland Young (Evanston, Ill.: Northwestern University Press, 1958), p. 53.

21. Philippa Strum and Michael Shmidman, *On Studying Political Science* (Pacific Palisades, California: Goodyear, 1969), p. 58.

22. *Ibid.*, p. 59.

23. *Ibid.*, p. 60.

24. Robert Murphy, *The Style and Study of Political Science* (Glenview, Ill.: Scott, Foresman, 1970), pp. 26-28.

25. See, for example, David Easton, *A Systems Analysis of Political Life* (New York: John Wiley & Sons, 1965), especially Part One.

26. Richard J. Van Loon and Michael S. Whittington, *The Canadian Political System: Environment, Structure and Process,* 2nd ed. (Toronto: McGraw-Hill Ryerson, 1976).

27. R. MacGregor Dawson, *The Government of Canada,* 5th ed. rev. by Norman Ward (Toronto: University of Toronto Press, 1970).

28. R. MacGregor Dawson and W.F. Dawson, *Democratic Government in Canada,* 4th ed. rev. by Norman Ward (Toronto: University of Toronto Press, 1971).

29. Paul W. Fox, ed., *Politics: Canada,* 3rd ed. (Toronto: McGraw-Hill, 1970).

30. Rais A. Khan, Stuart A. Mackown, and James D. McNiven, *An Introduction to Political Science* (Georgetown, Ont.: Irwin-Dorsey, 1972).

31. Orest M. Kruhlak, Richard Schultz, and Sidney I. Pobihushchy, eds., *The Canadian Political Process,* rev. ed. (Toronto: Holt, Rinehart and Winston, 1973).

32. Frederick Vaughan, Patrick Kyba, and O.P. Dwivedi, eds., *Contemporary Issues in Canadian Politics* (Scarborough, Ont.: Prentice-Hall, 1970).

33. J.R. Mallory, *The Structure of Canadian Government* (Toronto: Macmillan, 1971).

34. W.L. White, R.H. Wagenberg, and R.C. Nelson, *Introduction to Canadian Politics and Government* (Toronto: Holt, Rinehart and Winston, 1972).

SELECTED REFERENCES

Despite the widespread reliance on the institutional approach, political science literature contains very little explicit analysis on the topic. However, the following works should be useful, especially for the beginning student.

APTER, DAVID E. *Introduction to Political Analysis.* Cambridge, Mass.: Winthrop, 1977. Chapters 6 and 7 provide a useful description of the role of institutions, especially in Western democracies.

CHARLESWORTH, JAMES C., ed. *A Design for Political Science: Scope, Objectices, and Methods.* Philadelphia: The American Academy of Political and Social Science, 1966. Three major essays, together with responses, dealing with the aspects mentioned in the title.

———. *The Limits of Behavioralism in Political Science.* Philadelphia: The American Academy of Political and Social Science, 1962. The best treatment of the topic in a concise form.

DAHL, ROBERT A. *Modern Political Analysis,* sec. ed. Englewood Cliffs, NJ: Prentice-Hall, 1970. A good discussion of major concepts and issues with some references to approaches,

HYNEMAN, CHARLES S. *The Study of Politics: The Present State of American Political Science.* Urbana, Ill.: University of Illinois Press, 1959. A useful analysis of the major questions and conflicts in American political science.

IRISH, MARIAN D., ed. *Political Science: Advance of the Discipline.* Englewood Cliffs, NJ: Prentice-Hall, 1968. Six original essays dealing with basic concepts in political science traditions, methodologies, and emphases.

MURPHY, ROBERT. *The Style and Study of Political Science.* Glenview, Ill.: Scott, Foresman, 1970. An elementary introduction to the fields of political science and a cursory survey of the major approaches set mainly in an American framework.

SIMEON, RICHARD. "Regionalism and Canadian Political Institutions." *Queen's Quarterly* 82 (Winter, 1975), pp. 499-511. A first-rate analysis that challenges some traditional assumptions about Canadian regionalism.

SOMIT, ALBERT, AND JOSEPH TANENHAUS. *The Development of American Political Science: From Burgess to Behavioralism.* Boston: Allyn and Bacon, 1967. A very informative account of the development of American political science; contains a major section on behavioralism and its limitations.

STRUM, PHILIPPA AND MICHAEL SHMIDMAN. *On Studying Political Science.* Pacific Palisades, Cal.: Goodyear, 1969. A primer about political science; major concepts, major divisions, and major approaches are described briefly; very elementary.

VAN DYKE, VERNON. *Political Science: A Philosophical Analysis.* Stanford, Cal.: Stanford University Press, 1960. This wide-ranging and very useful introduction to the study of politics has an excellent, but brief, section on approaches.

YOUNG, ORAN R. *Systems of Political Science.* Englewood Cliffs, NJ: Prentice-Hall, 1968. A very useful, short introduction to some of the major approaches; several chapters deal with the nature and utilization of approaches.

YOUNG, ROLAND, ed. *Approaches to the Study of Politics.* Evanston, Ill.: Northwestern University Press, 1958. Twenty-two essays dealing with various approaches but not specifically with institutions except for one chapter on "structural-functional" analysis; assumes considerable knowledge of basic concepts.

9

Federal-Provincial Relations

J. Peter Meekison*

INTRODUCTION

There is an oft-told anecdote that describes very perceptively one of the most significant features of Canadian politics. Once upon a time an international committee was established to study the elephant. After agreeing on the terms of reference each delegate was asked to propose a tentative title for the final report. The delegates made the following suggestions:

Great Britain:	The Elephant and the Commonwealth
United States:	The Elephant and Free Enterprise
France:	The Love Life of the Elephant
U.S.S.R.:	The Elephant and Marxism
West Germany:	An Introduction to the Study of the Elephant
Canada:	The Elephant: A Federal or a Provincial Problem

To a great extent Canadian politics is the politics of federalism. Few, if any, issues discussed in Canada today do not in some fashion involve federal-provincial relations. As such, the anecdote says more about the realities of Canadian politics than one might realize.

The literature on federalism today is extensive, ranging from broad theoretical works to specific studies of individual states. In these writings federalism has been characterized as a network of legal relationships, as a process, as a sociological phenomenon, and as a bargain.[1] Given the number of federal states and the emergence and collapse of many new federations, such studies deserve careful scrutiny for the insights they give into the problems and pitfalls of governing under this complex system.

*Deputy Minister, Department of Federal and Intergovernmental Affairs, Alberta; Professor of Political Science (on leave), the University of Alberta. Portions of this paper were given at a conference at the University of Saskatchewan in March, 1977.

In approaching a study of Canadian politics from the perspective of federalism one encounters terms such as: classical federalism, quasi-federalism, decentralized federalism, economic federalism, executive federalism, dual federalism, emergency federalism, flexible federalism and cooperative federalism. While the qualitative differences among these particular terms are often hard to isolate, their usage suggests that Canadian federalism means different things to different people or that only a particular characteristic or phenomenon of the federal system is being analyzed. While each commentary is describing an aspect of Canadian politics and certain common characteristics may emerge, the qualification attached to the word federalism suggests that each author has a different perspective on the problem.

Instead of attempting to develop an ideal prototype, it is more useful to begin with the widely recognized structural approach of K. C. Wheare. Wheare defined a government as federal when there exists "a division of power between general and regional authorities, each of which, in its own sphere is coordinate with the others and independent of them."[2] The federal principle, according to Wheare's analysis, has three main components: the division of powers, two orders of government, and a statement of the relationships between them.

Although the cornerstone of a federal constitution may be the division of powers, these divisions are usually not sufficiently clear to prevent disputes from occurring over their precise meaning. These disputes arise as governments endeavor to fulfill their obligations and either trespass or are perceived to have trespassed on another's territory. Conflicts over the interpretation of the British North America Act provide an excellent example. The number of times that the courts in Canada have had to determine whether a question is a matter relating to "peace, order and good government" (national) or "property and civil rights" (provincial) are too frequent to mention. Regardless of the outcome of such cases, their existence serves to confirm the fact that perceptions of the division of powers change over time. Whether the changes in the division of powers occur as a result of judicial interpretation, amendment, convention, attrition, delegation, or something else, significant changes do take place in the relationship between the two orders of government. Thus the initial equilibrium within the federation, usually achieved after painstaking negotiation, is disturbed.

The factors contributing to change are reasonably well documented and need not be dealt with extensively. Cataclysms such as war, depression, or inflation have had a profound influence on Canadian federalism. Canada's transformation from an agricultural and rural society and economy to an industrial and urban one has greatly affected the system. Other forces such as advances in technology, improvements in communications, and the increased mobility of the population have also contributed to changes in Canadian federalism. Nor can one ignore the existence and development of cultural awareness in Quebec. Another factor that has created many problems and led to piecemeal adjustment is the disparity between the fiscal means and the fiscal needs of provincial governments. Each of these factors has contributed to adjustments in, or strains upon, the division of powers.

Adjustments within Canadian federalism have been made as the need for them has arisen. What has been the principal effect of these changes? At first glance one might conclude that governments are simply doing more and as a result clash more as they attempt to redefine the boundaries of their respective areas of jurisdiction. A more careful analysis indicates that decision making in many areas of public policy once believed to be within the exclusive jurisdiction of either government is now shared. Interdependence more than independence is one of the chief characteristics of Canadian federalism; consequently we need to be concerned not only with the division of powers but also with the processes by which the adjustments or, if one prefers, accommodations are reached.

Regardless of what changes have occurred, politicians usually premise their behavior on the assumption that their legislative authority is exclusive. If necessary, harmonization of federal and provincial policies will come later. The concept of exclusive powers, or autonomy, was present in 1867 and continues as an important factor influencing public policy development. Thus, while interdependence is recognized, governments often work on the premise that they have exclusive jurisdiction over a particular subject. Accordingly, policy development frequently requires the meshing or blending of exclusive powers; that is, governments must cooperate to achieve a common objective.

At this juncture it is necessary to emphasize the difference between the legal and political dimensions of Canadian federalism. Under the British North America Act (1867) the federal and provincial governments were assigned particular responsibilities. The distribution of legislative powers is contained in Sections 91-95 of the BNA Act. Other provisions of the constitution establish or confer certain powers, rights, or privileges on either the federal or provincial governments. For example, Section 101 authorized Parliament to establish a general court of appeal—the Supreme Court of Canada. Under Section 109 provincial proprietary rights over land, mines, minerals, and royalties were established. Section 125 provides that "no lands or property belonging to Canada or any province shall be liable to taxation." In analyzing the federal system, therefore, one must be conscious of what the constitution, either as amended or interpreted, means. In this respect the constitution serves as a reference point. Only if we understand the importance of the legal basis of the federal system can we comprehend the political aspects of Canadian federalism.

Having established the nature of each government's powers we can then examine intergovernmental relations and the interdependence that has become more and more apparent. Presenting the legal basis for developing and expanding a policy represent only part of the story. For example, Alberta's ownership of its oil and natural gas does not mean that provincial policies can be developed independently from the policies of the federal government. The federal government controls oil and natural gas exports through the National Energy Board; it has maintained a uniform national price for crude oil; it regulates interprovincial marketing of oil and natural gas; and it has established a tax policy under which companies can and will participate in exploration and development. Another example is that of health and hospital services where the federal government established national goals and standards. To have these translated into services, however, provincial governments had to develop and maintain the necessary administrative machinery, train health personnel, and plan and develop related services. The list of areas where policies of one government affect or influence the policies of the other is endless. The consequences of these influences have changed dramatically both the character and the functioning of the federal system. Initially governments were concerned about invasions of their exclusive jurisdictions, invasions that, to a great extent, came about as both the federal and provincial governments developed the basic legislation necessary to fulfill their constitutional obligations. While governments still jealously guard their jurisdictions they have also become conscious of the effects of policy interdependence. For example, the provincial finance ministers in December, 1976 presented their collective views to the federal government on its proposed revisions to the Bank Act, spelling out the effects, both desirable and undesirable, these revisions would have on provincial financial institutions.

In summary, Canadian federalism has a legal basis but is also a complex and dynamic system continually being subjected to pressures for change. That the Canadian political system has been able to adapt to meet new challenges and conditions represents a significant achievement. Change in any political system is inevitable and federal systems are no exception. While formal amendments to the constitution are infrequent and usually difficult, incremental changes do take place through a variety of techniques.

Before discussing the main focus of this chapter, which is the nature and relative significance of federal-provincial relations, brief attention should be given to the effects of federalism on a number of other Canadian political institutions. The composition of both the Senate and the House of Commons reflects the federal system. The Canadian Senate incorporates regional but to some extent also provincial representation. Representation in the House of Commons is also influenced by the federal system in that constituency boundaries are limited by provincial boundaries. The unit for redistribution of seats within the House of Commons is the province. Provinces are guaranteed that their representation in the House of Commons will not fall below their representation in the Senate. As a result of this policy Prince Edward Island has four members of Parliament, a membership greater than its entitlement under representation by population.

Perhaps the most federalized of Canadian political institutions is the federal cabinet. One of the chief tasks of any prime minister in putting together his cabinet is ensuring that each province has representation, a practice that began with Sir John A. Macdonald and has continued to the present. For example, when James Richardson resigned from the cabinet in the fall of 1976, the only other Liberal M.P. from Manitoba was appointed to the cabinet, thereby ensuring a continuing presence from that province. In instances where a province does not have any members in the governing party, such as in Alberta after the 1974 election, a senator may be appointed to act as the spokesman for the province. The cabinet ministers for each province act as spokesmen for that province in the cabinet, as spokesmen for the government in that province, and as patronage conduits for the governing party.

The composition of the Supreme Court of Canada is also affected by the federal system. Under the Supreme Court Act three judges are to be appointed to that court from the bar of Quebec. By convention, the remaining six are appointed as follows: three from Ontario, two from the West and one from Atlantic Canada.

The Canadian party system is also influenced by federalism. In some provinces one finds separate federal and provincial party organizations with different constitutions, finances and, sometimes, even supporters. For example, the Liberal party in Quebec split into two different organizations, a provincial and a national, in the early sixties. Interestingly, some of the great federal-provincial disputes have been between individuals ostensibly within the same party, such as the Hepburn-King debate over the war effort and the Lesage-Pearson debate over the Canada Pension Plan. Various theories have been developed over time to relate the party system to the federal system. Some of these have attempted to explain why voters support different parties federally and provincially. They have tried to show why, in January, 1977, although the Liberals formed a majority government in Ottawa, only two provinces, Nova Scotia and Prince Edward Island, had Liberal governments in office. Others have tried to demonstrate that the opposition's function in Canada is now performed largely by provincial governments. The success of third parties such as the Union Nationale, the CCF/NDP and Social Credit, at the provincial level, has also been the subject of several studies. Finally, some observers suggest that opposition parties in Ottawa are far more sensitive than the government to provincial rights and claims.

In short, the structure and operation of Canadian political institutions have been greatly influenced by the existence of the federal system. Indeed, to a great extent politics in Canada is determined by the restraints imposed by the federal arrangement. In considering federal-provincial relations one should not overlook the broader aspects of the political system and the profound effects that federalism has had on their development.

THE FEDERAL SYSTEM:
THE DEVELOPMENTAL STAGE—1867-1940

At the time of Confederation the constitutional draftsmen did not approach the division of powers with great precision. The criterion used was a relatively simple one: important subjects were given to the central government while those relating to local matters were assigned to the provinces. It is no secret that Sir John A. Macdonald cherished the idea of a unitary state but had to settle for something else—a system that Wheare describes as quasi-federal. Describing the division of powers, Macdonald said:

> We have given the General Legislature all the great subjects of legislation. . . . [W]e have expressly declared that all subjects of general interest not distinctly and exclusively conferred upon the local governments and legislatures, shall be conferred upon the General Governments and Legislature. . . . We have avoided all conflict of jurisdiction and authority.[3]

In addition to the broad grant of legislative power, the federal government exercised partial, but still significant, control over the provinces through its powers of disallowance and appointment of lieutenant-governors. Although the provinces were given taxing powers, their revenue position was fairly weak and a complex system of federal subsidies and grants was written into the constitution. There is little doubt that at its formation, Canada had a highly centralized form of federalism with the provinces being in a subordinate position to the federal government. That it has changed from the highly centralized quasi-federal system of 1867 to one where central and provincial governments are roughly equal is not really questioned today. Whether the change has been for good or bad is another matter entirely.

Those who cherish the notions of 1867 have one view of the Canadian federal system while others harbor other attitudes. Professor Cairns, in his usual perceptive style, expressed this concern as follows:

> With the passage of time the intentions of the Fathers unavoidably became an increasingly artificial concept with an ever attenuated contact with reality. Their visions were responses to the problems they faced in the light of prevalent conceptions of the role of government. Many of the conditions to which they addressed themselves faded away, to be replaced by conditions they could not predict. In such circumstances deference to their intentions became impossible, for they had none.[4]

While one cannot ignore the roots or foundations of any federal system, to base all current decisions only on a strict historical interpretation is to invite disaster.

The mechanisms of change have been fully discussed elsewhere and do not require too much elaboration. From 1867 to 1940 judicial interpretation by the courts would appear to have been the single most important device for refining the division of powers. The 1896 decision in the Local Prohibition case was the first in a series of cases that greatly reduced the scope and importance of the peace, order, and good government clause.[5] In 1925 in *Toronto Electric Commissioners* v. *Snider,* the general grant of power was reduced to an emergency power only.[6] This trend, favoring the provincial governments, continued through to the Depression, with the rejection by the Judicial Committee of most of the Bennett New Deal legislation.

At the same time that the scope of federal legislative power was reduced, the privy council also gave recognition to the status of provincial governments. They were more than local governments. In *Liquidators of the Maritime Bank* v. *Receiver General of New Brunswick* their lordships stated:

> The object of the Act was neither to weld the provinces into one nor to subordinate provincial governments to a central authority, but to create a federal government. . . . each province retaining its independence and autonomy.[7]

On the fiscal side, the intricate system of grants and subsidies was attacked by provincial governments shortly after Confederation and the pressures built up for a redistribution of the nation's wealth. After two interprovincial meetings, one in 1887 and another in 1902, the federal government succumbed to provincial pressures and an amendment to the constitution was passed in 1907 increasing the level of the subsidies. Speaking to the amendment in Parliament, Sir Wilfrid Laurier appreciated the futility of asserting that the settlement would "be final and unalterable," an assumption that had been expressed in 1867.

A detailed examination of both the development of Canadian society and the evolution of the federal system up to 1940 yields certain observations about its operation. In the first place, provincial powers had taken on a new significance—a prominence they did not have in 1867. Provincial governments developed and expanded their education and social assistance programs. Highway systems were being built. The migration from farm to city had increased the responsibilities of municipal governments. If anything, the transformation in Canadian society had required the provinces to assert themselves more than ever. This transformation had been reinforced by judicial interpretations which confirmed provincial responsibility for labor legislation, unemployment assistance, and a wide range of controls over commercial transactions. Macdonald's belief in the importance of federal powers failed to meet the test of time. As the urban, industrialized, social-welfare state emerged, the provincial governments assumed or were given the major responsibilities for meeting the needs of the citizens. This assessment does not suggest that the federal powers were insignificant. It is just that over time the relative relationship between the two governments shifted with the junior partners becoming full partners.

A second observation was that by 1940 there had been no corresponding shift in fiscal responsibilities between the two governments. By the late

1930s it was evident that the fiscal responsibilities of the provincial governments exceeded their fiscal capacities. The constitutional grants and subsidies, which were a condition of Confederation and which had represented a significant portion of provincial budgets in the period immediately after 1867, were inadequate to meet the needs of the provinces. To fill the gap, the provinces had developed their own systems of taxation, but their capacities were limited.

A third observation is that intergovernmental cooperation, although in its formative stages, had already emerged as a fact of life. Conditional grants or shared-cost programs had been initiated in 1912. Federal-provincial and interprovincial conferences had been held. Because delegation of powers was not possible, the practice of parallel legislation developed. In reviewing the emergence of federal-provincial interaction, the Rowell-Sirois Commission stated somewhat critically that:

> The evolution of political policies within the framework of the constitution is leading to joint activity between the Dominion and the provinces. This contrasts sharply with the original conception of federalism as a clearcut division of powers to be exercised separately, and experience indicates that it is injurious both to sound public finance and efficient administration.[8]

The Commission argued further that: "The experience with conditional grants leads us to doubt whether joint administration by the Dominion and a province is ever a satisfactory way of surmounting constitutional difficulties."[9]

The Rowell-Sirois Commission Report presented a comprehensive review of the federal system and its problems, and its recommendations were designed to make corrective adjustments in the federal system. The Commission suggested that provincial responsibilities in areas such as unemployment insurance and contributory old-age pensions be transferred to the federal government. Broadly speaking, these programs were expensive and involved policy areas where some uniformity of service levels appeared to be essential. The commissioners also recommended that a system of unconditional subsidies be introduced which would allow recipient provinces to provide services at the national standard.

An amendment to the British North America Act in 1940 transferred the responsibility for unemployment insurance to the federal goverment and in 1951 it assumed the principal responsibility for old-age pensions as well. However, at the 1941 federal-provincial conference several provinces rejected the basic proposal in the report and the sweeping reforms recommended by the Commission were not implemented. The Wartime Tax Agreements gave the federal government temporary authority to collect and administer both personal and corporate income taxes. In retrospect many of the ideas of the Commission have been implemented, perhaps not in precisely the manner suggested and not all at once, but nonetheless many were eventually accepted.

In summary, during its first seventy years, the federal system was dramatically altered. The ascendancy of the provinces could neither be denied nor reversed. Nonetheless, the realignment of the division of powers combined with the fiscal needs of the provinces created the need for an assessment of the federal system and its future direction.

THE FEDERAL SYSTEM:
CHANGE AND ACCOMMODATION—1940-1976

From the Depression up to the present several issues have shaped the federal system. Perhaps two of the most critical to the effective functioning of the federal system are the constitution and federal-provincial financial relations. Knowledge about these two areas gives one a reasonable understanding of change and accommodation within the federal system and tells us much about the workings of Canadian politics in general.

While these two matters raise fundamentally different questions, they share certain common characteristics. The financial arrangements have become far more than a tax-collection agreement and are now the single most important feature of fiscal federalism. Discussions on an amending formula have transcended that specific question and have attempted to come to grips with the broader problems of constitutional reform. Closely intertwined with this debate has been Quebec's concern about its role in Confederation. Today, with the shadow of Quebec separatism hanging over the country, the constitutional debate has taken on a new and urgent importance. Central to all these themes is the question of provincial autonomy—whether it be fiscal, constitutional, or cultural. That these should be recurring concerns indicates that the federal system is continuing to adapt and adjust to new circumstances.

Before analyzing these two themes a brief overview of the period in question may be useful. In 1957 Professor Corry, in "Constitutional Trends and Canadian Federalism," described the centralizing trend within the federal system.[10] Corry commented on the nationalistic sentiments among business and labor elites and the integrative effects of the transportation and communications infrastructure. Along with a powerful federal government, nationally oriented institutions or organizations influenced the centralization of Canadian federalism. Preponderant federal influence flowed from the powers and resulting policies acquired and developed by the federal government during the Second World War. To this had been added program responsibilities resulting from the spiraling number of shared-cost programs and the economic centralization resulting from the tax agreements.

Around 1960 the forces of centralization peaked and a process of decentralization began. The pendulum of power gradually swung back toward the provinces, gathering momentum as it moved. The election of John Diefenbaker, the death of Duplessis, the Quiet Revolution, a series of minority governments in Ottawa, and the power of well-entrenched provincial governments were factors influencing this transformation. In 1964 Smiley characterized this metamorphosis as a change from joint to consultative federalism, in which administrative relationships were replaced by principles of diplomacy.[11] In 1966 Black and Cairns discussed the emerging confidence of provincial governments and suggested that while Canada as a nation had evolved, so had the provinces.[12] Collectively they rivaled the federal government in the development and initiation of new directions in public policy. Writing in 1968, John Saywell stated: "In 1965, when the extension of provincial autonomy threatened to destroy legitimate federal power, he [P.E. Trudeau] entered federal politics as a defender of constitutionalism and Canadian Federalism."[13] Over the last ten years the decentralizing tendencies of the early sixties have been halted, with the federal government regaining much of its influence. It is probably correct to say that at present the pendulum appears to have come to rest, at least momentarily, at dead center.

The Courts and the Constitution

Central to the theme of constitutional change are judicial interpretations of the constitution, the search for an amending formula, and, more recently, the wide-ranging reviews of the constitution. If, during the first seventy years of Canada's federal experiment, the courts were active in shaping the federal system, it would appear that in the past forty years this process has been less significant. Many observers, including Chief Justice Laskin, have noted the tendency on the part of governments to avoid referring matters to the courts for resolution. While much of the present-day constitution is a direct result of judicial interpretation, solutions of today's problems are developed through what Professor Simeon has called federal-provincial diplomacy. (This particular question will be discussed later when intergovernmental relations are considered.)

Though the role of the courts has been modified, they still play an important part in shaping the constitution. With the abolition of appeals to the Judicial Committee of the Privy Council in 1949, the Supreme Court of Canada has become the umpire of Canadian federalism. While the number of constitutional cases heard by the court over the past few years is relatively minor in relation to their total caseload, some very significant decisions have been made. For example, in 1967 the court decided in the *Off-Shore Mineral Reference* that Canada, and not British Columbia, owned the offshore mineral resources.[14] In 1974 the court upheld the constitutionality of the Official Languages Act, 1969, in *Jones* v. *A-G Canada.*[15]

In one of its most recent decisions in July, 1976, the court confirmed the constitutionality of the federal government's Anti-Inflation Act.[16] This case may be described as the most important constitutional law case heard by the Supreme Court since it became the final court of appeal in 1949. Why? The court's task was to assess or reassess the current relevance of the Judicial Committee's previous interpretations of peace, order, and good government as it had evolved since 1896. The court had three basic choices to make. It could declare the Act unconstitutional, or it could declare the Act constitutional on one of two grounds—that inflation was a matter of serious national concern or that inflation could be considered an emergency. A majority of the court decided that the Act was constitutional on the grounds that inflation in Canada in the fall of 1975 constituted an emergency. Had the majority of judges accepted the argument of serious national concern, the existing equilibrium within the federal system would have been considerably altered. Provincial governments that presented their views on the Act's constitutionality argued that the law could be upheld only on the grounds of an emergency. The importance of this decision lies not only with the actual opinion but also with the reality that the Supreme Court has, and will continue to have, an important role within the federal system. This role may become even more significant as a result of amendments to the Supreme Court Act in 1975 which gave the court more discretion over the cases it will hear.

The Amending Formula and Constitutional Reform

One of the main preoccupations of governments in Canada is the lack of an amending formula in the constitution. Within most other federations the provincial governments were given a role in the amending process, with the decision outlining the extent of provincial participation being made at the time of federation. Attempts have been made since 1927 to develop an amending method acceptable to all governments in Canada. What are the problems? The crucial issues appear to be flexibility versus rigidity, the position of the populous central provinces of Ontario and Quebec, and questions about the cultural integrity of Quebec.

Reduced to its basic elements the argument revolves around whether a majority (50 percent), a special majority (2/3), or unanimous consent of the provinces is required before an amendment can be passed affecting the powers and privileges of the provinces. On the side of the majority principle one finds those who argue that anything else would place the constitution in a straitjacket, making it impossible to amend. To satisfy this principle, as well as the federal principle, amendment proposals have usually included a provision requiring that the provinces favoring an amendment must represent at least 50 percent of the population of the country. The other position, that of unanimity, also has its supporters. They contend that since all provinces are legal equals it follows that provinces should have an equal say over those amendments that would affect their legislative powers.

Before considering some of the proposals for an amending formula it is necessary to see how the constitution is amended today. From the outset, when amendments to the BNA Act were required, the actual amendment was enacted by the Parliament of the United Kingdom. The Canadian government made the request for the amendment after securing approval by resolution of both Houses of the Canadian Parliament. After the 1907 amendment revising the scale of constitutional subsidies, the practice of consulting the provinces emerged. The 1940 amendment transferring jurisdiction over unemployment insurance to the federal government was not enacted until all provinces had given their consent.

In 1949, Parliament secured an amendment that gives it authority to amend "the Constitution of Canada." The section reads as follows:

> Section 91. (1) The amendment from time to time of the Constitution of Canada, except as regards matters coming within the classes of subjects by this Act assigned exclusively to the Legislatures of the provinces, or as regards rights or privileges by this or any other Constitutional Act granted or secured to the Legislature or the Government of a province, or to any class of persons with respect to schools or as regards the use of the English or the French language or as regards the requirements that there shall be a session of the Parliament of Canada at least once each year, and that no House of Commons shall continue for more than five years from the day of the return of the Writs for choosing the House: provided, however, that a House of Commons may in time of real or apprehended war, invasion or insurrection be continued by the Parliament of Canada if such continuation is not opposed by the votes of more than one-third of the members of such House.

At the time this amendment was being discussed in Parliament some provincial governments expressed the view that they should have had a say in the matter. The federal government argued that it was seeking no more power than what the provinces had over their constitutions, as provided for in Section 92(1) of the BNA Act.

Three amendments affecting those matters that, according to the 1949 amendment, must still be enacted by the United Kingdom Parliament have been enacted since that date. The issues involved were old-age pensions in 1951, retirement of judges in 1960, and the 1964 amendment to the old-age pensions clause. All three amendments were enacted only after the unanimous consent of the provinces had been secured. Other amendments have been made to the constitution by Parliament acting alone. Recent examples are the 1975 amendments granting senate representation for the Yukon and Northwest Territories and increasing the size of the House of Commons. The latter amendment prompted Professor J. R. Mallory to write an essay entitled "Amending the Constitution by Stealth."[18] He indicates that few people were aware of the fact that the matter under discussion was in fact an amendment to the British North America Act.

While it should be clear that the constitution can and has been amended, the fact remains that parts of it can be amended only by legislative action of another country. For many Canadians this situation is one that needs rectifying. Successful resolution of this matter is intended not only to assuage feelings of Canadian nationalism but also to provide a measure of flexibility to the constitution.

After the failure to reach a consensus on an amending formula in 1950, this subject remained dormant for ten years. Between 1960 and 1964, under the auspices of both the Diefenbaker and Pearson governments, an amending formula, which became known as the Fulton-

Favreau formula, was developed. This formula provided for two general amending procedures: Parliament in conjunction with two thirds of the provinces representing 50 percent of the population; and Parliament in conjunction with all the provinces. Those areas where unanimous provincial consent was required included provincial powers, rights, privileges, and language rights. In addition to an amending formula, the Fulton-Favreau proposal provided for a new clause to be added to the constitution, a clause authorizing the delegation of powers between the federal and provincial governments. However, it stipulated that before delegation could be exercised at least four provinces had to be in agreement. Delegation between a single province and the federal government was not permitted. Although all eleven governments agreed to the formula in 1964, the Lesage government later changed its position, thereby bringing that episode to a halt. The cause-and-effect relationship between the Quiet Revolution and the decision by the Quebec government is an important one.

During the sixties, the concept of "cooperative federalism" dominated the thinking of Canada's political leaders. The term was used to describe all that was good and all that was bad with the federal system during this period.[19] The frequency of federal-provincial conferences and the range of matters discussed during this period indicated the growing interdependence that characterized our federal system. The Quiet Revolution and the concerns expressed in the Preliminary Report of the Royal Commission on Bilingualism and Biculturalism made it clear that severe problems existed within the political system. The increasing isolation of Quebec, the dissatisfaction of provincial governments with their fiscal position in the mid-sixties, and the rapid development of federal-provincial shared-cost programs precipitated a review of the Canadian constitution during the period 1967-1972.[20]

The proceedings of the 1967 Confederation of Tomorrow Conference and the First Constitutional Conference in 1968 indicated the crisis atmosphere that existed at that time. At the 1968 conference the eleven governments agreed to undertake a comprehensive review of the constitution including such matters as a bill of rights, language rights, the division of powers, institutions related to federalism (such as the Senate and Supreme Court), regional disparities, an amending formula, and mechanisms of federal-provincial relations.[21] While it was agreed that seven broad areas were to be discussed there was no clear statement about how this task would be approached. At the second meeting of the conference in February, 1969 the priorities of the review were more clearly defined but the issue of review versus reform was not resolved. This federal-provincial review consisted of seven meetings of first ministers, fourteen meetings of officials, and nine meetings of ministerial subcommittees. The culmination of all the study, negotiation, and soul-searching over the constitution and its adequacy as Canada entered its second century was the Victoria Charter of 1971. With the government of Quebec's rejection of that Charter in late June, 1971 the subject of constitutional reform quietly faded; it was raised once again by Prime Minister Trudeau in 1974, although then he restricted his concerns to "patriation" and the amending formula.

Much of the Victoria Charter dealt with structural matters such as an annual conference of first ministers, provincial participation in the appointment of Supreme Court of Canada judges, and an amending formula. A few substantive issues were contained in the Charter such as entrenchment of political rights and language rights. A special concern of Atlantic Canada was partially met through a section outlining the responsibilities of governments to reduce regional disparities. Many of the issues discussed by governments during the three-and-one-half-year review did not find their way into the Charter. Matters such as limits to the federal spending power, modifications to provincial taxing powers, Senate reform, and recognition of a provincial role in international affairs were discussed but not resolved. The only change in the division of powers was described as "revised Section 94A." At the urging of Quebec the provisions of Section 94A were extended to include "family, youth, and occupational training allowances." It should be pointed out that agreement was not reached on the most sensitive issue—a redistribution of government powers.

No other country has approached the reform of its political institutions in the manner Canada did during the period 1968-1972. Most countries discuss these fundamental issues at the time that they are founded; no other federation has undertaken a constitutional review one hundred years after the fact. The assessment was conducted at a leisurely pace and without any clearly defined objectives or timetable. In this sense the review in Canada is unique.

Parliament's involvement in the exercise began when it established a Special Joint Committee early in 1970. Thus one could argue it had benefited from the constitutional conferences and the materials prepared for them. But a time problem existed for the parliamentarians. By September, 1970 the members of the constitutional conference were anxious to produce some results. Up to that point the discussion had covered a wide range of topics, but impatience with the lack of results had been expressed. Thus the Special Joint Committee, if it was to have any impact on the outcome, had to accelerate its proceedings.

The first two recommendations of the Special Joint Committee were as follows:

1. Canada should have a new and distinctively Canadian constitution, one which would be a new whole even though it would utilize many of the same parts. . . .

2. A new Canadian constitution should be based on functional considerations, which would lead to greater decentralization of governmental powers in areas touching culture and social policy and to greater centralization in powers which have important economic effects at the national level. Functional considerations

also require greater decentralization in many areas of governmental administration.[22]

In support of the second recommendation the committee stated: "We are
convinced that there is a consensus among Canadians in favour of a more
functional federalism." Unfortunately the specific reasoning justifying
this position was not contained in the committee report.

The parliamentary committee indicated that they were "not discour-
aged by the apparent deadlock of [the Victoria] Conference. . . . We believe that the very lack of complete accord at Victoria points the way to
final success for it indicates the necessity of a broadening of perspective to
include the totality of constitutional problems."[23] The committee argued
that:

> The people now want a new constitution. The limited goal of
> "constitutional review" established by the first Federal-Provincial
> Constitutional Conference in 1968 has long been outmoded. The
> only goal which is now acceptable to most Canadians is a new con-
> stitution. An expectation of change has been built up and, in our
> view, cannot be frustrated without serious consequences for the
> national psyche. The process of review, once undertaken, must
> lead irreversibly to a new constitution.
>
> We are convinced that a new constitution is essential to a
> Canada with the kind of future Canadians envisage. The present
> constitution needs a fundamental recasting. It needs to be re-
> thought and reformulated in terms that are meaningful to Cana-
> dians now. For this reason we call for a new constitution: one that
> is a new whole, even though it may utilize many of the same parts.
> Our aim is not novelty, so we have no hesitation in adopting what
> is functional in the present constitution. But we insist on a new
> perspective which will embrace all the constituent parts in a whole
> that is at the same time distinctively Canadian and functionally
> contemporary.[24]

One is struck by the close similarity between many of the clauses of the
Victoria Charter, June, 1971, and the recommendations of the Special
Joint Committee, March, 1972. One might argue that the committee was
influenced more by what the first ministers had agreed to than by what
the public suggested at the hearings.

Unfortunately the committee report was never discussed in Parliament although Senator Forsey did comment on it in the Senate. A minority report on Quebec's right to secede was published in *Canadian Forum*.[25]
Given the events of 1976, both the Quebec provincial election and the interprovincial discussions on the constitution, the parliamentary committee report appears to have been prophetic. Whether their recommendations are considered in the future remains to be seen.

That the development of an acceptable amending formula remains a
goal of at least the federal government is indicated by Prime Minister
Trudeau's speech to the House of Commons on October 2, 1974, and his

letter of March 31, 1976 to the ten provincial premiers outlining his objectives for "patriation" of the constitution and an amending formula.[26] The amending formula favored by the federal government was the one developed in 1971 and is contained in the Victoria Charter.

The general amending formula proposed in the Victoria Charter is as follows:

> Amendments to the Constitution of Canada may from time to time be made by Proclamation issued by the Governor General under the Great Seal of Canada when so authorized by resolutions of the Senate and House of Commons and of the Legislative Assemblies of at least a majority of the Provinces that includes:
>
> (1) every Province that at any time before the issue of such Proclamation had, according to any previous general census, a population of at least twenty-five percent of the population of Canada;
> (2) at least two of the Atlantic Provinces;
> (3) at least two of the Western Provinces that have, according to the then latest general census, combined populations of at least fifty percent of the population of all the Western Provinces.

This formula represents a significant departure from previous proposals in a number of ways. Of perhaps greatest importance is the deletion of a unanimity rule for certain kinds of amendments. Up to this time all formulas that had been considered had had a unanimity requirement, the most recent example being the Fulton-Favreau formula of 1964. A second change is that the provincial majority is structured on the basis of region as opposed to a straight majority of provinces. Clause (3), of course, ensures both Ontario and Quebec a perpetual veto over amendments.

It is this formula that was presented once again to the provinces for their consideration by the prime minister in 1976. Significantly, his letter of March 31 of that year left the door open for some substantive changes to the constitution, including entrenchment of French language rights, provincial participation in the appointment of Supreme Court judges, a nonconstitutional obligation to reduce regional disparities, and certain safeguards designed to protect Quebec's cultural sovereignty. With the exception of the cultural guarantees to Quebec, the other provisions are to be found in the Victoria Charter.

The provincial governments reviewed the federal proposals during the summer and fall of 1976. Their discussions extended far beyond the limited goal of "patriation" and an amending formula. They discussed and reached unanimous agreement on a number of changes to the constitution, including entrenchment of language rights, an expansion of the provincial role in immigration, increased taxing powers over minerals, and limits to the federal government's declaratory powers under Section 92(10)c.

On the topic of the amending formula, the provinces were divided with the majority favoring the Victoria formula. Alberta took a strong position on having a unanimity requirement for any amendment that would reduce provincial powers found under Sections 92, 93, and 109 of the British North America Act. The province of Newfoundland, while not supporting this position initially, did so later. British Columbia advocated a five-region Canada which would have the effect of giving that province a veto along with Quebec and Ontario.

In January, 1977 the federal government responded to the proposal from the provinces. In his commentary on the provincial suggestions, Prime Minister Trudeau stated that these were either too little or too much. They were too little in that they did not address the total range of constitutional problems facing Canada. They were too much in that the proposals went far beyond the limited goal of "patriation" and adoption of an amending formula. The prime minister gave the provinces two alternatives: constitutional review by stages, or the undertaking of a global review similar to and building on that which had taken place from 1968 to 1971.[27]

The option of a comprehensive review would, of course, subject all aspects of the constitution to scrutiny. This alternative was probably proposed as a result of the November 15, 1976, Quebec election. At the time of writing there has been limited provincial response to the prime minister's January, 1977 letter.

Regardless of which alternative is selected it would appear that some assessment of the federal system is essential. As Prime Minister Trudeau told the nation on November 24, 1976, the debate on the future relationships between French- and English-speaking Canadians cannot be postponed any longer.[28] This debate transcends the question of language rights and will encompass an analysis and assessment of the entire federal system. The Parti Québecois states that federalism is not working. The debate must attempt to answer this charge at least in the minds of the Quebec electorate. It is in this context that solutions to Canada's constitutional problems must be found. Unlike the situation in previous eras, there now exists a degree of urgency.

Intergovernmental Fiscal Relations

A survey of federal-provincial fiscal relations in Canada since the Depression gives us considerable insight into the functioning of the federal system and the nature of Canadian politics. A key problem in any federal state is balancing the division of powers with the assignment of revenue sources between the federal and provincial governments. Put another way, the fiscal capacities of governments should be sufficient to allow them to meet their fiscal needs. For governments to finance services such as roads, schools, defense, and family allowances, they must have certain sources of income available to them such as taxation, borrowing, charging for services, or disposing of Crown assets. Taxation sources include personal and corporate income taxes, sales taxes, tariffs, gasoline taxes, and property taxes. Borrowing includes revenues raised from the sale of Canada Savings bonds, Ontario Hydro bonds, and municipal bonds. Governments charge for certain services for which the recipient or user pays. Examples of this form of financing include charges for postage stamps and premiums collected for hospital insurance and unemployment insurance. Revenue from disposal of government assets includes proceeds from the sale of public lands, royalty payments on resources, and stumpage rates for timber. Generally speaking, these are the major means by which governments derive the funds to finance their activities; taxation constitutes the principal source of revenue.

Before considering the present system of fiscal arrangements, a brief review of the financial arrangements at the time of Confederation is in order. Just as there was a division of legislative responsibilities there was also a division of fiscal responsibilities. Under Section 91(3), the federal government was given the power to raise "money by *any* mode or system of taxation." The provincial governments, however, under Section 92(2), were given only the power of "direct taxation within the province." Both governments were authorized to borrow money. Provincial governments, under Section 92, were also given legislative power over management and sale of public lands, licensing, and fines, each of which would generate certain revenues. Under Section 109 of the BNA Act the provincial ownership of "lands, mines, minerals and *royalties* belonging to the several provinces" was confirmed.

Even though the federal government assumed the "important functions of government," provincial revenues in 1867 were inadequate for them to meet their modest constitutional obligations. To fill the gap, a system of federal constitutional subsidies to the provinces was spelled out in Section 118 of the BNA Act, which was later superseded by the 1907 amendment to the constitution. What needs to be understood is that from the very beginning of Confederation there was a fiscal imbalance between provincial needs and means. It is for this reason that fiscal relations have so often been the subject of federal-provincial negotiations. In addition, the jurisdictional responsibilities of the provinces, such as health, welfare, education, highways, municipal institutions, libraries, and so on, have become far more important, and expensive, than they were in 1867.

Within the context of Canadian federalism the provinces have certain choices if they find they cannot finance their programs and services. They can reduce or eliminate certain activities; they can agree to constitutional amendments that transfer responsibilities to the federal government; they can demand a larger share of the tax pie; they can increase their taxes; or they can accept federal transfer payments. Reduction or elimination of services, while not impossible, is politically awkward as the government of Ontario discovered when it attempted to shut certain hospitals as a restraint measure. Two amendments have been made to the constitution transferring powers from the provinces to the federal government—unemployment insurance in 1940, and old-age pensions in 1951. It is unlikely that further amendments of this kind will take place given the current climate of federal-provincial relations. Provincial governments have demanded a greater share of income taxes collected and for a time were reasonably successful in their demands. Provinces have also resorted to increased rates of taxation as demonstrated by the gradual rise in sales taxes and personal income taxes. Additionally, both kinds of federal transfer payments have proliferated—unconditional grants, such as equalization payments, and conditional grants, such as the Canada Assistance Programme.

The Depression showed all too clearly the incongruity between provincial revenues and provincial responsibilities, both as established by the constitution and as interpreted by the courts. While the main responsibility for financing social programs was provincial, their revenue sources were severely limited. While this crisis accelerated the social consciousness of Canadian governments it also brought into focus more clearly than before many of the problems inherent in our federal system.

From 1941 when the first ministers' conference convened to discuss the recommendations of the Rowell-Sirois Commission, to December, 1976 when the first ministers' conference convened to discuss the renewal of the Fiscal Arrangements Act for the period 1977-1982, there has been a continuing series of federal-provincial meetings, discussions, confrontations, and agreements on fiscal matters. From the outset, the federal government desired a harmonization of federal and provincial tax policies. For approximately twenty years, from the 1941 Wartime Tax Agreements through to the end of the 1957-1962 tax agreements, the federal government collected personal and corporate income taxes and succession duties for the provincial governments.[29] These agreements permitted a centralized and uniform tax structure to develop in Canada. It was understood that the federal government was temporarily occupying the tax fields or "renting" the provincial taxes. The principal intergovernmental debate throughout this period was over what share of the taxes collected would go to the provinces. As might be expected, the federal and provincial governments had differing views on this fundamental question. While it is doubtful that the provinces ever received the full amount they requested, the trend over the twenty-year period was to increase the provincial proportion.

In 1955 an important addition to the tax agreements was initiated by the federal government. While the provinces are legally equal under the constitution, their economic capabilities are vastly different. Standard economic measurements such as per capita income and per capita yield from taxes illustrate the fiscal disparities in Canada. To assist in reducing this imbalance, the federal government established the equalization program. The principle of this venture was and remains the equalization, up to a certain standard, of provincial government revenues from selected sources. Through this program funds are transferred by the federal government to certain provinces without any strings attached. Today these transfers represent a significant percentage of the budgets of the recipient provinces.

Beginning with the 1962-1967 agreements, additional significant modifications to the tax agreements have been introduced. Perhaps the most important of these was the change from the idea of tax-sharing to joint occupancy. Up to this point the provincial governments had pressed for or demanded a greater share of the receipts collected from personal and corporate income tax. Whatever they were able to wring out of the federal government was transferred to them. As far as the general public was concerned all taxes were collected by Ottawa. Accordingly, if taxes were increased it was the federal government that received the criticism. Most people were unaware of the fact that a percentage of the taxes collected and a portion of any revenues resulting from an increase were transferred directly back to the provinces. For the provinces this situation was a good one from a political perspective. They benefited from federal policies and escaped all the criticism.

The principles governing the 1962-1967 agreement, which have been continued through to the 1977-1982 agreement, altered this situation. Instead of tax-sharing, a tax-collection agreement was proposed. The federal government proposed to reduce its personal and corporate income taxes and its succession duties. The extent of the reduction, which was the subject of intense negotiations, was calculated to give the provincial governments "tax room" roughly equivalent to what the provinces had been receiving as their share from these taxes under the previous agreement. Under the terms of the new agreement, the federal government would continue to collect provincial taxes, provided the provinces were willing to accept the federal government's tax system. Effective January 1, 1962, provincial governments were able to establish their own personal and corporate tax rates, which could be equal to or different from the size of the federal government's tax withdrawal. In other words, both governments were now free to establish their own tax rates, but each government now had to justify its taxes to its own taxpayers. By 1967 the federal government had withdrawn from the personal income tax field by 24 percent and from the corporation income tax by 9 percentage points of tax.[30] Some provinces chose to increase their tax rates. For example, Saskatchewan increased its rates and used the additional income to finance its Medicare program. Under the terms of the new tax agreements, or fiscal arrangements as they were now referred to, the provinces found themselves in a stronger fiscal position.

In 1966, when the renegotiation of the fiscal agreements was under way, the provinces pressed for further federal government tax withdrawal but the federal government adopted a hard line. The Minister of Finance, Mitchell Sharp, stated:

> We should get away from what is tending to become a conventional notion that the Federal Government can and should be expected to give greater tax room to the provinces when they find their expenditures rising more rapidly than their revenues. This has been possible, and has been done, in the past decade, but it cannot be accepted as a general duty. Our basic duty is the ancient one—to tax no more than we need, and to reduce taxes when we can and should.
>
> The second convention of federal-provincial fiscal relations that must be questioned is that there is some particular share of income tax . . . which is rightly federal or provincial. The fact is that both have constitutional rights in these fields.[31]

The federal position was premised on the belief that each government was responsible for its own taxing and spending decisions. In short, the federal stance was: If you want more money, raise it yourselves! Mr. Sharp argued that the federal government needed all its money to finance federal programs, many of which (such as equalization) were of direct benefit to the provinces. Provincial raids on the federal treasury were going to be repelled. The principles enunciated by the federal government in 1966 have been carried through to today.

The general philosophy governing fiscal arrangements has been essentially unchanged since 1966. This does not necessarily mean that intergovernmental fiscal relations have become more harmonious over the past decade than at previous times. What it does mean is that the federal government has maintained its firm position with respect to creating more tax room for the provincial governments.

Over the past few years, however, other adjustments to the Fiscal Arrangements Act have been made, which reflect a number of federal policy initiatives. One of these was the method adopted in 1967 to finance post-secondary education. From the early 1950s to 1966 the federal government provided per capita grants to help finance the operating costs of universities. Beginning in 1967 the federal government offered to pay half the operating costs of postsecondary education and did so by increasing the provincial share of personal and corporate income taxes by 4 percent and 1 percent respectively. This policy increased the total tax abatement received by the provincial governments on the personal income tax from 24 percent to 28 percent of the federal tax payable. It also raised the provincial corporate income tax from 9 percent to 10 percent of taxable income. If the revenue from these tax points was not equivalent to 50 percent of postsecondary education costs, the difference was met through federal cash grants.

In 1968 a temporary federal surtax on incomes was established and in 1969 a 2 percent social development tax was introduced. The federal government regarded these as nonsharable revenues. The federal government stated that it was adding to its revenues by developing specialized new taxes as opposed to general tax increases. Provincial governments criticized these measures on the grounds that they represented a departure from tax-sharing and reduced the scope of possible provincial tax increases. The federal government responded by contending that it was raising revenue for federal purposes. The effect was to complicate further the already complex tax system within Canada.

Another adjustment took place after the federal government's 1971 tax reform. Under the tax agreements the basic statute regulating the tax system is the federal Income Tax Act. One of the objectives of tax reform was to reduce or eliminate completely the tax burden on individuals at the lower end of the income scale. Any reform of this kind would also have the effect of reducing provincial government revenues since provincial personal income taxes are expressed as a percentage of the federal tax payable. To compensate the provinces for revenue losses resulting from federally inspired tax reforms, the federal government increased its tax abatement from 28 percent to 30.5 percent of the federal tax payable. Through this action the provinces were placed in the same fiscal position after the tax reform as they were before it came into effect. In addition the federal government established for the 1972-1977 agreements a revenue guarantee to the provinces which assured them of the same amount of money under the new tax policies as they would have received had there been no tax reform. The justification for this provision was that provincial governments should not be expected to subsidize federal tax reforms. By 1976 the cost of this revenue guarantee was estimated to be $1 billion. During the negotiations to renew the tax agreements for 1977-1982 the federal government announced the termination of this program. Predictably, the provinces were unanimous in their criticism of this action. The federal position was based on the premise that the revenue guarantee was a transitional measure, to act as a cushion, and that the provinces would now have to adjust their tax rates. In fairness to both sides it should be said that nobody realized that the sums involved would reach the magnitude of $1 billion.

The equalization program has also undergone a number of significant changes since it was first introduced. The number of different provincial revenue sources being equalized has increased from three in 1957 to twenty-nine, beginning with the 1977-1982 agreements. Items such as resource revenues, municipal taxes, liquor revenues, and sales taxes are now taken into consideration. Instead of being equalized to the per capita yield of the top two provinces, the standard used today is the national average per capita yield. Seven provinces currently receive equalization payments while three, Ontario, British Columbia, and Alberta, do not. While the nonreceiving provinces do not object to the principle of equalization, they do believe that limits are necessary.[32] Their concern is that their tax levels, partly because of equalization, may become so high that they become an impediment to their own economic development. Another criticism is that equalization does not take into consideration the costs of providing services. These arguments have never really been pressed too far if for no other reason than that no government, provincial or federal, wishes to see the gap between rich and poor provinces widen. There is no doubt that the equalization program will continue and that it has been of great benefit to the recipient provinces. In the 1976-1977 fiscal year equalization payments are estimated to have amounted to $2.2 billion, a significant increase over the $139 million paid in 1957-1958, the first year of the program.

With the increase in oil and natural gas prices since 1973 there has been a corresponding increase in provincial royalty income derived from these resources. Because resource royalties are one of the provincial sources of revenue included in the equalization formula, an increase in the one led to an increase in the other. The Minister of Finance, John Turner, announced that only one third (instead of 100 percent) of the provincial revenues resulting from the *increase* in oil prices would be included in the equalization formula. To do otherwise, he remarked, would make Ontario a have-not province, a reality the federal government could not accept.[33] The receiving provinces greeted this decision with little enthusiasm but were left with no alternative but to accept the policy. In negotiating the equalization program for 1977-1982 the governments agreed that 50 percent of income from all natural resources should be equalized. Thus the distinction between certain types of resources was eliminated. Nonetheless the policy developed in 1974 suggests that there are upper limits to the amount the federal government is willing to spend on this policy.

Shared-Cost Programs

Closely intertwined with the discussions on fiscal arrangements has been an ongoing debate over shared-cost programs; that is, those that are jointly financed by both levels of government. Health care, hospital care, social assistance, the construction of the Trans-Canada Highway, and postsecondary education are examples of areas where costs have been shared. To a certain extent federal reluctance to relinquish tax room to the provinces can be attributed to the existence of these shared-cost programs; the federal government requires a great deal of money to meet its shared-cost commitments.

Provincial criticisms of the shared-cost principle have been constant and have rested on the premise that these programs are primarily in areas of provincial jurisdiction. The provinces have also argued that the federal government has used its spending power to circumvent the constitutional division of powers. In addition, the provinces have argued that these federally inspired programs distort provincial priorities as the provinces that wish to participate in federally sponsored programs must adjust provincial priorities accordingly. Another provincial concern is the possibility that the federal government may terminate a program, leaving the provincial government the option of reducing services or filling the void, thereby possibly affecting the level of other programs.

The federal government has strongly defended its policies by arguing that under the constitution the exercise of the spending power is fully within the competence of Parliament. It has justified these programs on the grounds that society has become increasingly interdependent and that there are "national consequences of inaction" if provinces permit their standards to fall below a certain level. The federal government argues that in certain policy areas there exists a national interest. Two other justifications advanced for federal policy initiatives are the interdependence of government policies and the sense of community in Canada.[34]

The course of federal-provincial relations since World War II has been shaped to a considerable extent by the federal government's use of its spending power. Essentially the spending power is seen as the logical corollary to the taxing power. Parliament raises money through its taxing power and, so the argument goes, can spend that money for purposes and objectives not confined to the specific federal powers listed in Section 91. In short, this means that if the establishment of national standards is not possible through legislative action by Parliament, given the interpretation by the courts of peace, order, and good government and other clauses of Section 91, the same goal can be achieved through the exercise of the spending power. Throughout the postwar period, hundreds of federal-provincial conferences and meetings ranging from first ministers down to technical experts have been convened to discuss and assess policy initiatives relating to shared-cost programs. This phenomenon has been described as cooperative federalism and, more recently, by Professor D. V. Smiley as executive federalism.

The interdependence of shared-cost programs and the tax system was demonstrated in 1964 when, as a result of increasing criticism, primarily from Quebec, provincial governments were advised they could opt out of certain shared-cost programs. Any province choosing to do so would receive an appropriate additional tax abatement on personal income tax. The programs from which the federal government offered to withdraw were hospital insurance (worth 14 tax points) and certain health and social assistance programs (worth 5 tax points). While only Quebec accepted the offer, the precedent of federal withdrawal was established. Other provinces could see no direct benefit at that time since their actual cash position would not be affected.

The most recent development in shared-cost programs was the Established Programs Financing Proposal presented by the federal government to the federal-provincial conference in June, 1976.[35] The federal government took the position that the objectives behind Medicare, hospital care, and postsecondary education programs had been fulfilled and it was now time to place these programs on a different financial footing. These programs, according to Ottawa, were now established. National standards of service had been developed and it was doubtful that any province would depart from them in the future. If the main objective of a shared-cost program is to establish national standards, the rationale for continuing the program presumably disappears when that objective is achieved. Nonetheless the problem of financing the service remains. That the federal government had concerns about the escalating costs of these three programs is evidenced by the fact that ceilings were placed on the federal contributions to postsecondary education in 1972 and were announced for Medicare in the June, 1975 budget.[36] The federal government, in the June budget, also gave the required five-year notice that it would terminate the hospital insurance program in 1981. However, the federal government agreed to provide a certain level of federal payments regardless of program costs, provided that certain conditions, such as universality of coverage, were met. If economies could be effected, the provinces would be in a better position. If, however, program costs surpassed future federal payments the provincial governments would then be required to make up the difference.

It is doubtful that any perfect solution can be achieved to resolve the problems of fiscal federalism. Nonetheless the experience of the past twenty-five years suggests that approximate solutions can be developed. In the give-and-take of bargaining the provinces have generally been able to improve their financial position and a uniform, reasonable, and generally straightforward tax structure has been developed.

Areas for Further Study

The above presentation represents a generally traditional analysis of Canadian federalism; for one who wishes to probe deeper there are many fascinating questions still to be considered. For example, one might wish to study more fully general public awareness of the federal system. Are people familiar with the complexities and dynamic nature of the system? Do they care which government administers a program so long as services are provided? Do they know the extent to which federalism shapes Canadian politics? Our knowledge of public attitudes toward the federal system is surprisingly weak. Much more behavioral research is necessary if a more complete understanding of this complex subject is to be developed.

Another problem that should be considered is the meaning of the term "the provinces." On any given policy question one can expect to find a number of provincial viewpoints. Consider the problem of oil pricing. Alberta and Saskatchewan (producing provinces) have different views on oil pricing than do Ontario (a consumer of domestic oil) and Nova Scotia (a consumer of imported oil). Sometimes the interprovincial differences are so great that they cannot be reconciled; other times compromises can be achieved. One should not forget that while, under the constitution, legislative powers of the provinces are identical, their social, economic, and political climates vary considerably. When analyzing the federal system one should assess not only the similarities among provincial positions but also the differences. Indeed there is often a greater congruence between the federal position on a given matter and that of some provinces than among the ten provinces themselves.

While federal-provincial relations represent one facet of the federal system, interprovincial relations represent another. One cannot assume that all problems within the federal system are confined to the federal-provincial dimension. Interprovincial relations are becoming increasingly important. For example, since 1960 the premiers of the ten provinces have met annually to discuss problems of mutual concern. The matters discussed range from the economy, to resource taxation, to education. One consequence of the 1976 premiers' conference was the negotiation of a common provincial position on the renewal of the fiscal agreements. Whether this process will be repeated remains to be seen, but if it does continue both the content and dynamics of federal-provincial discussions will change considerably.

Another aspect of the federal system that warrants careful scrutiny is increasing regional cooperation among both the Western and the Maritime Provinces. Since the 1973 establishment of the Western Economic Opportunities Conference, the four Western Provinces have worked together closely to develop common positions toward the federal government on a number of matters such as transportation and economic development. The Council of Maritime Premiers also represents a significant achievement in the area of interprovincial cooperation. The three Maritime provinces have institutionalized their arrangement through joint legislative action. While still far short of Maritime union, the Council has a budget and employees and administers for the three provinces certain programs such as the Maritime Provinces' Higher Education Commission, the Maritime Municipal Training and Development Board, and the Land Registration and Information Service. The effects of this policy harmonization in the East and the West cannot help but have consequences for the federal system as a whole, either by presenting a common front to the federal government or by solving problems through interprovincial, as distinct from federal-provincial, mechanisms. Whether these regional groupings have resulted from feelings of alienation from the federal government or from a regional desire to cooperate, or some combination of both, is a matter for further study.

Another matter of continuing great importance in Canadian federalism is the question of Quebec. Concerns over English-French relations and the status of Quebec within Confederation are of long-standing duration. Indeed they are as old as Confederation itself. National unity, while always a fundamental dilemma confronting successive governments in Canada, is of more immediate concern today because of the 1976 electoral victory of the Parti Québecois in Quebec. The next few years will obviously be critically important for the future of Canada and the viability of its federal system. The federal system has proven to be remarkably flexible and resilient in the past and there is reason to believe that it will continue to be so in the future.

CONTEMPORARY TRENDS IN CANADIAN FEDERALISM

It was suggested at the beginning of this chapter that, speaking in terms of the centralization-decentralization dichotomy, the pendulum has come to rest. The preceding analysis supports this contention but also suggests that the centrifugal and centripetal tendencies inherent in Canadian federalism have not disappeared; indeed, they are very much in evidence. They are, however, approximately equal in force, maintaining the existing equilibrium within the system. Two characteristics appear to dominate the current federal scene. The first is interdependence of governments, as demonstrated by the fiscal arrangements. The second is the existence of a federal system in which one finds a strong central government and strong provincial governments more or less in equilibrium. These two phenomena are to some extent contradictory and lead to clashes between the federal and provincial governments.

The discussion on developments since 1940 has touched on two important features—the constitution, and intergovernmental fiscal arrangements. If the events of the past few years illustrate anything it is that the federal system is in a constant state of transition. The locus of much of the conflict has shifted from the courtroom to the conference. With the advent of conferences came also the establishment of federal-provincial committees, forging institutionalized links between the two orders of government. If anything has transformed the dynamics of the federal system in the past few years and greatly influenced Canadian politics in general, it is the emergence of the conference technique for resolving federal-provincial disputes. At first glance the notion of a high level of conference activity conjures up visions of harmony and cooperation. While this image is partially correct, it overlooks the fact that increased contact may also produce increased discord between the federal and provincial governments arising from intergovernmental competition. To a considerable extent the debate on energy policy has been a result of competition over control and development of natural resources. The dispute over cablevision between Quebec/Saskatchewan and Ottawa is another example. While these disputes have a jurisdictional dimension, they transcend the simple legal question of defining jurisdictional boundaries. The issues are more complex and relate directly to the relative power and responsibilities of the federal and provincial governments within Confederation.

During the fifties and sixties one frequently encountered criticism that the principle of cooperative federalism extended only to subject matters within provincial jurisdictions such as education, health, and social assistance. During the seventies there has been a phenomenal explosion in the range of issues subject to federal-provincial scrutiny. It is not just that governments are meeting more often but that there are now no limits to the subjects they consider. For example, in the past few years consultations, discussions, and/or negotiations have taken place on oil pricing, energy supply, international trade, demography, transportation, immigration, communications, municipal planning, banking, wage and price controls, scientific research, and consumer protection. In effect, no area of public policy can be placed outside the framework of federal-provincial relations.

The purposes of these interactions are many and varied. Sometimes an agreement is sought, such as with the anti-inflation program. Occasionally the federal government seeks provincial input, as with the revisions to the Bank Act. In some instances the provinces wish to modify existing federal policies, for example, concerning transportation. If the purposes behind intergovernmental discussions vary, so do the results. In some instances, such as the negotiations preceding the 1974 oil-pricing agreement, a specific result may be achieved. At other times no immediate or tangible conclusion may be reached, often leading to mixed reactions from the participants. Why was the conference held? What was behind the meeting? Was one government seeking political advantage? These are questions frequently asked in such instances.

Despite the apparent success of this means of accommodation, certain criticisms of it have been expressed. Perhaps the most fundamental of these is the possible effect such meetings may have on parliamentary government. To what extent does prior agreement between the executives of the federal and provincial governments erode parliamentary supremacy? Can either Parliament or a legislature undo what has been agreed on in the give-and-take of negotiation? Another concern is that most meetings are conducted behind closed doors. Critics are of the opinion that these meetings should be open to the public, although they often overlook the reality that certain portions of any negotiations will be carried on in private among the parties concerned. The conference of first ministers has been compared to a super-cabinet, but unlike a cabinet it is responsible not to one but to eleven legislatures. Finally, one must assess the effect of so many meetings and conferences on the climate of federal-provincial relations. Do they enhance or inhibit the decision-making capabilities of governments? Do they create or destroy the chance of reaching agreement within the federal system?

In conclusion, certain points merit careful consideration. While intergovernmental conflict may appear to be on the increase in Canada, it should also be recognized that governments now consult and cooperate on a much broader scale than ever before. Naturally, some conflict is inevitable, especially if new initiatives are involved. Finally, the stresses within the federal system appear to be a result of increased competition between the federal and provincial governments in achieving their respective policy goals. Sometimes these objectives can be harmonized; at other times, differences are irreconcilable. But if conflict appears endemic, so too is the desire to solve mutual problems.

The capacity for adjustment within the Canadian federal system is considerable. Federalism as a form of government is premised on diversity and the Canadian federal system is no exception. Problems and issues will continue to arise in Canada, given our social, cultural, and economic diversity. That solutions to these problems are forthcoming is demonstrated by the fiscal arrangements, which have been constantly adapted to meet changing circumstances. The inability of governments to resolve the dispute on the amending formula or to rewrite the constitution illustrates the difficulty in securing agreement on permanent changes. The distinction would suggest that governments are more willing to compromise and agree on short-term solutions to solve immediate problems than they are to go through the more fundamental process of restructuring the federal system. As new challenges confront governments, as new crises arise in Canadian politics, they must be met, reconciled, and resolved within the framework of our federal system.

By focusing on federalism we will not come to understand everything that we should know about Canadian politics, but if we do not study federalism we will be neglecting much of the most important information. After all, from 1867 to 1977, and beyond, many of the mundane as well as the vitally important aspects of Canadian politics can best be described and understood as the politics of a fascinating federal experiment.

ENDNOTES

1. See A.H. Birch, "Approaches to the Study of Federalism," *Political Studies* XIV, No. 1 (1966), pp. 15-33; and W.H. Riker, "Six Books in Search of a Subject or Does Federalism Exist and Does it Matter," *Comparative Politics* 2. No. 1 (October, 1969), pp. 135-146.

2. K.C. Wheare, *Federal Government*, 4th ed. (London: Oxford University Press, 1964), p. 33.

3. *Confederation Debates*, 1865, p. 40.

4. Alan Cairns, "The Living Canadian Constitution," *Queen's Quarterly* LXXVII, No. 4 (Winter, 1970), reprinted in J. Peter Meekison, ed., *Canadian Federalism: Myth or Reality*, 2nd ed. (Toronto: Methuen, 1971), p. 144.

5. *Attorney General of Ontario* v. *Attorney General of Canada*, [1896].

6. [1925], AC 396.

7. [1892], AC 437 at p. 422.

8. Royal Commission on Dominion-Provincial Relations, *Report* (Ottawa: Queen's Printer, 1954), Book I, p. 255.

9. *Ibid.*, p. 259.

10. J.A. Corry, "Constitutional Trends and Canadian Federalism," *Evolving Canadian Federalism*, ed. A.R.M. Lower, F.R. Scott, et al. (Durham, N.C.: Duke University Press, 1958), pp. 92-125.

11. D.V. Smiley, "Public Administration and Canadian Federalism," *Canadian Public Administration* VII (September, 1964), pp. 371-388.

12. E.R. Black and A. Cairns, "A Different Perspective on Canadian Federalism," *Canadian Public Administration* IX (March, 1966): pp. 27-45.

13. P.E. Trudeau, *Federalism and the French Canadians* (Toronto: Macmillan, 1968), p. xii.

14. *Reference Re Ownership of Off-Shore Mineral Rights*, 65 DLR (3rd).

15. *Jones* v. *A.G. Canada* (1974), 16 CCC (2nd) 297.

16. *Re Anti-Inflation Act* (1976), 9 NR 541 (Can.).

17. The comments were made in a paper distributed at the first ministers' conference on December 13 and 14, 1976, and were repeated in a speech delivered to the Canadian Club in Toronto on January 4, 1977. The case is known as the CIGOL case.

18. J.R. Mallory, "Amending the Constitution by Stealth," *Queen's Quarterly* 82 (Autumn, 1975), pp. 394-401.

19. See, for example, J.M. Leger, "Le fédéralisme coopératif ou le nouveau visage de la centralisation," in *Canadian Federalism: Myth or Reality?* ed. J. Peter Meekison (Toronto: Methuen, 1968), pp. 317-320; and Jean Luc Pepin, "Co-operative Federalism," in J. Peter Meekison, *op. cit.*, pp. 320-329.

20. The dates are based on the timing of the Confederation for Tomorrow Conferences which took place in 1967 and the presentation of the *Final Report* of the Special Joint Committee of the Senate and House of Commons on the Constitution of Canada.

21. For a comprehensive report and discussion on this subject, see *The Constitutional Review, 1968-1971*, Secretary's Report, Canadian Intergovernmental Conference Secretariat (Ottawa: Information Canada, 1974).

22. Canada, Special Joint Committee of the Senate and House of Commons on the Constitution of Canada, *Final Report,* Fourth Session, 28th Parliament, 1972, p. 1.

23. *Ibid.,* p. 5.

24. *Ibid.,* p. 7.

25. M. Asselin and P. DeBane, "Quebec's Right to Secede," *Canadian Forum* (May, 1972).

26. See House of Commons, *Debates,* April 9, 1976, pp. 12695-12705, for the complete text of the letter and draft proclamation.

27. The prime minister's letter of January 19, 1977, was tabled in the House of Commons, January 24, 1977.

28. For the text of the prime minister's speech see Toronto *Globe and Mail,* November 25, 1976.

29. Other than the Wartime Tax Agreements the province of Quebec has not participated in the tax-collection agreement. Ontario collects its own corporate income tax.

30. There is frequently confusion about the terminology used to describe the personal and corporate income tax percentages. The personal income tax of the provinces is expressed as a percentage of the federal income tax collected. For example, if the basic federal income tax payable by an individual was $1 000.00 the provincial tax would have been 24 percent × $1 000.000 = $240.000. With the corporation tax the 9 percentage points refers to a tax rate; that is, the corporation tax for provinces would be 9 percent × taxable income = provincial revenue.

31. *Federal-Provincial Tax Structure Committee* (Ottawa: Queen's Printer, 1966).

32. See, for example, the comments by Premier Robarts of Ontario at the finance ministers' meeting in September, 1966. *Ibid.,* pp. 45-46.

33. John Turner, *Budget Speech,* November 19, 1974 (Ottawa: Department of Finance, 1974).

34. For a full discussion of this question see P.E. Trudeau, *Federal-Provincial Grants and the Spending Power of Parliament* (Ottawa: Queen's Printer, 1969).

35. This proposal was tabled in the House of Commons by Prime Minister Trudeau on June 14, 1976.

36. See John Turner, *Budget Speech,* June 23, 1975 (Ottawa: Department of Finance, 1975).

37. The original federal offer was 12$1/2$ points of personal income tax. The most contentious issue during the negotiations was the termination of the revenue guarantee which the provinces estimated as being equivalent to 4 more tax points. As a sweetener the federal government added one more tax point and an equivalent amount to the per capita grant.

SELECTED REFERENCES

BLACK, E.R. *Divided Loylaties: Canadian Concepts of Federalism.* Montreal: McGill-Queen's University Press, 1975. An important work which analyzes a number of theories of Canadian federalism.

CAIRNS, ALAN C. "The Judicial Committee and its Critics." *Canadian Journal of Political Science,* Vol. IV (1971), pp. 301-345. An assessment of the quality of

Canada's jurisprudence through an examination and review of the Judicial Committee of the Privy Council's role as final authority for constitutional interpretation.

DUPRÉ, J.S. et al. *Federalism and Policy Development: The Case of Adult Occupational Training in Ontario.* Toronto: University of Toronto Press, 1973. An excellent case study examining the process of policy development in Canada's federal system.

GÉRIN-LAJOIE, PAUL. *Constitutional Amendment in Canada.* Toronto: University of Toronto Press, 1950. A history of amendments to the constitution to the time of writing, and the problems surrounding the "amending formula" debate.

JONES, RICHARD. *Community in Crisis: French-Canadian Nationalism in Perspective.* Toronto/Montreal: McClelland and Stewart, 1967. A good account of Quebec politics during the "Quiet Revolution."

LÉVESQUE, RENÉ. *An Option for Quebec.* Toronto: McClelland and Stewart, 1968. The book presents Mr. Levesque's case for a sovereign Quebec associated with the rest of Canada in an economic union.

MEEKISON, J.P., ed. *Canada Federalism: Myth or Reality,* 3rd ed. Toronto: Methuen. 1977. A collection of articles and documents which gives the reader a feel for the dynamics—both theoretical and practical—of the Canadian federal system.

MOORE, A., J. HARVEY PERRY, AND DONALD I. BEACH. *The Financing of the Canadian Federation: The First Hundred Years.* Toronto: The Canadian Tax Foundation, 1966. An analysis of the efforts to keep the division of revenue sources and revenues responsive to the growth of federal and provincial responsibilities from 1867 to 1966.

MORIN, CLAUDE. *Quebec versus Ottawa.* Toronto: University of Toronto Press, 1976. A presentation of the Quebec case for its consistent provincial autonomist stand in negotiations with the federal government.

ROWELL-SIROIS REPORT. *Report of the Royal Commission on Dominion Provincial Relations.* Ottawa: King's Printer, 1940. An important work which examines in detail the economic and financial basis of Confederation and the development of the distribution of powers and responsibilities from 1867-1940. It remains one of the most important analyses of federal-provincial relations.

RUSSELL, PETER H., ed. *Leading Constitutional Decisions,* Rev. ed. Toronto: McClelland and Stewart, Carleton Library, 1973. An excellent survey of the key judicial decisions regarding the Constitution, it deals specifically with the key cases on the division of powers. *See also his bibliography.*

SIMEON, RICHARD. *Federal-Provincial Diplomacy: The Making of Recent Policy in Canada.* Toronto: University of Toronto Press, 1972. Through an examination of the negotiations involving three important issues, the process of bargaining between the federal and provincial governments is examined.

SMILEY, D.V. *Canada in Question: Federalism in the Seventies,* 2nd ed. Toronto: McGraw Hill-Ryerson, 1976. Provides an overview of a number of aspects of the federal system of Canada, including the constitution and federalism, the evolution of the system, mechanisms for federal-provincial relations, fiscal and economic federalism, cultural duality, and the author's observations on national unity. *See also his bibliography.*

———. *Conditional Grants and Canadian Federalism.* Toronto: Canadian Tax Foundation, 1963. Provides a concise analysis of the evolution of federal grants to provinces and municipalities in Canada, as well as the implications for federal-provincial relations.

SPECIAL JOINT COMMITTEE OF THE SENATE AND OF THE HOUSE OF COMMONS. *Constitution of Canada: Final Report.* Ottawa: Queen's Printer, 1972. A two year study, including public meetings across Canada, was undertaken by a special joint committee: the report is the summary of their findings, and their recommendations regarding Canada's Constitution.

WHEARE, K.C. *Federal Government,* 4th ed. London: Oxford University Press, 1964. A book which examines what a federal system is and how it works, by examining the workings of the federal systems of the U.S., Canada, Switzerland, and Australia—in theory and practise.

Part Four:
Processes: The Essence of Canadian Politics

In studying Canadian politics we are very much interested in actual events, in the dynamics of political activity. The first chapter in this section describes the extent to which the democratic Canadian political system is based on the operation of political parties and electoral activity. The analysis may well substantiate the hypothesis that without a free and viable party system with its periodic and uncoerced elections, there can be no continuing democratic system. This approach, as Professor Engelmann points out, does not explain everything about Canadian politics but it does tell us a great deal.

In the second chapter, Professor Cameron identifies, describes, and assesses a continuing and now critical dimension of Canadian politics —English-French conflict and cooperation. This process of interaction has never been more important than it is today for, with separatists in office in Quebec, the very existence of the country is at stake. Surely no one understands Canada until he understands the processes by which the two largest segments of our society formed a country, worked together to develop it, and must now reconcile some basic differences if the country is to survive.

The third chapter in this section draws our attention to the complicated and Byzantine process of how public policy is shaped and administered, and makes a strong case for multidisciplinary analysis. As Professor Wilson demonstrates, the conventional dictum that "politics determines policies" is largely valid but equally valid is the opposite notion that "policies determine politics." He argues convincingly that since the public policy process involves virtually every institution of government, and its results impinge in countless ways on all of us, we cannot comprehend the reality of Canadian politics without studying public policy. For the approximately 1.4 million Canadians who are employed by our national, provincial, and municipal governments, the topic will naturally have special significance.

10

Canadian Political Parties and Elections

Frederick C. Engelmann[*]

INTRODUCTION

"Party" is one of the few household words in the political vocabulary of Canadian students. All are likely to know about Liberals, Progressive Conservatives, and New Democrats, and that they are political parties. Those who know a little about parties tend to identify them, as Edmund Burke did two hundred years ago, as groups tied together by similar ideas. In fact, modern political parties have come to be both less and more than this definition: less, in that supporters of a party may disagree among themselves, and to some degree even with their leaders; more, in that parties are in fact concerned with people more than with policies. Parties mobilize voters at election time, hire professional politicians, recruit potential leaders, nominate candidates for office and for top leadership posts, and attempt to elect these candidates so they can, as a final goal, furnish the political leaders of the nation.

In any country in which parties compete, the election is the arena of competition, Here, the ruled select their rulers. Each voter may simply vote for the representative from the constituency he or she lives in, as in Canada, or voters may have candidates for all kinds of offices to vote for, as in the United States. In any case, elections make it possible for people to vote for representatives and thus have representative government. If, as in Canada, their vote for a member of Parliament helps determine which party governs the country, there is responsible government.

The earlier definition of party should make clear that not all political groups are parties. Many political groups raise demands for public policies; these groups represent particular interests, and they are therefore called interest groups. Such groups will be discussed in Chapter 15.

*Professor of Political Science, University of Alberta.

What distinguishes parties from other political groups is that parties contest elections.

Several functions of parties were mentioned in the initial definition. The principal ones are recruiting and selecting leaders, mobilizing voters, and providing policy decisions. Of these, the first two, selecting leaders in part and mobilizing voters entirely, are connected with elections. Parties recruit potential leaders all the time, but they normally nominate candidates just prior to an election. Insofar as parties deal with policy decisions, they do so in an overall, general way when they prepare the election platform. The party needs to win the election or become part of a governing coalition (a highly unlikely event in Canada) in order to put into effect policies contained in its platform.

Where parties compete—we usually designate such countries as democracies—the competing parties make up the party system. The number of parties with at least a realistic hope of gaining legislative seats determines the system's designation. Thus, we have a two party system in the United States and multiparty systems in France and Italy. Canada had a pure two-party system until the First World War. Since then, it has become difficult to designate. A later section of this chapter will show why this is so.

RELEVANCE TO CANADA

Post-Confederation Canada has always been governed by a political party. With a brief exception in 1925, the leader of the strongest party in the House of Commons has always been the prime minister of Canada. As elections in Canada have become more and more a plebiscite between leaders, the importance of parties, whose leaders compete for the political leadership of the nation, has been maintained throughout the past 110 years.

The united colony of Canada, based on representative government, achieved responsible government in 1849. Responsible government means that the ministers of the Crown are in office only so long as they enjoy the support of the majority of the House of Commons. It also means that these ministers actually try to maintain such support. Not surprisingly, the Liberal Conservative party (now the Progressive Conservatives) was formed in the legislature to support a ministry as early as 1854. After Confederation, the task became one of governing the young Dominion of Canada, and the organization of a second party became necessary, certainly to provide alternate leaders. By 1878, those who had successfully opposed John A. Macdonald over the Pacific Scandal and had come to govern under Alexander Mackenzie were permanently organized into the Liberal party.

The culmination of a party choosing a leader may be to give the country a prime minister. He may come to dominate the party, but no prime minister has attempted to stay in office without his party's support. Parties have provided not only prime ministers and provincial premiers, but also leaders of the opposition and usually all the ministers in federal and provincial governments.

Beyond and including these visible leaders, Canadian political parties recruit virtually anybody who can be called a professional politician, whether this person sits in a legislative body or works for a political party. In addition, most people who aspire to candidacy for elective office work through political parties. Wherever political appointments are made—to the Senate, to the judiciary or to some, usually provincial, administrative posts—these of course come about through political parties.

Canadian parties have had considerable impact on the style of Canadian politics. Both Tories (Conservatives) and Grits (Liberals) have done their share in defining leadership roles. Conservatives have usually been led by a *primus inter pares*—a parliamentary colleague who became first among equals—or by a successful provincial premier who was seconded to the Ottawa scene. For most of the time since Confederation, the Liberals have been led by men who have not come up through party ranks but have been recruited and selected by the party after becoming well-known as administrators, lawyers, or writers. This difference in recruitment has produced a more independent and less controlled style on the part of Liberal leaders, all of whom, in this century, have become prime ministers. In this century, all major party leaders died in office or resigned voluntarily, except for John Diefenbaker, who was removed as leader by the Progressive Conservative party in 1967. In the CCF/NDP, leaders have to rely more on formal consultation with councils representing party members and with party bureaucrats. Wherever the CCF/NDP has been important, its leaders have been in real or potential conflict with the organized party faithful, but the leaders have tended to win such conflicts. In other important parties—Social Credit or the Union Nationale—such conflicts hardly, if ever, existed.

Until the end of the nineteenth century, it looked as though Grits and Tories would continue to be the parties of all Canadians, sharing a generally common electoral base. Since the 1890s, however, the parties' sources of support have differed. The Liberals have been French Canada's principal representative in Ottawa. Though this seems strange in the 1970s, the Liberals were for decades essentially the party of the Canadian farmer, a position occupied by the Conservatives since the late fifties. Both parties have continued to compete for the support of the Canadian worker. Since the Great Depression they have had to compete with the CCF/NDP which, at least nationally and to a large extent also provincially, has not so far been able to realize its objective of becoming the party of Canadian labor.

The parties' interaction with Canada's federal system has not been a clear and simple one. It is true that Liberals have not done well recently in most provincial elections, but we cannot speak of an anti-Liberal provincial front facing Ottawa. The strong current emphasis on Canadian federalism is not due to the parties. Party has been found to make little or no difference in federal-provincial conflicts. Yet, the federal system gives

Canadian parties eleven arenas to compete in, not just one as in the United Kingdom or France. Because third parties can score regionally, they have strong-to-moderate success in all but the four Atlantic Provinces. Provincial success of third parties helps to keep Canada from reverting to its original two-party system. In this way, third parties provide more variety in Canadian politics, but they often prevent the formation of alternative majorities.

Readers who expect the Canadian party system to generate much policy conflict will be disappointed. Liberals, Progressive Conservatives, and western Social Credit all support the prevailing economic system, though the captains of free enterpise are not happy with the taxing and regulating efforts of any of them. The NDP, while critical of the distribution of ownership and the management of the economy, has not attacked the prevailing economic dogma frontally when and where it was in a position to do so. As I will show later, the federal anti-inflation program is a nearly perfect example of the limited impact of party on policy.

Elections in Canada are now waged, with minor provincial exceptions, in single-member constituencies in which the candidate with the largest number of votes wins. Not only does the electoral system distort party strength in favor of the party getting the largest vote, it also gives undue representation to parties having regional strength in a country as regionally varied as Canada. Because of this, no party has had a majority of seats in Parliament in five of the eight elections since 1957.

PARTIES AND ELECTIONS IN CANADA

Origins and their Consequences

During the first fifty years of Confederation, party functions in Canada, federally and provincially, were performed by the Conservative and Liberal parties. The former had existed since 1854, the latter organized in the early years of Confederation. The party names are British; their sources, however, are a British-Québecois-American mixture. The Conservatives represented Macdonald's and Cartier's successful amalgamation of conservative interests in Quebec, Montreal, and Toronto, of the Tories of Canada West (now Ontario)—often descendants of Loyalist refugees from the American Revolution—and of the *bleu* faction of French Canadians with close ties to the Roman Catholic Church. The Liberals represented the farm proprietors of Canada West—known as the Clear Grits—and the smaller *rouge* element in Quebec, the liberals opposed to church leadership. To some degree, the parties reflected the split between the main body of *habitants* and the few followers of the French Revolution; they did not reflect the British split between Conservative landowners and Liberal merchants. There was a reflection among the Tories of the nation-building impulses of the early American Federalists, and among the Grits of the small-landowner base of the American Jeffersonians. Twenty years after Confederation, the Liberals under Wilfrid

Laurier made peace with the Catholic Church in Quebec; from then on, the Liberals have been successful in representing French Canada.

The two original parties, as mentioned before, developed within the structure of government and for decades the sole function of the parties was to support or oppose the government. After Manitoba and British Columbia came into Confederation, delayed voting in the West swung votes to the "Ministerialists," members of Parliament who would support the government in return for favors for their region. Only from the 1890s on, with some development of constituency organization on both sides, did the two parties compete on more equal terms.

Western agriculture was the first social segment to create, outside of Parliament, organizations that were more than pressure groups. These organizations went about persuading large groups of voters to elect people who were neither Conservatives nor Liberals. Western farmers were alienated by Canada's rejection of free grain trade with the United States just before the First World War. As the War ended and an agricultural depression set in, more farmers became disenchanted. The United Farmers movement spread east, where it had its first flash success in the Ontario election of 1919. Nationally, the movement joined with fragments of the Liberal caucus to form the Progressive Party, which came out second strongest in Parliament in the 1921 election but refused to accept the responsibility of becoming the official opposition. Partly as a consequence of this, the party declined during the twenties. The most lasting effect of the United Farmers movement was in Alberta, where it formed the government from 1921 to 1935.

The drive of western farmers to form parties had consequences during the Great Depression. In 1932, it was the main force, with some workers and a few intellectuals, behind the formation of the Cooperative Commonwealth Federation (CCF). A generation later, in 1961, this party, by now supported by an important segment of the labor movement, reformed as the New Democratic Party (NDP). It is significant, however, that the CCF/NDP had its steadiest support in still heavily rural Saskatchewan.

A second depression offshoot of western agriculture was the Social Credit movement which, led by the messianic evangelist Aberhart, swept Alberta in 1935 and governed that province till 1971. Though much of the later Social Credit in Alberta, and Social Credit in British Columbia, had little to do with the western farmers' movement, it was the original vehicle for Social Credit.

French Canada had developed a nationalist movement around 1900, but only during the Great Depression did it result in the formation of a party, the Union Nationale of Duplessis. It had no real impact on federal politics, but governed Quebec for two decades. The Bloc Populaire went federal in the forties, but was not important. The now-governing Parti Québecois, being separatist, does not at this point see itself as a competitor on the federal party scene.

Everywhere else in the democratic world, except in the United States, industrial labor—some would say the working class—has launched important parties. In Canada, this effort has been restricted to the CCF/NDP, which has never drawn overwhelming labor support; to the only worker-based Social Credit party in Canada, the one in Quebec; and to the perennial but infinitesimal Communist party.

What difference has it made to Canadian politics that two parties originally within Parliament existed from the beginning, and that parties developing outside Parliament did not emerge until at least fifty years later? As I will show later, Liberals and Conservatives have organizations dominated by their parliamentary leaders, much of the time they have received the support of all social groups in Canada, and their appeal to voters has, in most instances, been pragmatic; that is, they have claimed to have the leaders most likely to succeed in governing Canada. None of the other parties has had the same breadth and flexibility. One may disagree about the virtues of such qualities, but one cannot deny their success. Liberals and Conservatives have been government or opposition in Ottawa throughout, and in the provinces most of the time. They have persisted and at present most Canadians would probably agree that they will continue to compete for the prize of federal office for some time to come.

Support and its Relevance

While splinter parties existed in various parts of the country, an average of 98 percent of Canadian voters supported Conservative and Liberal candidates until the First World War. The period showed variations of support between the two parties. From the time both parties had a firm identity, 1878, through the election of 1891, the Conservatives under Macdonald had a majority of the vote, not only overall but also in each region of the country. In 1896, Laurier's Liberals won the election by winning in Quebec, but in the three subsequent elections they had majority support everywhere except in Ontario. In terms of the popular vote all victories since 1878 had been fairly close; it took only minor vote changes, mostly in Ontario and British Columbia, for Borden's Conservatives to emerge victorious in 1911.

If we had had public opinion surveys during the first fifty years of Confederation, we would probably find that the vote of both parties was spread fairly evenly not only over Canada's regions and provinces, which we do know, but also over the country's major social groups. Before the Empire went to war in 1914, there was every reason to believe that Canada would have the kind of stable two-party system for which the United States has been known for more than a century.

The First World War and the struggle it occasioned in Canada, the Conscription Crisis, changed all that. The Conservative Borden government formed a coalition with war-supporting Liberals and passed the Wartime Elections Act, which dropped Quebec's share of the Canadian vote from the normal 25 percent to a bit above 15 percent; this was partly done by enfranchising females related to men fighting the War. In that election, 73 percent of Quebec voters supported Laurier's Liberal opposition, while 64 percent of voters in the rest of Canada supported the government. This polarization of the vote between Quebec and the other provinces was unprecedented and has never recurred to the same extent. Whatever else it did, this crisis put an end to the established pattern of competition in which the two parties had social support spread broadly over society. Significantly, this coincided with the rise of electorally important third parties, especially in Western Canada.

After 1921, peremptory two-party competition seemed to regenerate, with only Alberta voting Progressive. But the founding of the CCF and the Social Credit party has kept support of the major parties down. Since 1935 in the West and 1962 in Quebec major party support has been below 85 per cent and usually significantly lower. Exceptions were the "Diefomania" election of 1958, and the "Trudeaumania" election of 1968.

Of the major parties, the Conservatives have lacked adequate support in French Canada since 1917, 1958 being the sole exception. Conservatives also did poorly in the West between the Depression and Diefenbaker; since 1957 the Liberals have lacked adequate western support. What we find, or at least found before the anti-inflation program and the victory of the Parti Québecois, is that Liberals do well mobilizing voters in Quebec and southern Ontario, and Conservatives do well mobilizing voters in the West and parts of the Atlantic Provinces. What is more, Liberal dominance of the Quebec federal vote and Conservative dominance of the western federal vote have been fairly stable phenomena; a far cry from the all-Canada competitive elections before 1917.

Surveys of the postwar years have given us a picture of the support social groups give to parties. Professional and white-collar people tended to support Conservatives until Diefenbaker; since then they have favored the Liberals. Workers have tended to support Liberals a bit more than Conservatives; despite its ties to organized labor, the NDP ranks third in ability to mobilize workers. Conservatives have consistently done the best job of mobilizing farmers.

Mobilization of the highly educated goes with mobilization of those in nonmanual occupations: before Diefenbaker, the Conservatives did best with that group; since then, the Liberals do. Until the last decade, the NDP had among its supporters the highest proportion of those without a high school degree. With regard to religion, the Conservative and NDP voters strongly tend to be Protestant, while Liberals show a small Catholic majority. That francophones vote heavily Liberal is not surprising; nor is the fact that postwar immigrants to Canada also support the Liberal party.

The relevance of the party support pattern to political competition will be discussed in a later section. I want to emphasize at this point that the parties are different in their social composition, but more along religious and ethnic than along social class or occupational lines. Both Conservatives and New Democrats are strongly English-speaking, Protestant parties; the supporters of the Liberals, however, especially in recent decades, have come from both of the two major faiths and both of the two founding races, complemented by the bulk of recent immigrants.

Leadership

Political parties do many things: they mobilize the electorate; they help develop programs to deal with the demands of interest groups; they help produce policies if called upon to govern; and they perform a number of tasks aimed at organizing the political government and providing effective government for society. The one thing any party does, even in countries where there is only one party, is to recruit people for political leadership. Where, as in Canada, there is more than one party, each party nominates candidates for public election to office.

In Canada, of course, the parliamentary system channels the nomination of party candidates and their election to Parliament. Since party leaders are selected by leadership conventions and not, as in the United Kingdom, by their parliamentary party (caucus in Canada), they need not be, although they usually are, members of Parliament to begin with. The system of responsible government gives great power to the leaders of the parties in Parliament, certainly to those with any chance of forming the government. The leader of the strongest party remains prime minister only so long as he retains the support of his party in the House of Commons. This need for support is less of a check than it is a weapon. It enables the leader of the governing party to lead his party with the near-assurance that all his followers will follow him on every issue that comes to a vote in Parliament. This caucus discipline is almost as strong in the principal opposition parties and in other parties represented in the House of Commons as it is in the governing party.

But as Canada's constitution—the meaning of the term as used here goes well beyond the provisions of the British North America Act—gives power to the prime minister and to the leaders of the other parties, so it also detracts from these powers. It does so through the operation of Canada's highly decentralized federal system. Each party considers itself one unit, but the national leader, even when the prime minister, may have to let himself be influenced more by the party's provincial leaders, especially by those holding office, than by anyone else. At this time in Canadian history, prime ministers have to deal diplomatically not only with premiers from other parties, but also from their own, and leaders of the opposition have to use language considerate of their provincial party leaders in office.

While the selection of leaders and the conduct of electoral campaigns will receive brief discussion later in this chapter, I want to point here to the role of the party leader vis-à-vis the electorate. The leader of the opposition, the prime minister, and other national party leaders, most likely in that order, are engaged in an ongoing mobilization of the electorate, even when there is no likelihood of an early election. This is one leadership role that has been magnified by television. Clearly, the interests of the media and the leaders are served equally when a network representative interviews one of the leaders: the leader of the opposition to tell us what he would or would not have done had he been in office, the prime minister to tell us why he did what he did, and other party leaders to give us the whys and wherefores of their views on the matter. On television, a party leader's status is greatly reinforced.

Structure

Political parties are organizations, and their organizational structure is relevant to the functions they perform. These functions, especially leadership selection and voter mobilization, can be undertaken in Canada only by adapting to our federal and electoral systems. If parties are to compete successfully on a nation-wide basis, and if they are to compete in several or all the provinces, they need organization at the provincial as well as the national level. By offering leaders for provincial government, the provincial structure of Canadian parties gains and maintains its importance. This importance leads Donald Smiley[1] to assert that Canadian parties are to a large degree confederal; that is, their provincial structures have a great deal of autonomy. The electoral system, based as it is on single-member constituencies, requires at least rudiments of party organization at the constituency level, both for nominating candidates and for mobilizing voters, especially on election day.

Party structure also has to face up to Canada's parliamentary system, but here the story is less uniform. In the early parliamentary parties, and Liberals and Conservatives certainly are among the world's early parliamentary parties, the parliamentary leaders enjoyed a historical priority: the party's parliamentary structure was in place first, and the electoral (also called associational or extragovernmental) structure of the party was created to serve this parliamentary party by nominating candidates and mobilizing voters to elect them. With the exception of short-lived fragment parties, all parties arriving on the scene after the development of the Tories and Grits formed outside Parliament and worked their way in. Their electoral structure, therefore, was established prior to their parliamentary structure. But election to office enhances the standing of legislators within any party structure, and gaining official opposition status and especially forming the government—and in some provinces some third parties have done either or both—does so even more. These parties thus have tended to join Liberals and Conservatives in becoming "cadre" parties, where the electoral structure serves as a cadre, or a group of helpers, for the parliamentary party.

Only a strong commitment to the rights and significance of individual party members has been able to halt the trend toward this cadre development, and of important parties in Canada only the CCF/NDP has shown such a commitment. No matter how small the number of individual NDP members, each is given rights to participation by the party's constitution. The emphasis on members' rights and influence makes the NDP's structure that of a mass party. Electoral success generally, and election to office in three western provinces, has, however, obliterated much of the structural difference between the NDP and the other parties. It is important to remember, nonetheless, that Saskatchewan, where the party has attained most importance, has a special tradition of lay participation in politics, which helps to keep the entire NDP structurally distinct.

The actual structure of parties having parliamentary representation on the federal or the provincial level is anchored in the parliamentary, or legislative, caucus. Whether participation of lay members is important or not, there is a federal, or provincial, convention, with appropriate executive bodies, which oversees the electoral operations of the party. Only the NDP seriously adds the overseeing of broad policy to the task of its conventions. The federal, or provincial, office, a headquarters employing at least a skeleton professional bureaucracy, is formally responsible to conventions or the executive, actually to the leader or caucus. In constituencies held or seriously contested by a party, there may be a permanent constituency executive. Only in the NDP do party members in a constituency meet to try to influence party policy; in other parties, members who may have bought a single-shot party membership meet mainly to nominate candidates.

The use of the terms "federal" or "provincial" in this discussion should remind the reader that there tends to be provincial autonomy in political parties, which means that the federal-provincial links are generally weak. In all democratic federal systems, provincial parties have a certain amount of autonomy. It should not surprise us that this is very much the case in present-day Canada, where the importance of provincial government is so great that a provincial career is sufficient for many ambitious and able political leaders.

Appeal and Ideology

Initially I pointed out that Edmund Burke described political parties as groups tied together by common ideas, but that they were in fact doing a number of things not necessarily on the basis of common ideas. I know, however, that most students, and much of the general public, continue to believe that Burke was correct. There is an element of truth in his definition that applies to Canadian parties, but it applies least to Liberals and Conservatives. For these parties, a certain style connected with their past is much more important than a definite set of ideas. But largely because of their long-standing success in competing for office, their appeal to the voters, especially at election time, is primarily one of trying to demonstrate that they will do better in office than their opponents.

Liberals and Conservatives, then, appeal to voters largely in terms of the alleged quality of their candidates for office, and of the way in which they do, or would, handle the issues of the day. This kind of appeal is termed "pragmatic." As Pierre Elliott Trudeau demonstrated between 1974 and 1975, it is quite possible to retain office promising that Canada would be kept free from the wage and price controls proposed by the Conservatives, and then to impose those same controls, with cosmetic changes, one year later. Whether one considers such action flexible genius or electoral perfidy, it is a glorious example of pragmatic politics.

The opposite of a pragmatic appeal is one based on ideology, on a coherent set of party principles. In its pure form, such an appeal exists in Canada only in the various Communist parties, each of which selects issues and presents them in terms of its dogma. These parties, however, run few candidates and get only a few votes. The only Canadian party competing nationally and electing members that displays anything approaching ideological appeal is the NDP. Its predecessor, the CCF, adopted a socialist program in 1933. Some of its appeal to the voters was based on this program; to other aspects of its appeal, for instance the support of the North Atlantic military alliance, the program was irrelevant. In 1956 the party gave up doctrinaire socialism. If the appeal of the NDP has been ideological, this ideology has been confined to trying to create a general atmosphere favoring the wage earner and people on fixed incomes rather than those enjoying the fruits of the profit sector.

Does this mean that federal elections have been tweedledum-tweedledee games? Not quite, despite the limited impact of parties on policies, which I will discuss in the next section. The nearly century-old identification of French Canada with the Liberal party has, on balance, given the Liberals more electoral credibility in Quebec, even when French language rights are not an issue. What we have here is more a difference of style than of policy. There are other style differences of more recent vintage. The West used to be a Liberal preserve, but since Diefenbaker, that region has responded to Conservative and not to Liberal cues. Attitudes toward federalism also make a difference in major-party appeal, based on style rather than substance. Of all provinces, Quebec, strongly Liberal in federal elections, raises the most demands. Outside Quebec, however, those jealous of provincial rights are being appealed to more by Conservatives than by Liberals, often regardless of the issue.

In the absence of important ideological appeals to Canadian voters, policy differences between parties have been products of situation rather than dogma. Most of the parties' appeals to Canadians have been based on differences in style or simply on seeking office.

Programs—Federal and Provincial

I have just said that dogmatic differences in party policies have been unimportant in Canada. On the federal level, there appears to be one important difference: external relations. It is true that from the Boer War of 1900 until the Statute of Westminster in 1931, the Conservative party had been more colonial, imperial and pro-British, and the Liberal party more autonomous and thus nationalist. It is equally true that, certainly from the reciprocity crisis of 1911 till the missile crisis of 1963, the Liberal party has been the more pro-American of the two. That this is not clearly an ideological matter is shown by the Trudeau era, in which the Liberals have been more insistent on an independent Canadian foreign policy, and at times more worried about U.S. domination in general, than the Conservatives.

The Liberals have placed more emphasis on bilingualism than the Conservatives, but their major support base in Quebec has encouraged this emphasis. Multiculturalism finds as much encouragement under Trudeau as it did under Diefenbaker.

In the area of economic redistribution, massive programs have been in effect for the past two decades, regardless of the governing party. If there has been dogma, it has been the belief that programs should be undertaken within the framework of the free-enterprise system and it has been shared by both major parties. A Conservative-appointed royal commission suggested taxation of nonworking income at a rate as high as that of wages and salaries. The proposal was turned down by the Liberal government at that time, but there is no certainty that the Conservatives would have adopted it. A universal prepaid health-care program was adopted by the Liberals after the recommendation of a Conservative-appointed royal commission and a pioneering effort of the CCF government of Saskatchewan.

The CCF/NDP has formed the government in three western provinces, but most of its policies have been similar to those of other provincial governments. Saskatchewan's Medicare policy of 1962, and public automobile insurance in Saskatchewan, Manitoba, and British Columbia are exceptions. Saskatchewan is appropriating some of its resource industries, while Alberta coinvests in its resources with some of the proceeds going into public royalties and public profits. The provinces, one governed by the NDP, the other by right-wing-liberal Progressive Conservatives, are protecting their provincial resource rights with similar vigor.

The emphasis in this brief section should perhaps be more on Liberal-Conservative similarity than on their similarity with the NDP, which has not held federal power, and is not expected to be the chief competition in the foreseeable future. The absence of effective federal competition by a leftist party will be taken up briefly later.

Electoral System, Elections and Participation

The House of Commons and the provincial legislatures are subject to quinquennial acts, which means statutes ending them after five years unless they are dissolved earlier. These days, executives at both levels are expected to dissolve the legislative body no later than four years after its election. Dissolution is timed by prime ministers and premiers with the strategic aim of winning the next election, and favorable circumstances may not arise close to the five-year limit. Canadians, therefore, can expect to be called upon to vote in an important election, provincial or national, on the average, every two years or less.

Since 1966, all members of the House of Commons are elected from single-member constituencies; the candidate with the most votes is declared elected. After each census, seats are distributed among provinces and territories according to a complicated formula, with population having the most important influence on how the seats are distributed. Constituency boundaries are drawn by provincial commissions of essentially nonpartisan composition. In establishing the provincially agreed-upon constituencies, the House of Commons has but little leeway to differ.

Canadian citizens of both sexes, aged eighteen years or more, have the right to vote. They are placed on voters' lists by enumerators nominated by the parties that have polled the highest and second-highest vote in the constituency.

Canada's electoral system favors the party first in electoral strength over the second party. It favors both of these parties even more over all other parties. Only the geographically unequal distribution of party strength gives third, and sometimes fourth or even fifth, parties a chance to gain seats. Alan Cairns[2] rightly points out that the realities of geographic distribution of party strength among constituencies affects the balance of parties, and of parties within regions, in the House of Commons. In the Thirtieth Parliament, more than forty percent of the Liberal caucus came from Quebec, and 20 percent of the Conservative caucus (and zero percent of any other caucus) from Alberta.

It is up to the parties contesting an election to mobilize the voters. This they do by various means: they canvass promising voters, help individuals to vote by transporting them to the polls and/or baby-sitting, randomly distribute literature, conduct campaign meetings, and spread propaganda over radio and television. The latter, because of its range, is usually done by federal or provincial headquarters; the other activities center on the constituency. Central headquarters is in charge of the campaign schedule and itinerary of the party leader, and possibly of other party luminaries.

Campaigns, being a competition for votes, deal only to some extent with attempts to convert the opposition. Stronger efforts are made to persuade the undecided and, even more important, to make sure that as many as possible known supporters go to the polls.

Who does go to the polls? On the average, about 75 percent of those eligible to vote in federal elections, 70 percent in provincial elections. Data from the 1965 federal election survey show that those with higher socioeconomic status and those with more education tend to vote more regularly. Interestingly, strong participation among the highly educated is found in federal but not in provincial elections.

Leadership Selection: Nominations and Recruitment

Since 1961, all federal parties have selected their leader in a federal leadership convention. Originally, they all selected them in a more traditional mode, in the parliamentary caucus. The Liberals, with an almost all-Quebec caucus, decided to hold the first leadership convention in 1919. The Conservatives followed in 1927. The CCF had all along used their convention to confirm their caucus-selected leader; in 1961 the NDP also chose the convention as the way to select their leader.

Conventions of all parties have complex rules of representation. Invariably, all members of the parliamentary caucus are seated. The other delegates represent the party from all over the country. Voting is by individuals and by secret ballot. In all conventions a majority of delegates' votes is needed to select the leader. On each ballot, the lowest candidate is dropped, though additional ones may withdraw.

Smiley[3] finds leadership conventions help to make Canadian parties more national. Unlike their famous American model, they are not bargaining places for the provinces. However, the person selected as leader will spend most of his/her time, if appointed prime minister, bargaining with the provinces. In any case, leadership conventions usually end in a show of unity. The presence of the candidates and their staffs on the floor of the convention sometimes makes such shows more credible than the American model, where some of the principals may prefer to stay in their hotel rooms.

Who gets to be federal leader of a major party? By and large, leaders are closer to the American pattern of inexperienced politicians than to the British pattern of experienced ones. Liberal conventions have always chosen a man with little experience in federal politics, though King and certainly Pearson had considerable experience in the federal bureaucracy. Conservative conventions have selected men with varying experience in the House of Commons, and provincial premiers.

Virtually all the candidates for party leadership, federal and provincial (where the convention process is like the federal one), have been successful nominees of their party for at least one legislative body. In order to gain a party nomination to the House of Commons or a provincial legislative assembly or parliament, a person needs to be selected by a constituency nomination meeting. This may be open to all members or to elected delegates. The former is the usual mode employed in the Liberal and Conservative parties, and it is here that these parties acquire many of their formal members who simply buy a membership in order to vote for one of the candidates vying for the nomination.

Most of the candidates for constituency nominations have something in common: they have been recruited for an active political life by a political party. Some who do not make it try again, but the political system allows for only one nomination in a constituency, and for only one victor among those getting a party nomination. Parties have few bureaucrats, and there are few places indeed for those who choose, as Max Weber[4] called it, "politics as a vocation."

Party Competition and Party System

As long as there were only two parties in Canada and the provinces, party competition was simple. Conservatives and Liberals were sufficiently evenly matched in all the political arenas so that power changed at least a few times in every jurisdiction. In addition, both parties were pragmatic, using office-seeking appeals.

The federal election of 1917, the United Farmers' victory in Ontario in 1919, and the federal success of the Progressives in 1921 seemed to have changed all that. But this change did not last; the UFO disappeared, the Progressives lost their importance, and by 1926 the old competitive pattern appeared to have been restored everywhere except in Alberta and Manitoba. What did change, however, was the loss of the Conservatives' competitive position in Quebec.

Up until the Great Depression the two major parties were at least assured of dividing the lion's share of the vote between them. But after the creation of the CCF and Social Credit they were not able to do that anymore, least of all in the West. Only the unique success of John Diefenbaker, the charismatic western Conservative in 1958, gave the two parties more than eighty-five percent of the vote; the rest of the time they had to be satisfied with 5 to 20 percent less than that.

The increased number of parties denied the governing party a parliamentary majority six times between 1925 and 1974. But in all of these situations except one, there were enough members of loosely organized caucuses generally supportive of the government to keep it in office. From 1972 to 1974, when Trudeau's Liberals needed the support of the NDP under David Lewis's leadership to stay in office, the fate of the government depended on the disciplined caucus of a strong third party. Neither Liberals nor NDP wanted a coalition; in fact, federal coalitions seem to have fallen into disrepute after Borden's coalition during the First World War. The NDP really held the balance of power between Grits and Tories and brought down the Trudeau government over the 1974-75 budget.

In the wake of Diefenbaker's triumph, many observers assumed that the CCF/NDP would go away, and that the two-party system, desired by many supporters of a traditional parliamentary system, would reappear. This did not happen. Despite the ups and downs of the NDP, that party probably is here to stay. At the same time, it is difficult to imagine how it could, in the foreseeable future, push either of the major parties into a position as weak as the one it now holds.

In these days of change between majority and minority government, Canada has adopted a qualitative party competition which, though unique in the parliamentary world and different from that of the United States, will probably be around for a while. Everywhere else, one of the two competitive parties is, in terms of support at least, what we usually call "left of center." By this, political scientists mean that the party draws most of its support from wage and salary earners, and that about two thirds or more of the wage and salary earners support it. Canada does not have such a party competing effectively for federal office. Everywhere else wage earners could punish the Trudeau government at the polls for the full-wage, partial-profit control program of 1975. In Canada alone, such action is politically impossible; the NDP, the sole appropriate vehicle for such action, shows no signs of mustering the strength to serve as a left-of-center alternative. Canadians owe such welfare innovation as they have received, Medicare is foremost here, to well-meaning Liberals and "red" Tories, not to demands organized from the left or from below, at least as far as federal implementation is concerned.

Now, if this is the state of party competition in Canada, what kind of a party system do we have? We do not have a two-party system like the Americans, who really have no third party, and not even like the British, though their nationalist parties seem about to spoil the traditional government-opposition dialogue. We do not even have a two-major-party system with one reliably placed third party, because as recently as 1962 a fourth party, Social Credit, had more than 10 percent of the Commons seats.

Our party system, then, is not best described by numbers. It has two main characteristics. The first is that there is only one third party with organizational stability, the NDP. Any party needing the NDP to support a minority government can pretty well predict what it is getting. And second, while the major parties hardly differ in appeal, especially in economic matters, they do differ ethnically and regionally. Party competition based on these two factors, in which by definition there can be little rational persuasion, is incapable of providing real contests over innovative policies. If it serves to bring on redistributive policies, it does so by accident rather than design. Canada is ill served by party competition in which ethnic, religious, and regional support outweighs policy demands.

LIMITATIONS OF THE USEFULNESS OF POLITICAL PARTIES IN EXPLAINING THE CANADIAN POLITY

It is exactly because political party is a household word in Canada that it is easy to exaggerate the role of parties in the Canadian polity. In this section I want to point out which aspects of the Canadian polity are explained adequately by the study of political parties and which are not.

The limited role of parties in policy making has been discussed earlier. Since relatively little policy can be explained by the party approach, and since this holds true of the federal as well as most provincial governments, the party approach also explains little about Canadian federalism. There are many confrontations at federal-provincial conferences, but we have yet to have one in which the federal government and its partisan friends in provincial government unite to face the provinces governed by partisan foes. Rather, particular issues, finances, and the distribution of powers under the British North America Act channel the course of federal-provincial policy making. Richard Simeon[5] has shown conclusively that party plays an insignificant role in conflict or negotiation between federal and provincial governments. There has been much federal-provincial conflict since Simeon made this observation, but it is still valid.

Along with the limited policy impact of parties goes, usually, a limited policy effect of elections. The onset of the Great Depression had something to do with R. B. Bennett's victory over the incumbent Mackenzie King in 1930, but voters had no idea of how Bennett might fight the Depression; nor did they have an inkling of the far-reaching measures he would attempt several years later. In 1974 many of those voting for Trudeau and the Liberals may have done so because Trudeau opposed Stanfield's proposal to cure the economy through wage and price controls. Little did they think that voting for Trudeau would lead to wage and price controls fifteen months later.

Does the parties approach tell us very much about governing Canadian society? Two recent phenomena show that it does not. The first of these is western alienation. It would be simple to say that the West shows its alienation by voting against the party that governs Canada. But this is partially false, as the Liberals did well in British Columbia in the federal election of 1974. Party tells us even less when it comes to the behavior of the Western Provinces: the western stance of the leftists, Blakeney and Barrett, is very similar to that of the rightists, Lougheed and Bennett, and the latter two do not even belong to the same party.

More seriously, it is not at all clear what the parties approach can tell us, in early 1977, about the future of Quebec in Confederation. The overwhelming federal Liberal representation from Quebec, from 1962 past the Parti Québecois victory in 1976, fails to give us telling clues about future outcomes, or even options, in the most fateful confrontation in Canadian history.

An area in which the parties approach is barren because of an almost universal nonperformance is that of government and elections below the provincial level. In most Canadian cities elections to council are nonpartisan. Sometimes, but not too often, municipal elections are fought by one or more ad hoc tickets.

Lack of parties in municipal government need not, however, stop the party-oriented analyst. He can point out that party labels, if introduced, could split the propertied or property-brokerage interests that tend to have an above-average interest and influence in our cities. Where there are demands for, or attempts at, partisan activity in municipal politics, they are likely to come from the NDP, the party most often opposed to urban landed interests. Yet such efforts are exceptional. There is a semblance of democracy in our cities: to hold office, one needs to be elected. But the master broker between the governors and the governed, the political party, normally is not on the scene. Our approach, then, cannot tell us what goes on in city politics, and it cannot even tell us how the chief actors came to occupy their leading position.

SCOPE OF THE APPROACH USED IN THIS CHAPTER

This chapter has given a general introduction to the subject of Canadian parties and elections. It has discussed the subject in its various aspects in some detail, and examined briefly the limits on party functions themselves, the desirability of parties, and their potency in explaining Canadian politics. In this final section, I shall attempt an overall evaluation of the performance of Canadian political parties and, incidentally, of Canada's electoral system. This evaluation will lead to an assessment of the importance of studying parties and elections.

An outsider might think that parties perform *too* well in Canada. Though there are occasional oddballs and occasional intentional absentees on opposition benches, why do Canadian legislators almost always vote with their party? Do government members always think the government is right, and do opposition members almost always think the gov-

ernment is wrong? I do not believe so; but I also do not believe that, in
Canada at least, a vote on a bill is an exercise in the search for truth.
Rather, it is an exercise in following one's leader, after having had a
chance at attempting to exercise influence on those few issues that really
matter to the individual member. The reasons why we tolerate this nearly
perfectly predictable performance are the following: first, only by voting
for the leader can a member of Parliament carry out the leadership mandate of the governing party; and second, deviations, as they accumulate,
would destroy either governmental stability or responsible government
itself.

Another outsider, coming from a country where the principal parties
provide clearer policy alternatives, might think that our parties perform
very poorly. This criticism has been leveled by many political scientists
and other informed Canadians. Yet, in fairness, it must be admitted that
Liberals and Conservatives do not have a constitutional or statutory
duopoly on political competition. After all, at the time of writing, all provinces west of New Brunswick have at least one third party as chief competitor on the provincial level, making for more meaningful competition
than we have in Ottawa. However, it may be exceedingly difficult for the
NDP, or another different party, to become number two in federal politics, and thus one of the chief competitors. It is also improbable that the
Liberals will emulate the U.S. Democrats and become the left-of-center
party of the employed, of economically dependent Canadians, thus making major-party competition more meaningful. Meanwhile, Canadians
have the kind of political competition they evidently want and therefore
deserve, and we cannot fault political parties as such for failing to present
more in the way of policy alternatives.

Critics of an institution should be prepared to develop a scheme without it. I am not a critic of political parties; but those who are critics, here
and elsewhere in democracies, fail to provide serious schemes without
parties. Let me therefore try briefly to develop one. There would be little
difficulty in having specific policies worked out by interest groups and
bureaucrats, and in having them enacted by legislators elected in nonpartisan elections. There is, likewise, no need to have parties mobilize voters;
we could have elections in which only those who felt inclined voted, and
these people would presumably find ways of informing themselves. For
me the unanswerable questions are: How would we find political leaders,
how would we remove them; and, should we find answers to these questions, how would we as voters make sure that there is any kind of long-
term influence on our governors, the kind of influence that is sanctioned
by what we call "responsibility"? Until someone can persuade me how to
accomplish all this without political parties, I insist on considering them a
good thing for democracy.

How well does our electoral system work? Looking at the federal
scene in the seventies so far, it looks as though in most of Quebec only
Liberal votes count, in Alberta only Conservative votes, and that the election is decided by one or two million voters in southern Ontario. This
means, looking at it cynically, that Alberta does not count while the Grits
are in office, and that the only reason why Quebec might count while the

Tories are in office is that Quebec has so many seats. But let us consider the alternative, some form of proportional representation where, technicalities aside, a party gets about as high a percentage of seats as its percentage of the vote. This may be satisfactory on the input side: each Liberal vote, for instance, would be equally significant, whether cast in Alberta or in New Brunswick. Yet such a system fails us on the output side: in the past fifty years we would have had majority governments only twice, having come close another three times.

But do we need majority governments? Lester B. Pearson's minority governments gave this country many constructive policies, including Medicare, the Canada pension, and the flag, but they could do so only because with their silent partners, the Créditistes, they had a majority. The cabinet system, to have any stability at all, needs reliable majorities. Through the good offices of the governing party, majorities tie the government to Parliament and to the people. Alternatives such as the American or Swiss systems are possible for Canada, but they would require a massive reorientation for everyone actively and passively engaged in the political process. Intellectually, there may be a lot wrong with the cabinet system, especially the phenomena of the disciplined government caucus and the disciplined opposition. Yet, to take the American alternative, there would be two prices to pay: first, prolonged trust in an essentially sole-ruling chief executive; and second, giving up most of what little remains of a connection between party and policy.

I hope I have demonstrated that parties and elections are important to the functioning of the Canadian polity. But then, so are buildings in which government is housed and the paper flow of government communications. Political scientists do not make a special effort to study such matters, but they do study and analyze political parties and elections. Let me now present the argument that the student of Canadian politics needs to study parties and elections to get to know and understand his subject.

Canada is a representative democracy. With the monarchy serving only as a symbol and to maintain the rules of the game, the government is entrusted to elected representatives, their executive leaders, and their administrative appointees. Representation in Canada implies, as it does in all democracies, the public election of representatives. Beyond this, it implies the competitive election of representatives. As I have shown throughout this chapter, in Canada, and in other democracies, parties are the active agents in this competition. It is, in sum, the election that gives us our governors, and the parties that compete in the elections.

The structure of Canadian government, its policy processes, even its policies, can be studied without using the parties and elections approach. However, people who form part of a system of representative government such as Canada has, whether elected members, candidates, managers, election workers and, last but not least, voters, can be fully understood only through the study of parties and elections.

ENDNOTES

1. Donald Smiley, *Canada in Question: Federalism in the Seventies* (Toronto: McGraw-Hill Ryerson, 1976), Ch. 4.
2. A. C. Cairns, "The Electoral System and the Party System in Canada," *Canadian Journal of Political Science*, I, No. 1 (March, 1968).
3. Donald Smiley, "The National Party Leadership Convention in Canada," *Canadian Journal of Political Science*, I, No. 4 (December, 1968).
4. Reprinted in H.H. Gerth and C.W. Mills, *From Max Weber* (Oxford University Press, 1958), pp. 77-128.
5. Richard Simeon, *Federal-Provincial Diplomacy* (Toronto: University of Toronto Press, 1972).

SELECTED REFERENCES

After the pioneering efforts of John Meisel, C.B. Macpherson, S.M. Lipset and a few others, there was a lull in writing on Canadian parties until the mid-sixties. Since then, there has been a veritable explosion. Two recent, extensive and not completely overlapping bibliographies are available. These can be found in the following volumes:

ENGELMANN, FREDERICK C., AND MILDRED SCHWARTZ. *Canadian Political Parties: Origin, Character, Impact.* Scarborough: Prentice-Hall, 1975.

VAN LOON, RICHARD J., AND MICHAEL S. WHITTINGTON. *The Canadian Political System: Environment, Structure and Process.* Toronto: McGraw-Hill Ryerson, 1976.

In using these bibliographies, I want to call attention especially to the periodical literature, much of it in the *Canadian Journal of Political Science*, where a good deal of original research has been published.

There are three standard books on Canadian political parties in general. One important differentiation is that the first title listed is co-authored, the second a mixture of co-authorship and co-editorship, and the third a collection of readings. All three expand on, and illustrate, materials discussed in this chapter. These books are:

ENGELMANN, FREDERICK C., AND MILDRED SCHWARTZ. *Canadian Political Parties: Origin, Character, Impact.* Scarborough: Prentice-Hall, 1975.

WINN, CONRAD, AND JOHN MCMENEMY. *Political Parties in Canada.* Toronto: McGraw-Hill Ryerson, 1976.

THORBURN, H.G., ed. *Party Politics in Canada*, 3rd ed. Scarborough: Prentice-Hall, 1972.

11

Dualism and the Concept of National Unity

David R. Cameron*

INTRODUCTION

How does one understand one's country? This is a question that citizens of many lands confront from time to time; it is never a simple question to cope with and, in times of domestic strife or crisis, the search for an answer can be an acute and pressing business. The way a person understands his country will guide the way he acts as a citizen. For example, during Alexander Dubcek's period as premier of Czechoslovakia, many of the country's citizens were struggling to realize in political activity their understanding of Czechoslovakia as a free, socialist country; others, however, viewed Czechoslovakia as a member of the Soviet bloc of countries and, finally, as subordinate to the will of the U.S.S.R. As we all know, the issue was authoritatively resolved in favor of the latter view, with the help of Russian military force. A survey of the international scene will reveal the extent to which many countries of the world face a set of painful questions about their character and future. Canada's is but one case among many and, in global terms, is far from being the most critical.

Canada is currently experiencing a period of profound disagreement among its citizens about the nature of the country; disagreement not just between French-speaking and English-speaking Canadians, although this is the most significant line of conflict, but between various regions, groups, and provinces. This is in no sense an unprecedented occurrence in Canada, for the country's history has been marked by alternating periods of conflict and relative tranquility. It is, however, the most serious crisis the country has had to face so far and its primary source lies in the relationship of the French-Canadians of Quebec to the rest of Canada. The commissioners of the Royal Commission on Bilingualism and Biculturalism made precisely this assertion more than a decade ago, and there is even less room for denial today than there was in 1965.[1]

*Associate Professor of Political Studies, Trent University; and Director of Research, Task Force on Canadian Unity.

A major obstacle hampering both understanding and action in such an area is the sheer variety and complexity of most countries. In this, Canada is no exception. Practically speaking, it is impossible to create an image or provide a summary account of the country which will be easily understood by others but which, at the same time, will not simplify or neglect the diversity of the land and its people. If a foreigner asks you what kind of a place Canada is, what do you say? If you are like most of us, you attempt an answer, listing several of the features or qualities you deem to be most important, leaving an enormous amount unsaid, and at the end of it all feeling very unsatisfied with your reply. This is in fact about all that any of us can do. We work out a simplified account, a caricature, that will help us to come to terms with our country, to communicate our understanding of it to others. We develop theories that highlight those features we think are most important at the expense of those features we believe are less significant. The selection of an approach is as necessary for the political scientist or historian as it is for the ordinary citizen.

Since this is an explicit theme of this volume, let us expand upon it briefly. One definition of a fact is "a thing perceived." Whatever may be its deficiencies, either as a definition or as an expression of a philosophical theory, this rendering at least has the virtue of underlining the degree to which the so-called observer of the world of facts is himself a participant in and to a marked extent a creator of that universe of empirical reality. Does the sun "rise" or is the earth turning? Each view has received scientific support at different periods of our history. If this is a factor to be borne in mind even in our perception of natural objects such as stones and plants and animals, how much more important is it in our study of countries and nations? Indeed, such concepts as "nation," "country," and "class" are themselves intellectual constructions which we impose upon the world and which help us to render the chaos of social phenomena intelligible. In the absence of the ordering vision of the observer-participant, what exists is a nameless mass of people; it is the identification of significance—*this* collectivity is a people, a nation—which invests a mass with character. In naming or denoting, one is in part creating. Many Canadians, especially French Canadians, see Canada as a country composed of two nations; many others see it as a single nation. That this is more than a simple linguistic confusion will become apparent in the balance of this chapter.

A person's perception, not only of his country, but of the world itself may well depend heavily on his social, economic, geographical, or cultural position. The angle of vision is likely to vary according to his position or standing in the social and political world. Our social universe is composed, not simply of "natural" facts and objects, but also of opinions about those facts and objects, and a student of politics and social life must be sensitive to both these dimensions. It is not enough to establish in socioeconomic data the empirical existence of a class structure; it is equally important to determine what, if anything, the members of the community think about that structure. It is not sufficient to identify the linguistic and cultural affiliations that distinguish a specific group of people; it is also necessary to examine the cultural consciousness of the members of that national group and the importance they attach to those affiliations.

This volume contains not simply approaches to Canadian politics but approaches to an understanding of Canada itself. Theories of regionalism, continentalism, and class advance our understanding of the nature of our country while at the same time assisting us in comprehending its politics. Given the intimate connections that abound, this is only to be expected. The function of this chapter is to identify, describe, and assess one of the major avenues of understanding Canadian politics, namely, the theory of cultural dualism. It is one of the most significant ways of accounting for Canada and its politics, and it has the virtue of enjoying an existence not only in the data which are the subject matter of political analysis, but in the beliefs and sentiments of the country's political leaders and citizens.

I should like to begin this discussion by examining a concept which lies near the center of most Canadian political rhetoric and debate and much political analysis, namely, the idea of national unity. National unity is the broad intellectual framework within which the theory of dualism may be best understood.

THE CONCEPT OF NATIONAL UNITY

I suspect that the phrase "national unity" is the most frequently used expression in the Canadian political vocabulary. That this is a plausible contention at once tells us a good deal about the country and the character of its politics. For a start, it suggests, at least at the formal level of identifying a major problem area and a consequent national objective of high priority, that there is a fair amount of agreement among citizens, politicians, and analysts; not by any means unanimity, but a conventional understanding sufficiently broad and powerful to set the terms of much Canadian political discussion. National unity identifies what is most problematic about Canadian life, at least as it is perceived by the country's citizens, and delineates the major factor that politics in this country must take into account. But there are two points that need to be made at this stage.

First of all, in the absence of further specification, the phrase is a formal statement lacking any substantive content. It indicates that a major problem Canadians face is keeping the country together, but it does not show why this is a problem, what the primary disintegrative forces are, what the constellation of public opinion on the subject is, how unity is to be achieved, or even why it should be achieved. There is, of course, a broad range of possibilities with respect to any of these points and these must be filled out in the course of any discussion or study.

The second point arises out of the first. We have suggested that there is a conventional preoccupation with national unity, but not necessarily any agreement about the substantive issues that should engage our attention under this rubric. In terms of our earlier discussion, what this implies is that we Canadians have not so far been successful in establishing an authoritative answer to the question of what kind of a country this is. There is a variety of competing responses or conceptions of what Canada is, or should be, some of them clearly incompatible with the continued existence of any kind of country at all; but none has succeeded in establishing itself generally and gaining broad acceptance throughout the country. Our naming and creating has not been a collective, national activity, nor has it led toward any coherent national identity; it has rather been carried on within relatively distinct regional and cultural groups, and often in surprising isolation from the efforts of understanding which were being made elsewhere.

Indeed, to the extent that there is any nationally accepted vision of the country these days, it appears to be found in the residual and formally paradoxical idea that there is *no* nationally accepted vision and that this is a defining characteristic of the society. For some people, this is a fact to be applauded and supported; for others, it is to restate in the form of a solution what had formerly been articulated as the problem.

Canada is indeed an extraordinarily diverse country, and it is one which has sustained, and perhaps in some ways even increased, the range of diversity over the period of its national existence. For a variety of reasons, it has run counter to the historic trend toward increasingly centralized and homogeneous forms of political community and society. The federal system of government was established in the nineteenth century in response to the brute fact of politically significant diversity, and this political structure has itself helped to maintain and advance diversity.

Even a cursory examination of the British North America Act,[2] Canada's major constitutional document, makes it clear that there was not just one, but several different lines of cleavage that the Fathers of Confederation deemed to be sufficiently significant to warrant attention in the proposed federal system. This is not to say that they necessarily liked having to take account of them—indeed, Macdonald and others would have preferred a legislative union, could they have had it—but that they saw that these cleavages could not be avoided. Thus they were moved to support the principle of a federal rather than a unitary system of government, but bent their efforts to ensuring that the balance of power lay decisively with the central government. The American Civil War was, in this context, a critical event in the minds of most of those who discussed the construction of a Canadian confederation.

One major cleavage was, of course, the regional and political differentiation expressed by the British colonies of Nova Scotia, New Brunswick, and Canada (composed of Canada East and Canada West, subsequently Quebec and Ontario), the original members of the new confederation. The necessary recognition of these claims to regional autonomy provided the context in which the federal system grew, eventually extending from coast to coast and including ten provinces and two territories in its political framework. The acute problem of communications in the mid-nineteenth century constituted a further incentive to recognize the principle of decentralization in a large territory with a very small population.

Another cleavage of great significance at the time was that of religious belief. It was, arguably, the most important cultural matter to be considered in the making of Confederation, although inevitably it was entangled with language questions. There appears to have been a belief, which proved wrong in the event, that if religious rights, particularly in the area of education, were protected, then linguistic rights would follow. Constitutionally, the major provision protected the existing separate school rights of Protestants and Catholics. Section 93 of the BNA Act, dealing with education, became a major clause around which French and English conflict was to revolve in subsequent years. The Manitoba schools question at the end of the last century was perhaps the most dramatic demonstration of the extent to which the interlocking considerations of religion, language, and culture lay at the very center of Canadian political life.[3]

The overlapping but distinguishable linguistic cleavage between French and English was recognized as a fact of Canadian life by the 1860s. It was by then evident that a policy of assimilating the French Canadians to the English-speaking world of North America would not work without intolerable costs, and it was therefore understood that at least minimal formal protection of language was necessary. This was reflected in Section 133 of the BNA Act which provided for the use of the English and French languages in Parliament and the courts of Canada and the legislature and courts of Quebec.

A final division that received some modest attention in the British North America Act was that which separated the native population of British North America from the European settlers. The lines of coexistence between the aboriginal and European cultures were not developed in any detail; it was thought constitutionally sufficient to vest authority for the care of aboriginal peoples in the federal government. In Section 91 (24) of the British North America Act, the federal government is granted jurisdiction over "Indians, and Lands reserved for the Indians." Subsequent judicial interpretation has determined that Inuit are to be considered "Indians" within the meaning of Section 91 (24).

No mention was made of other cultures. The theory of multiculturalism as a significant aspect of Canadian life had to await the waves of immigration, primarily European, that began in the late nineteenth century and continued up to the present. To the extent that multiculturalism was a factor in mid-nineteenth century thought, it tended to be a matter of French Canadians and the "races" of Great Britain; the Scots, the Irish, and the English.

The point to be made here bears on our discussion of dualism for it suggests the broader social, economic, and cultural context within which dualism must be considered. A variety of politically significant cleavages were recognized in the nineteenth century, cleavages that any political structure would have to take into account. The French-English question, although the most important in the event, was only one of a number that confronted the colonial politicians in the 1860s.

If anything, the range of cleavages and their significance have increased since then. We have today the increasingly acute question of the country's Inuit and Indian peoples, and their relationship to the rest of society. We have theories of multiculturalism, arising out of the persistence of distinctive subcultures, vying for attention and public support with theories of biculturalism. We have a number of energetic and thriving regional economic and social systems, in many instances led by highly sophisticated provincial governments. And we have a more acute sensitivity to what has been described as the "two nations" of the rich and poor, whether the dividing line is drawn in regional terms or horizontally in class terms. One might say that Canada is not so much a mosaic, but a collage in which qualitatively different elements and objects are distributed rather haphazardly within a single frame. This makes the political world within which citizens and politicians function an inordinately complex one, and rules out as inadequate any simple analysis of Canadian politics.

So the question remains: In view of this diversity, what image of Canada do people have in mind when they speak of the need to foster national unity? They cannot mean that we should become a unified country in the juridical sense, that is to say, a state, for assuredly we are that already. There is no gainsaying the existence and authority of our constitutional structure as stated primarily in the British North America Act, nor is there any doubt about the actuality of our federal and parliamentary system of government, the general efficacy of our legislative, judicial, and administrative systems, nor about our standing and reputation internationally.

But neither can people, when they speak of promoting national unity, mean that in Canada we should try to make ourselves a single people, a nation with one national culture and a single dominant mode of life. If that is what people mean, then they are surely pursuing a chimera. The United States of America has been neatly described as "the American people organized," a state which is "co-extensive with a particular culture whose interest it is its primary responsibility to serve and protect."[4] It would be folly to claim the same for Canada, whose political system is a framework within which the various peoples and communities can seek their respective goals.

René Lévesque has made the derisive comment that 'Le Canada, c'est un soufflé qui n'a pas pris.' The comment conveys Lévesque's main point clearly enough, namely, that in his judgment the Canadian "experiment" has been a flop, but the analogy he employs is at once malapropos and highly revealing. To think of Canada as a soufflé that did not rise is to intimate that one holds the view that the historic task which faced the country was to create out of the constituent elements of the population a new compound, a Canadian people in which all the elements would be transformed and homogenized. It is, in other words, a Gallic (and a gastronomic) rendering of the American melting-pot idea, and, while it may speak in some way to the political experience of a French Canadian who is a member of the only fully articulated cultural nation in the country, it misses the point as far as Canada as a whole is concerned. With the exception of a few abortive attempts, which proved the inadvisability of the effort, the Canadian experience has never involved the wholehearted pursuit of a national mission or ideology, and to impose upon it a standard drawn from cultural nationalism is to misrepresent and distort its character. Canada is a country and a state; it is not a nation-state.

What, then, might be meant by the phrase national unity? What Canada possesses is the apparatus of a federal state (legislatures, courts, "national" and provincial public services, and so on). But no regime (except perhaps one based on terror) can survive if it does not enjoy the allegiance or, minimally, the apathetic acceptance of the population. Since most Canadians seek something more than bare survival, most discussions of national unity involve the quest for the proper ground of allegiance, for that form of allegiance appropriate to a diverse, federal country. And the type of allegiance most likely to be appropriate is as superficially paradoxical as is the principle of federalism itself; it is the support of a common political framework, and a loyalty to it, that make it possible for distinctive subsystem groups and associations to continue and flourish although they may have other distinctive loyalties. It is the broad community of sentiment and interest within which the primary loyalties of the Maritimer, the Québécois, or the Westerner may find security and room to live. An allegiance, a unity of sentiment or conviction, which by design and by its nature corroded these other loyalties and interests would be at odds with the principle of federalism itself.

I have said that federalism and the form of allegiance proper to it are both paradoxical in their character, but only superficially so. It may be that it is difficult in an era of exclusivist and competing ideologies to resist the belief that federalism is an inept and archaic political form condemned to languish in a historical backwater. There is often little room for alternative visions and competing claims in the sweeping world views of nationalism, liberalism, or Marxism. But surely, while it may be difficult, it is not impossible. We are all aware of the distinctive loyalties which attach to the various associations of which we are members, be they the family, a church, a trade union, or a political party. What federalism seeks to do is to take account of the diversity of a society and to build into the political system itself a multiplicity of claims and a number of loci of power. It may be said that, as a political system, federalism fails not only when it collapses as a result of secession, but also when it effectively disappears into a unitary state as a result of unrestrained centralization.

One might suggest with pardonable exaggeration that the reason there is a crisis in Canadian federalism today is that Canadian federalism has been so successful. We *are* a diverse country, and we have, and have sustained, a political system that reflects and protects much of that diversity. National unity will be problematic so long as federalism is vital.

Before the Canadian federal system was created, George Etienne Cartier stated in a few words the continuing challenge that was to face the country in the century that followed. He claimed that, should British North Americans achieve a union, they "would form a political nationality with which neither national origin, nor the religion of any individual would interfere." It is that form of national unity which is suggested by the evocative phrase, political nationality, which Canadians have been attempting to fashion for themselves for more than a century.

Many Canadians have sought to specify what the content of national unity might be, and it is obvious that it is no easy task. But enough has been written and spoken to make it clear that the recognition of a common fate and the common satisfaction of interests have a lot to do with it. While it is an unhappy oversimplification to identify federalism with reason and nationalism with emotion,[5] it is nonetheless true that the appeal of federalism is not in any straightforward way to those primary emotions frequently composing the regional, cultural, linguistic, or religious loyalties which flourish, or should be permitted to flourish, within the general framework of a federal state.

An example may help to make the point clear. It is always possible for a French Canadian to consider whether or not it makes sense for him and his community to remain a part of Canada; indeed, this question has arisen in acute form in recent years. But it is barely intelligible to suggest that a French Canadian might raise the question whether he should be a French Canadian. Membership in the Canadian association is in substantial degree a matter of choice, grounded in principle on calculations of interest, judgments about the satisfaction of needs, the consultation of preferences, and so on. But one does not choose in any significant way to be or not to be a French Canadian. That is the unquestioned base, part of the personal identity in terms of which one calculates interests and benefits, rather than an element in the calculation itself. Symbolic of the politicizing of this national sentiment in Quebec is the gradual transmuting of French Canadians living in Quebec into Québécois, a people with a legally defined territory who already, in their provincial capacity, possess many of the attributes of statehood. It is the unrestrained expression of this political dimension of national sentiment, that is to say, it is nationalism, which constitutes a secessionist movement, in its nature destructive of federalism itself.

Nothing is simple in federalism, and one of the complicating factors that must be kept in mind is not just that there is diversity, but that there are different kinds of diversity. I have suggested that French Canada is, in cultural terms, the only nation in the country. This is clearly a matter of degree, and to some extent a matter of semantics, but it seems to me a reasonable proposition that there is no other cultural group with the size, the concentration in a territory, the history, language, and distinctive way of life to warrant description as a nation. English Canada is in some ways more of an anticategory, created in contradistinction to French Canada; this is a point we shall need to consider later on. For the rest, we have a bewildering array of communities and loyalties, grounded sometimes in language and culture, sometimes in region, sometimes in common weakness or in distance from the center, sometimes in occupational and economic similarities, sometimes in the enjoyment of shared political forms.

Even Ontario, which if frequently seen by the rest of the country as the homogeneous heartland of English Canada, is in fact extraordinarily varied. A day in central Toronto will attest to this fact, and the Franco-Ontarian and native populations of the province provide further testimony. A few hours' drive north, out of the heavily populated urban

south of the province, will disclose a second world that has little, if anything, to do with the national image of the province, a world that has more
in common with northern Quebec and Manitoba than it does with the
urban, industrial, and manufacturing life of Toronto or Hamilton.

National unity, then, is likely to be expressed in terms of some such
concept as Cartier's "political nationality," that is to say, a system of belief
and sentiment that will sustain the country and make it intelligible to its
citizens, and will preserve the diversity of the land and the federal system
of government which is its political expression.

But Canadians understandably seek some greater clarity and detail as
an aid to understanding their country. There are two conceptions or images of the country which are germane to our discussion at this point, each
of them constituting a further specification of the conditions within which
national unity might be defined, and each of them implying a normative
judgment about the things it is worthwhile for the political system to sustain and protect. The first is the conception of Canada as a bicultural
country, and the second is the conception of Canada as a multicultural
country. One hardly need say that there are a variety of other ways of con-
ceiving of the country: for example, as an urban, industrialized society
with a developed capitalist economy and a population divided along class
lines; as a hinterland of the American empire; as a conservative, tradi-
tionalist community that defines itself in contradistinction to the democratic republicanism of the United States and claims continuity with the parliamentary and monarchical principles of Great Britain and British society.

However, the multicultural and bicultural or dualist images of Canada
are among the most widely accepted and influential conceptions of the
country currently in existence, and it is helpful to consider them together.
Because the focus of attention in this chapter is on dualism rather than on
multiculturalism, I shall employ the latter primarily as a means of illuminat-
ing and explicating the former.

DUALISM AND MULTICULTURALISM

When the Royal Commission on Bilingualism and Biculturalism was established in 1963, its terms of reference were recorded in privy council minutes as follows: "To inquire into and report upon the existing state of
bilingualism and biculturalism in Canada and to recommend what steps
should be taken to develop the Canadian Confederation on the basis of an
equal partnership between the two founding races, taking into account the
contribution made by the other ethnic groups to the cultural enrichment of
Canada and the measures that should be taken to safeguard that contribution."

The first part of the terms of reference postulates a theory of dualism
or biculturalism, while the second, dealing with "other ethnic groups," implies some theory of cultural pluralism or multiculturalism. These distinct
conceptions of Canadian society existed in uneasy relationship with one

another throughout the life of the B and B Commission. They were reflected in the composition of the Commission itself; that is to say, in the cultural and linguistic background of the commissioners, in the Commission's research activities, in its hearings, and in its reports.

While there is, at many points, considerable overlap between these two conceptions of Canadian society, they pull in quite different directions at several critical junctures, and the uneasy relationship referred to within the Royal Commission has been paralleled by a similar uneasiness and, at times, tension in the society at large. This is something we shall explain further in the pages that follow. Our first task is to describe the theory of dualism.

Dualism in Canada may be generally described as the view which holds that the most significant cleavage in Canadian society is the line dividing English from French, and which identifies as the major challenge to domestic statecraft the establishment of harmonious and just relations between the English-speaking and the French-speaking communities of Canada. It is an understanding of the Canadian situation that has its origins in the British defeat of the French forces at Quebec in 1759; since that time, the reconciliation of French and English has been a continuing preoccupation of Canadians and their political leaders.

Those who would assert the importance of the dualist approach to an understanding of Canadian politics need do little more than point to several of the major events of Canada's history. Again and again, one finds either that the explicit issue is one which involves French-English relations, or, if it begins as something else, it is soon transmuted into that kind of conflict. Quite apart from the years of accommodation and adjustment that followed the British assumption of civil authority in the eighteenth century, there have been a series of significant occurrences which have extended up to the present: the 1837 Rebellion and Lord Durham's *Report* which was a response to it; the controversy between Upper and Lower Canada and the increasingly obvious unworkability of the united-province system; the recognition of the two communities in the Confederation debates and in the new federal system; the Riel Rebellion; the Manitoba schools question; the controversy over French-language schools in Ontario during the First World War; and conscription as an issue in the two World Wars. Since 1960, Canada has experienced the cultural awakening of the Québécois people, an awakening that has gathered force and momentum until we now have a government in Quebec City committed to achieve sovereign independence for its people. It is events such as these that provide empirical support for the contention that questions of dualism lie at the center of Canadian public life.

Dualism, however, is a slippery concept to catch hold of, for it contains several equivocal elements and the way in which these elements are defined and interrelated establishes the particular theory of dualism the individual or group in question holds. The most important of these elements, of course, are the two things about which one is speaking when one speaks of dualism: namely, French Canada, or the francophone community, or the province of Quebec on the one hand; and English Canada, or the anglophone community, or the other nine provinces, or the other nine plus the federal government on the other hand. The way in which one defines these two entities is of signal importance in determining the type of dualist theory which is advanced. Another critical element is the set of relationships, political and other, that connect the two entities to one another.

One can see, then, that dualism is by no means a straightforward, self-explanatory view of Canada. It involves, first of all, choosing an angle of vision that will bring into prominence one set of characteristics of the country and neglect others; then it requires that one specify the meaning of the various critical elements and what that viewpoint can be expected to show.

For purposes of illustration, one might identify two broad strains of dualist thought in Canada. Each overlaps the other extensively, but they are characterized by a distinct focus or orientation and they lead on to distinguishable policy alternatives. We might call them the "sociological" and "institutional" approaches to dualism.

The sociological approach defines the two communities in noninstitutional terms. All those whose native tongue is French or all those who are French Canadian by origin are part of one community; those who speak English or whose origin is not French-Canadian are part of the other community. In recent times, and in part, perhaps, because of the unacceptable implications and, indeed, inadequacy of any attempt to understand an ethnically diverse population in terms of just two ethnic categories, the sociological approach has tended to define the two communities in terms of language rather than ethnicity. For example, while the B and B Commission's terms of reference spoke of two founding races, the commissioners in fact concentrated their attention primarily on the two communities defined as francophone and anglophone.

It is this sociological approach to dualism that has been adhered to consistently by the federal government and by Prime Minister Trudeau. It takes seriously the demographic data showing extensive interpenetration and geographic dispersion of the two linguistic communities, and the consequent fact that no single political jurisdiction can be considered to be solely responsible for one of the linguistic communities or for policies relating to dualism. Thus there is an assumption that in provinces where both communities are strongly represented the respective provincial governments must assume partial responsibility for making appropriate arrangements. The protection of English-language minority rights in Quebec, and the protection of Franco-Ontarian and Acadian minority rights in Ontario and New Brunswick are perfectly consistent with this sociological approach to dualism. To the extent that responsibility is distributed, at least in principle, among all the provincial governments, there is a corresponding reduction, relatively speaking, in the importance of any single provincial government's role.

There is, of course, a practical recognition of the special tasks facing Quebec in nurturing the well-being of the francophone community, but always on the understanding that there are reciprocal obligations on the part of all governments in Canada to attend as best they can to the needs of both language groups. Thus, embedded in this approach, there is a bias against recognizing any one provincial government as having a special standing or responsibility that might properly receive constitutional recognition. Quebec, as a matter of constitutional principle, is a province like the others, and any arrangements or liberties extended to her must in principle be applicable to the others as well.

A practical implication of the sociological approach to dualism is the strengthening of the federal government's role in the area of bilingualism and biculturalism, since it is the only government in the country with obligations to all Canadian citizens. It is the federal government that has comprehensive responsibility for the population as a whole, and it is therefore reasonable for citizens and provincial governments to look to the federal government to assume leadership in developing and implementing policies relating to dualism. Broadly speaking, this is what has happened during the past decade and a half, at least so far as English Canada and the provinces other than Quebec are concerned. The central government has been looked to for leadership in these areas and has helped to define broad policy directions that both levels of government might pursue.

Within its own area of jurisdiction, virtually all the steps taken by the federal government have been consistent with the sociological approach to dualism. Many of the specific policies have their origin in the recommendations of the Royal Commission on Bilingualism and Biculturalism, although that body itself did not in fact adopt the sociological approach to dualism unequivocally. One of the reasons why there has been a high degree of consistency in federal cultural policy is that it is the expression of the firm convictions of a prime minister who has enjoyed a virtual monopoly on federal policy formation in matters of dualism for almost a decade. The Official Languages Act of 1969, the principle of establishing bilingual districts where the size of the francophone or anglophone minority group warrants it, the bilingualization of the federal civil service, and the effort to provide service to the citizens of the country in whichever official language they customarily use, the general encouragement of bilingualism throughout the country—these are all emanations of the sociological approach to dualism.

What of the approach to dualism we have called institutional? This interpretation of dualism starts from the same premise; that is to say, from a belief that the two communities compose the basic elements of Canadian society, but its development from that point on is significantly different from that of the sociological approach. While recognizing the demographic facts of interpenetration and dispersion, the institutional approach makes a hardheaded judgment, namely, that a minority culture that does not enjoy concrete expression in a set of political institutions is unlikely in the long run to endure.

The institutionalists are inclined to view the sociological approach with suspicion because it neglects the issue of political power in working out accommodations between the two cultures. Where everyone is said to be responsible, no one is responsible; where the federal government and perhaps half the provincial governments are deemed to have responsibility, no government has genuine responsibility, at least not in the direct, painful sense in which a political regime accountable to its people will find it difficult to avoid vigorous action on behalf of the citizenry.

Who is responsible for the welfare and advançement of Canada's French Canadians? The federal government asserts this responsibility, but its sense of obligation must inevitably be blunted by the demands and claims of the myriad other interests and groups to which it has to attend, not least of which are those of the majority English Canadian community. It cannot push the claims of French Canada, but must balance them off against others. For the provinces other than Quebec, the French-Canadian question is necessarily—however warm their sympathies may be—a relatively peripheral issue (New Brunswickers, I presume, would not accept this assertion for a minute). What political jurisdiction other than the province of Quebec can wholeheartedly take on as its primary responsibility the protection and well-being of French Canada?

So those who adopt this view are inclined to see the historical continuance of French-Canadian culture in North America as being in very great measure the product of a set of arrangements that gave room in the political organization of Canadian society to the existence and the claims of French Canada. During the past century, this has taken the form of a federal system that, at least informally, vested in one government, that of the province of Quebec, direct obligations with respect to French Canada. This has ensured the expression and protection of French Canada's interests, in part, no doubt, because there is a definable government that can be held accountable by the electorate for its actions. The particular role of Quebec has also been a factor in combating the forces of centralization and in maintaining a genuinely federal system of government.

It can be seen that there are some close connections between this institutional approach to dualism and many theories of nationalism. Most important is the fact that both take seriously the question of political power, and assume that cultural vitality depends on a suitable distribution of power and must, for its continued health, enjoy political expression. A minority culture cannot depend on the goodwill of the majority for its support; it must be in a position to command fair treatment. It must, in all likelihood, find a way of turning itself into a majority. The logic of federalism in this respect is that a minority can be given political power, can be turned into a majority, in those culturally sensitive areas that require it, but can be treated as a portion of the population as a whole in those matters which are deemed to be common throughout the system and not intimately related to culture. Understandably, there is great difficulty in distinguishing clearly between those matters which are common and federal and those which are local and provincial, and there is traditionally controversy between the two spheres of government over whose judgment is to prevail. Where there is persistent conflict between the minority and the majority about matters of significance, it is frequently the case that a theory of institutional dualism held by the minority culture will be transformed into a theory of nationalism and national independence; certainly, the institutional approach lends itself more easily than the sociological to this type of change.

Another important connection between institutional dualism and nationalism is the collective dimension. Both see that the vitality and welfare of the individual depends heavily upon his active membership in the cultural group or the nation. The sociological approach to dualism, in contrast, tends to be more concerned with the protection of the individual's linguistic and cultural rights rather than with the well-being of the collectivity as a whole.

There are, at this point, several important implications to be drawn from the institutional approach. First, the adoption of this way of understanding dualism leads one to downplay the significance of those minorities that do not constitute a political regime of some sort. In the Canadian context this means that there is less concern for the well-being of francophone or French-Canadian minorities outside the province of Quebec, or, perhaps more precisely, a fatalism about the chances of survival of such politically unprotected minorities. The sociological approach is seen to be pretty much beside the point, for it is believed that the issue is not so much how well the various governments in Canada cope with the requirements of individuals who speak one or another of the two official languages, but rather how well two relatively coherent collectivities can live together "within the bosom of a single state."

Secondly, neither the federal government nor any of the other nine provinces is deemed to have nearly so important a responsibility for the direct working out of arrangements for French Canadians as is the case in the sociological approach. The important actions in this sphere belong to the government of Quebec so far as French Canadians are concerned, and to the other governments of Canada so far as English Canada is concerned. The relationships between Quebec and the rest of Canada become quasi-diplomatic in character, with the provincial government at Quebec City speaking for French Canada and seeking to represent and protect its interests.

I would hazard the guess that the English-speaking citizens of the country and the francophone minorities outside Quebec find the sociological approach to dualism congenial, whereas the Québécois, the French Canadians within the province of Quebec, approach the question of dualism much more in institutional and political terms and with a much more acute sensitivity to the connection between cultural well-being and political power. This is yet another sign, manifested in the very images of Canada that Canadians hold, of the 'Two Solitudes' of which Hugh MacLennan has spoken.

Let us complicate the picture further by examining one assumption that supports both these conceptions of dualism. Whatever version of dualism is held, two entities are seen to be in relationship with one another—the two nations, the two nationalities, the two cultural or linguistic groups, or whatever. It is assumed that there are two collectivities, and that they each possess an identity of some kind, a set of specifiable characteristics and orientations.

This assumption appears to work reasonably well in the case of French Canada or the francophone community, but what of English Canada? Indeed, what is English Canada? We seem to be able to talk intelligibly about English Canada so long as we do not examine too carefully what it is we are referring to. But when we do undertake such an examination, what we seem to discover is diversity which reaches so far and so deep that it forces us to call into question the very concept that we have been happily employing. English Canadians are distributed throughout all the ten provinces; vast numbers of them are not Anglo-Saxon in ethnic origin; many speak English as a second language. Diverse religions, cultural practices, and languages teem beneath the placid surface of English Canada. What is more, the economic, occupational, and social composition of this collectivity varies not only in class terms but also by region, and increasingly strong loyalties are developing which attach segments of the Canadian population to provincial governments and subsystem political cultures.

How are these phenomena to be fitted into a theory of dualism? How, for example, is the contribution of the other ethnic groups to be taken seriously if the country is to be developed on the basis of an equal partnership between the two founding races? How might we reconcile cultural pluralism with dualism? It is, I think, fair to suggest that so far we have not succeeded in effecting either a conceptual or a practical reconciliation of these two. While it is probably true to say that the existence of a large French-Canadian community in British North America created the conditions within which both the form and the theory of cultural pluralism could take root in Canada, and while it is most certainly true that the other ethnic groups share many of the same concerns with the French-Canadian community, it is nevertheless the case that, as theories and as social patterns, pluralism and dualism tug in quite different directions, and each poses a problem for the other.[6]

If bilingualism and biculturalism are to be the defining concepts for Canadian life, then the possibility of adequate institutional recognition and support of pluralism is markedly diminished. If one is preoccupied with French-English relations, it is difficult to bring into bold relief those social facts and relationships which are neither French nor English. Where do the native people fit into such a scheme? Where might the Italians of Toronto be placed? The Greeks of Montreal? The Ukrainians on the Prairies or the Asians of British Columbia? If dualism is the explanatory model that is employed, then concern for and sensitivity to multiculturalism in Canada will necessarily be reduced. Politically, the choice of model can have serious ramifications, because the two-nations theory opens up, at least in principle, the possibility of a set of relationships and political structures that reflect the two dominant cultural entities. How does that fit with a federal system of ten provinces and a central government?

If, to take the opposite position, multiculturalism is accepted as the dominant norm, with English as the de facto lingua franca, then the French-Canadian fact will tend to be assimilated to that theory of pluralism, and French Canadians will tend to be regarded simply as members of one of the several minority cultures that together compose the Canadian mosaic. This is, I think, a frame of mind much more likely to prevail in Western Canada, where the demographic facts of life encourage and support it. The divergent principles of dualism and multiculturalism lie at the center of a good deal of misunderstanding in Canada; it is in many ways difficult for Westerners to understand and appreciate the way in which central Canadians define the cultural composition of Canada, but it appears to be equally difficult for the citizens of Ontario and Quebec to comprehend and respect the angle of vision that Westerners employ to understand their community and its culture.

The principle of multiculturalism, then, is a useful aid, in that it helps us to appreciate the limitations of dualism as an approach to Canadian politics, limitations that will, in fact, be duplicated in some form by any coherent theory or explanatory principle. Each, if it is any good, is like a searchlight which brings some things of significance into bold relief and which helps us to explore unfamiliar territory. But like any bright light on a dark night, it blinds us to other things and may, if we are not careful, lead us to overlook things that should not be neglected. So it is with the theory of dualism. It is most appropriately treated as a tool to help us understand, and as a guide and reference point for some of our activities as citizens and political actors.

As an approach to Canadian politics, dualism has the signal virtue of directing our attention toward what is undeniably a major and continuing issue in Canadian social and political life. As we have indicated, there is massive evidence throughout our history to support the view that English-French relations cannot be ignored in any serious attempt to understand the Canadian people and the country's political institutions. The importance of dualism is undeniable, so much so that, if the country founders in the next few years, it will be the problems between French Canada and English Canada that will have brought it to the ground.

On the other hand, the theory does have its limitations. It is ambiguous in that it covers at least two distinguishable orientations, the institutional and the sociological, which lead in quite different directions and toward distinct conclusions. The particular version which one is employing needs to be specified and handled with care. More significant is the fact that, while the dualist approach encourages sensitivity to some aspects of Canadian life which are profoundly important, it has the effect of obscuring other aspects which are by no means inconsequential. We have attempted to show this by contrasting it with the theory of cultural pluralism.

There is even a geographical bias in the theory to which many Westerners in particular have taken exception; they argue, not without some justice, that to concentrate on French-English relations is to concentrate on central Canada, particularly Ontario and Quebec, at the expense of the Maritimes, the Prairies, and British Columbia. They claim that the idea of national unity should not be exhausted by the notion of achieving harmony between the two cultures, but should involve granting a square deal to the various regions and provinces of Canada. Freight rates, tariffs, agricultural and natural resource policy—these are the stuff of which national unity is made, or not made.

This last point suggests a broader limitation to which we might refer in closing. It applies to both the theory of dualism and the theory of multiculturalism. Each is concerned with culture and with the relationships between culture and political life. As such, each approaches the social world with a particular concern for such cultural artifacts as language, religion, ethnicity, and, broadly speaking, the constellation of attitudes and sentiments which cluster around these artifacts.

But there are many other avenues by which we may seek to understand the world in which we live. Several are explored in this volume, and they may depend little or not at all upon the cultural factors that have loomed so large in this chapter. It is, I think, unhelpful to deal with this variety of explanation by asserting that one approach is right and the others are wrong. Instead, it is wiser to think of these theories as one would tools in a box, indispensable aids in accomplishing certain things, but radically dependent upon the craftsman's intelligence and sensitivity. The effectiveness of a theory, or of a tool, will depend upon the user's sophistication, upon his skill in manipulating the instrument, his familiarity with the material he is working with, the clarity of his objectives, and a sense of limitation. These, I think, are some of the talents that it is important for the student of politics to possess. Certainly, it is in this spirit that one might properly employ the theory of cultural dualism as an approach to Canadian politics.

ENDNOTES

1. The Royal Commission on Bilingualism and Biculturalism, *Preliminary Report,* (Ottawa: Queen's Printer, 1965), p. 13.

2. The text of the British North America Act may be conveniently consulted as an appendix to R.M. Dawson, *The Government of Canada,* 4th ed., revised by Norman Ward (Toronto: University of Toronto Press, 1963). Part I of that volume provides a brief historical sketch of constitutional development in Canada while Part II examines the framework of the constitution itself.

3. Lovell Clark, ed., *The Manitoba School Question: Majority Rule or Minority Rights?* (Toronto: Copp Clark, 1968). This book provides a useful collection of contemporary and critical material on this issue.

4. Allan Smith, "Metaphor and Nationality in North America," *Canadian Historical Review* (September, 1970), p. 274.

5. For an example of the vigorous development of this line of thought, see P.E. Trudeau, "Federalism, Nationalism, and Reason," in *Federalism and the French Canadians* (Toronto: Macmillan, 1968).

6. The relationship between pluralism and dualism is discussed in D.R. Cameron, *Nationalism, Self-Determination and the Quebec Question* (Toronto: Macmillan, 1974), Ch. 7, esp. pp. 110-112.

SELECTED REFERENCES

There is extensive literature on Canadian dualism, particularly focusing on Quebec's position in Canada. The volumes listed below are examples of those a student will find most useful. Many contain excellent bibliographical information. The list should be regarded as illustrative rather than systematic.

BURNS, R.M., ed. *One Country or Two?* Montreal: McGill-Queen's University Press, 1971. A balanced and thoughtful collection of essays by a group of English-speaking Canadians reflecting on the question of Quebec separation and its consequences for Canada.

CAMERON, DAVID. *Nationalism, Self-Determination and the Quebec Question.* Toronto: Macmillan, 1974. Concentrates on nationalist theory, the principle of self-determination of peoples, and the way in which they bear on Quebec.

COMMISSIONER OF OFFICIAL LANGUAGES. *Annual Reports,* 1970-71 and onward. Ottawa: Information Canada. An annual review of the development of institutional bilingualism in Canada. Written in a lively and readable style.

COOK, RAMSAY. *Canada and the French-Canadian Question.* Toronto: Macmillan, 1967. This book and the one below are important collections of essays on nationalism and history in Quebec and Canada by one of the country's most distinguished English Canadian students of Quebec.

———. *The Maple Leaf Forever.* Toronto: Macmillan, 1971.

———., ed. *French-Canadian Nationalism.* Toronto: Macmillan, 1969. A useful anthology of work by French Canadians writing about themselves and their community.

DION, LÉON. *Quebec: The Unfinished Revolution.* Montreal and London: McGill-Queen's University Press, 1976. A collection of essays on Quebec by a prominent French-Canadian political scientist.

GRANATSTEIN, J.L., gen. ed. *Issues in Canadian History* Series. Toronto: Copp Clark. This series contains a substantial number of thin volumes which make such topics as the Manitoba school question, Louis Riel, Henri Bourassa, Quebec and Duplessis readily accessible to the student interested in the history of Canadian dualism.

MCROBERTS, KENNETH, AND DALE POSTGATE. *Quebec: Social Change and Political Crisis.* Toronto: McClelland and Stewart, 1976. An examination of Quebec politics and social life from the point of view of modernization and political development.

ROYAL COMMISSION ON BILINGUALISM AND BICULTURALISM. *Reports.* Ottawa: Queen's Printer.
Preliminary Report, 1965.
Book I, *The Official Languages,* 1967.
Book II, *Education,* 1968.
Book III, *The Work World,* 1969.
Book IV, *The Cultural Contributions of other Ethnic Groups,* 1969.
The B and B reports, published in the last half of the 1960s, are perhaps still the main empirical study for those who would explore further the themes of

this chapter. See also the studies of the Commission, recording research done on a variety of more specific topics.

SMILEY, DONALD V. *The Canadian Political Nationality.* Toronto: Methuen, 1967. This book and the one which follows are thoughtful, penetrating studies of contemporary Canadian federalism in the light of the challenge from Quebec.

———. *Canada in Question.* 2nd ed. Toronto: McGraw-Hill Ryerson, 1976.

TRUDEAU, P.E. *Federalism and the French Canadians.* Toronto: Macmillan, 1968. This is an indispensable source, for the obvious reason that Trudeau has been a central figure in recent Canadian public affairs, and for the less obvious reason that it is provocatively argued and explicitly related to an important intellectual tradition.

In addition, the serious student might wish to consult the following:

BOILY, ROBERT. *Québec, 1940-1969: Bibliographie.* Montreal: Les Presses de l'Université de Montréal, 1971.

COTNAM, JACQUES. *Contemporary Quebec: An Analytical Bibliography.* Toronto: McClelland and Stewart, 1973.

FULFORD, ROBERT, et al. *Read Canadian: A Book About Canadian Books.* Toronto: James, Lewis and Samuel, 1972.

12

Some Perspectives on Public Policy Analysis

V. Seymour Wilson*

Men at some time are master of their fates.
The fault, dear Brutus, is not in our stars,
But in ourselves, that we are underlings.
Julius Caesar
Act I Scene II

INTRODUCTION

A Story with a Moral

Many centuries ago, the Roman poet Ovid in the *Metamorphoses* chronicled a beautiful mythological tale which, to this day, has captured the imagination of romantic writers among us. Pygmalion was the king of Cyprus in Greek legend, and also an accomplished sculptor and a man of high moral values. Disgusted by the slatternly quality of the women in his kingdom, the bachelor monarch consistently refused to be tempted by their physical attributes, but instead carved for himself an ivory statue of a perfect woman with which he promptly fell madly in love. In answer to his fervent prayers for life to enter his creation, the goddess Aphrodite changed the ivory statue into a living creature called Galatea. Unlike so much of Greek mythology, this tale had a happy ending with Pygmalion marrying the virtuous and beautiful Galatea, who eventually bore him a fitting male heir to the throne of Cyprus. And they all lived happily ever after.

*Associate Professor, School of Public Administration, Carleton University.

This Greek myth embodies a series of life's analogies. There are, of course, the humorous ones. The brilliant Irish playwright, George Bernard Shaw, many decades ago wrote a successful play on this Greek theme, and the recent Broadway musical hit, *My Fair Lady*, is also based on Pygmalion mythology. For the purposes of this essay, however, I am going to be less sanguine but no less analogous. Like Pygmalion, many of us social scientists in Canada view our environment as capricious, "nasty and disputatious."[1] Similarly, we are like sculptors in that we create instruments to help us seek the objectives of knowledge, beauty, and truth. The creation of sculpture presumes purpose; so too does the construction of modes of social inquiry. The analogy can be extended even further, for the social scientists' search for knowledge is, in the final analysis, a Pygmalion search for the instruments that can be used to achieve human purpose.

But is this where the analogy ends? The discussion of public policy in the 1970s has seen a decided shift in emphasis: the arguments vacillate between the selection of priorities to controversy over the choice of goals. This is a shift from means to ends, from economics to political philosophy and sociology.[2] The beginning student of public policy could easily be bewildered by the complexities of the phenomena to be analyzed, studied, and understood. Indeed, it is legitimate for the student to ask whether any social science knowledge about public policy is worth studying. Given the chaos twentieth-century man has created for himself and his environment, has this knowledge been beneficial, or has it simply been snake oil bottled and sold to unsuspecting politicians and others involved in the policy-making process? Or, to put it another way, how good are our methodological constructs for understanding and providing answers to the problems of society such as pollution, conservation, or political stability? In the social scientists' quest for knowledge in a world of "blooming buzzing confusion" have we, in effect, created aphrodisiacs for ourselves, or have we, like Ovid's Pygmalion, constructed graven images that do have the potential of coming alive and enlightening us and our societies as well? Students of public policy analysis have increasingly realized that the problems they have been attempting to understand are terribly complex, and that previous solutions, based on the naive simplicity and hopeless unsophistication of these earlier understandings, must now be almost all relegated to the ragbag of historical curiosities. Will the experience with the social sciences then be, as the Pygmalion tale, happy ever after, or will it evolve into a typical Greek tragedy, leaving us all bleeding on the stage as the curtain falls on the last act?

These questions are not posed for melodramatic reasons. The dichotomies presented in my queries may be construed by some as naive Manichean perspectives, but this, I contend, is simply hindsight, for modern social sciences can be faulted for not having posed them decades ago. Events in North American society, particularly in the last decade, have raised serious questions about the human capacity to achieve social ends

and the role the social sciences have played in this quest. As Lance Liebman has expressed it, success after success:

> . . . stimulated the traditional hubris: We have done much, there-
> fore we can do anything, therefore we shall do it. . . . The idea was
> both that institutional arrangements could be imagined (indeed
> could be selected by reason) which would produce whatever social
> circumstances were desired, and that technology had infinite
> capacity to produce the good life, at low cost. The last decade has
> witnessed the steady tension between this powerful confidence
> and its antithesis: the idea that nothing works, that man has fallen
> and cannot be raised by conceptions of his own devising.
>
> A second theme is closely related to the first. This is the ten-
> sion between commitment to the economic market and dissatis-
> faction with the market's product. By 1960, economists had a-
> greed on a party line: The market is ideal for allocating resources,
> for determining what should be produced, from what raw mater-
> ials and for whose consumption. Performance of this task by the
> market is value-neutral, and except for an occasional obligation to
> deal with "externalities" (costs or benefits that the market cannot
> easily consider), all deviations from market allocation are mis-
> takes, for which consumers must pay. . . . Over the last ten years,
> this simple position has crumbled. Environmentalism expanded
> the small problem of externalities into a major challenge to the
> validity of market decisions. The words that have emerged are
> *power* and *influence.* The new recognition is that power and influ-
> ence flow from the fabric of social and economic institutions and
> ideas, and cannot be calibrated and redistributed as easily as dis-
> posable income.[3]

The sense of profound shock and dismay occasioned by this experience seems to have had a severe effect on the intellectual climate in North
America; in the 1970s one senses a readiness by scholars in the field of
public policy to explore, almost from scratch, the mechanisms of interactions among *economy, state,* and *society.* It is as if we knew nothing or very
little about the interactions between and among these systems. This, at
least, is how I choose to interpret the proliferation of detailed studies of
the determinants and consequences of public policies, a motley collection
of case studies and theorizing material, enough to scare all but the lion-
hearted among beginning students of public policy. More will be said on
this aspect a little later.

My task in this chapter is to explain what public policy is and how
focusing on it can help us to understand the reality of Canadian politics.
In the next section I will discuss definitions, dimensions of these definitions, and the concerns that, in my opinion, emerge from these dimensions. I will then expand, with illustrations, the definitions already given.
Having come thus far in exploring how we can better understand Cana-

dian politics by the study of public policy I will then concentrate on one of the major dimensions: the effect or impact aspects of public policy analysis. One of my major concerns here is relevance. At a time when the interrelationship and complexity of economic, social, and political questions has become so evident, we are confronted by an increasing intellectual reductionism in the social sciences—a body of knowledge that exists primarily, in my view, to help unravel the complexities of these questions. I explore this theme with illustrations from law, economics, and political science. Implicit in my discussion is a plea to the beginning student of public policy to avoid this reductionism by engaging in as much multidisciplinary work in the social sciences as possible. Finally there will be a discussion of some of the alleged limitations of public policy analysis and a few answers to these allegations.

CONCERNS, DEFINITIONS, AND CLARIFICATIONS

For the present, let us return to some basics: What is public policy and how should we study it? Simply stated, policies are actions taken by governments.[4] This very wide definition can accommodate actions by government to provide public services, the regulation of economic and social activity, the celebration of symbolic events that legitimize the political system, and the control of the policy-making process or other political actions. For purposes of this chapter the study of public policy (or public policy analysis) is the application of *social science knowledge* to public policy questions. More specifically, public policy analysis is concerned with how the policy-making process, including institutions and levels of government, determines policy, and with the impact or effect of policies once they have been adopted and implemented. The definition of the "how" of the policy-making process reminds me of the image of Janus—there are two faces to be viewed, studied, and understood. Beginning students in political science are all taught the familiar-sounding dictum that "politics determine policies." In this chapter, we intend to explore this theme by evaluating Canadian examples. But the opposite is equally true, namely, that policies determine politics, and this chapter will also explore this basic insight of policy analysis.

A second theme in our definition of policy analysis deals with the impact or effect of public policy making. As the Liebman quotation indicates, there has been a pervasive, apocalyptic gloom about policy makers' abilities to solve the complex issues of the day. Economic issues have come to the forefront for essentially one very important reason. Given an assumed scarcity of resources, policy makers must be vitally concerned with the relative and conflicting urgency of demands and the relative costs of production. Numerous specific social problems await solution in every Western, not to mention Third World, country—education, tax distribution, urban renewal, utilization of renewable and nonrenewable natural resources, housing, poverty, agricultural problems, the environment

—the litany seems almost endless. Given a surplus of problems and a scarcity of resources, the economists were bound to be interested and eager, and the politicians and their advisers quite naturally looked to them for bold and innovative solutions.

And the economists were not bashful in supplying that advice. For three decades after the Depression, economists in North America remained the most important group of social scientists from whom governments continually sought policy advice. Here in Canada, the 1940s and 1950s were the heyday of the federal deputy minister of finance, Dr. W.C. Clarke, and his boys; a coterie of brilliant economic and finanical advisers to the Canadian government. Consider, for example, the tremendous influence the economist Dr. W.A. MacIntosh exerted in the preparation and marketing of perhaps the most important economic policy proposals ever to have been prepared and instituted in this country, the White Paper on Employment and Income of 1945. In this document the Liberal government of the day committed itself to a unique and immutable set of centralist principles which it considered relevant to postwar economic policies. The consequences of this commitment are now Canadian political and economic history. But what is extremely interesting is Dr. MacIntosh's personal account of the genesis of these economic proposals:

> The suggestion . . . was my own. I had for some months been worried by the preoccupation of ministers with immediate matters, the uninformed proposals emerging from various sources, and the lack of comprehension among industrialists.

After having made suggestions to his minister, C.D. Howe, about the proposed scope and pattern of the economic commitment required of the Canadian government, MacIntosh was asked by Howe to prepare draft proposals. However, realizing the scope of these proposals, Howe, then minister of reconstruction and supply and one of the most dynamic and powerful ministers in the cabinet, got cold feet: "more than once . . . Mr. Howe had second thoughts. The scope was too broad; the commitments were too far-reaching, the language was not that of a plain engineer." Finally, however, Howe acquiesced:

> The White Paper as it appeared was written entirely by me except for two easily identifiable paragraphs added by Mr. Howe. *The scope and pattern were mine.* When I say the Paper was written by me, this covers all degrees of writing from genuine authorship to the work of an amanuensis. Such simple ideas as were expressed were drawn from a common pool, and I can recollect no basis for copyright.

Closeting himself in a boardroom with the three most influential members of the cabinet, Howe, St. Laurent, and Ilsley, Dr. MacIntosh, fully determined that "it [the White Paper] was to be no back room pronouncement issued by an information service, nor any hasty commitment of a minister sniffing the election air," proceeded to drill them in the nuances and full implications of the document. He was, he explained, "forearmed with a text in which [he] had underlined in different colours the special commitments, the general statements of policy, the implied commitments and all statements in the name of the Government. [He] *required specific approval to each, or alternatively amended wording.*" By the end of the day he had accomplished his mission, and the three ministers had obviously had enough lessons in economics from Professor MacIntosh:

> . . . they were visibly wearied by my schoolmasterish drill, but they approved the text for *formal acceptance by the Cabinet,* having made no change of substance . . . I knew I was accomplishing my prime object, viz., that no important paper should ever have gone to Cabinet with a fuller understanding and realization on the part of the key ministers of what they were committing the Government to.[5]

Economic policy advice in Canada had reached its apogee; it could not have been more influential. But those halcyon days of the influence of economists are now gone. Economic advice at the major levels of government in Canada today is, more than ever before, also concerned with the societal variables of power, influence, authority, and legitimacy—terms almost unknown in the economists' lexicon. Today, a senior economist like MacIntosh would have to spend many sleepless nights worrying much more about the intended and unintended scope of his economic proposals and their impact on Canadian society if adopted by the federal cabinet. Moreover, because these proposals must run the gauntlet of a number of power centers before adoption, our economist would also have to worry a great deal more about his federal counterparts and their ministers in certain strategic departments of government, about senior advisers ensconced in the privy council office, and last, but certainly not least, about the provincial governments and how they might react to these policies. The policy process has become much more complicated; bureaucratic and political forces must each get their share of the action. To quote Liebman once more on this change:

> When the economic market is rejected as a mechanism for translating individual decisions into collective ones, it can only be replaced by a *political* market supplemented by *bureaucratic* implementation. To pose the problem in simple terms, it is much easier to reject an economic market which places no value on pollution from a smoke stack than it is to decide how much consumers of the factory's product should be forced to pay for a cleaner production process. Similarly, it is easier to reject the distribution of income that would result from a free labor market than it is to invent either a theoretical standard of distribution commanding wide assent or a satisfactory political process for making a decision on "proper" distribution periodically.[6]

Strange as it may seem, this insight into the second part of the definition of public policy analysis—that is, the impact or effect of public policy—is one that has barely begun to receive systematic attention. For example, it is only in the last few years that a new conservatism has emerged in the social sciences, stressing the limits of social policy and the counterintuitive nature of social systems, and which warns against any such simple-minded onslaught on social problems as simply building houses and freeways to solve the urban crisis, or attempting to solve the welfare problem by simply increasing welfare payments to people without means of support. This literature has made us keenly aware of profound complexities of social engineering; we now know that too often new problems emerge when old problems get solved and that, because of some positive feedback loop, too often the old problems actually get worse as a result of these well-meaning but hopelessly unsophisticated attempts at social cures.

I shall not attempt in this chapter to deal with all the intricacies of this aspect of impact or effect. Part of the problem, however, is of vital concern and interest to beginning students of public policy and that is the relevance of social science to public policy analysis. A cursory reading of the Liebman quotation, and what I have already said about the impotency of so much public policy analysis and advice, should elicit, among others, the following elementary questions: Why should this state of affairs exist? Is there something inherently wrong with the social sciences if answers for our social problems are not adequately forthcoming? If so, why? In the latter part of this chapter, I will attempt to answer some of these questions. But before proceeding, a number of assumptions upon which this chapter is built should be made more explicit.

Some Assumptions

First of all, I make the important assumption that, by and large, the study of public policy belongs in that category Aristotle classified as "practical sciences," namely, investigations into the realm of practical reason.[7] Practical reason, in turn, assumes two crucial understandings: that theory and practice cannot be arbitrarily separated; and policy analysis cannot ignore the practical and moral consequences involved in both the areas of process and performance (or impact). Aristotle, therefore, always assumed that studying public policy could only be worthwhile if it is constantly related to action. For this reason, students of public policy can never be logically amoral; it is impossible to engage in a meaningful study of policy questions, or of politics in general, and ignore the practical and moral implications of one's endeavors.[8] The comedian, Tom Lehrer, neatly sums up the perils implicit here in his song about the ethics of the American rocket scientist, Wernher von Braun: "Once the rockets are up, who cares where they come down?/'That's not my department' says Wernher von Braun." In the physical sciences, the classic case at the moment is the tremendous progress being made in genetic engineering in molecular biology, and the bitter controversies and factional divisions this has caused.

Until recently, scientific advances have always been viewed in amoral terms but many prominent physical scientists are now publicly declaring that the development of such awesome technology carries with it uncomfortable responsibilities that can no longer be fobbed off by the scientific community as a societal problem. The theoretical vision of the policy theorist must be continually corrected by a vision that takes him back to the practical world in which men must make political judgments. As Michael Polanyi has so effectively argued, practical skills and practical experience embrace much more information and understanding than scientific experts are sometimes willing to concede and to heed.[9]

The second assumption is no less important than the first. Policy questions arise in the context of human purposes, needs, and aspirations. What this means in the study of public policy is that no one social science discipline can be a Pygmalion unto itself. What is more, this search must go beyond the questions of means-ends relationships; social scientists must also be prepared to examine critically the context in which the action is contemplated, and evaluate it from a moral standpoint. The study and practice of public policy must of necessity be multidisciplinary, and, furthermore, ethical assumptions must also be questioned and made explicit. Too often we forget this basic fact. Harry Boyle, the former chairman of the federal regulatory communications agency, the CRTC (Canadian Radio-television and Telecommunications Commission), made this essential point in his usual folksy way, and it is worth quoting him at length. Relating a recent experience involving an application before the Commission, the chairman declared:

> I've never in my life seen such an array of expertise. The leading lawyer in the case is now on the bench, a tremendous lawyer. They must have had 50 other people in there, executives, technical people, management. They'd prepared a massive bloody brief, and everyone looked at me as though I were a brass-bound idiot when I said my piece at the end of their presentation.

Like the innocent youngster gazing at the naked emperor, he continued:

> "Gentlemen, I congratulate you. I compliment you on your perfection and I compliment you on your technical and your financial skills. But I notice you have never mentioned one thing about what your project is going to do. You've never mentioned programming, you've never mentioned content. Can you tell me what this is going to do for humanity?"
>
> Well, that just stopped everything dead, and the lawyer said to me afterwards, "You shouldn't have asked that question. You know I couldn't answer it." But that's really the question you have to ask now. Are we just going to go on chasing after technology? What's it all going to do for humanity?[10]

Indeed, what is it all about if it is of no relevant value in seeking the larger answers we are ultimately after? Social scientists, like the technologists, financial experts, and lawyers in Mr. Boyle's scenario, must be continually reminded of this basic fact. Our quest for better professional expertise and methodological elegance might inadvertently make Pygmalions of us all, but with fatal consequences for our understanding and practice of public policy. This chapter, therefore, throws out a basic query: Are the methodological tools we use in the social sciences impediments to our deeper understanding of social reality? Does that famous sage, Pogo, sum up the predicament of the social sciences when he pronounces, "We is met the enemy and he is us"?

A third assumption addresses itself to the malaise of the 1970s outlined earlier in this chapter. The overly optimistic vision of the 1960s should not, in my view, be succeeded in the late 1970s by the opposite and equally unrealistic stance of intellectual constipation in the face of the complex problems confronting us. Making choices for others is at the very heart of public policy making, but it fits uneasily with the search for strict personal meaning and nonauthoritative behavior. The beginning student, in examining specific case studies of public policy situations, will soon find himself confronted with ethical questions: Given the facts, how would I react in making a decision? Will the decision be fair? Will it take into account as many of the complexities and nuances of meaning and implications as is humanly possible? Am I capable of appreciating these complexities and nuances?

It is easy to see how, in the face of these questions, the decision could be taken to make no decision at all on the matter. In a word, a nondecision has been made. Yet a continued disinclination to act only exacerbates rather than solves the problems. A vacuum could be created, passing on the problems to people and groups who are less fastidious about making choices for others.[11] This chapter is therefore action-oriented but with an emphasis on caution and humility. Commenting on the process whereby recondite theoretical tools in the social sciences are unwarily applied to solve complex sociological phenomena in our body politic, Daniel Patrick Moynihan sums up, with his customary eloquence, the limits and possibilities of our present knowledge in public policy analysis:

> Government . . . that would attempt many things very much needs the discipline of skeptical and complex intelligence repeatedly inquiring "What do you mean?" and "How do you know?" . . . The consequence of such a sensibility is not so much great *caution* as great *care* . . . [for] the great questions of government have to do not with what *will* work but what *does* work. The best of behavioural sciences would in truth be of no great utility in a genuine political democracy, where one opinion is as good as another, and where public policies emerging for legislative-executive collaboration will constantly move in one direction, then another, following such whim, fashion, or pressure that seems uppermost at the moment.
>
> What government and the public most need to know in the aftermath of this process is whether there was anything to show for the effort, and if so, what. Causal insights of the kind that can lead to the prediction of events are interesting, absorbing, but they are hardly necessary to the management of a large, open political system. All that is needed is a rough, but hopefully constantly refined, set of understandings as to what is associated with

what. A good deal of medicine is no more than this, yet people are healthier as a result, and so might be the consequence for the body politic.[12]

Finally, one caveat is in order here. Earlier in this chapter, I spent some time arguing about the defects of the social sciences and the possibilities of a multidisciplinary perspective, or, as it is called in Canada, a political economy perspective. The beginning student should assume that I am referring to some adequate exposure and study of economics, political science, law, and psychosociological phenomena, and the ability to bring these insights together to study and apply to public policy. A multidisciplinary perspective for studying public policy means much more than this, however. Scholars must do some serious preparatory work in mapping the parameters for formulating basic questions about the relationships between economic and political systems; the flexibility of the concepts, the variability of the environments explicitly or implicitly pictured in questions about systems' interrelationships, and the flows of causation of interposing concepts in analysis. Some of this is already being done, as evidenced in some of my footnotes. However, I shall have more to say about these preparatory labors a little later in the chapter. Every human field of endeavor has its problems, and the social sciences have even more than their fair share. The beginning student should, therefore, not worry about the magnitude of these problems now, for, as he proceeds in study, there will be ample time to confront them.

POLITICS AND POLICIES

In a remarkably candid lecture given at Acadia University, Nova Scotia, on February 8, 1977, Robert Stanfield, the former federal leader of the Progressive Conservative party, had this to say about the decision-making process at the federal level:

> Parliament is not fitted for controlling the kind of all-pervasive government we have today. It cannot cope with it effectively. . . . Frankly, I do not know how the House of Commons can be restored to effective supervision of the government; how we can restore government really responsible to Parliament. . . . Consequently, more and more is for all practical purposes being decided by and implemented by the bureaucracy. This is inevitable in view of the broadening scope of federal government activities.[13]

Mr. Stanfield's speech on the Canadian Parliament and its role in the public policy process in part mirrors the basic assumption in traditional writings on liberal democratic politics, that the legislature is the keystone of our democratic system.

This view has, of course, been increasingly challenged by both academics and politicians, as Mr. Stanfield's remarks testify. As further examples, consider the views of Professor J.M. Mallory, given to the prestigious Royal Society of Canada three years ago:

> . . . in spite of universal suffrage, the mass of citizens is perhaps as far away from the real decisions of government as they were two hundred years ago, and the cabinet system provides strong institutional barriers to the development of more democratic ways of doing things.[14]

Parliament under a majority government is thereafter described as "a groaning beast of burden for the government's legislative system."[15] One opposition member of Parliament went even further in his pointed criticisms of the Canadian public policy process. Douglas Roche argued that:

> Our political process is scandalously deficient in resolving problems and creating a society of peace and social justice. . . . The key issues today are not being settled in Parliament. Federal-provincial conferences settle the price of oil and gas as well as apportion the cost of social progress. The federal bureaucracy settles the big spending questions in defence and CIDA.[16]

The little empirical work done in Canada on the topic of political influence on public policy making generally agrees with the views expressed above, although some qualifications have recently appeared in the literature. One aspect of this debate involves the extent to which determinants of government expenditures on various programs have been affected by political considerations.[17] Economist Richard Bird, in addressing himself to this problem, finds that the study of the determinants of government expenditure cannot be in any way conclusive because of major gaps in social science knowledge. There is, for example, an almost total absence of studies examining the relationship of political factors to either total levels of government expenditures or differential expenditures in different policy areas.[18]

Since Bird's study, however, Falcone and Whittington have argued that political variables do not explain much of the variation in government output. They qualify their assertions, however, by acknowledging that their negative results may be attributable to defects in their approach, such as their inability to measure bureaucratic influence, or their assumptions about the declining or noninfluential role of Parliament in the policy-making process. Dale Poel, in his comparative study of a large range of policies across Canada, found that both socioeconomic and political variables are important determinants of provincial legislation.[19]

Clearly the empirical evidence remains inconclusive. Comparative evidence from other countries, however, shows that the questions of political influence on public policy formation can be classified on an ascending scale. As Heidenheimer, Heclo, and Adams point out:

> Sometimes the counterbidding of parties in elections contributes to a "higher level of public partisanship," but has little identifiable

effect on the creation or adjustment of policies. At other times parties contribute by organizing general predispositions and moods, facilitating the adoption of reform plans worked out by others. Party competition can also lead to unplanned searches for policy alternatives, which may turn out to be productive if linked to bureaucratic supports. In some reform struggles, finally, parties may go beyond facilitation to actual creation of policy choices.[20]

The attempt to measure "general predispositions and moods" which make it easy to adopt party policy proposals will undoubtedly be a difficult task but the few case studies we have in Canada dealing with political influence on public policy issues seem to confirm the conclusions of Poel and Heidenheimer. My own case study on the adoption of language policy at the federal level, for example, indicates that political influences from the prime minister, the party, and Parliament, were substantive and decisive in the adoption of a major and enduring policy stance on the issue in the 1960s and 1970s.[21]

Another very important illustration of politics affecting policies is the manner in which the concept of cooperative federalism was developed and put into effect in Canada in the early 1960s. By the late 1950s Ottawa's centralist policies, developed during and after World War II, and reflected in the MacIntosh approach to economic policy formation described earlier in the chapter, were facing serious challenges from the provinces, particularly Quebec and Ontario.[22] Thrown out of office in 1957, the Liberal party was faced with the difficult task of continuing to provide some measure of federal presence throughout the country, while at the same time accommodating Quebec's demands for greater provincial autonomy. Political expendiency, therefore, dictated that the appeal to the country should be two-pronged: an appeal to the have-not provinces with a promise of more funds from the federal treasury (called equalization payments), while at the same time allowing provinces to opt out of shared-cost programs, an arrangement geared to appeal to Quebec which was concerned about federal interference in fields of provincial jurisdiction. To quote the Liberal campaign pamphlet, *Policies of the Liberal Party,* published for the 1963 general election:

> . . . A new Liberal government will make equalization payments which will bring the other provinces up to the level of the richest in revenue per head from shared taxes. If some provinces wish, they should be able to withdraw, without loss, from joint programs which involve regular expenditures by the federal government and which are well established. In such cases, Ottawa will compensate provinces for the federal share of the cost, by covering its own direct taxes and increasing equalization payments. This will be done also if some provinces do not want to take part in new joint programs.

Thus cooperative federalism was born and given full legitimacy by party ideologues writing numerous "think-tank" pieces on the topic.[23] At the same time, the Liberals did not entirely abandon their former position of, as John Meisel puts it, "a national cast of mind." Hence their election proposals for a Canada Pension Plan, youth allowances, student loans, municipal winter works assistance—a veritable penumbra of policies to accommodate all points of view in the country. The rest, of course, is now history, for Canadians received all these election promises, in one form or another.[24] Politics did determine the policies to be followed.

Recently students of public policy analysis have been made aware of the fact that the exact opposite is also true; namely, that sometimes policies determine the politics to be followed. In other words, policy in this case becomes the independent variable and politics the dependent. Theodore Lowi, the most important exponent of this point of view, argues that "a political relationship is determined by the type of policy at stake, so that for every type of policy there is likely to be a distinctive type of political relationship."[25] Although other social scientists have referred to this insight previously, to my knowledge Lowi is the first social scientist to develop it as a dominant perspective.

Lowi essentially argues that we should discover the structural characteristics or stable patterns of politics common to different types of policy in order to pinpoint the normal patterns associated with various expected outcomes. In other words, policy is a cause of politics. Lowi's work in public policy becomes very important for students because it enables us to understand and to differentiate what part of political behavior (dependent variable) is structured by the policy (independent variable), and what remaining variation of policy may be due to other factors such as resources, goals, and tactics. Thus we will have isolated that part of the variation due to policy. However, Lowi argues that to understand fully the reality of the policy process we should encompass both aspects of the policy-politics equation (politics→policy, and policy→politics).[26]

This is a very simple outline of a complex but extremely suggestive line of analysis in public policy. An example of this theoretical insight occurring in practical politics in Canada is furnished by the experience of the Local Initiatives Program (LIP) and Opportunities for Youth (OFY) policies in the early 1970s.[27] When these programs appeared in 1971 they and the government were the subjects of much public derision. John Meisel, in his analysis of the 1972 federal election, assessed the programs as intelligent, competent, innovative, and conceived independent of the whims and caprices of the political environment. However, both policies:

> . . . became an electoral liability not so much because of what they were but because they were not made acceptable and were thus permitted to contribute to the impression many had of the government as an inefficient organization spending public funds on the mindless, and even dangerous schemes of young and/or irresponsible people.[28]

Space precludes a full examination of these public policies, but both Best and Blake indicate that for the first year of LIP's operation, (1971-72), both citizen participation and bureaucratic procedures were carefully devised and approved to reduce the possibility of politics interfering in the projects approval processes. By 1974, however, this appeared to be no longer the case as the politicians discovered the great political benefits inherent in LIP in their constituencies. To quote Donald Blake on this point:

> There seems to be evidence that partisan considerations may have influenced allocations during the second and third years of the program. Douglas Fisher in one of the more elaborate examinations of the 1972-73 program notes that (prior to extensions) "constituencies with sitting Liberal members averaged $781,000 in LIP grants, Tory ridings averaged $454,000, NDP ridings $529,000 and Creditistes' ridings $813,00." Not content with that evidence, he probed a little deeper and discovered that in all provinces except Alberta and Manitoba, Liberal ridings did better on average than did those held by members of other parties. In Alberta, where all seats were held by the Conservatives, no comparisons are possible, but in Manitoba Liberal ridings were second to those held by the NDP, a finding which Fisher attributes to the aggressiveness of Stanley Knowles whose riding received $1.6 million. Calculations omitting Knowles' riding put the Liberals in first place. Similar questions were raised about the 1973-74 program. In addition, in each program year isolated charges have been made about interference of politicians on behalf of or in opposition to particular projects.[29]

Using multiple regression techniques and controlling for economic need (unemployment and educational levels, the presence of Canada's indigenous populations), Blake, allowing for a few cautionary caveats, found that per capita riding allocations in 1972-74 were positively related to support for the Liberal party. Furthermore, what is even more interesting is that certain ridings held by cabinet ministers and Quebec Liberals received a further bonus of LIP funds. The independent variable of policy devised in 1971 was certainly, by 1974, determining the nature of political activity surrounding it.

Another important insight derived from studying public policy and its relationship to Canadian politics is the connection between understanding a public policy problem and motivation to attack and solve it. Karl Marx once said, in an obvious reference to his belief that understanding precedes motivation, that "mankind always takes up only such problems as it can solve." The style of public policy formation in the 1960s was too often the other way around. Flushed with the successes of our technological endeavors every problem seemed to be amenable to instant solution: "If we can put a man on the moon, why can't we solve the problem of the ghetto?"[30] And, to return to my opening comments, the human capacity to achieve social ends seemed to have infinite possibilities.[31] Technique and rational human reasoning were the yardsticks for this upward and onward road to progress.

We now know better in the 1970s. As Nathan Glazer reminds us.

> . . . social policy itself, in almost every field, creates new and, I would argue, unmanageable demands. It is illusory to see social policy only as making an inroad on a problem; there are dynamic aspects to any policy, such that it also expands the problem, changes the problem, generates further problems. And for a number of reasons, social policy finds it impossible to deal adequately with these new demands that follow the implementation of the original measures.[32]

Part of the problem can be laid at the doorstep of the typical North American confidence in rationality and its usual accompanying impulsive pseudo-solutions to all public policy questions. That is another theme by itself, fit for another chapter. In this chapter, however, I shall limit myself to what I consider another fundamental part of the problem; namely, the increasing reductionism in the social sciences creating intellectual blinkers within each field, and an inability to see the whole of the problem in all its ramifications—economic, sociopsychological, and political. In the words of the popular dictum: "We are unable to see the forest for the trees." I shall return to this theme later.

But to continue our discussion of the style of public policy in which motivation outruns understanding. In a very provocative and perceptive essay on environmental policy making, economist Anthony Downs has elaborated on this phenomenon, so prevalent in the recent policy-making style on the North American continent. He identifies what he calls the "issue-attention cycle" in politics, and he distinguishes five phases of that cycle:

1. The "pre-problem stage" during which the problem exists, but not much public attention is paid to it.

2. Then comes "alarmed discovery and euphoric enthusiasm," when the problem is considered a priori fully solvable "if only we devote sufficient effort to it."

3. In the next phase, it is realized that solving the problem may be costly and goes against the immediate interests of large and influential groups of people.

4. As a result of this realization, there is then a gradual decline of intense public interest, which is helped by the providential appearance of another problem that will occupy the limelight.

5. Finally, there is the "post-problem stage" which differs from the "pre-problem stage" in that a number of efforts and agencies that have been set up to solve the problem in Phase 2 continue to exist and may actually make some quiet progress.[33]

Moreover, according to Downs, once the problem has passed through the cycle, it will continue to receive a modicum of public attention. It seems to me that Downs's paradigm, with suitable modifications for the Canadian environment, can give excellent insights into the vicissitudes of many policies vigorously pursued and then laid peacefully to rest in Canada during the last decade. An illustration of this is the considerable interest and optimism engendered by urban policy solutions in the 1960s: the problem existed for years without adequate attention; Mr. Paul Hellyer's highly visible task force of experts headed by himself sought quick solutions to the problems; that was followed by Mr. Hellyer's resignation from the Trudeau cabinet and his bitter attacks on the government inaction on urban policy; and finally we have the bureaucratization of the problem in a ministry.[34] Undergirding this whole cycle are two themes I have continually stressed: the optimism or overconfidence that all social problems are solvable, and the blinkers of experts who find technical solutions to public policy questions in complete isolation from other realities.

Consider, for example, the views of economist N.H. Lithwick who was one of the chief architects of the "post-problem stage" of the urban crisis phenomenon in Canada (Stage 5 of Downs's cycle). In building the bureaucracy he was in complete command of the economic understanding of the urban problem but, in his words, "incredibly naive" about the political realities of urban problems in Canada. Thus he confesses:

> Certainly I was excessively optimistic about the prospects for governmental reform both internally in the Federal Government, and in the extent to which the Federal Government would move to establish a national framework within which it would operate. The kind of organization I helped set up reflects this. . . . What we sought was a distinctly professional, non-bureaucratic agency, where the necessary cross-disciplinary, comprehensive approaches to urban policy could be taken. . . . That these plans were overly-ambitious is attested to by the fact that within six months I came to the conclusion that they would not work.[35]

Urban problems within our constitutional framework are essentially a provincial responsibility. Also, given the political climate in Canadian federalism and the growth of the provinces' political power during the last two decades, it is no surprise that political realities would preclude or make exceedingly difficult any strong federal initiatives on an urban crisis. Any second-year student in political science would and should be aware of these basic realities of Canadian politics.

To sum up so far, I have argued that public policies are, broadly defined, a variety of actions taken by government. Public policy analysis is concerned with how the policy-making process, including institutions and levels of government, determine policy, and the impact or effect of policies that are adopted and implemented. Thus, to understand how the study of public policy can help us to comprehend the reality of Canadian politics we must of necessity be students of public policy analysis.

The how of public policy analysis compels us to look at policy making from two dimensions. One dimension is almost axiomatic: policy patterns reflect the distribution of power and influence within the polity, forcing us to explore in what ways politics affect policy. While this is undoubtedly true, and I have given a few illustrative examples, it is equally true that another dimension reveals that, in a great deal of politics, the pre-existing definition of the policy is the framework within which the actors attempt to influence government. In a word, policy also affects politics, and I have attempted to illustrate why and how this second relationship occurs.

The question of impact or effect forces us to be concerned with the relevance of policy advice. While this is not the only concern, it is, in my view, one of the major concerns, and I have chosen to concentrate on exploring some of its implications. During the past decade Canadian public discourse has moved toward confronting real social issues, but the social sciences have too often been found wanting in their contributions to this discourse. It is at this juncture between impact or effect and the questions of relevance that we confront serious difficulties of inadequate knowledge and intellectual reductionism on a discipline basis. It is to an exploration of this theme that I now address myself.

POLICY ANALYSIS, RELEVANCE, AND THE SOCIAL SCIENCES

As we enter the late 1970s, it is my observation that the social sciences are becoming increasingly so segmented and specialized that the public decision maker who turns to them for much-needed advice risks "either hearing little but noise or receiving 'fractional advice to deal with whole policy' as William T.R. Fox expresses the problem presented by the natural sciences."[36]

David B. Truman, in my view, raises a significant aspect of the problem of relevance when he pinpoints the important dimension of the "degree of effectiveness in focusing or merging the technical elements of these sciences so the gap between them and the policy problem as a complex whole is reduced to minimal and hopefully manageable proportions."[37] But, one might sensibly ask, why is this of relevance to the beginning student of public policy? Should this not be a problem for the experts who should be expected to bridge the gaps of the disciplines in presenting public policy analysis and advice to senior advisers and our political masters?

I personally could not agree more. However, to bridge gaps, one must have some understanding of the modes of analysis and outstanding intellectual problems in at least one or two of the other social sciences, apart from one's specialty. The traditional multidisciplinary perspective in Canada has been political economy, but in recent years we have witnessed, as Alan Cairns expresses it, the "conspicuous neglect of previous Canadian scholarship, including works in the political economy tradition, the existence of which is virtually unknown to possibly the majority of English Canadian political scientists who are cut off from the domestic past of their discipline."[38] Implicit in my examination of the problems of reductionism in all the social sciences is a plea for beginning students to commence multidisciplinary studies as soon as possible in one or two other areas of the social sciences, apart from their own specializations, to diminish this problem of reductionism and "fractional advice to deal with whole policy."

The Case of Economics and Law

A multidisciplinary perspective was considered a necessity decades ago when the social sciences were still in their infancy in Canada. Political scientist, Donald V. Smiley, provides us with an explanation for this:

> Public problems which agitated and continue to agitate Canadians—problems of external trade and natural resource development, of immigration and transportation and fiscal policy and so on—almost invariably presented themselves with both political and economic aspects, and if we add the complications of a division of powers between federal and provincial governments, usually a legal-constitutional dimension as well. Thus Canadian scholars discovered early what has become the necessary working assumption of those now studying the developing nations, i.e. that the disciplinary boundaries between economics, politics, and sociology could be maintained only in those geographical areas where there existed a relatively high degree of sub-system autonomy in respect to economy, polity and society.[39]

Smiley is, in effect, reaffirming a basic fact: the interrelations between legal-political and socioeconomic processes are indeed the most fundamental areas of concentration in public policy studies. Thus, political economy was revitalized as a necessary focus in public policy studies, and so too were the legal-political aspects of constitutional studies, delegated legislation, and administrative law. Such illustrious scholars as Harold Innis, Frank R. Scott, Alexander Brady, Robert A. Mackay, W.A. Mackintosh, R.M. McIver, J.A. Corry, C.B. Macpherson, and W.A. Angus represent a small portion of that earlier rostrum of social scientists who recognized completely why this approach to understanding public policy was so necessary.

Political economy studies and legal constitutional analyses represented a substantial core of the social sciences in the 1930s, this being highlighted by the professional contributions made to the famous Royal Commission on Dominion-Provincial Relations (the Rowell-Sirois Commission) in the late 1930s. Political economy drew heavily on the inquiries of both orthodox neoclassical microeconomics, more commonly called market economics, and institutional or macroeconomics.[40]

Economic choice, from a microeconomic perspective, conceives government as an economic variable, its decisions and activities are analyzed in terms of a maximizing model in which individuals and groups attempt to maximize their private welfare. Government's performance is therefore assessed in terms of the market economy, dominated by studied calculations of advantage: constitution making, the politics of internal bureaucratic organizations, and, indeed, general political activity, are all viewed as maximizing processes in a market economy.

Institutional economics, on the other hand, was much more concerned with macroeconomic problems: the organization, control, and evolution of the economic system, whether it be market or nonmarket. Chief among these concerns for political economists were the factors and forces governing the distribution of economic welfare (the controversial field of welfare economics), and the historical development of societal institutions such as property, corporation, and the state. This tradition in economics produced an understanding of the impact of government in the economic system, analyses of capitalism and Marxism, and theories of the economic system viewed as a system of organization and control.

The study of law also added realism to public policy analysis by stressing the procedural and structural aspects of government. Moreover, it added a realistic consideration as to why governmental structures evolved in the manner they did, and how society, even with all its imperfections, coped with the operative aspects of such concepts as the public interest, justice, equality, injustice, and so on. Furthermore, public law gave students of public policy a strong sense of the limitations of government action: why, for example, the Canadian federal government cannot single-handedly confront the multitudinous problems involved in urban policy, or education, or health and welfare. An understanding of law, as it relates to the regulatory activities of government, gave public policy students some knowledge of the substantive policy areas of antitrust, utilities and communications regulation, conservation, and taxation, to name a few areas.

But there were profound problems, both in law and economics, which have been exacerbated partly because of academic reductionism in both disciplines. Let us briefly look at law first. Harry Jones, in an excellent article on this subject some time ago, argued that while the broader aspects of public policy may be of some interest to some law professors, the majority of lawyers, as in the incident related by Harry Boyle, are mere technicians.[41] Because of its primary interest in disputes and the settlement of disputes, the study of law tends to be "fact-minded and problem oriented." This, he argues, is evidenced by a lawyer's distrust of generalizations, and by the overwhelming inclination of research in law to select problems already shaped by society. Moreover, few law professors know the methodology of empirical research: their preparatory research labors are mainly concentrated in searching library sources and precedents, logical analysis, and armchair speculation. The lawyer's background in training, and, after graduation, socialization in his profession, lead to a strong conservative bias, an exaggerated reliance on stability, and a penchant for the status quo.

Economics, however, has suffered from an entirely different malaise which, interestingly enough, has led to some of the same symptoms exhibited by law. The oldest of the social sciences prided itself on its rigorous, precise, pragmatic methodology which has led to a highly developed theoretical structure based on equilibrium analysis. Adam Smith's murky theorizing in political economy had been finally replaced by the methodological rigor advocated by the likes of Alfred Marshall. True, other social scientists kept insisting that the behavioral assumptions of conventional economic theory—maximizing behavior, rationality, hedonism—and the main components of "economic man," on which the theorizing of economics essentially rested, were fatally oversimplified.[42] These criticisms were, however, simply ignored, but like Banquo's ghost, the consequences of this neglect have been increasingly disturbing the neat, elegant world of neoclassical economics in particular.

The first major problem faced by economics was this increasing distance between the real world of economic allocation and valuation, and the economist's almost total preoccupation with equilibrium analysis and quantitative procedures. Without in any way denying the real advances made by quantification, nevertheless this almost total preoccupation with scientific method, rigor, and precision led to the unconscious acceptance of equilibrium analysis as normatively good in economics because in physics, from whence it came, it was natural. Therefore, as intellectual refinements of recondite theoretical tools proceeded, there was a corresponding separation of economic and political concerns which, economist Richard Bird contends, denied

> . . . everything we think we know about the interdependence of human behaviour and is refuted by a good deal of evidence. In contrast to this position, one can, I think, argue that the day of the analytical political economist—who is concerned with the systematic analysis of both economic and political aspects of non-market decisions—has arrived, and that the field of political economy (or policy analysis), after some years in the professional doldrums is slowly regaining, because of its sheer importance in the lives of all of us, the intellectual status needed to attract capable people to it.[43]

But what were some of these refinements that brought about this separation of economic and political considerations? Both market and institutional economics do not begin with human relationships but rather stress individual things and people. The individualistic ethic prevails, for the individual is presumed to be motivated continually to maximize his utility—a purely self-interested assumption. Moreover, a fetish is made of each economic commodity, treating it as having an inherent value aside from the particular social relations involved in its production and consumption. As economist Michael Reagan points out in his book, *The Managed Economy,* this reification of economic concepts, in this particular instance property, stresses qualities that are in effect absent; property is not tangible but a socially defined bundle of rights based on human relationships. Thus, "the hired managers of property . . . exercised rights of use and disposition that in fact affected not just the property holders, but also the employees, the consuming public and the community in which the firm was located."[44] A related problem, of course, is that the neoclassical economists assume that individual consumer preferences are somehow given, but never consider how society shapes these preferences. In contrast, political scientists would never make such assumptions—hence the proliferation of attitudinal and socialization studies in the discipline.

Another major problem of neoclassical economics is its complete dependence on the harmonious and optimal outcome of market competition. Optimal equilibrium in economics suffers from exactly the same problems as functionalism in political and sociological thought; there is an emphasis on status quo conditions in society, and a very pronounced bias against societal pressures for change in the overall system. As economist Sherman Krupp puts it:

> Functional theory commonly predisposes analysis to those equilibrating forces which make for cooperation and harmony. . . . The stress of functional theories on goal-maintenance markedly reduces their capacity for dealing with conflict-ridden systems.[45]

Krupp argues that this overwhelming stress in the neoclassical paradigm, given economics' natural bent toward stability in the system, leaves no room for the analysis of power or conflict in the societal system. This is a fact of which economist John Kenneth Galbraith makes much in his 1972 presidential address to the American Economic Association. Neoclassical economics, he argues "offers no useful handle for grasping the economic problems that now beset the modern society. [It thus] destroys its relation with the real world."[46]

The above assumptions, and many others not enumerated here, lead to some readily admitted biases by leading economists, biases that make these otherwise eminent men look foolish in the eyes of the decision makers they advise. For example, a leading economist, George Stigler, is proudly on record arguing that economic training is by nature conservative, and young minds in training are captured by this orientation of the discipline. The young economist, he argues, is "drilled in the problems of all economic systems and the methods by which a price system solves these problems. . . . He cannot believe that a change in the form of social organization will eliminate basic economic problems."[47]

Another example is supplied by Professor Gordon Tullock in his important book, *The Logic of the Law.* Tullock essentially argues in this study that legal rights should not be decided by ethics, but by efficiency to expedite the legal process.[48] The logical conclusion of this argument is that many of the procedural safeguards we do have under the law at present will and should be eliminated in the name of efficiency if Professor Tullock had his way.

In many instances, the assumptions about rational behavior border on the ludicrous. Let us take a commonplace example: discrimination in hiring. If one notes that little hiring of women or minorities such as blacks or Indians has taken place in our liberal democratic society and asks why and what will the consequences of this be for our society, a leading economist like Milton Friedman, for example, would answer in the following vein: If an employer does not choose the most qualified people because of his irrational preferences, then he will lose money, and competition will put him out of business. Ergo, capitalism automatically eliminates discrimination and produces the best of all possible worlds sooner or later.

Economist Mancur Olson sums up this predicament rather neatly when he states that "economic (more precisely microeconomic) theory is in a fundamental sense more nearly a theory of rational behaviour than a theory of material goods."[49]

The Case of Political Science

Part of the foregoing comments represents somewhat of an indictment of conventional economics. It is contended that a large part of that discipline tended to limit itself to a consideration of the economic impacts or consequences of public policies, with policies being taken as given. Only incidentally has economics as a discipline involved itself with the political determinants of policy or the political consequences of economic policies.

The same can be said of the behavioral approach in political science. Those political scientists who wished to study individual decisions, specific personality factors, and other individual causal factors behind individual political decisions found precious little in studies on the constitution or in the cumulative precedents of *stare decisis* in law. They therefore started a revolution that, according to Theodore Lowi, has had some unforeseen consequences in the understanding of public policy:

> Individuals in their politics do not directly experience constitutionality and standing to sue, or agency and delegation or statutes and administrative rulings, or collective responsibility. Therefore, it was probably inevitable that the public law aspects of traditional knowledge would have to be thrown out altogether. They, in fact, were thrown out, and were only brought back in through the study of the individual behaviors of judges.
>
> Justifiable as that . . . may have been, something indispensable was sacrificed in the larger framework of political science in which behavioralism was only one source of theory. One might, for example, still ask whether it is possible to talk about public policy at all without some knowledge of the oil industry, without some grasp of how members of the chemical industry compete, without some sense of why and how the agriculture industry was politicized. . . . It would have been indispensable—why not now—to know a little something about property and capitalism. It is also difficult to understand how one can speak of policy and policy analysis without some sense of law and of the laws that make big policy. . . . Policy must have something to do with the long-range intentions of governments and government agencies, public commitments that are going to be implemented, however crudely with inducements and sanctions over a lot of space, time and population. It may be more difficult to be precise and systematic about this level of knowledge, but our knowledge of this level is not improved by rejecting it in favor of micropolitical approaches merely in order to get more systematic analysis.[50]

I shall not attempt to construct here a list of benefits political science has derived from the behavioral persuasion. Other chapters in this book bear, I think, ample testimony to the fact that the changes introduced in the study of politics, while perhaps necessary, were hardly as momentous as the original foes feared and the behavioralists hoped. For example, the behavioralist persuasion had nothing to offer political economy, the precise area where public policy studies have such crucial concerns and queries. The very eclectic nature of this meeting between politics and economics would have fostered an "academic concern with the inextricably related political economic dimensions of public policy in contradistinction, so far as political scientists are concerned, to our recent preoccupations with the input side of the political process."[51] In other words, it is being claimed that this tradition would dispose us to ask fundamental questions concerning the nature of both outputs and outcomes in the system. David Easton attempts to differentiate between the two:

> In formulating systems approach I have also suggested that we need to distinguish carefully between *outputs* and *outcomes*. . . . Recent concern for the generation of social indicators to estimate more reliably the effects of outputs on bringing about changes in society—of crime, poverty, safety, political apathy and involvement, health and the like—represents a first step toward formally differentiating outputs (laws) from outcomes (social effects).[52]

The questions involved in social effects coincide with Harold Lasswell's "who gets what, when, how," but it is clear from the literature how little theorizing and research from a political economy perspective is actually directed to these notable universal choices. Trained political economists with a strong orientation toward economics as a science of valuation could identify and measure the incidence of benefits that governments create and distribute, which is no easy task. Some distributive public goods are, by definition, impossible to measure in distributive terms, but nevertheless the attempts to measure them can and should open up new vistas of political and economic understanding.

Let us take an example. One reason for measuring received benefits is to give another dimension to the power attribution debates in political science and political sociology. Perhaps it might be more instructive to identify power structures by determining who gets what and how much of the outputs than to expend a great deal of intellectual effort in trying to identify the power structures in society by determining who governs. Indeed, another dimension of power is to identify not the decision makers per se but who gets how much from the system. New vistas as to why and how this is so will, then, certainly be crucial. If this is going to be the case then new techniques of power attribution, such as budgetary and cost-benefit analysis, will complement the conventional interviewing schedules and other tools used in behavioral studies.

In the postbehavioral period, much has been written in political science to show the importance of both values and facts in social science, but nowhere do we see a thriving body of systematic, explicit normative propositions developed for those who wish to receive such advice. Already a small beginning has been made in economics. Those economists concerned with welfare economics and public finance are beginning to develop a systematic body of knowledge dealing with economics as a science of valuation. The political scientist, Aaron Wildavsky, thought it prudent to warn political scientists that this impetus is bound to "swallow up political rationality . . . if political rationality continues to lack trained and adept defenders" in political science.[53]

Thus political scientists with sound training in economics and law should have a lot of relevant things to say about conflicting demands in the polity. How a person or a society should rank efficiency against other values is something economists have traditionally often ignored, but political scientists know this area as their stock in trade. At least they should. According to Austin Ranney, most political scientists in North America "have focussed their professional attention mainly on the processes by which public policies are made and have shown relatively little concern with their contents."[54] This is undoubtedly true. Traditionally, political scientists have had little interest in or knowledge of substantial policy fields. Economics, or, with the exception of political science, the rest of the social sciences, for that matter, is a discipline well-known for the development of content expertise: public finance, agricultural economics, labor economics, natural resources, welfare economics, public utilities, and so on. Economists will continue to dominate in public policy content not only because they have something to say to government, which, I have argued, is a deficient contribution at any rate, but because political science of the 1970s has virtually abdicated the field entirely to them. Public policy content expertise seems to be avoided or, if convenient, shunted off to the subfield of public administration, recently described in a prominent Canadian political science publication as a "hole."[55]

What, then, is to be done? I have tried to argue that the questions of public policy must rely on the social sciences for meaningful sustenance, despite the fact that each area of the social sciences has problems. Nevertheless, multidisciplinary paradigms, techniques, and so forth must be marshaled to enlighten us as to who gets what, when, how, and why. Lowi's questions along these lines are very suggestive because they focus on the integrity of political science qua political science, yet they strongly suggest the need for a multidisciplinary orientation. First, what is the policy as a policy? That is, what is a policy, defined not in terms of an individual decision but as part of a long line of intention to which a government or an agency of government is committed? Second, what is the policy as law? Behind every public policy is a specific type of legitimate coercion. How are these coercive instruments applied, when are they applied, and why? Most of my previous work in public policy, and the work of G. Bruce Doern in regulation, has focused on these central questions.[56]

Third, what is the impact of the policy on the political system? Lowi suggests that impact analysis would generate the following questions in political science: What will policy alternative *x* do to the capacity of that government to change later to policy alternative *y*, if *x* fails? What will a given type of sanction do to the capacity of law enforcement officers to operate, or what effect will a given type of sanction have on the actual structure of law enforcement? Will an independent regulatory approach, versus a departmental approach, reduce or increase legislative participation in future policy making in that area? Do the new fiscal approaches to welfare militate strongly in favor of executive dominance of government decision making? All of these questions, I contend, necessitate a good working knowledge and understanding of economics, law, and sociology, to emphasize the more important social sciences in public policy analysis. Analysis of public policy content with an emphasis on political is, or should be, one of the central concerns of political science. Austin Ranney's comments on this score should therefore be salutary:

> In my opinion, political scientists will—and should be—called upon to advise policy-makers to the degree that they are perceived to have special professional knowledge and skills. If all we can offer is common sense or a passion for social justice, then we have no claim to and will not receive any special attention not paid to any other citizen enjoying these admirable but widely diffused assets.[57]

At this juncture, it is important to emphasize that the too facile distinction made between policy theory and policy analysis in political science must not cloud the central fact that both theory and analysis in the study of public policy must go hand in hand. In my view, to favor one over the other would be disastrous. Policy theory would become stunted and useless if, like neoclassical economics, relevance is sacrificed on the altar of theoretical elegance. That approach may, in the short run, make a few professional reputations, but in the long run it will become a primrose path for social science. Similarly, policy analysis would be sterile and would certainly degenerate into mere technical training if it is not allowed to feed and sustain itself on policy theory. This is a danger that confronts all the social sciences relevant to the study of public policy.

A CONCLUDING NOTE ON LIMITATIONS

I have tried to demonstrate the importance of the public policy analysis perspective. However, a few queries remain about the limitations of this perspective in studying Canadian politics.

Because of the focus I have emphasized here, public policy analysis is open to the charge that it encourages trespassing on what are supposed to be the territories of other disciplines. The student, in effect, ends up as a "jack of all trades and master of none." This charge is a difficult one to answer and refute fully because the dangers it points to are real and cannot be ignored. However, there are aspects of evidence that must be weighed in coming to a conclusion about the charge of multidisciplinary gloss. First, as a political scientist, I am naturally best able to cite fellow political scientists who have made significant contributions to other social sciences. There is no doubt in my mind that such luminaries as Daniel Patrick Moynihan, Aaron Wildavsky, Herbert Simon, Robert A. Dahl, Robert E. Lane, David Easton, and Harold Lasswell, among others, have made significant contributions to psychology, economics, and other specialized subfields of the various social sciences. It is also possible to compile similarly long lists of scholars in each social science who have made major contributions to other social sciences. Economists who have made significant contributions to political science and sociology include Kenneth Arrow, Charles Lindblom, Thomas Schelling, Kenneth Boulding, Anthony Downs, James Buchanan, Jerome Rothenberg, Albert Hirschman, and many others. If these social scientists are able to cross the imaginary disciplinary barriers, then the potential exists for all of us.

Moreover, most of us are not going to be experts in any social science field. Many, if not most, of the beginning students of public policy are not training to become university professors, but wish to gain a modicum of understanding of the policy process. Many will go on to become professionals either engaged in activity tangential to the public policy process, or become public administrators with a need to understand the ramifications of a wide variety of events influencing their work. Under such circumstances a multidisciplinary perspective cannot be construed as a disadvantage. On the contrary, it should be an asset.

The most fundamental answer to the charge of multidisciplinary gloss, hower, is the fact that the differences among the social sciences involve not the subjects they study but rather the preconceptions they have inherited, the methods they use, and some of the conclusions they reach. Thus as Mancur Olson has indicated:

> To distinguish the defining features of the social science disciplines, we must look at the ways in which scholars in various disciplines work, rather than at the nature of the phenomena they study. For the theories or tools of thought of the social science disciplines are so general that each discipline's theory encompasses objects or problems that convention puts in the reservation of some other discipline.[58]

In other words, there is nothing inherent in one discipline that prevents the study of phenomena usually considered the province of another discipline. I have, I believe, adequately argued this fact in the body of this chapter.

Public policy analysis has also been open to the charge of being too closely linked to the study of bureaucracy and public administration whose main concern, it is contended, is the narrow framework of efficiency and effectiveness.[59] In my mind this charge is simply a red herring. Public policy analysis must of necessity be wide-ranging in considering factors that might influence policy. Indeed, my implicit plea in this chapter is for a multidisciplinary perspective that, by its very nature, will preclude narrow conceptualization. Students of public policy must examine prevailing traits of administrative agencies and bureaucracies, levels of economic development as these levels pertain to their scholarly insights, the political culture of their environment which might shed many clues on intrabureaucratic behavior, social and economic characteristics of voters or the bureaucracy's clientele, and historical experiences which can and do have profound implications for both the structure and processes of administration.[60]

One concluding caveat to the student. The literature on public policy analysis is submerged by a tremendous amount of theorizing and navel gazing. Theories abound in the field because every student who writes for the professional journals on the subject usually considers himself to be an expert. Others are intellectually constipated; they are forever "getting ready to get ready" to accomplish the great theoretical work. Yet others are serious scholars, plowing away in the vineyards of theory to enlighten the majority of us who are not as theoretically adept. It takes time but the student will eventually learn who are the best scholars he should be reading. What is needed in policy analysis is more testing and refinement of the numerous elegant paradigms and other insights we have of the policy process. The beginning student might find it very profitable to select some theoretical insights in areas in which he is interested and concentrate on refining these insights. He might find this more profitable.

At this stage of the development of public policy analysis there are still some dangers. Despite my arguments dismissing the charge of multidisciplinary gloss, I believe that at this point in time there is some danger that this charge could be correct. Thus I started this chapter with a moral tale, and I conclude by referring to that Greek myth once again. In his twentieth-century updating of the story, the playwright, George Bernard Shaw, inserted quite a bit of irony into *Pygmalion*. Shaw's fair damsel was a working-class girl, transformed into a beautiful Galatea, with new finery and adopted higher-class pretensions. But appearances were deceptive, for the beautiful woman was never able to make the leap from her past into a present life style that was beyond her. The attempt to make a silk purse from a sow's ear was doomed to failure. Similarly, a gloss of multidisciplinary pretensions in the study of public policy will ultimately have disastrous effects. It is not going to be an easy task for those of us interested in public policy analysis, but I am convinced that it must be done. Multidisciplinary work demands sustained dedication and training, and must be pursued with vigor and imagination. The alternative, in my view, is a stark reality that if we fail, the social sciences, in the final analysis, face the real danger of becoming pygmy Pygmalions.

ENDNOTES

1. See the comments of Professor Douglas Hartle, a former deputy secretary of the Treasury Board of Canada. Sandra Gwyn, "Refugees from Ottawa: Five Public Servants and Why They Left," *Saturday Night* (March, 1976), pp. 19-28, especially pp. 20-22.

2. For a recent excellent overview of this shift and a concern for both means and ends see the whole issue of *The Public Interest,* No. 34 (Winter, 1974); and *Canadian Public Policy* II, No. 4 (Autumn, 1976), especially the contributions by J. Meisel, W.A. MacDonald, R. Simeon, and H.I. Macdonald.

3. Lance Liebman, "Social Intervention in a Democracy," *The Public Interest,* No. 34 (Winter, 1974), pp. 15-16.

4. Ira Sharkansky, ed., *Policy Analysis in Political Science* (Chicago: Markham, 1970), p. 1.

5. W.A. MacIntosh, "The White Paper on Employment and Income in its 1945 Setting," in *Canadian Economic Policy Since the War* (Ottawa: Canadian Trade Committee, 1965), pp. 15-16. A series of six public lectures in commemoration of the twentieth anniversary of the White Paper on Employment and Income of 1945.

6. Liebman, *op. cit.,* p. 16.

7. John Ladd, "The Place of Practical Reason in Judicial Decisions," in *Nomos VII: Rational Decision,* ed. C.J. Friedrich (New York: Atherton, 1964).

8. John Ladd, "Morality and the Ideal of Rationality in Formal Organizations," *Monist,* 54, No. 4 (October, 1970).

9. Michael Polanyi, *The Study of Man* (London: Rutledge and Paul, 1959), p. 33.

10. Silver Donald Cameron, "What Makes Harry Boyle?" *Weekend Magazine* (March, 12, 1977), p. 9.

11. For an excellent exploration of this theme within the context of social programs and public income distribution see Hugh Heclo, "Frontiers of Social Policy in Europe and America," *Policy Sciences,* 6, No. 4 (December, 1975), pp. 403-421.

12. Daniel Patrick Moynihan, *Maximum Feasible Misunderstanding* (New York: The Free Press, 1969), pp. 193-194.

13. R.S. Stanfield, "Ottawa's Power Upsets System," *The Globe and Mail,* Toronto, Tuesday, February 8, 1977, p. 7.

14. J.R. Mallory, "Responsive and Responsible Government," Royal Society of Canada, *Transactions,* Series IV, XXII (1974), p. 208.

15. *Ibid.,* p. 209.

16. Douglas Roche, *The Human Side of Politics* (Toronto: Clarke, Irwin, 1976), p. x.

17. For a brief discussion of this debate, see G. Bruce Doern and V. Seymour Wilson, eds., *Issues in Canadian Public Policy* (Toronto: Macmillan, 1974), pp. 1-7.

18. Richard M. Bird, *The Growth of Government Spending in Canada* (Toronto: Canadian Tax Foundation, 1970).

19. Dale H. Poel, "The Diffusion of Legislation Among the Canadian Provinces: A Statistical Analysis," *Canadian Journal of Political Science,* 9, No. 4 (December, 1976), pp. 605-626.

20. Arnold J. Heidenheimer et al., *Comparative Public Policy: The Politics of Social Choice in Europe and America* (New York: St. Martin's Press, 1975), p. 272.

21. V. Seymour Wilson, "Language Policy" in Doern and Wilson, *op. cit.,* pp. 253-285.

22. John A. Meisel, "The June 1962 Election: Break-up of our Party System?" *Queen's Quarterly,* LXIX, No. 3 (Autumn, 1962), pp. 332*ff.*

23. The transcripts (Volumes I and II) of the 1960 Kingston conference of Liberal thinkers provide ample evidence of this developing policy trend. See in particular the pieces by Sharp, Pickersgill, Lamontagne, and Tom Kent. See, for example, Jean-Luc Pepin, "Co-operative Federalism," *The Canadian Forum*, 44, No. 527 (December, 1964), pp. 206-210; a skeptical view is provided by J.M. Leger, "Le fédéralisme coopératif ou le nouveau visage de la centralisation," *Le Devoir*, Montreal, Mardi 3, Septembre, 1963. These articles are essentially reproduced in J. Peter Meekison, ed., *Canadian Federalism: Myth or Reality?* (Toronto: Methuen, 1968).

24. For an analysis of some of these outputs, see Richard Simeon, *Federal-Provincial Diplomacy* (Toronto: University of Toronto Press, 1972); J. Stefan Dupré, "Contracting Out: A Funny Thing Happened on the Way to the Centennial," *Report,* 1964 Conference (Toronto: Canadian Tax Foundation, 1965), pp. 215-17.

25. T.J. Lowi, "American Business, Public Policy, Case Studies and Political Theory," *World Politics*, XVL, No. 4 (July, 1964), p. 688. For a more critical evaluation of the utility of Lowi's insights in the study of Canadian public policy, see Doern and Wilson, *op. cit.*, especially Chs. 1 and 6.

26. Lowi first conceptualizes policies in "terms of their impact or expected impact on the society." (Lowi, *op. cit.*, p. 689.) Later, in discussing redistributive policy he argues that "expectations about what it can be . . . are determinative." (Lowi, *op. cit.*, p. 691.)

27. The best analysis so far of these programs has been done by Robert Best in his "Distributive-Constituent Policy and its Impact on Federal-Provincial Relations: The Case of OFY and LIP," unpublished MA Research Essay, Carleton University, 1973. An abridgement of his analysis of the OFY program appears in Doern and Wilson, *op. cit.*, Ch. 6. For a further analysis testing propositions about partisanship in the allocation process of LIP see, Donald E. Blake, "LIP and Partisanship: An Analysis of the Local Initiatives Program," *Canadian Public Policy—Analyse de Politiques*, II, No. 1 (Winter, 1976), pp. 17-32.

28. John Meisel, "Howe, Hubris and '72: An Essay on Political Elitism," in *The Canadian Political Process*, ed. O.M. Kruhlak et al., rev. ed. (Toronto: Holt, Rinehart and Winston, 1973), pp. 206-207.

29. Donald E. Blake, *op. cit.*, p. 21.

30. Richard R. Nelson, "Intellectualizing about the Moon-Ghetto Metaphor: A Study of the Current Malaise of Rational Analysis of Social Problems," *Policy Sciences*, 5, No. 4 (December, 1974), pp. 375-414.

31. See the quote by Lance Liebman in note 3.

32. Nathan Glazer, "The Limits of Social Policy," *Commentary*, 52, No. 3 (September, 1971), p. 53.

33. Anthony Downs, "Up and Down with Ecology—the 'Issue-Attention Cycle,' " *The Public Interest*, No. 28 (Summer, 1972), pp. 38-50, especially pp. 39-41.

34. Canada's urban policy as a case study has been investigated by N. Lloyd Axworthy in his Ph.D. Thesis, "The Task Force on Housing and Urban Development—A Study of Democratic Decision-Making in Canada," Ph.D. thesis, Princeton University, 1972; Lloyd Axworthy, "The Housing Task Force: A Case Study" in *The Structures of Policy-Making in Canada*, ed. G. Bruce Doern and Peter Aucoin (Toronto: Macmillan, 1971), pp. 130-153; David M.

Cameron, "Urban Policy," in *Issues in Canadian Public Policy*, ed. G. Bruce Doern and V. Seymour Wilson (Toronto: Macmillan, 1974), pp. 228-252. Peter Aucoin and R. French, *Knowledge, Power and Public Policy*, Background Study No. 31, (Ottawa: Science Council of Canada, 1974).

35. N.H. Lithwick, "Political Innovation: A Case Study," *Plan: The Town Planning Institute of Canada*, 12, No. 1 (1972), pp. 52-53.

36. David B. Truman, "Maturity, Relevance and the Problem of Training," *Political Science and Public Policy*, ed. Austin Ranney (Chicago: Markham, 1968), p. 282. Truman was in effect quoting W.T.R. Fox's keynote address, "Science in International Politics," given to the eighth annual convention of the International Studies Association, April 14, 1967.

37. *Ibid.*, p. 283.

38. Alan C. Cairns, "National Influences on the Study of Politics," *Queen's Quarterly*, 81, No. 3 (Autumn, 1974), p. 335.

39. D.V. Smiley, "Contributions to Canadian Political Science since the Second World War," *Canadian Journal of Economics and Political Science*, 33 (1967), p. 569.

40. See the exchange between James Buchanan and Warren Samuels in "On Some Fundamental Issues in Political Economy: An Exchange of Correspondence," *Journal of Economic Issues*, 9 (March, 1975), pp. 15-38.

41. Harry Jones, "Law and Politics," *Perspectives in the Study of Politics*, ed. Malcolm Parsons (New York: Rand McNally, 1968), pp. 63-76.

42. Quite a few economists have been somewhat uncomfortable about the notions of equilibrium analysis, but these disquieting problems were simply ignored. For example, "Equilibrium economics describes a community without economic problems, because so far as it affects him, everybody knows how everyone else is going to behave." T.W. Hutchison, *The Significance and Basic Postulates of Economic Theory* (New York: Augustus M. Kelley, 1965), p. 164.

43. Richard Bird, *The Growth of Government Spending in Canada* (Toronto: Canadian Tax Foundation, 1970), p. 4.

44. Michael Reagan, *The Managed Economy* (New York: Oxford University Press, 1963), p. 55.

45. Sherman Krupp, "Equilibrium Theory in Economics," *Functionalism in the Social Sciences*, ed. Don Martindale (Philadelphia: American Academy of Political and Social Science, 1965), pp. 65 and 78.

46. John Kenneth Galbraith, "Power and the Useful Economist," *American Economic Review*, 63 (March, 1973), p. 2.

47. Quoted in Robert Lekachman, "The Conservative Drift in Economics," *Transaction* (Fall, 1973), p. 300.

48. Gordon Tullock, *The Logic of the Law* (New York: Basic Books, 1971).

49. Mancur Olson, "Economics, Sociology and the Best of All Possible Worlds," *The Public Interest*, 9-17 (1967-68), p. 99.

50. Theodore J. Lowi, "What Political Scientists Don't Need to Ask About Policy Analysis," *Policy Studies and the Social Sciences*, ed. Stuart S. Nagel (Toronto: D.C. Heath, Lexington Books, 1975), p. 270.

51. D.V. Smiley, "Must Canadian Political Science be a Miniature Replica?" *Journal of Canadian Studies*, 9, No. 1 (February, 1974), pp. 38-39.

52. David Easton, *The Political System: An Inquiry into the State of Political Science*, 2nd ed. (New York: Knopf, 1971), pp. 374-375.

53. Aaron Wildavsky, "The Political Economy of Efficiency: Cost Benefit Analysis, Systems Analysis, and Program Budgeting," *Public Administration Review*, XXVI (December, 1966), p. 310.

54. Austin Ranney, ed., *Political Science and Public Policy* (Chicago: Markham, 1968), p. 3.

55. Richard Simeon, *op. cit.*, p. 549. Reading Simeon's "Studying Public Policy" reminded me of that Jean Renoir film, "Rules of the Game," in which the house party sallies forth from La Colinière on a Sunday morning and shoots every bird and rabbit in sight for miles around. Bang! Bang! Bang! go the pointed criticisms and down they crash. Before long the landscape is littered with the corpses of academic marksmanship.

56. See, for example, G. Bruce Doern and V. Seymour Wilson, eds., *Issues in Canadian Public Policy* (Toronto: Macmillan, 1974); G. Bruce Doern, ed., *The Regulatory Process in Canada* (Toronto: Macmillan, 1977).

57. Austin Ranney, *op. cit.*, pp. 17-18.

58. Mancur Olson Jr., *op. cit.*, p. 99.

59. See, for example, the article by Richard Simeon, "Studying Public Policy," *Canadian Journal of Political Science*, IX, No. 4 (December, 1976), pp. 548-580.

60. For a good Canadian example of an attempt to bring together a wide variety of social science research and offer some theoretical links see J.E. Hodgetts, W. McCloskey, R.A. Whitaker, and V. Seymour Wilson, *The Biography of an Institution: The Public Service Commission of Canada 1908-1967* (Montreal: McGill-Queen's University Press, 1972).

SELECTED REFERENCES

POLITICAL SCIENCE

AUCOIN, PETER, AND R.D. FRENCH. *Knowledge, Power and Public Policy.* Background Study No. 31. Ottawa: Science Council of Canada, 1974. This analytical study examines one recent aspect of the machinery of government changes in Canada—the ministry of state concept. While it concentrates on the federal level, there is also an examination of major reforms in the Ontario provincial government. Somewhat advanced for beginning students, but excellent reference to illustrate problems of organizational change and innovation.

DOERN, G. BRUCE, AND PETER AUCOIN, eds. *The Structures of Policy Making in Canada.* Toronto: Macmillan, 1971. Concentrates on such aspects as instruments of policy making (white papers, task forces), techniques (budgetary tools, advisory councils), and evolutionary changes in structure and philosophy in cabinet structures. Excellent reference.

DOERN, G. BRUCE, AND V. SEYMOUR WILSON, eds. *Issues in Canadian Public Policy.* Toronto: Macmillan, 1974. Concentrates on the political dimensions of public policy analysis. Examines policy making from the vantage point of both values and governing instruments and from an analysis of several policy areas concurrently. Excellent reference but for more advanced students.

DYE, THOMAS R. *Understanding Public Policy.* Englewood Cliffs, N.J.: Prentice-Hall, 1972. A good, general, comparative treatment of public policy. Heavy on American examples, but nevertheless highly recommended for its theoretical treatment of public policy analysis.

HOCKIN, THOMAS, ed. *Apex of Power,* 2nd ed. Scarborough: Prentice-Hall, 1977. Focuses on the relationship of the prime minister of Canada to the Canadian political and governmental system. Balanced collection of readings of prime ministerial restraints, assets, and policy influence. Highly recommended.

HOLDEN, MATTHEW, AND ENNIS L. DRESANG. *What Government Does.* Beverley Hills, Cal.: 1975. Sage Yearbooks in Politics and Public Policy, Vol. I. Designed to deal with a variety of policy problems from a political science perspective —environmental concerns, economic regulation, housing, welfare, and so on. Somewhat advanced but generally good.

MOYNIHAN, DANIEL PATRICK. *Maximum Feasible Misunderstanding.* New York: The Free Press, 1969. An excellent and much-maligned study (because of its use of the term "benign neglect") of the bureaucratic nightmare of social welfare programs during the Kennedy "Great Society" years. A case study of the limits of social policy and the application of social science to policy questions from the vantage point of one of the chief participants in the policy-making process of that period. Excellent and highly recommended.

NAGEL, STUART S., ed. *Policy Studies and the Social Sciences.* Toronto: D.C. Heath, Lexington Books, 1975. General readings on the scope of the social sciences and application to policy studies. Helpful and informative but not essential reading.

RANNEY, AUSTIN, ed. *Political Science and Public Policy,* Chicago: Markham, 1968. This book starts with the question: What professional expertise and obligations, if any, have political scientists to study, evaluate, and make recommendations about the contents of public policies? Covers a broad array of problems from concepts and issues to substantive case studies of U.S. domestic and foreign policy. Highly recommended, in particular Parts I and IV. Somewhat advanced for beginning student.

RIPLEY, RANDALL B., ed. *Public Policies and Their Politics.* New York: Norton, 1966. This book concentrates on the instruments or methods that government uses in implementing its program, or the techniques of government control. Covers such subjects as techniques of regulation, subsidy, and manipulation. Advanced case studies in American politics, but excellent book. Highly recommended for the beginning student, however, is the piece by Theodore Lowi.

SHARKANSKY, IRA, ed. *Policy Analysis in Political Science.* Chicago: Markham, 1970. Its stated purpose is to introduce students to the wide concerns of policy analysis—the variety of concepts, techniques of investigation, and findings in the literature. Good book but for advanced students of public policy.

ECONOMICS

Three books are specifically recommended. In addition, I would suggest that students will find it extremely profitable to read the general political economy works of Robert Heilbroner and J.K. Galbraith.

ANDERSON, WILLIAM H. *Financing Modern Government.* Boston: Houghton-Mifflin, 1973. An excellent introduction to public finance. Written to emphasize the need for government activity, the concept of scarce resources in the public as well as in the private sector, and the necessity for allocating resources optionally between both private and public sectors. Highly recommended.

FROMM, GARY, AND PAUL TAUBMAN. *Public Economic Theory and Policy.* New York: Macmillan, 1973. Good book dealing with such topics as the criteria of governmental intervention, normative theory of public expenditures, cost-benefit analysis, and so on. Advanced textbook, but highly recommended for its rigorous treatment of issues in public finance. Too advanced for beginning student but good text.

PHELPS, EDMUND S. *Private Wants and Public Needs.* New York: Norton, 1965. This is an excellent introduction of political economy readings covering such diverse topics as private versus public spending, and the role for government expenditure in the economy. The readings are juxtaposed so that the student obtains different points of view on the same subject. Highly recommended.

Part Five:

Canadian Politics: The Exercise of Power

The philosopher, Hobbes, once stated, "I put for a general inclination of mankind, a perpetual and restless desire of power after power, that ceaseth only in death." Whether or not we agree completely with Hobbes, the most elementary observation of Canadian society tells us that some people exercise political power and that others strive to displace them.

Numerous writers have commented on this fact. Some years ago Frederick Watkins asserted that, "The proper scope of political science is not the study of the state or of any other specific institutional complex, but the investigation of all associations insofar as they can be shown to exemplify the problem of power."[1] More recently William Robson declared, "It is with power in society that political science is primarily concerned—its nature, basis, processes, scope and results. . . . The 'focus of interest' of the political scientist is clear and unambiguous; it centres on the struggle to gain or retain power, to exercise power or influence over others, or to resist that exercise."[2] The four chapters in this section define and assess four explanations of who holds political power.

The first chapter draws our attention to the individual wielders of power; the leaders who have championed causes, dominated political parties, headed governments, and sometimes personified the nation. As Professor Young explains, these political leaders, partly because of television exposure, have become the focal points of our political system. "We may be forever unable scientifically to measure and explore the psyche of our political leaders, yet we ought to be properly aware of the impact of human behavior on the political system, especially in the office that is the vital center." He concludes: "Politics is, after all, about control of the levers of power—or the allocation of scarce resources authoritatively, if you must—and that, surely, is what leadership is all about."

In the second chapter we encounter the concept of elites, a notion some observers have explained as describing nothing more than the insight that any social form of action involves division of labor and influence. The idea that societies are dominated and manipulated by elites has been around for centuries. In our day, with the pervasive arm of government reaching ever wider afield, and with obvious connections existing between the political and economic elites, that notion is held with firm conviction by many people. Are such impressions rooted in fact? Professor Forcese assesses that orientation and suggests that, while the study of elites is an important approach to politics, we should always study elites in terms of their interaction with nonelites.

The third chapter focuses on groups, specifically political interest groups. As pointed out by Professor Schwartz, group activity is widespread and involves both cooperation and conflict. We are reminded that "politics is inherently a group process" and that group analysis can tell us much about Canadian politics. It may even serve us well as an integrating concept, but if we try to make it all-inclusive we will probably find it inadequate.

Our last chapter challenges many of the key arguments advanced by other contributors. A Marxist analysis, we are told, "transcends the parochialism into which so much of the discussion of Canadian politics and economics descends." Only by asking the basic questions about Canadian society can we really come to grips with what Canadian politics involves. Marx has written: "The ultimate causes of all social changes and political revolutions are to be sought, not in the minds of men, . . . but in changes in the mode of production and exchange." And again, "The mode of production of the material means of existence conditions the whole process of social, political, and intellectual life." Given space limitations, Professor Resnick is not able to explain all the subtleties of a Marxist analysis but he states clearly why he believes that "Marxism poses an integrated social, political, and economic theory" that best explains Canadian politics. At least implicitly he suggests that in analyzing politics, theory, in this case Marxist theory, can be a vitally important starting point as well as an end point. Is he right?

ENDNOTES

1. Frederick M. Watkins, *The State as a Concept of Political Science* (New York: Harper, 1934), p. 83.
2. William A. Robson, *The University Teaching of Social Sciences: Political Science* (Paris: UNESCO, 1954), pp. 17-18.

13

Leadership and Canadian Politics

Walter D. Young*

*No matter what the form of government the universal
fact is the rule of the many by the few.*

Gaetano Mosca
The Ruling Class

As an approach to the study of Canadian politics, there is much to be said
for an analysis of political leadership, not because our leaders are or have
been men of heroic proportions and not because they and they alone have
been the movers of events, but because the nature of our political institutions in both the broad and narrow sense places them at the center of political consciousness. Although they are as much shaped by events as they
shape them, political leaders are nevertheless the focal point of our political system. And however much the level of political awareness and sophistication advances, the importance of leadership moves in advance of it.
Television may make the people more aware of what is happening, but it
also makes them more aware of who appears to be making it happen.
Leaders are more effective because they have access to a highly effective
and extremely malleable means of communication.

The very complexity of modern politics places heavy demands on
political leaders. Not only must they deal with the problems of government at the purely executive level, they must also make government intelligible to the people governed, a people more conscious of national and
international concerns than ever before. The citizens of the modern state
rely on their leaders to provide some kind of order from the chaos of information with which they are constantly bombarded. Before the days of

*Professor and Chairman, Department of Political Science, University of Victoria.

radio and television, the job of the leader was a good deal easier and the problems, in some respects, a good deal simpler. Not only were the people less informed about national issues, but they expected less from their leaders, in large measure because they read and heard less about politics from both sides, apart, of course, from election campaigns.

It is customary to think of a democratic system as one in which men are free to govern themselves, and in which popular participation precludes the rise of dictators. We are, it is true, some distance from the wicked days of absolute monarchy; but we are no less enthralled by our leaders, however much we limit their terms of office and their behavior by the elaborate trappings of constitutional government. Modern democracy has not lessened either the need or the demand for leadership.

Our history is written very largely in terms of the men who led parties or led the nation. Eras are defined by the men who dominated them: the reign of Henry VIII, the Mackenzie King era, the Diefenbaker period, the Eisenhower administration. This does not mean that these men made all the decisions; it does mean that they were the focus of government. By virtue of the office they held, they were at the center of events and exerted a major influence. It is natural to view a particular period as characterized by the most prominent leader. Some scholars have argued that the kind or quality of leadership a state enjoys at any particular time is indicative of the quality of the political system itself.[1] It was once a popular view that history is really the biography of great men and it is still true that popular writers tend to reduce historical events to personal triumph or tragedy.

While it is obvious that no leader functions in isolation from the political system in which he operates, it is also clear that democratic leaders have a great deal of power and that this power is not only a reflection of the constitutional framework within which they operate, but also a reflection of the innate need people in modern society have for leadership. The need tends to vary directly with a number of factors, the most obvious of which is political tension: war, insurrection, severe economic or social disorder, and so on. The need for leadership is not reduced by increasing the availability of structures for participation; indeed higher levels of participation tend to heighten the need for leadership.[2] Different circumstances demand different kinds of leaders, but leadership is always an essential ingredient of politics. There is no evidence to suggest that higher levels of political awareness and literacy diminish either the need for or the reliance upon leadership. Indeed, the more complex and sophisticated life becomes, the more people seem to need someone or some group to provide direction and coherence.

A great deal has been written about leadership in general and about the different kinds of leadership.[3] Basically the relationship we define as leadership is one in which one person or group of people exercises influence and another person or people submits to that influence willingly.[4] Coercion is not leadership, although political leaders stand at the apex of that agency which has a monopoly of coercive power within the state.

There is both more and less to leadership than the above definition implies. In Canada, as in most political systems, leadership does not consist in simply getting large numbers of people to do what the leaders want them to do. It is more a matter of getting large numbers of people to accept what the leaders have done or seem to have done, to accept it not merely as being legitimate but as being appropriate as well. The tacit acceptance of our political system as legitimate is what gives law its effectiveness; in other words, our obedience is not a function of our being led by the current prime minister. After all, many people disliked Mackenzie King intensely and disparaged his kind of leadership, but still obeyed the law. Within the modern constitutional framework, however, leadership lends comprehensibility and additional legitimacy to the political system. Instead of the vast and faceless bureaucracy, there is a prime minister who speaks for and to the nation. At a time when the engine of state at both the federal and provincial levels is large and complicated, the existence of a single individual as the functioning head of the apparatus provides a much needed focus and credibility. The need for such a figure increases with the growth of the machine, and the power of such a figure increases accordingly.

When the Liberal government decided to invoke the War Measures Act during the FLQ crisis in 1970, the decision was not taken by the prime minister alone. In the cabinet system of government, prime ministers do not enjoy the solitary decisiveness of, for example, the American president. But for the nation the identification of one person with a crucial decision is an important part of their willingness to accept the decision as legitimate. As the nation's leader, Mr. Trudeau was not getting the people of Canada to do anything; he was exercising his influence by having them accept and support what his government was doing.

What is important to keep in mind is that in most contemporary leader-follower relationships in government, apart from the prime minister-cabinet relationship, the follower is passive and is led to accept what the leader is doing or what he represents. In other words, being a follower does not mean doing what the leader asks as much as accepting what the leader has done. And what the leader or the government is doing can be done to someone else; for example, the FLQ members and the many others who were arrested under the War Measures Act; or it can be done to the followers themselves, for example, the citizens whose incomes were restricted by wage and price control. For the most part, then, the follower is merely a passive observer or recipient. This is perhaps less so in the case of a party leader and party members when leadership may galvanize members into doing more canvassing, giving more money, and so on. The difference, of course, is that in this instance the followers have a choice.

The willingness of well-educated and sophisticated people to accept the leadership of a single individual can be explained, at least partially, as a normal response from men and women whose earliest experience was of the authoritarian hierarchy of parent and child. A willingness to be led and, in times of crisis, an eagerness to be led, is as much a trait of man in civilized society as in primitive society. In both circumstances the individual's first conscious experience of organized society is within the family hierarchy. The relationship between the child and the parent through the most influential years establishes an authority pattern that is carried over into adulthood. Adults not only behave deferentially toward those in a leadership role, but actively seek individuals to fill that role. There is no evidence to indicate that levels of sophistication and maturity bear an inverse relationship to the need for leadership.

The relationship of leaders and followers in modern society is complex. It was popular at one time to view leaders as men of a particular sort, men who "bore the stamp of greatness" and were in some way or other of heroic proportion and therefore born to lead or "born to be great." This concentration on the personality of the leader formed the basis of the great man thesis of history and led to leadership being seen as simply a reflection of the singular personal traits of the leader.

It is important to understand the personality of any given leader because obviously a leader is not simply the person who happened to be closest to the phone when the cry went up: "Who will save the country?" But it is equally important to understand that circumstance is a major part of the equation. It has been aptly put that "leadership is a function of personality and of the social situation and of these two in interaction."[5] Winston Churchill's ability to lead the British people during the Second World War was as much attributable to the political and social circumstances of the time as to his own peculiar qualities. Once circumstances changed, as he so eloquently put it himself, he was "immediately dismissed by the British electorate from all further conduct of their affairs."[6]

At this point it is necessary to inject a cautionary note. It is almost too easy to discuss leadership with reference to such colossi as Churchill, to those figures who bestride human history as signal examples of leadership: Stalin, Roosevelt, Hitler, Mao Tse-tung, Ghandi, Kennedy. In each case the interaction of personality and circumstance is not difficult to discern. But there are other leaders and other circumstances. Mackenzie King was hardly a colossus but was nevertheless the leader of his party and his nation for longer than anyone else in Canada, before or since. The exercise of such leadership is perhaps more difficult to discern but it is still leadership. The lesser lights lead but in a less obvious fashion.

There is little that can be said about the personalities of leaders that would survive any rigorous analysis by a psychologist. Mackenzie King left a voluminous diary that is proving a veritable mother lode for psychohistorians and psychobiographers determined to explore the mental processes of such a significant figure in his country's history.[7] For most leaders, however, the data for such analysis is inadequate. They may, however, be characterized by the kind of leadership they provide. Max Weber's categories of charismatic, patriarchal, and bureaucratic leadership are still the most useful.[8] The three are not mutually exclusive. Charismatic leaders are those who lead by virtue of some special personal quality or gift they possess; patriarchal leaders are those who lead because of their status based on experience, traditions, achievements, and seniority; and bureaucratic leaders are those who lead by virtue of the legal and purely rational situation in which they find themselves. John Diefenbaker was a

charismatic leader in Canada during the period 1956-1969; after his de-
position as leader he remained a patriarchal leader for many in the Conservative party and was therefore somewhat of a nuisance for his successor, Robert Stanfield, who was the formal and bureaucratic leader of the
party, although never of the nation.

The charismatic leader is the most interesting and obvious sort of
leader largely because the great men have all been, in one way or another,
charismatic leaders. Charismatic leadership is the least stable but most
spectacular kind of leadership. Charismatic leaders are those who have
special gifts; who are able to embody the goals or desires of the group they
lead; who are, in some significant respects, larger than life and inspira-
tional in their appeal. As Schiffer points out, charismatic leaders are not
perfect men, but they exemplify the characteristics most desired by their
nation at the time of their leadership.[9] The success of John Diefenbaker
and the subsequent phenomenon of Trudeaumania[10] are useful demonstrations of charismatic leadership in a modern society. While the enthusiasm generated by Diefenbaker and Trudeau cannot be compared
with that produced by the Bay City Rollers, for example, both phenomena
show that the advance of civilization and the increased levels of sophistication that such progress brings do not reduce either the need for or the
reliance upon leadership and the continued need for idols.

Because he seems to answer a need, or because he seems to personify
the goals of the bulk of the people, the charismatic leader is able to exercise authority that a bureaucratic leader would lack. This authority is the
product of a marriage of exceptional personal traits and propitious circumstances that is usually fortuitous. The aura that surrounds such a
leader generates deference and obedience and enhances his power.
Normally a party leader has certain prerogatives by virtue of the office
itself. The charismatic leader has these powers plus those generated by his
charisma. And if his charisma is successful nationally and he brings the
party he leads to power, then as prime minister he is in a commanding
position for it will be clearly seen that victory was due to his appeal and not
to that of the party per se. Until the government's fortunes begin to slide,
he will remain in a position of considerable authority.

It is possible to overdo the notion of charisma and to attempt to find
this elusive characteristic in every successful leader. It may be the case,
indeed probably is more often than not, that a successful leader happens
to be someone who has a good mind, quick wit, a flair for oratory, and
above average ambition. These characteristics may or may not be part of a
mixture that spells charisma, but they can often be just as useful as
Weber's concept as explanations for a leader's success. What is important
for the student of Canadian politics to keep in mind is that a leader's personality is consequential and may be a major source of his authority within
the party or within the nation.

The bureaucratic leader is the individual who holds an office that
confers on its occupant the highest level of authority within the particular
organization. While the election or appointment of the individual to that
office can be taken as evidence of some superior qualities, it is often the

case that seniority alone will ensure that an individual reaches the top. In the case of political parties, longevity may serve as the ladder for internal party officials—one becomes national president of the New Democratic Party in some measure because of yeoman service—but it does not offer much assistance to the man who would be leader. Yet all political parties in Canada have at one time or another been led by men who were bureaucratic leaders in that their authority came more from the office than from some particular qualities they possessed.

For the Conservative party, John Bracken is perhaps the outstanding example. Recruited directly by the party's patriarch, Arthur Meighen, he left the comfort of the premier's office in Manitoba to become one of the more uninspiring leaders of that party.[11] Louis St. Laurent succeeded Mackenzie King as leader of the Liberal party and, although elected over other contestants by a leadership convention, he was the hand-picked successor. Until he assumed the avuncular image that characterized his final years in office, a kind of patriarchal charisma, he was a bureaucratic leader in that his authority stemmed more from the office he held than from any outstanding personal trait. He was, after all, prime minister, and that does do something for a man's influence.[12]

The successful leader is constantly watching himself being watched. Few people study the behavior of leaders more carefully than do the leaders themselves. They must be constantly aware of how well or badly they are doing in their various constituencies: cabinet, caucus, party, nation. There is always a danger that they may be getting the wrong information; some leaders make the fatal error of surrounding themselves with people who will bring only good news. But since leadership is a process of interaction between leader and led, leaders must be sensitive to the effect they are having on the people around them.

Never before has the apparatus of communication been so beneficial to the successful leader. The assistance lent by television to the dramaturgy of leadership is quite remarkable. The elaborate attention to costume and behavior that was such a large part of Trudeaumania was successful very largely because television enabled several million Canadians to see the prime minister at the Grey Cup game in a wide-brimmed black impresario's hat with flowing scarf and cape or emerging from Parliament in an open-necked shirt and sandals. All the devices designed to declare to the public that here is someone special are heavily dependent on the news media, principally television. When Parliament is in session, and especially since the televising of sittings began, the prime minister has a daily opportunity to impress himself on the nation and, it follows, on his party. But reaching those commanding heights is difficult, and staying there no simple task, television and a hungry audience notwithstanding.

Leaders often appoint to their personal staff men and women with experience in communications, usually former newspaper or television journalists, or people from the advertising trade, to advise them and ensure that their personality and behavior are consistent with public expectation. As Dion has put it, "The successes of great political leaders in the past have been closely related to their ability to understand and express the sentiments of the followers."[13] If a leader is elected because he is perceived as a model or ideal figure, he must work to ensure that the voters will retain that perception. The elaborate public relations apparatus that exists in the prime minister's office or within the staff of a provincial premier is best understood in this context. The influence of men like Keith Davey in the Liberal party and Dalton Camp in the Conservative party attests to the importance placed on advice from experts in the arcane techniques of public relations.

The personality of the leader and his ability to choose men and women to work with him serve to enhance his authority further. A loyal bank of "right-hand men" will serve to reinforce the position of the leader. The growth of the prime minister's office under Pierre Trudeau provides a useful example of a leader bolstering his position in the several constituencies within which he must work: cabinet, caucus, party, nation. By providing him with his own administrative apparatus to keep him abreast of developments within each of these constituencies, and with expert advice as well as the public relations services discussed above, the PMO is a crucial adjunct to the role of the leader.[14] The prime minister must be careful, however, to ensure that the PMO does not become a barrier to his supporters who would quickly resent it if it served to insulate the leader from his immediate followers or if it was seen to be usurping those positions usually filled by cabinet members or cabinet committees.[15]

The PMO may help the prime minister with the constituencies he must serve but the ordinary party leader does not have such an apparatus and even the prime minister must, from time to time, substitute his own judgment for that of his professional advisers. His first constituency must be the party that chose him. And that constituency has two dimensions: the party itself in its federal riding-by-riding manifestation; and the party in Parliament, the caucus.

The party leader is chosen by the party membership through delegates to national leadership conventions after a vigorous and costly campaign.[16] The stakes are high for, in the case of the two major parties, the victor is either leader of the opposition or prime minister. The convention itself is a demonstration of the significance of the national party and the successful leader is the one who does not ignore the rank and file. But his contact with the party at the local riding level is inevitably sporadic and, from the point of view of the leader as party decision maker, of little value. The parliamentary party or caucus is the most important party body. It is within this body that a leader must demonstrate his political skills at close range in order to maintain his stature and authority.

The caucus will usually include most of the leader's rivals for the office he holds and, possibly, the previous incumbent. It will also reflect the ideological divisions within the party as well as the regional antagonisms that are so typically Canadian. Caucus-leader relations are more difficult for a leader of the opposition than for a prime minister for the latter carries with him both the aura of his office and the potential for making ministers of backbenchers and senators of the weary—a not inconsiderable asset in encouraging loyalty and support.

By being chosen leader of the party, the individual is placed in an institutional situation that provides him with a degree of authority that the ordinary party member does not possess. Rank and file members will, as a rule, defer to the leader. The loyalty of party members to their leader is perhaps surpassed only by a fan's loyalty to the local hockey team. The leader's role in policy making is pre-eminent and through the press and television he becomes the party's most visible electoral commodity. If the party is not in power, he is number two in any debate as leader of the opposition, number three if leader of the NDP.

Not only does the office of party leader confer on its holder a major portion of authority within the party structure, but that authority is further enhanced by the externalities of the office. To the outside world he *is* the party. He is expected to make definitive statements on matters of national and international concern in Canada and will be criticized both within his party and nationally by press and party members alike if he consistently fails to do this effectively.

An interesting and useful example of this particular phenomenon would be the career of Joe Clark. In the space of eighteen months he passed from anonymity to national prominence. By any objective standard it would be difficult to deduce from examining the early career of Joe Clark that he was destined to be leader of the Conservative party, leader of Her Majesty's opposition, and wield the power that those offices confer on their holder. Apart, perhaps, from his mother, few would have discerned anything that might have been taken for a mark of greatness. His meteoric career provides a useful example of the marriage of ambition with circumstance.

Clark was helped by a contest in which there did not appear to be any obvious winner, by his finely tuned organization, and by the added bonus derived from the fact that his most serious opponent represented Quebec—not in itself a difficult thing for the Conservative party to digest, but Claude Wagner had been a Liberal as well. As victor, Clark had the customary period of grace in which he enjoyed a kind of immunity from both internal and external criticism. The last phase of this period coincided with a series of political misfortunes for the Liberal government of Prime Minister Trudeau, which served admirably to catapult the fortunes of the Conservative party and its new leader into a commanding lead in the Gallup poll.

The point, of course, is that circumstance served not only to cement his position as party leader after a somewhat divisive campaign, but to enhance his authority within the party despite the fact that he did relatively little as leader during his first year in office. The fact remained that he was the only leader that the party had, the stock in trade of every new leader, and a new leader, by virtue of that fact alone, is able to command the allegiance of the rank and file of the party and of the party caucus itself. The Liberals' difficulties were a bonus.

But the fickle nature of Dame Fortune was revealed when the Parti Québecois came to power in Quebec in November, 1976 and the populace veered back to a position that had largely contributed to Robert

Stanfield's discomfiture, namely, the belief that Pierre Trudeau was probably the best man to deal with a difficult Quebec. The low profile Joe Clark had adopted and that served him well as long as the Liberal government seemed bent on self-destruction, became a liability. Pundits and editorial writers took him to task in the winter and spring of 1977 for his failure to state the policy of the official opposition. His tactic was largely designed to give the party time to heal the wounds from the leadership campaign but it served instead to make him a target. The rapid decline in his party's position in the opinion polls as reported in March, 1977 considerably weakened his position as leader. The loss of Jack Horner, M.P., who had contested the leadership against Clark and sat as a Tory from Alberta for nineteen years was another blow. Horner crossed the floor in April, 1977 and became a Liberal cabinet minister. In the same way that circumstance may work to catapult a politician into the highest office in his party, it may also undermine his position. The test of effective leadership is, then, longevity and the ability to take advantage of good winds and be close to a snug harbor in the storms.

Clark's predecessor, Robert Stanfield, had mixed results as party leader. He led the party through three general elections but was unsuccessful in each. The intriguing feature of his career was not his inability to win elections for his party—there have been Conservatives in the past who also excelled in that respect—it lay, rather, in the universal affection and respect in which he was held among his intimates, his caucus, and the press.[17] Unable to project his undeniably sterling qualities to the multitude of Canadian voters and faced with a Liberal government that was, at that juncture, relatively free from those peculiarly Liberal signs of age, arrogance and bad management, he failed.

He had as well a particularly awkward burden for a party leader, namely, the presence in his caucus of his predecessor, John Diefenbaker. Diefenbaker was propelled out of the leadership by a cabal within the party apparatus and actually contested the leadership against Stanfield and others. He remained in the caucus emitting all the baleful radiance of a whore at a family wedding. Clark was not spared this numbing presence, but the eight years intervening served to dim the Diefenbaker effulgence. Moreover, Clark was not associated with the anti-Diefenbaker coup that had begun in the final years of the Diefenbaker administration.

What this serves to show is the extent to which the interweaving of man, circumstance, and followers serves both to create and to undermine leadership. The authority the leader exercises over his immediate followers and over the rank and file of his party in the nation is a product of his capacity to turn events to his advantage; of his capacity to maintain his authority in the party caucus by the skillful management of men and the effective utilization of events; and of his popularity in the nation itself as demonstrated by opinion polls, press coverage, and the response to his public appearances. There is much that is under the control of the leader himself, but equally there is much that is beyond his personal control.

For the party leader who is also prime minister the process is both easier and more difficult, with the edge going to the former. He has the formal power of his office which places him at the apex of the apparatus of government.[18] In an order-in-council to his cabinet, Mackenzie King outlined the prerogatives of the prime minister which included the appointment of all cabinet ministers, dissolution and convocation of parliament, and a number of other appointments including Treasury Board, senators, and deputy ministers. According to John Diefenbaker, "More important in many ways was the convention that gave the Prime Minister total control of cabinet discussion."[19] Both aspects of the prime minister's authority are important to the effective performance of his tasks as prime minister; they also serve to enhance his effectiveness as party leader.

The interests of the party and the government frequently intersect. The prime minister, by virtue of his prerogative of appointment, is in a position to reward the faithful party servant or the tired parliamentarian with appointments to the bench, to the Senate, or to the diplomatic service. As the key figure in the administration of this kind of patronage, the prime minister as party leader is able to keep his fences mended and his troops loyal. The national president of the Liberal Federation of Canada, on assuming that office, is virtually assured a seat in the Senate if he is not already there. The Conservative party functions in the same manner although it has enjoyed fewer years in office and hence has not been able to make the most effective use of that particular device. In summary, the prime minister uses the powers of his office to serve his purposes as leader of the party.

The parliamentary system provides that before one can be a leader of the nation, that is, prime minister, one must first be the leader of the party. There are two types of party in Canada, roughly speaking: those that exercise fairly strict control over the party leader, and those that elect a leader and are prepared to follow, always assuming that victory lies in the direction he leads. There is really only one party in the first category, and that is the NDP, successor to the CCF. Describing itself as a democratic party, the NDP not only elects its leader democratically, as the other parties do, it does so at every biennial convention. It is most unusual, however, for the leader to be challenged during what must be described as a ritual expression of democratic intent. It has happened, however, at the provincial level where the party leader must subject himself to the decision of the delegates at annual conventions. In British Columbia in 1967 and in Ontario in 1968 the incumbent was challenged. In both cases the challenge was beaten back but the message was clear and in both cases the incumbent resigned within two years and a new leader was chosen. The challenge produced a deep rift in both provincial parties, a rift that was slow to close.

What seems important about the party that provides for the regular review of its leadership, whether that opportunity is regularly used to challenge the leader or not, is that this constitutional provision reflects a spirit or ethos in the party that makes demands on a leader which other parties do not make and poses unique problems for that party's leader when in power. The democratic norms that such procedures reflect are themselves an indication of the party's commitment to a specific ideology and of the membership's commitment to an individualist ethic in the interpretation and expression of the party ideology. The kind of person attracted to such a political organization and the kind of behavior these norms elicit—active, vocal, antiauthoritarian—demand a kind of leadership that is managerial, conciliatory, and consensus oriented. The leadership typified by M.J. Coldwell in the era of the CCF and by Ed Schreyer of Manitoba and Alan Blakeney of Saskatchewan in the case of the NDP reflects this feature of the CCF/NDP.

In this instance leadership is a useful indicator of the character of the party. To the extent that a party has more on its agenda than winning elections, the party's leader will necessarily reflect these interests. The selection of a leader will be influenced by factors that are a product of the party's internal needs. No party is going to ignore the need to choose a leader who will be able to increase the party's support among the electorate at large, but in a party such as the NDP the order of priorities is different and the kind of leader chosen will reflect this difference.

In the case of the NDP these priorities include the expression of a socialist philosophy, the provision of a political agency through which the members may express their own interpretation of that philosophy and, as important as the preceding two, the provision of a vehicle that gives its members well-defined roles for taking part in the policy making and organization of the party. People do not, as a rule, join the NDP to advance their status in Canadian society. They do not join to ensure either advancement or the ear of the government unless, of course, the party has been in office for a reasonable period of time; for the most part people join parties such as the NDP to share in the business of politics. It follows that the kind of leader they select would be one who encourages this kind of membership, whose style of leadership does not pose a threat to the democratic norms of the party, and who does not interfere with the established rights of the members to participate in policy making. Where the NDP has formed the government and the leader has not behaved in a manner consistent with the party norms, the party reaction has been hostile, especially among the most active members. This was the case in British Columbia during the second year of the NDP term of office under the leadership of David Barrett.

With the Liberal and Conservative parties, a different game is played. The objectives of these two parties are more clearly understood and in some ways more basic: winning power and keeping power. Membership is of lesser importance and the norms of democracy are less rigidly adhered to; both Liberal and Conservative parties accord defeated candidates the right to be delegates to conventions which the NDP does not do. This may be more a reflection of the relative numbers involved than of inherent differences although it is not likely. Moreover, the kind of people who do join the Liberal or Conservative party are less likely to be anxious to play so active a part as many who join the NDP. They will tend, by and large, to be more subservient to authority and therefore more readily led. Membership in the Liberal and Conservative parties is more a statement of interest than a declaration of intent.

Accordingly, the leaders of these two parties have a somewhat easier time of it, especially if they are successful. Success is measured by two criteria. One, which is obvious, is the number of elections won; the other, which is more important to the leader who is in opposition, is the track record in the opinion polls. These are not the only means whereby party members judge their leaders; other less obvious measures range from the ability of the leader to accommodate the conflicting interests within the party's ruling cliques to his control over his cabinet colleagues.

The selection of party leader by a convention of party delegates alters the traditional assumptions about the source of a prime minister's power. As the choice of his party at large, the prime minister sees himself and is seen by his colleagues in Parliament as having an additional authority base because he was chosen by party members outside Parliament. As a leader moves from success at the convention to success at the polls, as Pierre Trudeau did in 1968, it is not difficult for both the leader and his followers to view his authority as stemming from these two electoral contests and not from his position in Parliament. Accordingly, he would pay less attention to Parliament, and have less respect for the institution.[20]

With the leaders of the Liberal and Conservative parties, their mastery of the arts of management need only be displayed in three arenas, whereas the leader of the NDP has a fourth. The Liberal or Conservative leader who is also prime minister needs to lead in his cabinet and in his party caucus. Neither is a particularly difficult task although the standard view would seem to indicate that it is in these two forums that he is most seriously restrained. The evidence, for the most part, would seem to indicate the opposite. It is one of the more interesting features of cabinet government that ministers are often prepared to accept quite appalling behavior from their leader presumably because he holds their political future in his hands, and they are unwilling to jeopardize their careers to further some principle that the voters are not likely to appreciate in any case.

Perhaps one of the most classic instances would be Mackenzie King's sacrifice of his defense minister, J.L. Ralston, in 1944.[21] Ralston had submitted his resignation to King in 1942 on a point of principle; the principle being that the national referendum on conscription indicated that the government should take immediate action to reinforce the overseas contingents when the exigencies of battle demanded it, without recourse to Parliament. King, no lover of immediate action on any question, disagreed with this point of view and refused to accept Ralston's resignation, but kept his letter. Two years later when it suited King's purpose to replace Ralston with General A.G.L. MacNaughton, he resurrected the letter, flourished it before a stunned cabinet, and Ralston was out. None of his colleagues made a move to protest.

Maurice Duplessis was unquestionably the most dictatorial of our provincial premiers. His control over his cabinet colleagues was absolute, even to the point of gross and unrelenting interference with their portfolios and, in some cases, with their personal lives. Antonio Barrette, who later succeeded Paul Sauvé as premier and leader of the Union Nationale, was barred from cabinet meetings, although he kept his portfolio as minister of labor, for over a year because Duplessis was annoyed with his behavior in connection with a construction contract. Duplessis even issued orders that the Château Frontenac Hotel not serve Barrette any meals so that Barrette, who lived in the hotel, had to go out to eat.[22] Duplessis made all the major decisions, expected and received abject declarations of fealty from his ministers, each one of whom was clearly unwilling to make even the slightest move to resurrect his own dignity in the face of possible dismissal from a cabinet in which, undoubtedly, access to the pork barrel was a function of total obedience.[23]

In both cases the authority of the party leader was absolute. No one within the caucus or the cabinet was willing to challenge such authority. Such concentration of power may be explained by the personality of the leader; by the personalities of those he selected to serve under him; after all, a leader would not knowingly place in his cabinet all those he saw as his chief rivals unless he felt that they were less harmful inside than out; or by the circumstances prevailing at the time. Without more evidence than that currently available, an explanation based on the analysis of personalities and motives is likely to be inconclusive. What is clear, however, is that the nature of the party and parliamentary systems in Canada serves to enhance the position of the prime minister, and especially so if the external political circumstances are propitious.

The prime minister, who is seen by his colleagues in the cabinet and in the House or legislative assembly as being both the architect of victory and the talisman for continued success, is in a virtually impregnable position. As long as he is able to be or appear to be indispensable, there are few checks to his authority as long as his cabinet colleagues are prepared to accept his direction. The House of Commons cannot limit the power of the prime minister with a solid cabinet and a loyal caucus, and these two are virtually synonymous. Unlike the American president, who must reckon with Congress as well as with a precise and limited term of office, premiers and prime ministers who are the undoubted masters of their parties have an almost medieval power. No other explanation seems reasonable for the kind of power exercised by Mackenzie King, W.A.C. Bennett, E.C. Manning, Maurice Duplessis, or John Diefenbaker in the early months of his first ministry.

Joseph Wearing has suggested that such instances as the dismissal of Ralston and other examples of prime ministerial autocracy, such as R.B. Bennett's New Deal addresses or Pearson's secret meetings with Quebec officials on the pension plan, are best seen as indications of a "pathological condition in the Canadian political system."[24] These and other examples showed a leader working desperately to stave off collapse, collapse that was itself a product of his failure to generate consensus among his colleagues by persuasion and firm leadership. Undeniably these specific acts were taken during difficult times for the governments concerned. The fact remains, however, that the power to take action unilaterally was not challenged in most cases. Indeed, in the case of Pearson and King, and even Bennett, the moves demonstrated the kind of decisiveness that the government and nation yearned for. Having set the machine in motion, the party and nation expect it to be driven. It is in the absence of decisive leadership that the pathological condition develops and in its presence that it is ameliorated.

By focusing attention on the apex of the pyramid, it becomes clear that the political system in Canada generates a demand for leadership. There seems to be little doubt that the politicians who have remained longest in office have demonstrated early in their careers as premier or prime minister a capacity for fairly authoritarian leadership within the structure of government itself, particularly at the provincial level where the ability to lead is enhanced by the relatively higher incidence of amateurism in politics.

Equally important, however, is the extent to which the premier or prime minister uses his authority to delegate power to his cabinet colleagues. Duplessis and W.A.C. Bennett did little or no delegation. In the case of the former, virtually all major decisions, regardless of the department, were made by *le Chef*. Mackenzie King, on the other hand, gave to colleagues like C.D. Howe and J.G. Gardiner almost a free hand within their areas of responsibility. Gardiner was the prime minister for the Prairies. It was small wonder then that ministers would be loath to give up their fiefdom in support of a colleague who was foolish enough to place his in jeopardy. The art of skillful delegation and management of the barons so created is the art of leadership and when well handled undoubtedly enhances the authority of the man in charge.

When the prime minister begins to lose his grip, when he no longer has those tokens that denote power, when his mistakes begin to outnumber his triumphs, then his power begins to dissipate. It was only four years from Diefenbaker's triumphant and overwhelming victory in 1958 to the ignominy of 1962, which saw the largest parliamentary majority in Canadian history reduced to a minority government of 119 seats. Within the party and within the cabinet there was growing dissatisfaction with the leadership of John Diefenbaker, a man whose electoral charisma far exceeded his capacity to manage a government. By 1962 he had succeeded in alienating the business community, antagonizing the United States, and annoying the British government. In his cabinet, ministers were moving uneasily on the balls of their feet, waiting for the first sign of collapse and ready to jump with the majority.[25]

The most common explanation for Diefenbaker's failure is that he suffered from a lack of decisiveness and an overabundance of ambition. Unlike Mackenzie King, he was unable to delegate effectively, a weakness that was multiplied by his almost pathological suspicion of most of his colleagues, notably those who displayed anything remotely approaching an independence of mind. A touch of paranoia may indeed be a salutary defect in a leader; an excess, however, can make a wreckage of a ministry in short order.[26] In Diefenbaker's case the collapse of his government in 1962, following the resignation of Douglas Harkness from the cabinet, set the stage for his subsequent removal from the leadership itself some five years later. This was the direct result of the party's national president, Dalton Camp, actively campaigning against him.

Diefenbaker's experience, however painful it may have been to him, is nevertheless instructive for students of Canadian politics. By 1962, he had failed to establish a Conservative foothold in Quebec; he had lost a large portion of his party's power base in Ontario by alienating the business establishment which had previously supported the Conservatives; and he had weakened the party's hold on the West Coast. Only in the Prairie Provinces was the Tory party's hold firm. Once his party was defeated in 1963, Diefenbaker was vulnerable in the extreme. His failure to recoup his losses in 1965 against the remarkably lackluster Pearson government sealed his fate. He could no longer lead the party because he had nothing to offer it.

His record as prime minister was not distinguished beyond the fact that he had brought the party from the wilderness to power. But he had successfully led it back into the wilderness in less than five years. His inability to satisfy the power brokers in central Canada gave him only very limited leverage on the party machinery. A party leader in the Canadian system, indeed in most political systems, must have some currency in his pockets, so to speak. A bankrupt leader cannot lead. Diefenbaker had the party's highest office but it was of no use to him. He became the first party leader and former prime minister to be defeated in convention by his own party as a candidate for the office of which he was the most recent incumbent. His defeat was prefigured by the successful reelection of Dalton Camp as party president in 1966 on a clear and specific commitment to an early leadership convention.[27]

The Canadian political system does not, then, deal kindly with defeated leaders. What, after all, is a better measure of an individual's capacity for leadership than his record of defeats? This is not the case with the minor parties, for there the scale of victory is much smaller: an increase in the number of seats, an upward shift in the Gallup poll, or the steady growth in the popular vote. These and other lesser advances are the stuff of success for the individual who leads the NDP or Créditiste parties.

The Conservative party has had to cultivate a taste for defeat and this has induced a degree of brittleness in the party so that it cannot abide leaders who do not succeed and chooses its leaders with what some would describe as an almost desperate anxiety to find someone with the talisman of victory about his person. This helps to explain the Conservative tendency to reach down into provincial politics to recruit a successful provincial politician in the hope that the same trick can be turned at the federal level. The typical Conservative leader does not have the same parliamentary background as does his Liberal counterpart. With the exception of Borden, Manion, Meighen, and Diefenbaker, the remaining four Conservative leaders since the turn of the century had most of their experience in provincial politics. Bracken, Drew, and Stanfield had no federal experience. Joe Clark was virtually an unknown junior backbencher when he became leader. Stanfield's principal opponent for the leadership, Duff Roblin, was, like Stanfield, a successful provincial premier with no federal experience. Clark's opponent at the last ballot, Claude Wagner, had made his reputation in provincial politics in Quebec as a Liberal.[28]

Unlike the Conservatives, the Liberals are the party of power in

Canada and have the resilience that constant exercise of power brings. Moreover, by virtue of their long tenure, they have built up a backlog of experienced politicians and administrators at the federal level. Persistence in power breeds cohesion in the same way that it blurs principle. Parties that are unable to win power, although they are in the position of the alternative government, are constantly looking both for scapegoats and panaceas. Parties accustomed to power know that retaining power requires unity and unity becomes very important. A party out of office will find itself badly divided over a policy issue and its leader weakened by his support for one side or another because the issue is seen by both sides as crucial to success. The Conservative party's adoption of wage and price controls as a plank in the 1973 election divided the party. The Liberal rejection of the policy in the campaign and its subsequent implementation of the policy was accepted by Liberals with equanimity. Those in power live in the world of expediency and thereby, it would seem, stay in power. Those out of power sample every potion available in the hope that one will prove to be the elixir of victory and they readily fall to quarreling over which holds the most promise.

The task, then, of the leader of the opposition party is the more difficult and more fraught with danger. So much does the system emphasize the office of the party leader in power, that it is only an extraordinary leader of an opposition party who is able to appear to be either innovative, devastating, or in any way a strikingly attractive alternative. For one thing, he does not have the aura of a prime minister in the eyes of the viewing public; for another, it is difficult for him to avoid giving the appearance of desperation from time to time as he struggles to get a flash of the limelight. His counterpart in the American system emerges only during the election year when conventions and primaries generate the atmosphere of elemental battle in which all bets are open. Not for the presidential candidate the role of the weary challenger about to make one more attempt at the title. Few candidates have made two runs at the presidency, and succeeded. Robert Stanfield, in contrast, became leader in 1967 and led his party through three campaigns before calling it a day after the 1974 election.

The leader of the party out of power has a difficult task. His stock in trade consists of the mandate his party has given him by electing him leader; the possibility that he may become prime minister and therefore have portfolios at his disposal; and the abilities and internal support that brought him to the leadership in the first place.

CONCLUSION

As an approach to the understanding of Canadian politics, the study of leadership has much to recommend it, particularly in that it will illuminate much of the reality behind the traditional facade of parliamentary government. Much that a study of the institutions of parliamentary government in Canada will necessarily leave out can be provided by an examination of the role and power of the party leader and the prime minister as party and national leader. In the same way that one cannot really understand our politics without some understanding of the party system, so too an understanding of the party system is dependent in some measure on an understanding of the role of the leader. And in the areas of administration and communications in politics, once again the position of the leader is of some significance. Premiers and prime ministers alike must be aware of the tendency of their advisers and senior bureaucrats to sift and shape information before passing it up.[29]

How is it possible for us to understand how decisions are made in government without understanding the impact of a single figure at the apex of the mechanism? If everything in government is political, then the overarching concern must reflect the awareness of the demands, real or imagined, of the leader. The importance of this element in our political system is not diminishing; it is growing.

It is nevertheless wise to keep in mind the need to understand the relationship between the leader and led; between the leader and his support mechanisms; between the leader and his cabinet colleagues, his party caucus, his party members, and the public at large; as well as between the leader and the party elite who are not necessarily in cabinet or caucus. Those who finance parties and, of greater importance, those who finance and run large and powerful corporations that dominate major industries, have an important relationship with party leaders that may be either symbiotic or antagonistic. For the Liberal and Conservative parties, the economic elite wields a significant influence on the leader; for the New Democratic Party the leaders of the major trade unions cannot be ignored. The relationship between these elites and the purely political elite, especially the party leaders, is an important element in Canadian politics.

There is also a further advantage in an approach to Canadian politics through leadership, and that is that it ensures an awareness of the practical, earthy, intensely human reality of politics. The precision and clarity of a well-modeled systems analysis, or the charm of institutional description derived from historical precedent tend to conceal the impact of greed, envy, ambition, and deference. Because a good deal of emotion swirls around the office of leader, this approach does retain some of that quality of what is, after all, an intensely human endeavor. As was indicated above, we may be forever unable to measure and explore the psyche of our political leaders scientifically, yet we ought to be properly aware of the impact of human behavior on the political system, especially in the office that is the vital center.

The danger in the approach is a function of the fascination for the great individual which can cloud judgment and mask the significance of the other elements of government. The exercise of leadership is a multidimensional exercise that involves both action and reaction to the forces that are the results of decisions taken at other levels of government and at other centers of power in society. No leader acts in isolation. So it is of major importance for students of Canadian politics to have some understanding of the other parts of the system over which the political leader towers. Approaching Canadian politics through the examination of leadership alone would result in a somewhat one-sided view of the system; approaching it without looking at leadership would produce a somewhat unrealistic view of Canadian government. Politics is, after all, about control of the levers of power, or the allocation of scarce resources authoritatively if you must, and that, surely, is what leadership is all about.

ENDNOTES

1. Karl Deutsch, *Politics and Government: How People Decide their Fate* (Boston: Houghton-Mifflin, 1970), p. 204.

2. See Robert Michels, *Political Parties* (New York: Dover, 1959), especially Ch. 5.

3. See the bibliography at the end of this chapter.

4. Léon Dion, "The Concept of Political Leadership," *Canadian Journal of Political Science* (March, 1968), p. 3.

5. Cecil Gibb, "Leadership," *The Handbook of Social Psychology*, eds. Lindzey and Aronson (Don Mills: Addison Wesley, 1969), 2nd ed., Vol. IV, p. 268.

6. Winston Churchill, *The Second World War, Vol. 1, The Gathering Storm* (Boston: Houghton-Mifflin, 1948), p. 526.

7. See, for example, J.E. Esberey, "Personality and Politics," *CJPS* (March, 1973); and John Courtney, "Prime Ministerial Character: An Examination of Mackenzie King's Character," and J.E. Esberey, "Prime Ministerial Character: An Alternative View," *CJPS* (March, 1976).

8. Max Weber, *The Theory of Social and Economic Organization*, trans. Henderson and Parsons (New York: Collier-Macmillan, 1947).

9. Irvine Schiffer, *Charisma* (Toronto: University of Toronto Press, 1973), pp. 29-34; ch. 2.

10. Donald Peacock, *Journey to Power* (Toronto: Ryerson, 1968); and J.T. Saywell, ed., *The Canadian Annual Review* (Toronto: University of Toronto Press, 1969).

11. See Jack Granatstein, *The Politics of Survival: The Conservative Party of Canada, 1939-1945* (Toronto: University of Toronto Press, 1967), p. 138*ff*.

12. See J.W. Pickersgill, *My Years with St. Laurent* (Toronto: University of Toronto Press, 1963); and Dale Thomson, *Louis St. Laurent, Canadian* (Toronto: Macmillan, 1967), *passim*.

13. Dion, *op. cit.*, p. 6.

14. See Joseph Wearing, "President or Prime Minister," *Apex of Power: The Prime Minister and Political Leadership in Canada*, ed. Thomas Hockin (Scarborough: Prentice-Hall, 1971), esp. pp. 256-257.

15. See D. Shackleton, *Power Town* (Toronto: McClelland and Stewart, 1977), Ch. 2 for a journalistic account.

16. See John C. Courtney, *The Selection of National Party Leaders in Canada* (Toronto: Macmillan, 1973); and Peacock, *op. cit.*

17. See Geoffrey Stevens, *Stanfield* (Toronto: McClelland and Stewart, 1976), pp. 5-11.
18. See Hockin, *op. cit.*, especially the articles by Hockin, Schindeler, Smith, and Wright.
19. John Diefenbaker, *One Canada, Vol. II* (Toronto: Macmillan, 1976), p. 50.
20. See D.V. Smiley, "The National Party Leadership Convention in Canada: A Preliminary Analysis," in Hockin, *op. cit.*, pp. 52*ff.*
21. See D.G. Creighton, *The Forked Road* (Toronto: McClelland and Stewart, 1976), pp. 93-95; and Bruce Hutchison, *The Incredible Canadian: A Portrait of Mackenzie King* (Toronto: Longmans, 1953), Ch. 37.
22. Conrad Black, *Duplessis* (Toronto: McClelland and Stewart, 1976), p. 315.
23. See Pierre Laporte, *True Face of Duplessis* (Montreal: Harvest House, 1960); and Black, *op. cit.*, p. 299*ff.*
24. Wearing, in Hockin, *op. cit.*, p. 249.
25. See Peter Newman, *Renegade in Power* (Toronto: McClelland and Stewart, 1963) and *The Distemper of Our Times: Canadian Politics in Transition, 1963-1968* (Toronto: McClelland and Stewart, 1968); Peter Stursberg, *Diefenbaker: Leadership Lost, 1962-67* (Toronto: University of Toronto Press, 1976); and Donald C. Creighton, *Canada's First Century* (Toronto: Macmillan, 1970).
26. See John Diefenbaker, *One Canada: The Years of Achievement, 1956-1962* (Toronto: Macmillan, 1976), pp. 3-4, 42-44, for example.
27. See Courtney, *op. cit.*, p. 102; Stursberg, *op. cit.*, p. 163*ff.*
28. Courtney, *ibid.*, p. 151.
29. Interview with T.C. Douglas, March, 1977.

SELECTED REFERENCES

GENERAL

DION, LÉON. "The concept of political leadership: an analysis." *CJPS* (March, 1968). A clear and helpful discussion of the process and character of leadership.

EDINGER, LEWIS J., ed. *Political Leadership in Industrialized Societies*. New York: Wiley, 1967. A useful collection of essays for the more advanced students.

GOULDNER, ALVIN W., ed. *Studies in Leadership*. New York: Harper, 1950. In some ways a minor classic in the field; some of the essays are dated, but worth careful reading.

MICHELS, ROBERT. *Political Parties*. New York: Dover, 1959. The analysis of leadership in democratic parties and the elaboration of the "iron law of oligarchy" make this required reading.

SCHIFFER, IRVINE. *Charisma: A Psychoanalytic Look at Mass Society*. Toronto: University of Toronto Press, 1973. An intriguing examination of leaders and led from a Freudian perspective.

TUCKER, ROBERT. "The theory of charismatic leadership." *Daedalus* (Summer, 1968). The best discussion of Weber's influential thesis.

CANADA

While a great deal has been written about the process of choosing and disposing of leaders in Canada, relatively little has been written about leadership per se in a Canadian context. Perhaps the best studies in this latter category are:

COURTNEY, JOHN C. *The Selection of National Party Leaders in Canada.* Toronto: Macmillan, 1963. This monograph is broader than the title implies and has a particularly good bibliography.

———. "Prime Ministerial Character: An Examination of Mackenzie King's Political Leadership." *Canadian Journal of Political Science* (March, 1976).

ESBEREY, J.E. "Prime Ministerial Character: An Alternative View." *Canadian Journal of Political Science,* (March, 1976).

HOCKIN, THOMAS, ed. *Apex of Power: The Prime Minister and Political Leadership in Canada.* Toronto: Prentice-Hall, 1971. This is a good collection of essays, a number of which were written especially for this volume. The essays by Hockin, Smiley, Wright, Smith and Wearing in particular are worthwhile.

BIOGRAPHICAL STUDIES WHICH ARE USEFUL INCLUDE THE FOLLOWING:

FERNS, HARRY AND BERNARD OSTRY. *The Age of Mackenzie King: The Rise of the Leader.* Toronto: Lorimer, 1976.

NEATBY, BLAIR. *William Lyon Mackenzie King, 1924-1932: The Lonely Heights.* Toronto: University of Toronto Press, 1963.

———. *William Lyon Mackenzie King, 1932-1939: The Prism of Unity.* Toronto: University of Toronto Press, 1976.

NEWMAN, PETER C. *Renegade in Power: The Diefenbaker Years.* Toronto: McClelland and Stewart, 1963.

PEACOCK, DONALD. *Journey to Power.* Toronto: Ryerson, 1968.

PEARSON, LESTER B. *Memoirs,* Vol. III. Toronto: University of Toronto Press, 1975.

PICKERSGILL, J.W. *My Years with St. Laurent.* Toronto: University of Toronto Press, 1975.

SHERMAN, PADDY. *Bennett.* Toronto: McClelland and Stewart, 1966.

STURSBERG, PETER. *Diefenbaker: Leadership Gained, 1956-62.* Toronto: University of Toronto Press, 1976.

———. *Diefenbaker: Leadership Lost, 1962-67.* Toronto: University of Toronto Press, 1976.

14

Elites and Power in Canada

Dennis Forcese*

INTRODUCTION

There is probably no other area of social science enquiry that has stirred as much public interest as the study of elites. To write about men of wealth and power is to titillate an audience ready to be intrigued by the secrets and the conspiratorial designs of "the establishment." A recent example is the phenomenal publishing success of Peter Newman's *The Canadian Establishment*, a Canadian best seller. Newman's work is not presented as an analytical or critical work, but an entertaining inside look at Canada's wealthy entrepreneurs and their remote and mysterious world of luxury and power.[1] Particularly in a period of our social history in which concepts such as "mass society" and "alienation" are bandied about by social scientists and the literate public alike, with implied or stated notions of helpless and manipulated citizens, the idea that we are controlled by a shadowy oligarchy is compelling. Thus, despite criticism, theories of society that emphasize the existence of a power elite have persisted in the popular and in the social science literature. There has always been a demand to know and understand the nature of power and privilege, and the people who exercise it.

Reduced to its most fundamental sense, power can be understood as the ability to get what one wants, regardless of what other people want. It means making the decisions that affect one's life, and the lives of others. At the societal level, power means governing, whether through formal and legitimated political institutions or through the control of resources and organizations that are not nominally or strictly political. It is no new

*Associate Professor and Chairman, Department of Sociology and Anthropology, Carleton University.

thing to suggest that in Canadian society, as in all other societies, there is a small and enduring group of people who exercise such control or government. In some literature such groups are called oligarchies; more often today they are called elites.

ELITISTS AND PLURALISTS

The theoretical basis of the elitist model of society has usually been understood to consist of the works of writers whom James Burnham called "the Machiavellians."[2] Vilfredo Pareto, Georges Sorel, Gaetano Mosca, and Robert Michels, although differing in important respects,[3] were so labeled by Burnham because each in his own way stressed the contest tor and consolidation of power by cohesive minority groups. Of these theorists, Robert Michels is perhaps most often read today.[4]

In 1911 Michels first published his now famous work in which he offered his "iron law of oligarchy." Michels sought to demonstrate the "autocratic tendencies of leaders," and the generalization that, once in power, men will seek to maintain themselves in power and do so successfully. Thus, in modern voluntary associations and organizations, whether political parties, trade unions, government, or society itself, a small minority will establish itself as those making decisions. As contrasted to the rank and file, the leadership group develops the information, the expertise, and the inclination to persist in decision making. It also comes to command the rewards and the material resources. For Michels, such an oligarchy was inevitable, a function of modern organization. Some such orientation remains the basis of all present elitist analyses.

The bête noire of the elitists has been the pluralist model of society. A pure elite theorist takes the view that at all times, in all societies, and in all subgroups of society, decision-making power is in the hands of a cohesive and persisting minority group. Such a view obviously contradicts any simple model of democracy as idealized in the notion of full and equal participation, or opportunity to participate, in the functioning of society and its political system. Elite theorists, in effect, argue that such a liberal democratic view of the diffusion and plurality of power is naive, and that where it appears to be true it is an artful illusion, an aspect of "symbolic politics."[5] It is, they assert, an ideological deception, created and manipulated by those in power.

In point of fact, it is difficult to find representatives of such a simple liberal pluralist view. Rather, one finds in the social science literature writers who do not insist on the reality of a truly open and egalitarian politics but on a plurality of elites. Such theorists insist that there are many groups exercising power in modern democratic society, and that the basis of effective democracy is to be found in the contention and countervailing influences of these several elites. There is competition, conflict, and a balance of power among contending elites, or what Riesman called "veto groups,"[6] with each elite having an expertise and a socioeconomic power base. Ironically, many of the pluralist theorists also find support for their perspective in the works of the Machiavellians. For example, Seymour Martin Lipset wrote in his introduction to the English paperback edition of Michels's *Political Parties* that the very oligarchic tendency that Michels saw as the antithesis of democracy was the essence of its character.[7] Thus, although elite groups do exist, Lipset contends that

> Democracy in large measure rests on the fact that no one group is able to secure a basis of power and command over the majority so that it can effectively suppress or deny the claims of the group it opposes.[8]

For the liberal pluralists, therefore, politics is a matter of contending interests and of the groups, or elites, that act for them. Where the elitists contend that a unitary group dominates, and that the idea of countervailing interests and groups is fictional, the pluralists find the concept of ruling elite no less a fiction, or, in Meisel's view, a myth.[9]

In the pages to follow we shall examine North American examples of elite theory and research, both of the ruling elite and the pluralist elite varieties. We shall then analyze the research findings as they pertain to Canadian society and politics, and we shall consider whether there is any resolution to be found in the elitist-pluralist dispute. Finally we shall assess the general significance and utility of the elitist perspective, focusing on strengths as well as limitations.

LEVELS OF ANALYSIS: COMMUNITY AND NATION

There are two well-established levels of elite research. In the first instance, there is the long tradition of social science research in community structure and leadership. This work is closely wedded to the study of social stratification, and can be found illustrated in early and influential works such as the Yankeetown series of W. Lloyd Warner[10] or Middletown by the Lynds.[11] Incorporating a methodological tradition familiar to social anthropologists, these and similar works depended on an amalgam of reported or printed material, as well as observation and interview, to piece together a view of class structure and leadership in towns and small cities.

The extremely provocative work of Floyd Hunter was a direct heir to this tradition.[12] Hunter's study of the power structure in the city of Atlanta stimulated numerous approving and critical researchers, intent on replicating or repudiating his findings. Representing the latter was Robert Dahl and his study of New Haven,[13] and a companion volume by Nelson Polsby.[14] The books by Hunter and Dahl are examples of community-level leadership or elite research. But they differ in very important ways, in research method and in interpretive ideology, and are ideally representative of the elitist-pluralist disagreement. While Hunter, a sociologist, concluded that there was a cohesive and well-defined power elite, Dahl rejected such a view and, in his own work, which came to be representative of such study in the discipline of political science, argued that there were several specialized decision-making groups.

A second level of elite analysis involves the entire nation. National elite analysis is most clearly in the tradition of the European social theorists whom we earlier designated the Machiavellians. The most influential such work in modern social science was C. Wright Mills's, *The Power Elite.*[15] Like his fellow sociologist Hunter, Mills insisted that a dominant elite characterized American society, occupying the "command posts" of vital decision making. Rather than a democratic society of effective interest groups and voluntary associations, with open and representative decision making, the United States was a mass society, with a citizenry helpless before the power elite. To Mills, power was vested in the principal institutions of the society. As his critics, such as Dahl[16] and the sociologist Daniel Bell saw it,[17] Mills thereby contrived to avoid the reality of decision making and politics. As Bell put it, Mills produced "a book which discusses power, but rarely politics,"[18] a view aptly summarizing the pluralist objection.

In Canada, John Porter produced a monumental contribution to the tradition of national elite analysis. In *The Vertical Mosaic,*[19] Porter reveals the influence of C. Wright Mills. But unlike Mills, Porter developed a much more thorough and carefully documented view of the class structure of Canada. And although Porter wrote of elites, he was disinclined to interpret his data as proving there was a unitary ruling elite, leaving the question of the degree of integration of the several Canadian elite groups open to research. Thus, although Porter worked in the tradition of elite analysis after the fashion of the Machiavellians and Mills, he stopped short of their conclusions, and reported findings akin to the pluralist model.

RESEARCH METHODS AND BIASES

At both the community and the national levels of analysis, but especially the former, a wealth of research findings have accumulated in the disciplines of political science and sociology. Along with this volume of research has emerged evidence suggesting a bias in research strategy and findings by discipline.

We previously suggested that there are two distinct theoretical or ideological approaches to the question of elite: the elitist model which tends to be associated with sociology, and the pluralist which tends to be associated with political science. These contrary theoretical predispositions are taught succeeding generations of students in the two disciplines, and the outlooks are reinforced and perpetuated. These learned views, in turn, orient one's definition of the research problem in leadership, of the appropriate data, and of the correct interpretation of the data. The disciplinary preconceptions thereby tend to result in elite findings in sociology, and multiple elite findings in political science. This shows not deliberate distortion but how the real process of research is shaped by theoretical inclination and preferred research method.

In general there have been three methods developed to investigate power structures. Finer distinctions may be made, but most elite research will use a variant of one or more of the positional, the reputational, or the decision-making methods.[20] Each is associated with disciplinary preference; political scientists favor the decision-making method, and sociologists the positional or the reputational. Each realizes findings consistent with the theoretical preconceptions of the researchers. Accordingly, several social scientists have been led to conclude that the only way in which valid empirical results are to be had is by triangulation, that is, the use of the several research approaches in the same research project.[21] Yet, as we shall consider, the disparity in research findings seems as much a matter of data interpretation as of data collection. That is, the theoretical position from which the researcher begins, as well as the method used, govern the conclusions, leading one to be satisfied, or not satisfied, that the data are sufficient to confirm the existence of a ruling elite.

The Positional Method

The most prominent example of a positional approach is the work of Mills. In *The Power Elite*, he argued the existence of an American national elite on the basis of the key roles or positions existing in the United States.[22] That is, certain positions such as the presidency, the military chief of staff, or the chairman of the board of directors of a major corporation such as General Motors, were obviously deemed positions of power and their incumbents, therefore, people of power. Accordingly, the power elite was comprised of those in the "command posts" of American society who "share decisions having at least national consequences."[23] Similarly, in a less well known work, Mills had identified a labor elite, the "new men of power," on the basis of occupancy of key positions of power in labor organizations.[24]

The positional method to this point is rather straightforward, and certainly not a social science innovation insofar as it depends on citing formal or institutionalized positions of significant power and the people who fill these positions. But the power elite concept implies much more than some number of individuals who are in positions of power; an elite is a group exercising coordinated power and collective decision making. Mills insisted that this collective group character of key decision makers existed in the United States. He took the view that the demands and skills associated with decision making in one top command post were much the same as in another, whatever the institutional setting. Thus the individuals who filled these positions were interchangeable, in theory and in practice. Individual men of power had had careers in which mobility from one sector of power to another was usual, thereby negating any possibility of institutional checks or balances of power.

Mills distinguished three important sectors of power in American society: the economic, the political, and the military. He claimed that the three were interdependent in interests and in personnel. Military officers moved to directorships in major corporations, or into politics and even the presidency, or corporate heads ran for and won political office, or politicians would move from Capitol Hill to the corporate boardrooms. Not surprisingly, corporate, military, and political interests coincided. Government policies and expenditures related to the magnitude of the military establishment; military expenditures on personnel and especially on innovative and more elaborate technology was good for big business and not infrequently for politicians whose constituencies were dependent on a military base or a big business, such as Boeing, locked into military production; and politicians depended on business largesse for their campaign funds and perhaps some personal income, as well as postpolitical careers.

In addition to this interchangeability and interdependence, Mills noted that the men of power shared a social class background and experience. They went to the same or similar schools, lived in the same or similar neighborhoods, played at the same or similar clubs. In short, they shared an interaction set and life style. Thus, they thought alike, had similar attitudes and decision predispositions, and, Mills thought, they did collaborate. Because of these features—the interchangeability of roles, the interdependence, and the similarity of outlook and experience—Mills spoke not of isolated men of power but of an elite. Thus, the positional method, as exemplified in the work of Mills, consisted of identifying power positions and the people occupying them. But, additionally, he spoke of an elite on the basis of reasonable inference of frequent contact and interaction.

The Reputational Method

The reputational method requires similar indication of collusion, but a different technique is used to identify the men of power. The method is premised on the view that leadership in important decision areas is not necessarily, perhaps not even usually, to be found in the formal roles or offices of major institutions. Rather, there are powerful people who influence and make decisions in the absence of such office, and such people may not operate in a publicly visible manner. But they will be known to people in key positions in a community or society, if not to the general public. The method that one adopts, therefore, is to poll a number of key informants who, in turn, may suggest other informants, in order to compile a list of these people who by reputation are most influential, whether holding office or not. The initial interviews lead the researcher in snowballing fashion to additional interviewees until a reputational consensus becomes apparent. The list of leaders may then be resubmitted, if the researcher wishes, to a panel of key informants to determine priority of power, probably already indicated by the number of times a person of power was cited. Quite literally, then, the reputational method entails eliciting the names of people who have a reputation for determining important decisions in a community or a society.

This method is obviously best suited for small systems, such as towns or moderately sized cities. However, it is quite conceivable that a panel of informants could identify at a national level those people in or out of formal office whom they deem of pre-eminent power. In fact, political journalists often do make such judgments. It is the case, though, that the method has been associated mainly with community-level analysis.

The principal innovator in reputational method was Floyd Hunter. In his *Community Power Structure*,[25] Hunter pioneered the method and identified a clear consensus on the people dominating decision making in the city of Atlanta. He found that they tended to be associated with business and that they appeared to be not isolated individuals but an effective group. They shared not only a similarity of interest but also of social background, socialization, residence, and recreation. And although in business and not elected office, they tended to maintain close ties with the state legislature. Thus, as in the positional method, once the men of power were identified, they were judged to constitute an elite by virtue of some indication and some inference of interaction and collusion.

The Decision-Making Method

As we indicated previously, many social scientists took exception to such elitist conclusions. Reacting initially to Hunter and then to Mills, the opposition was best represented by Robert Dahl. Dahl set out to demonstrate an alternative method, and he subsequently generated quite different conclusions. The decision-making method, as the designation implies, was premised on the argument that if one is identifying decision makers, then one must avoid reputations and suspicions and deal in real decisions. To Dahl and to other critics such as Bell,[26] the trouble with researchers like Hunter was that they accepted statements about power, but did not look at or analyze the real execution of power by demonstrating who really made specific decisions.

In his work in New Haven, Dahl set out to recreate, on the basis of documentary records and the recollections of witnesses and participants, the decisions made in the community over a period of years. Those people found to have been active in forming decisions were considered the leaders. Dahl found that the leadership structure was pluralistic. Different kinds of decision situations engaged different people, leading Dahl to conclude that there were several specialized leadership groups rather than one powerful elite.

Different Methods and Different Findings

The New Haven study and similar findings were not convincing to the elitists, who scoffed that Dahl was merely dealing in superficialities and trivial decisions. They did not concede that the "front men" in elected office, such as city council, were the real power in a community. Nor could public records ever disclose the true decision-making interaction and the impact of informal participants. To the elitists, the decision-making method, given its focus, could only identify lower-level or secondary leaders, and its advocates were naive in viewing such leaders as the real men of power.

Conversely, to those working in the pluralist mode and using a decision-making method, the reputational and the positional approaches must inevitably suggest an elite, whether one existed or not. The elitist conclusions were thus viewed as conspiratorial fantasy, ignoring the reality of political interaction

Both parties to the issue have a point. The theoretical models and the methods with which they are associated do, to a considerable degree, predefine the research outcomes, rendering the findings a function of the researcher's preconceptions and investigative technique. In the 1960s several social scientists published works empirically indicating that researchers selected a research method on the basis of their training in a discipline, political science or sociology, and that the method seemed almost to guarantee the findings.[27] It seemed that pluralist or elitist conclusions were artifacts of the methods used and the methods a function of the orienting model prevailing in the discipline. Terry Clark further suggested that even where the methods produced valid findings, there was a biasing preselection of target communities.[28] That is, sociologists tended to select communities with elitist or pyramidal power structures, while political scientists tended to select communities with pluralist or dispersed power structures. Thus, for example, the dispute was dealing in apples and oranges, as in Hunter's industrial Atlanta and Dahl's university town of New Haven.

Further complicating the research findings, Nelson published the results of his re-analysis of community power-structure studies, and the analyses of critics of the studies, Walton, and Curtis and Petras. Nelson's data, based on correspondence with community power researchers, suggest that the confusion in findings is a matter of "poorly communicated ideas" or ambiguously stated conclusions on the nature of the leaders or elite identified, whether they are one or plural.[29] The ambiguity is compounded by the predisposition of the critics, who expect to find sociologists preferring a reputational method and political scientists preferring a decision-making method. Accordingly, Nelson concludes that the bias reported by Walton, and by Curtis and Petras, is as much their bias as that of the primary researchers.[30]

The dispute lives on, in theory and in empirical findings. It is unlikely that the existence or nonexistence of a ruling elite will ever be conclusively established in a modern complex liberal-democratic society such as the United States or Canada. One can point to privileged and powerful people, whether at the community or the national level. But it seems inevitable that there will always remain reasonable doubt about the extent of deliberate collaboration among such men of power. The idea that such people form an active and cohesive group seems doomed to remain at best a matter of conjecture and circumstantial evidence, especially on the national level. Stated otherwise, whatever the theoretical and research bias or objectivity, the confirmed data are unlikely ever to take one beyond the finding of a plurality of elites, whatever one's suspicions to the contrary. The Canadian research data illustrate this conclusion.

CANADIAN FINDINGS: THE LOCAL LEVEL

The American tradition of investigation into community leadership does not have a strong counterpart in Canada. But there are some comparable data, usually dealing with single-industry company towns, agricultural communities, and communities in economically depressed regions subject to government intervention, as in the Newfoundland outports or the Manitoba interlake fishing villages.[31] The methodologies used in such studies were similar to those previously described, although much of the work was not exclusively directed on the leadership structure but on the character and organization of the total community.

Reminiscent of the American research, a clear generalization that emerges from the Canadian community-level research, and that we will rediscover in the national studies in Canada, is the strength of the economic variable. The leadership of communities in Canada tends to be associated with economic success and business status. For example, a study of the Manitoba interlake communities and the fishing industry found that the economic success of individual fishermen was generally translated into overall leadership status. In the communities and the fishermen's association, leadership, both by formal position and by reputation, was in the hands of the most successful and prosperous fishermen. Yet these were still secondary leaders. As in company towns, the owners and managers of the companies, in this instance the fish-packing and marketing companies who even owned the boats used by the fishermen, were conceded the obvious dominance in decision making. Similarly, in his very thorough survey of community studies, Lucas notes that small businessmen and a few professionals dominate formal positions of decision making and tend to be viewed as most influential.[32] Even in company towns, where by definition the company runs things, the nearest thing to a countervailing influence or opposition elite was found not among company workers, but among the few independent merchants and professionals in the towns. Similar findings are reported in prairie agricultural regions. In his study of Biggar, Saskatchewan, Richard Laskin reports that businessmen and professionals dominate community organizations.[33] In Alberta, Bennett finds that the reputational and formal leaders are the wealthy ranchers, the prosperous element of these mixed farming-ranching districts. These are characteristically the people engaged in provincial politics, making the big decisions, leaving overt local politics to their lesser neighbors, the farmers.[34]

An additional empirical generalization of note emerges from the

Canadian community-level research. In small communities, the pre-eminence of people from "correct" ethnic backgrounds is consistently noted. With very localized exceptions, such as the high status of the Icelanders in the Manitoba interlake region,[35] people of United Kingdom origins have been found in dominating leadership positions. Most researchers remark on the pattern of ethnic stratification in their communities, with Anglo-Scottish Canadians at the pinnacle, in wealth and in power.[36]

A study of the power structure in a large Canadian city also confirmed the business and ethnic pattern of dominance. Kelner's Toronto data led her to distinguish a primary or core elite level, and a lesser or secondary elite, both business dominated. At the lesser level, there was some penetration by the Jews and the Irish, but she reports the core elite was closed, and consisted of old monied families of British descent.[37]

The community-level empirical generalizations prove to be very consistent with national power-structure research findings. They constitute strong confirmation of John Porter's conclusions on ethnic advantage and power in Canada, and of the domination of national elite groups by people of British descent.

CANADIAN FINDINGS: THE NATIONAL LEVEL

The most influential work dealing in Canadian elites remains, thirteen years after its publication in 1965, John Porter's *The Vertical Mosaic*. As we noted earlier, although probably influenced by C. Wright Mills, Porter's work is far more thorough, theoretically and empirically, than *The Power Elite*. Porter's conclusions can most aptly be termed as qualified elitist; he does not deny, as the pluralists do, the possibility of a ruling elite, but empirically he can only demonstrate a plurality of elites.

Porter cites the critical sectors of power in Canada as being the economic, political, bureaucratic, ideological, and labor, and attaches the greatest importance to the economic. Like Mills, he examines the social class origins and life styles of people in positions of power in these sectors and finds sufficient coincidence of background, interaction, and interest to suggest similar or complementary decision making. But rather than insist that there is a unified and cohesive ruling elite dominating the nation, Porter resists such an inference and instead concludes that in Canada the several elites do not fully merge. Despite the degrees of identity among the powerful in the several elite sectors, they may, because of the specializations of the elites, not only cooperate but also compete. Porter persists in this view ten years after the publication of *The Vertical Mosaic* and writes:

> In *The Vertical Mosaic* I adopted what might be called a plural elite model which, very simply, stated that the power of economic, political, bureaucratic, military and other institutions tend to be separated because they perform different tasks for a society and,

in so doing, become specialized, and hence there is always a tendency for power also to be separated. At the same time the overall coordinating and guidance needs of the society require interaction between the various elite groups. It therefore becomes a matter of empirical investigation to discover the extent to which these coordinating and guidance needs lead to an aggrandizement of power, to the creation of what might be called a power elite.[38]

In his research, Porter found, as reaffirmed by later researchers, that the more privileged and more powerful Canadians tended to be people of United Kingdom descent. This was especially so in the economic sector. The political elite proved an exception, largely because of the structure of formal political organization in Canada, that is, federalism, and regional patterns of immigration. Canada has regionally specific ethnic concentrations, approximately coincident with provincial boundaries. The obvious example is the French in Quebec, but in addition, there are the Scots in the Maritimes, the Anglo-Irish in Newfoundland, the Anglo-Scots in Ontario, and the central Europeans in the Prairies. Within the structure of local, provincial, and federal politics, local ethnic representation, especially that of French Canadians, was inevitable by force of number, despite the economic privilege of Anglo minorities. Thus we find that the political elite is more ethnically heterogeneous than other elite sectors. Middle-class professional occupations lead to electoral success and cabinet positions,[39] but, significantly, for people of many ethnic groups. There is a class advantage, but an ethnic bias or advantage, which is a marked feature in nonpolitical sectors, especially the economic elite, is not an important factor in gaining access to the political elite except regionally, as described above.

Porter also remarked on the pattern of ethnic privilege in the federal bureaucracy. This finding was later supported in Beattie's work when he clearly demonstrated that francophones had only slight access to middle range executive positions, although there was indication that senior positions were becoming increasingly accessible to francophones.[40] In general, the bureaucratic elite has been a stable influence in Canadian politics, not subject to the turnover characteristic of elected political office, and thereby very often the object of the attention of corporate interest groups.

Olsen, who has been working with John Porter, also finds that the "state elite," that is, politicians such as federal cabinet ministers, provincial premiers, justices of the Supreme Court of Canada, and provincial chief justices, tend to be middle class in origin. He also finds that people of British descent still dominate the judiciary, although the proportion of francophones has been increasing.[41] Olsen reports that except for Quebec, where francophone politicians are obviously well represented, people of British descent dominate, especially in Ontario, British Columbia, and Alberta.[42] Olsen also looks at federal and provincial bureaucrats of the rank of deputy or assistant deputy minister and heads of Crown corporations or regulating bodies in the provinces. Again he finds people of middle-class origins and, by ethnicity, the British, very much overrepresented, with the francophones moderately underrepresented and all other ethnic groups considerably underrepresented.[43]

Clement, a student of Porter's, has attempted to replicate and update Porter's work. Concentrating on the economic or corporate elite, Clement confirms the ethnic pattern of representation but comes to quite different conclusions from Porter on the degree of access or mobility into the elite and the extent of elite integration.[44] Clement attaches major importance to the Anglo-dominated corporate and media elites that control the economy and the ideology of the nation, and thereby effectively dominate or rule Canadian society. Distinguishing by economic sector, Clement finds that there are significant variations in the extent of foreign penetration of corporate ownership in Canada. The mass media, transportation networks, financial institutions, and the utilities are Canadian-owned, and Clement hence speaks of an indigenous Canadian elite. Noting that the degree of foreign control of Canadian industry will have increased dramatically from the early post-World War II period of Porter's research, Clement distinguishes a second elite group of considerable importance, the comprador elite. These are the directors of foreign-owned corporations, resident in Canada and dominating the resource and manufacturing industries. He also identifies a third group, the parasite elite, nonresidents of Canada usually located in the United States, who direct the multinational corporations active in Canada. Both of the latter are associated with the branch-plant companies operating in Canada. Clement concludes that the members of the indigenous Canadian elite have essentially been go-betweens vis-à-vis the American and other foreign interests, and have thus developed a complementarity of interest and benefit, sanctioned and furthered by the state, that is, the Canadian government.[45]

Related to this division of function in the elite, Clement finds that access to and mobility into elite positions have become increasingly restricted since Porter's research. Although Clement is willing to speak of an effective ruling elite, he does not lose sight of the class basis of Canadian society and observes that the elite, with rare exception, now consists of people of upper-class social origins and is thereby more homogeneous and better integrated than in the earlier post-World War II period.[46]

> The existence of a powerful Canadian commercial elite controlled by the upper class and of a predominantly foreign elite in production means that Canada remains a "low mobility" society. Concentration and centralization in commercial sectors has been the result of indigenous forces while these same processes in the productive sectors have been imposed from outside. The result is an economy which is highly structured with few mobility avenues for those outside the upper class.[47]

Clement very explicitly seeks to distinguish his analysis from the pluralist conviction of representative politics in which interest groups contend with one another, effectively check one another, and in which their activities tend to be mediated by the federal and provincial governments. He is particularly critical of the work of Robert Presthus,[48] the major pluralist contributor to the Canadian literature on elite structure.[49] Unlike Porter who insists on the existence of such an elite, Presthus perceives countervailing elites. His model might be described as an interest-group concept of elites in Canada, much like that of Engelmann and Schwartz who write of economic, political, administrative, and ideological subsystems and elites.[50]

Presthus deals in three components of the political elite: legislators, bureaucrats or public servants, and interest-group leaders. His analysis seeks to relate the activities of elite groups in the economy to the provincial and federal bureaucracies, legislatures, and cabinets. Although he finds considerable corporate influence, an influence much greater than that of organized labor as an interest group, and some coincidence of corporate and government interest, Presthus insists on the effective autonomy of the state and that corporate interest groups and elites have not merged or integrated. This insistence upon the separation of elites is a feature of the pluralist interpretation, despite the fact that the pluralists are as aware as the elitists of some degree of harmony of interest and outlook between elites. In Canada we know that particular interests are associated with particular parties. For example, in his study of party financing, Paltiel reports that the Liberal party and the Progressive Conservative party are largely financed by big business, while the New Democratic Party tends to be supported by organized labor.[51] Few of us find such a relationship remarkable. As the pluralists would suggest, such financial connections are altogether reasonable and expected features in interest-group politics.

Presthus holds the view that elite competition and bargaining are essential in a viable political system. In the process of elite accommodation, he argues, contending interests reach a degree of accord that creates equilibrium in society and deters "disintegrative tendencies." Thus "elite accommodation may be regarded as a structural requisite of any democratic society."[52]

It is this theoretical premise that enables Presthus to come to quite different conclusions about the importance of elites in Canadian society. Like Clement and Porter, Presthus finds that, with the exception of the relatively open political elite, the economic-based elite groups are quite homogeneous insofar as class, ethnic background, and experience are concerned.[53] But the accommodation and cooperation among the socially homogeneous elite subgroups is vital to the stability of the socially heterogeneous society of Canada. Like other political scientists, such as Arend Lijphart and Kenneth McRae, Presthus believes that some measure of elite collaboration or rule must exist.[54] To the elitist, such "consociational democracy" is not democracy and deters necessary social change, while to the pluralist such elite accommodation ensures the continued existence of the national society. One thereby finds in the Canadian literature the essence of the elitist-pluralist dispute, rooted not so much in diverging empirical findings as in the theoretical meaning and importance attached to the empirical findings.

THE POWER STRUCTURE AND CHANGE

It is apparent when we consider the cumulative research findings dealing with the subject of elites that there is a fundamental theoretical divergence in the outlooks of people working in the genre. It is doubtful, given that the divergence is more theoretical than empirical, that the disputants can be reconciled. On the one hand, the theoretical or ideological predisposition of elitists stems from a critical and pessimistic view of modern capitalist democracies. The pluralist view, on the other hand, derives from an essentially satisfied view of the same sociopolitical systems. Research by each finds elite groups, but in the former instance these groups constitute an effectively integrated and ominously powerful ruling elite. In the latter instance, the several elite groups maintain a measure of subautonomy, and to the degree that they cooperate and share outlooks and interests, such cooperation is functionally necessary to maintain our society. Each school of elite analysis invokes the call to political realism, the reality of extreme power or the reality of political exchange. Finally, and conceptually important, both seem to concede, at times explicitly, that the ruling elite or the several specialized elites, are representatives of some larger social body, a privileged and influential upper or ruling class. In particular, the elitists are willing to make this explicit, perhaps because they are more apt to initiate their elite analyses from the broader theoretical and empirical standpoint of stratification of class analysis that is such a prominent interest in the discipline of sociology. Thus ultimately Clement not only makes clear that the thrust of his analysis is to point to a ruling class,[55] but also suggests that the concept of elite may therefore be of slight importance and a mere methodological tool.[56]

The elitist pessimism and the pluralist optimism fundamentally relate to the necessity for and the prospects of change in society. To the extent that one concludes that liberal democratic-capitalist societies such as Canada are desirable and even admirable social systems, whatever their imperfections may be, then one may logically emphasize structures and processes that maintain that kind of society. Given that point of view, such change as is desired must be gradual, allowing a stable evolutionary transition. We find such a sentiment in the work of John Porter who seems to bridge the elitist and pluralist extremes. Although Porter has explicitly decried the excesses and inequalities of stratified Canadian society, he rejects calls to change in Canada that are premised on radical or violent transformations.[57] His meritocratic Canada of equal opportunity is an ideal that he considers to be an achievable target, and one that will presumably not utterly eliminate privileged and powerful groups or elites.

To the pluralists, such a point of view must appear altogether sane and reasonable, as it must to some degree also appeal to any middle-class Canadians, whatever contrary radical beliefs they may hold from intellectual and ideological conviction.

But whatever the appeal, the elitists' critical rejection of such reasonableness fundamentally relates to their estimation of the probability of necessary social change. Class societies are stable societies, and, because of the cooperation of elite groups, the patterns of power and privilege in such societies are enduring; on this the pluralists and the elitists agree. But as far as the elitists are concerned, gradual changes are not likely to make the desired changes in wealth and power. The elites or the ruling class will not act in the interests of significant redistribution, but in the interests of perpetuating their advantage. Consequently, only massive, and perhaps violent, challenge can bring about the necessary change. In the end, the dissolution of ruling elites is to be had in class conflict and the destruction of capitalist classes in societies.

To expect a synthesis of these divergent views would be a naiveté of the magnitude of which each of the protagonists accuses the other. In Canada, as elsewhere, the conclusions one reaches about elites are a matter of the theoretical and ideological convictions one holds, realizing that no science, and certainly not the social sciences, are ever fully objective and value free.

CONCLUSIONS: THE SCOPE AND RELEVANCE OF ELITE RESEARCH

Investigation of elites is an area of study that extends over two academic disciplines: sociology and political science. The question of whether or not there are elites is of long standing and of fundamental theoretical interest, for it addresses the very nature of society and of power and government. It addresses the question of who rules, and for whom, a question elemental to political analysis. In the older literature in political science, the question was often taken up in terms of the existence, nature, and influence of oligarchies. The modern inclination is to substitute the concept of elite for oligarchy, but the end, determining the nature and process of the exercise of power, remains the same.

Elite analysis in the modern literature in political science and political sociology is in no part unique to Canadian scholarly research. Rather, as we have attempted to make clear, its origins and its cross references are to be found in European social and political theory as well as in American empirical research. To take but two prominent examples, we know that John Porter was much influenced by C. Wright Mills and his work in the elitist tradition, while Robert Presthus is an American who brought his pluralist outlooks with him when he took up a university appointment in Toronto, and applied them in his Canadian research. To understand empirical research and interpretations of research on elites in Canada, one must be aware of the non-Canadian history and context of the work.

In addition to the general ties to fundamental social and political theory, research on elites in Canada and elsewhere does relate to specific subfields or traditions of enquiry in social science. The best examples in sociology are to be found in the area of social-stratification research where the matter of elites is of intrinsic interest, and, in political science, in the study of interest group politics where researchers must inevitably come to terms with the question of elites. Once again, we may revert to the examples of John Porter and Robert Presthus: Porter, a sociologist, works in the subfield of social stratification, while Presthus orients his interest in elites within the broader subfield of interest-group politics.

Another growing area of social science research which involves elite analysis is especially pertinent to Canada; this is the study of multiethnic society and politics and, in particular, the increasingly popular concept and model of consociational democracy. The reformulation of the long-standing academic interest in the bases of social and political stability is a defining feature of the consociational model, and it cannot avoid coming to grips with the nature and role of elite groups. Other obvious links to subfields in political science and political sociology would include the study of political socialization, political ideology and culture, mass politics and political movements, political mobilization, and political development. In each of these areas, the problem of elite influence and manipulation is pertinent. In fact, it is all but impossible to conceive of a field of political enquiry that does not at some point have to deal with the question of elites, given that the study of politics is the study of the exercise of power.

We have argued that the study of elites is fraught with controversy. It has produced findings subject to alternative interpretations and will continue to do so. But, whatever the controversy in interpretation, the findings have been of value. Detailed empirical knowledge of the social characteristics and relations of "men of power" is obviously a necessary component of any complete social or political understanding. Thus, in Canada, we increasingly have useful empirical information that enables us to understand the character, composition, and the decision-making predilections of men of power.

But we must not lose sight of the fact that analysis of elites is but a fraction of the important research in political science or political sociology. It does not, for example, satisfactorily consider the nature and importance of formal and informal political institutions on the one hand, or of mass behavior on the other, although many elitists would have us believe that elites simply contrive political organizations and manipulate the masses. The so-called elites, or the ruling class, are but minorities of the mass of Canadian people and organizations. They represent vast wealth and power, but not autonomous power. Above all else, the one important matter with which elite analysis does not deal involves the degree of autonomy of such men of power or, conversely, the extent and manner in which a ruling elite or a plurality of elites are influenced by nonelite Canadians. It is not satisfactory to assume that in the study of political elites we have the essence of social and political explanation. Such an emphasis ignores mass behavior, fails to demonstrate the elite's manipulation of public behavior, attitudes, ideologies, or political cultures, and does not clearly demonstrate effective control of agencies of socialization in Canada or any society. Moreover, of increasing interest to political scientists, especially the Marxist theorists, is the degree to which the state and its governing organs have a power quite independent of elite or ruling-class interests. Thus, for example, in a very detailed work, Pierre Fournier writes of the Quebec ruling class, both French- and English-Canadian businessmen, who, in his view, shape Quebec society through the media, through education, and through government.[58] But—the point needs to be emphasized—he insists that the state is "not simply an instrument in the hands of business or private enterprise" but "relatively autonomous."[59]

In sum, the greatest weakness of elite analysis has been the widespread assumption that elites, integrated or plural, really run things, be it in collusion or in competition. In fact, however, all that is demonstrated is that elites are people of wealth who also make many important political decisions. But they do not do so in a social vacuum. Elites, too, exist in a larger society and are subject to influences. If we hope to gain anything close to a full understanding of society, of politics, and of sociopolitical change, we must study not only elites but also the interaction between elites and nonelites; anything less will be incomplete and inadequate.

ENDNOTES

1. Peter Newman, *The Canadian Establishment* (Toronto: McClelland and Stewart, 1974).

2. James Burnham, *The Machiavellians: Defenders of Freedom* (New York: John Day, 1943).

3. John Meisel, *The Myth of the Ruling Class: Gaetano Mosca and the Elite* (Ann Arbor: The University of Michigan Press, 1962).

4. Robert Michels, *Political Parties: A Sociological Study of the Oligarchical Tendencies of Modern Democracy* (New York: Collier Books, 1962).

5. Murray Edelman, *The Symbolic Uses of Politics* (Urbana: University of Illinois Press, 1964).

6. David Riesman, *The Lonely Crowd* (New Haven: Yale University Press, 1961).

7. Seymour Martin Lipset, "Introduction," in Robert Michels, *op. cit.*, p. 34.

8. *Ibid.*, pp. 36-37.

9. Meisel, *op. cit.*

10. W. L. Warner and P.S. Lunt, *The Status System of a Modern Community* (New Haven: Yale University Press, 1947).

11. Robert S. Lynd and H. M. Lynd, *Middletown: A Study in Modern American Culture* (New York: Harcourt, Brace and World, 1929).

12. Floyd Hunter, *Community Power Structure* (Chapel Hill: University of North Carolina Press, 1956).

13. Robert Dahl, *Who Governs? Power and Democracy in an American City* (New Haven: Yale University Press, 1963).

14. Nelson Polsby, *Community Power and Political Theory* (New Haven: Yale University Press, 1963).

15. C. Wright Mills, *The Power Elite* (New York: Oxford University Press, 1956).

16. Robert Dahl, "A Critique of the Ruling Elite Model," *The Search for Community Power*, ed. W. Hawley and F. Wirt (Englewood Cliffs, N.J.: Prentice-Hall, 1968), pp. 151-158.

17. Daniel Bell, *The End of Ideology: On the Exhaustion of Political Ideas in the Fifties*, rev. ed. (New York: Collier Books, 1962).

18. *Ibid.*, p. 74.

19. John Porter, *The Vertical Mosaic* (Toronto: University of Toronto Press, 1965).

20. Arnold Rose, *The Power Structure: Political Process in American Society* (New York: Oxford University Press, 1967), pp. 255-297; Wendell Bell et al., *Public Leadership* (San Francisco: Chandler, 1961), pp. 1-120; Delbert Miller, *International Community Power Structures: Comparative Studies of Four World Cities* (Bloomington: Indiana University Press, 1970), pp. 3-29; Ted Goertzel, *Political Society* (Chicago: Rand McNally, 1976), pp. 119-132.

21. Terry Clark, "Community or Communities," *Community Structure and Decision-Making: Comparative Analyses*, ed. Terry Clark (San Francisco: Chandler, 1968), pp. 83-90; Michael Nelson, "Community Power Structure: Fact or Artifact?" M. A. Thesis, Carleton University, Ottawa, 1972.

22. Mills, *op. cit.*

23. *Ibid.*, p. 18.

24. C. Wright Mills, *The New Men of Power* (New York: Harcourt, Brace and World, 1958).

25. Hunter, *op. cit.*

26. Wendell Bell, *op. cit.*

27. John Walton, "Substance and Artifact: The Current Status of Research on Community Power Structure," *American Journal of Sociology*, 71 (1966), pp. 430-438; Terry Clark et al., "Discipline, Method, Community Structure and Decision-Making: The Role and Limitations of the Sociology of Knowledge," *The American Sociologist*, 3 (August, 1968), pp. 214-217; James Curtis and John Petras, "Community Power, Power Studies, and the Sociology of Knowledge," *Human Organization* (Fall, 1970), pp. 204-218; Michael Nelson, *op. cit.*

28. Terry Clark, *op. cit.*, pp. 83-90.

29. Michael Nelson, "The Validity of Secondary Analyses of Community Power Studies," *Social Forces*, 52 (June, 1974), p. 535.

30. *Ibid.*, pp. 531-537.

31. Richard Laskin, *Organizations in a Saskatchewan Town* (Saskatoon Centre for Community Studies, 1961); Rex Lucas, *Minetown, Milltown, Railtown: Life in Canadian Communities of Single Industry* (Toronto: University of Toronto

Press, 1971); Dennis Forcese, "Leadership in a Depressed Primary Industry," M. A. Thesis, University of Manitoba, Winnipeg, 1964.

32. Lucas, *op. cit.*

33. Laskin, *op. cit.*

34. John Bennett, *Northern Plainsmen: Adaptive Strategy and Agrarian Life* (Chicago: Aldine, 1969).

35. Forcese, *op. cit.*

36. Lucas, *op. cit.*

37. Merrijoy Kelner, "Ethnic Penetration into Toronto's Elite Structure," *The Canadian Review of Sociology and Anthropology*, 7 (May, 1970), pp. 128-137.

38. John Porter, "Foreword," in *The Canadian Corporate Elite*, by Wallace Clement (Toronto: McClelland and Stewart, The Carleton Library, 1975), p. xiv, reprinted by permission of The Canadian Publishers, McClelland and Stewart Ltd., Toronto.

39. Dennis Forcese and John deVries, "Occupation and Electoral Success in Canada: The 1972 Federal Election," Department of Sociology and Anthropology, Carleton University, Ottawa, 1974; Dennis Forcese and John deVries, "Occupation and Electoral Success in Canada: The 1974 Federal Election," *The Canadian Review of Sociology and Anthropology*, 14 (1977), pp. 331-340.

40. Chris Beattie, *Minority Men in a Majority Setting: Middle-Level Francophones in the Canadian Public Service* (Toronto: McClelland and Stewart, The Carleton Library, 1975).

41. Dennis Olsen, "The State Elites," *The Canadian State*, ed. Leo Panitch (Toronto: University of Toronto Press, 1977), pp. 199-224.

42. Olsen, *op. cit.*

43. *Ibid.*

44. Wallace Clement, *The Canadian Corporate Elite: An Analysis of Economic Power* (Toronto: McClelland and Stewart, The Carleton Library, 1975); "Continental Capitalism: Corporate Power Relations Between Canada and the U.S." Ph.D. Thesis, Carleton University, Ottawa, 1976.

45. Clement, *The Canadian Corporate Elite, op. cit.*, pp. 344-366; "Continental Capitalism," *op. cit.*

46. Clement, *The Canadian Corporate Elite, op. cit.*, pp. 172-223.

47. *Ibid.*, p. 357, reprinted by permission of The Canadian Publishers, McClelland and Stewart Ltd., Toronto.

48. *Ibid.*, pp. 358-361.

49. Robert Presthus, *Elites in the Policy Process* (London: Cambridge University Press, 1974).

50. Frederick Engelmann and Mildred Schwartz, *Political Parties and the Canadian Social Structure* (Scarborough: Prentice-Hall, 1967), pp. 76-90.

51. Khayyam Paltiel, *Political Party Financing in Canada* (Toronto: McGraw-Hill, 1970).

52. Presthus, *op. cit.*, p. 34.

53. *Ibid.*, pp. 238, 394.

54. Kenneth McRae, *Consociational Democracy* (Toronto: McClelland and Stewart, The Carleton Library, 1975).

55. Clement, *The Canadian Corporate Elite, op. cit.*, pp. 357-358.

56. Clement, "Continental Capitalism," *op cit.*
57. John Porter, "Foreword," *The Canadian Corporate Elite, op. cit.,* pp. ix-xv.
58. Pierre Fournier, *The Quebec Establishment: The Ruling Class and the State* (Montreal: Black Rose Books, 1976).
59. *Ibid.,* p. 202.

SELECTED REFERENCES

BELL, WENDELL, R. HILL, AND C. WRIGHT. *Public Leadership.*San Francisco:Chandler, 1961. A thorough critical review of the several approaches to elite investigation, with a comprehensive pre-1960 bibliography.

BURNHAM, JAMES. *The Machiavellians: Defenders of Freedom.* New York: John Day, 1943. A provocative exposition of the works of Machiavelli, Michels, Mosca, and Pareto, and their conceptions of elite rule.

CLARK, TERRY, ed. *Community Structure and Decision-Making: Comparative Analyses.* San Francisco: Chandler, 1968. A good collection of comparative community decision-making analyses, attempting to represent the several methodological approaches.

CLEMENT, WALLACE. *The Canadian Corporate Elite: An Analysis of Economic Power.* Toronto: McClelland and Stewart, The Carleton Library, 1975. A detailed attempt to update John Porter's analysis of the corporate elite, with evidence of increased concentration of power. The book includes a good bibliography.

DAHL, ROBERT. *Who Governs? Power and Democracy in an American City.* New Haven: Yale University Press, 1961. The pathfinding work in the decision-making approach, and as such a "classic" work.

HUNTER, FLOYD. *Community Power Structure.* Chapel Hill: University of North Carolina Press, 1956. The empirical study of elites in North America effectively begins with this work in the reputational tradition.

MEISEL, JOHN. *The Myth of the Ruling Class: Gaetano Mosca and the Elite.* Ann Arbor: The University of Michigan Press, 1962. A detailed critique of the work of Mosca, and what Meisel considers the error of elite analysis.

MICHELS, ROBERT. *Political Parties: A Sociological Study of the Oligarchical Tendencies of Modern Democracy.* New York: Collier Books, 1962. The most famous, and oft-cited work in the European tradition of empirical elite analysis.

MILLER, DELBERT. *International Community Power Structures: Comparative Studies of Four World Cities.* Bloomington: Indiana University Press, 1970. A comparative analysis of power structure in America, England, and Latin America.

MILLS, C. WRIGHT. *The Power Elite.* New York: The Oxford University Press, 1956. This work was the ideological spur that prompted the spate of counter-efforts in elite analysis, and remains the most famous book in North American sociology.

MOSCA, GAETANO. *The Ruling Class.* New York: McGraw-Hill, 1939. Along with Michels, this work is the usually cited European theoretical reference for elite analysis.

NELSON, MICHAEL. "Community Power Structure: Fact or Artifact?" Unpublished M.A. Thesis, Department of Sociology and Anthropology, Carleton University, Ottawa, 1972. A very detached analysis of disciplinary and methodological bias in elite investigation, with an extensive bibliography.

PORTER, JOHN. *The Vertical Mosaic.* Toronto: The University of Toronto Press, 1965. The most influential work in Canadian social science, Porter's analysis offered systematic evidence of concentrated power in Canada.

PRESTHUS, ROBERT. *Elites in the Policy Process.* London: Cambridge Press, 1974. A comparative analysis of elites and interest groups in Canada and the United States.

———. *Elite Accommodation in Canadian Politics.* Toronto: Macmillan, 1973. An analysis of interest group politics and elites in Canada, with considerable empirical detail.

ROSE, ARNOLD. *The Power Structure: Political Process in American Society.* New York: Oxford University Press, 1967. An explicit attempt to speak against the pluralist interest group conception of elite behavior in the United States.

15

The Group Basis of Politics

Mildred A. Schwartz[*]

REASONS FOR STUDYING GROUPS

To the contemporary social scientist the call to a "group basis of politics" seems self-evident. Politics is inherently a group process since it involves the definition of collective goals, particularly those pertaining to the allocation of scarce resources. Politics does not concern isolated individuals; the political process gets underway only when there are a number of people whose collective existence leads to the development of political leadership, institutions, and organizations. Yet to the extent that groups in politics may no longer connote anything special, we risk missing the innovative potential generated through the group approach, and the battles fought and won that gave the group approach much of its lasting impact and its inability to excite us now.

A necessarily brief picture of trends in the intellectual history of the group approach must give pre-eminence to the rejection of nineteenth-century views of sovereignty, in which authority was confined to the state.[1] Among the major figures producing a shift in emphasis was the German exponent of historical jurisprudence, Otto von Gierke (1841-1921), who argued that the state had many similarities to other social groups, and, in particular, shared with other groups in making and enforcing laws. In other words, he treated law and authority as general social processes operating in the life of all organized collectivities, and not just exclusive attributes of the state.[2] Translated into English, von Gierke's work influenced a broad range of scholars, including Harold Laski (1893-1950), himself highly influential in his early writing in furthering the "pluralist theory of the state" in which power was seen as residing in a number of associations, of which the state is but one.[3]

*Professor of Sociology, University of Illinois at Chicago Circle.
Author's Note: My colleagues Paul Pross, Fred Engelmann, and Léon Dion kindly reviewed this chapter, though time did not permit adding specific suggestions. They are not responsible, however, for my interpretations.

This new emphasis, attuned to the spread of popular sovereignty and growing limits on the authoritarian state, was attractive to political thinking then current in the United States, but an even stronger impetus there was empirical rather than normative. That is, Americans were probably less concerned with the locus of authority, since their system made it evident that the state was not a monolithic center of power, but rather with how government actually operated. This is the origin of the "behavioral revolution," which began with a shift away from juridic and institutional emphases to a focus on how governments work. The crucial figure was Arthur Bentley whose *The Process of Government*, published in 1908, was the American version of a group emphasis.[4] For Bentley, the task was straightforward: to explain political behavior we cannot spend time dissecting laws, constitutions, or treatises; nor can we concern ourselves with individual psychological qualities.

> The raw material [of government] can be found only in the actually performed legislating-administrating-adjudicating activities of the nation and in the streams and currents of activity that gather among the people and rush into these spheres.[5]

In the United States as well, the move to a group approach, describing things as they were, found an outlet in the writings of "muckrakers," those concerned with exposing political corruption and venality to the public. The relation between the study of groups and the muckrakers lay in their revelations of how special group interests affected the course of governmental decisions.[6] This direction is also found in the work of economic historians, in particular Charles Beard, who placed a new emphasis on the impact of business interests on party politics.[7]

To the extent that these various threads can be brought together, they share a common concern with the place of the individual in his social and political milieu, and constitute an affirmation of the liberal democratic state. The contemporary view is stated most carefully by the eminent Laval University political scientist, Léon Dion, in his two-volume work.[8] It is no longer primarily concerned with the dominance of the state, nor with the rather simple-minded solutions suggested by Bentley that defining groups and their interests tells us everything we need to know about politics, nor does it have the conviction that a plurality of interests protects the individual from the tyranny of any one of them. Yet it does recognize that groups serve as a buffer between the isolated individual and his vulnerability to the manipulations of elites. It questions the arguments of neorationalists such as Mancur Olson,[9] who give pre-eminence to the individual as the unit of political analysis but omit collective experiences and aspirations. From the perspective of political theory, then, we can begin with Dion's contention that the group approach is not all there is to politics; but to ignore groups is to ignore the fundamental issues raised by a liberal society concerning the role of the individual and his place in the polity.

There are really only a few Canadian group theorists. Canadian political thought was not engaged by the issues of historic concern to the originating theorists, even though Harold Laski taught at McGill University during World War I. Nor were there notable followers of Bentley here, such as David Truman or V. O. Key in the United States. Certainly Canadian students are now unusually fortunate to have available Dion's impressive work on the subject. But Dion is too comprehensive in his review of the literature and too fair-minded in his assessment to be characterized as a whole-hearted group theorist. Dion doubts whether the study of groups can even be termed a theory. Moreover, his two-volume work is relatively thin on Canadian material, and in that sense one would be hard-pressed to describe him as a theorist of Canadian groups. None of these points, however, detracts from our debt to Dion, whose work provides the framework for this chapter.

In the one major political science text that takes seriously the group approach, Van Loon and Whittington begin their relevant chapter with an assertion on the pervasiveness of groups in Canada:

> Wherever government turns its hand, there it will find some kind of organized group operating—and whatever groups operate they find that government activities overlap their own.[10]

Nevertheless, they still show considerable reservation about the effectiveness of the group approach and its applicability to Canada.

In the pages that follow, there will be references to a variety of group studies, some of individual groups and some comparative. These provide the basic sources for our knowledge of political groups in Canada. Yet the authors of these studies are not readily characterized as group theorists, in the sense of a Bentley or a Truman. The one clear exception is Robert Presthus, currently professor of political science at York University.

THE MANY MEANINGS OF GROUPS

One of the most irritating experiences in reading Bentley's now classic work is a vagueness of language, an unwillingness to define concepts, and a lack of guidelines for those who would follow him. He could say, with alarming inclusiveness, "When the groups are adequately stated, everything is stated. When I say everything I mean everything,"[11] and yet not tell us what an adequately stated group is, or even more precisely, what is not a group. It is simply not useful to consider all groups. At most, we need take into account only those groups that pursue political interests. Our working definition of the elements characterizing such political interest groups is derived largely from Dion.[12] An interest group is first of all an association in which members are organized in more or less stable relationships with assigned roles. It is here that Dion differs with some other students of interest groups who are prepared to include unorganized entities in their definition, recognizing their potential for political action.[13] The appeal of Dion's approach lies in its affirmation that if interest groups are going to perform their central task they must be able to act, and while individuals can act in concert without prior organization, as in a mob, this is too uncertain and ephemeral a basis of social action to be part of our concern. An interest group derives from a larger collectivity, which may not itself be organized, but with which it shares some characteristics and hence some interests.

Interest groups are more or less voluntary associations. Why "more or less"? They are voluntary in the sense that people do not belong because of some ascribed status but have to join deliberately. However, there may be little option but to join. This can be illustrated in the case of trade union membership in a closed shop. The union is a voluntary association, and membership is a positive act, but refusing to join may preclude the possibility of employment. Membership in business or professional associations may not be completely coercive, yet it too may be essential for establishing contacts with clients, providing specialized services as in the case of physicians who depend on referrals, conforming to licensing regulations, and achieving substantial success in a given field. Given these limitations, one may wonder why it is still so important to stress the voluntary nature of interest groups. The answer lies in their comparison with similar groups that have a totally involuntary membership. These are generally termed corporate groups. They are found in many undemocratic societies, and are indeed the hallmark of fascist-style politics. Under fascism, all major interests in the society, such as farmers, industrial workers, owners, or students, are organized and people with the appropriate characteristics or qualifications are automatically a part of that group. This organization has a political goal, enabling the authoritarian regime to control these interests. However, it is true that in democratic societies there are also corporate groups in which membership is essentially automatic. The instance already cited of trade union membership in a closed shop would be a case in point. Such corporate groups differ from the fascist example in not being organized by some central political authority and in existing independently of it. Moreover, they may be called upon, in a cooperative spirit, to participate with other organized interests, such as business and labor agreeing on voluntary wage restraints. We follow the tradition here of speaking of interest groups and not of corporate groups since the latter are involuntary or ascribed, while the voluntaristic nature of the former is always an essential characteristic, even if not empirically present in all instances. Moreover, they differ from corporate groups in not always having a recognized place in the political process.

We referred earlier to the central task of interest groups without specifying what this might be. It is, fundamentally, the promotion or defense of the group's welfare. An interest group comes into being when a number of individuals with shared characteristics recognize they have the same concerns and unite to further them, either because of a perceived threat from others in the society, or because they believe they can, through organization, enhance their share or access to valued goods and services. The collective objectives or goals that develop in this way may be simple or complex, few or many, and may involve a great deal of or little organized activity; the goals, however, remain as the raison d'être for the group's existence.

Interest groups are distinguished from other groups their primary orientation to the political system, coupled w and distinct organizational existence. It is in this sense that w interest groups are different from corporate groups, at least v ter are creatures of the political authorities. They are also d⎯ ⎯⎯om political parties. Parties exist to attain power, whatever other purpose they may pursue, but interest groups do not. The political concerns of interest groups come through pressures on decision makers, not through direct participation in the political decision-making process.

EMERGENCE AND CHARACTER OF INTEREST GROUPS

The search for interest groups remains entirely ad hoc unless it is guided by a theoretical framework for predicting sources from which interests are likely to emerge. Further discussion of the nature of interest groups remains largely descriptive unless there is some theory for deriving hypotheses about likely activities and effects. Thus far, the problems associated with the absence of the first kind of theory appear largely insoluble, but the second has received some limited attention.

Reasons for the absence of a suitable theory for dealing with interest group origins are suggested in Engelmann and Schwartz's work on Canadian political parties. They find one useful theory in a framework for isolating and ordering social cleavages, which can then be used in discussing the formation of political parties, organizing sources of support for parties, evaluating party efforts in mobilizing the electorate, and in contributing to an evaluation of party influences on society.[14] It is instructive that they make no use of this scheme in discussing interest groups. One apparent reason is the nature of interest groups, which may represent an almost limitless variety of interests. Social cleavages, in contrast, are stable, enduring, large-scale, and fundamental divisions in society, so that virtually the entire population can be classified. Social cleavages are not immutable, but they can be altered only through major social changes. While interest groups are often associated with social cleavages, as for example the Canadian Manufacturers' Association with the business community, they are not necessarily an expression of consensus in that community. More significantly, some cleavages may exist without the organization of interest groups. This would be the case where there were class divisions in the society without working-class organizations. Such instances have been treated by others (such as Truman and Key) as potentials for interest groups, but we have deliberately excluded them from our definition by insisting on some actually organized entity. And finally, one can find large numbers of interest groups that have come into being and continue to exist with only the most peripheral relation to social cleavages. These encompass interest groups with some immediate purpose, often with a single goal. Examples include health-related groups, such as the Canadian Mental Health Association, and social action groups, such as Pollution Probe, Ban the Bomb, and the Canadian Union for the Rights of

Biafra. We may then follow David Truman, who confronts the problem of interest-group origins, but deals with it empirically in terms of the broad range of influences, governmental stimuli, immediate circumstances, and underlying cleavages that can give rise to interest groups.[15]

Efforts to deal with the character of interest groups by building on some general theoretical scheme are more frequent and appear in the development of typologies. By far the most successful effort of this sort, by A. Paul Pross, was designed to have both analytical and descriptive uses. Pross suggests that we treat interest groups as organizations that can be placed along a single continuum, ranging from institutionalized groups to issue-oriented ones.[16] One could, more precisely, divide his single dimension into two, since it encompasses both the objectives of the groups and their organizational makeup, but in either case this does not affect the usefulness of his approach. The most institutionalized groups are those with well-developed organizational structures that enable them to retain stable memberships and maintain ready access to government. They tend to have a range of concerns, be adept at bargaining, and place strong emphasis on maintaining the organization itself. In contrast, issue-oriented interest groups are loosely organized, and are often dependent on volunteer and intermittent assistance. They often have a single issue as their focus, and it is this that determines their activities, not any particular concern for the continuity of their organization.

This typology aids in classifying, and hence understanding, existing groups, although no single group may exactly conform to either extreme. At the institutionalized end we can place the Canadian Manufacturers' Association, the Consumers' Association of Canada, and the Canadian Federation of Agriculture. We can also find examples of institutionalized groups among local ratepayers' associations and neighborhood businessmen's groups. Groups that have a less coherent organizational structure and greater focus on particular issues include those operating on the local level, inspired by concerns with housing, education, transportation, or environment. A famous Toronto example is the Stop Spadina group. Nationally, issue-oriented groups may come into being in response to an equally broad range of issues. Among recent examples are the pro-abortion and aid to Biafra groups.

The typology is also useful for generating hypotheses about additional relationships. For example, one of the functions of interest groups is to communicate their program and objectives. This may be done in a number of ways, ranging from media-oriented activities to access-oriented ones. In the former, emphasis is on efforts to influence public opinion as well as exert pressure on government. Pross then goes on to argue, in a way that can be subject to further test and elaboration, that the Canadian political system emphasizes direct access, not publicity. Case studies can then be examined to see whether they support the notion that:

> The Canadian political system . . . tends to favour elite groups, making functional accommodative, consensus-seeking techniques of political communication, rather than conflict-oriented

techniques that are directed towards the achievement of objectives through arousing public opinion.[17]

While recognizing that Pross provides a set of guidelines that can aid the search for further relationships, for the purpose of this chapter it is the descriptive quality of his typology that is most helpful.

RELATIONS WITH GOVERNMENT

The principal justification for studying the role of groups in the political process lies in their relations to government. In the Canadian setting, it is apparent that there are three loci of possible influence: cabinet, legislative bodies, and the public bureaucracy. Agreement on these loci has not produced similar judgments, however, on where the greatest contact is between interest groups and government, the level at which efforts to influence are most effective, or the ways in which these efforts can be made influential.[18] It appears that some of the disagreements, or perhaps more properly, differences in emphasis, are associated with difficulties in obtaining information on the processes of contact and in evaluating outcomes.

Cabinet

Institutionalized interest groups maintain contacts with the cabinet through the submission of annual briefs. According to Helen Dawson, whose work on interest groups represents one of the few long-standing commitments to the topic among Canadian political scientists, Canadian cabinets, at both federal and provincial levels, are readily accessible to interest groups, and even welcome contact as a means of obtaining information on public demands and possibly as a counterweight to the demands of their own public servants.[19] Probably more significant than formal briefs are regular contacts with individual cabinet ministers. Such contacts are made not only with ministers responsible for departments that are directly relevant to a particular group, but also with ministers from the same region as the affected interest group. The importance of such contacts becomes apparent when studying groups without easy access to cabinet. Thus Chant argues, in studying efforts to bring about pollution control, that pressure on cabinet is one of the necessary ingredients for success for issue-oriented groups.[20] Dawson suggests that cabinets in minority governments are more vulnerable to pressure from interest groups than during a strong majority. Yet Engelmann and Schwartz question just what impact interest groups' tactics in fact have. Interest groups by definition present their own concerns; even where individual cabinet members have a strong commitment to the same goals, the cabinet as a whole, charged with governing the country, will always be hard-pressed to satisfy all groups that place demands on it.[21]

Legislature

Until recently, there was general consensus that interest-group contacts with individual members of Parliament were not likely to lead to productive interchanges. Some reevaluation has occurred, partly through the success of issue-oriented groups which are dependent on the publicity they can achieve, either through broad-gauged contacts or through members of Parliament, and the indirect payoff from favorable publicity through the mass media. As Van Loon and Whittington point out, one could easily overlook the possible impact of interest groups on Parliament, in the sense that we are speaking of two analytically distinct sources of political action, when many M.P.s, either themselves or through their families, are also members of interest groups. This means that, for example, spokesmen for consumer interests are not solely concentrated in the Consumers' Association, but find many allies and even members among M.P.s. Robert Presthus also requires us to consider the impact of relatively frequent contact between M.P.s and interest group representatives with whom there is already some affinity of interest.[22] As a result of recent changes in the committee structure and powers in Parliament, Dawson predicts that we may see more direct contacts with M.P.s, and a lessened emphasis on cabinet. At present, however, interest groups rarely supply information to parliamentary committees and continue to have a somewhat touchy relationship with M.P.s.

Even more contradictory are assessments of contact with the Senate. Dawson states that her research gives little support to the notion of strong lobbying of senators, and indeed, sees little point to such efforts by interest groups. Yet now that the government plans to introduce more legislation through Senate initiative, it may well be, she suggests, that the Senate will grow in importance to interest groups. Senators, however, cannot be dismissed so readily, if Van Loon and Whittington's judgments are accepted. They see the most effective lobbyists as those with strong connections with the executive and administrative levels of government. Among those with such contacts are included current members of the Senate, opening a whole new avenue of access for interest groups.[23]

Public Service

The downgrading of members of Parliament as targets of interest groups is consistent with the Canadian parliamentary system. When legislation is introduced in Parliament, it is already too late for much influence to be exerted. Moreover, the ordinary member is unlikely to introduce significant legislation, which remains the prerogative not just of the party in office, but of the cabinet. In a real sense, then, even lobbying cabinet members can come too late to influence legislation where the government has already made a policy commitment. It is for these reasons that the public service is a prime target for interest groups. At this point, there is still the opportunity to influence pending legislation and its eventual implementation. Presthus, and Van Loon and Whittington consider access to the bureaucracy as the most important activity for interest groups.[24] Efforts to influence include direct contacts and briefings. These often come through the personal ties that develop after civil servants and interest group officials have been in office a long time. Employing representatives from interest groups in the higher echelons of the public service would hardly be in keeping with the spirit of an impartial bureaucracy, let alone with the bureaucracy's demands for employees' commitment, which could easily run counter to the interest group. This is contrary to Presthus's interpretation of the pressure for a "representative bureaucracy."[25] Interest groups, however, are accustomed to press for representation in agencies that can impinge more immediately on their fate. These are regulatory agencies and royal commissions, the latter being important because of the probability that their recommendations will be incorporated into legislation.

Interest groups in this process often appear to have special legislative advantages because, once they are identified as interested parties yet prepared to be constructive in their advice and criticisms, they can be shown drafts of instructions for legislation, which is not the same as the legislation itself. After a bill has gone through first reading in the House, they may also be sent a pending bill and solicited for comments.

Many factors enter into an interest group's success in accomplishing its policy goals. Number of members, control over financial resources, monopoly over important technical knowledge, and the prestige of its leaders all bear on whether it will be taken seriously. It also appears that a willingness to cooperate and to avoid outright confrontation and personal criticism are important elements in success, if not on a particular issue, at least on the chances of continued easy access to the loci of power. Regional centers of support can aid interest groups where they are effective in first convincing provincial authorities of their cause, and where these in turn are prepared to help argue their cause nationally. Bucovetsky, for example, demonstrates how mining and oil interests with a strong provincial base were able to make their case counter to apparent government intentions on tax reform.[26] As Bucovetsky shows, the public bureaucracy is not a monolith, but incorporates a diversity of perspectives and goals. The autonomy of government departments is then an important independent element in an interest group's successful challenge. Where there is not sufficient evidence of overwhelming public support and hence political expediency, bureaucratic interests are every bit as likely to win as the challenging interest group. Thus Barry shows how, despite concerted efforts on the part of an issue-oriented group founded to aid the plight of Biafrans and aided by such institutionalized groups as the Presbyterian Church and the Canadian Red Cross, the Department of External Affairs was able to maintain its position. Barry judges that this was possible because the government did not feel there was sufficient public pressure to create a change in policy on Biafra.[27]

Perhaps the most telling factor preventing a full assessment of the relation between interest group and government and, in particular, the bureaucracy, is the attitude of secrecy under which these activities are conducted. This is not to say that there is anything illegal in what occurs, or even of questionable legitimacy, but it is a reflection of the style of Canadian government, and the manner in which the bureaucracy operates. This situation has made judgments difficult and the most careful students of this topic cautiously avoid explicit conclusions without much more empirical evidence.[28]

Government Control

As these comments have implied, relations between interest groups and government are really reciprocal. Neither is passive and both try to influence the other. We have already suggested that cabinet members will make use of information supplied by interest groups in deliberate efforts to thwart the control of their own bureaucracies. Members of Parliament also appear to welcome interest group contacts as a means of obtaining information they can use for their own purposes. While interest groups try to obtain places on regulatory agencies and royal commissions, government agencies actively recruit them as members of advisory committees. These may then become tame experts, tools of a government department. Governments see a real value in interest groups that provide information and demands through recognized channels, and where they do not exist, may even aid in setting them up. It is certainly no secret that many such interest groups accept government grants to ensure their continuity. While this does not necessarily make them tools of government, their independence can be compromised more readily. In this sense, we see how the thin line separating voluntaristic interest groups from centrally organized corporate groups is easily bridged. It has led some Canadian interests to be at least reluctant to locate in Ottawa, where chances for cooptation are greatest, if only through flattering appeals for their appearance and the ties they forge with governmental agencies.[29]

Federalism

Perhaps the greatest impact of government on interest groups stems from a feature of the political system that lacks the deliberate features of contact and control we have suggested above. It is a structural feature of Canadian political life, affecting interest groups equally with government: the federal nature of the Canadian polity. Major interest groups with some national focus normally adopt a federal structure, mirroring the structure of government.[30] This is a necessary characteristic so that they can mobilize their members and effectively deal with different governments with jurisdiction over them.

According to Dawson, this federal structure of interest groups themselves, as well as the need to involve themselves in the federal structure of the government, is generally a source of considerable strain on the potential impact of interest groups.

> The fact that the national organization's executive or board of directors or both is often composed of regional or provincial rep-

resentatives (usually branch presidents), means that the achievement of consensus on desirable national, as opposed to regional
or provincial, policies often verges on the impossible. Consequently the national headquarters is frequently unable to present
a vigorous, consistent, or sometimes even united front to the federal government. Furthermore, for reasons that are not always
clear, provincial branches and other affiliates tend to keep re-
electing the same personnel to the national executive, board of
directors and committees. Not surprisingly, many organizations
have the same personnel for years at a stretch. This has two consequences: an ageing executive body and difficulty in initiating
policy changes.[31]

Dawson goes on to say that the national executive is largely dependent on
the popularity of provincial components, who in turn need to make their
appeals in terms of their local members or clientele. All this effects consistent and united policy making, and contributes to a frequent lack of
unity among the components of the organization. Moreover, when the interests served are covered by more than one governmental jurisdiction,
the ability of the national executive to deal with the federal government is
often impeded by local considerations. Where uniformity in regulations is
sought, the organization becomes a victim of the political maneuvering
characteristic of federal-provincial relations in Canada. All these symptoms contribute to and enhance the likelihood of financial weaknesses,
fed by members' resentment at the costs of financing a national headquarters. Indeed, because some interest groups rely on federal grants, they are
reluctant to have a national headquarters, or at least one in Ottawa,
where, it is feared, the executive would be unduly influenced by the federal government.

Not all students of interest groups in Canada echo this essentially
negative assessment of the consequences of federalism. There are those
who see some positive advantages, reflecting David Truman's assessment,
made earlier in the context of the American federal system:

> Groups that would be rather obscure or weak under a unitary ar-
> rangement may hold advantageous positions in the State gov-
> ernments and will be vigorous in their insistence upon the exist-
> ing distribution of powers between State and nation. As the ad-
> vantage of access shifts through time, moreover, groups shift
> from defenders to critics of the existing balance.[32]

Bucovetsky, for example, records the ways in which the mining industry,
as an interest group, took advantage of its crucial role in the economies of
the Western Provinces to further the bargaining power of the provinces
themselves in affecting federal tax legislation. Kwavnick presents case
study material from two interest groups, associated with students and
labor, to argue that the means available under a federal system enable interest groups to enhance their position. This is demonstrated through the
rivalries between the Canadian Union of Studens (CUS) and the Union
Générale des Etudiants du Québec (UGEQ). The latter was able both to

become an independent organization and to promote its bargaining position when the federal government in effect defined the interest of French-speaking students as lying solely under the jurisdiction of the Quebec government. There was then no major need to participate in a national organization. Perhaps illustrating even more clearly the impact of federalism were efforts by the Canadian Labour Congress (CLC) and the Quebec-based Confederation of National Trade Unions (CNTU) to increase their roles through two opposing approaches. The CLC attempted to alter the balance of power between provincial and federal governments by pressing for more centralizing policies. In contrast, the CNTU was concerned with enhancing the position of provincial governments as a means of consolidating its own position.[33]

We will leave this discussion of federalism without firm conclusions. It is clear, in any case, that federalism has a major effect on interest groups in Canada. Dawson is undoubtedly correct in assigning considerable weight to the deleterious consequences for interest groups. But we should also be alert to the possibilities, suggested above, that just as interest groups do not passively accept governmental efforts at control, neither are they passive in accepting the structural consequences of federalism.

RELATIONS WITH POLITICAL PARTIES

Any discussion of the relation between interest groups and political parties is affected by the conceptual problems of adequately distinguishing between the two. Presthus, for example, is prepared to subsume political parties under interest groups.[34] Many political scientists are more comfortable with Almond's distinction on the basis of function. "Interest groups articulate political demands"; that is, they raise demands, seek support for them, and attempt to influence policy makers to satisfy them. "Political parties . . . are aggregative"; that is, they combine articulated interests and assign priorities in ways that permit the selection of political authorities and the making of policy decisions.[35] Empirically, the distinctions between the two may not always be clear-cut, but analytically their separation is a necessary part of understanding the political process in any system where there are competitive parties. Unless we wish to give unnatural flatness to our political analysis, we must emphasize that parties, unlike interest groups, are exclusively engaged in politics and exist to acquire governing authority directly.

The form and character that relations between parties and interest groups take is closely tied to their social and political milieu. Dion, for example, beginning with a threefold distinction among parties (not particularly relevant here), is able to develop a twenty-celled typology of possible relationships.[36] The closest ties occur where the politicization of an interest group leads to the development of an organizational arm specifically devoted to political action. Instances of such cohesion existed between trade unions and the British Labour Party and the founding of confessional parties in the Netherlands.

In Canada, it is alleged that the relationship between parties and interest groups is very tenuous, with one notable exception.[37] That one exception, and even it is not of the character of its British counterpart, concerns the connection between organized labor and first the CCF and then the NDP.[38] For the most part, reasons for assuming a nonpartisan stance seem overwhelming. Most crucially, overt attachment to a single party will preclude much government favor when that party is out of office. Some groups, notably the wheat pools, had political difficulties when their party, the United Farmers, faded into oblivion. As a result, many interest groups follow a policy of avoiding partisan attachments. In the past, for example, the Canadian Manufacturers' Association (CMA) and, more recently, the Retail Manufacturers' Association (RMA) have shown strong proclivities for the Conservative party. Yet they have still been restrained by the necessity of continued dealings with a Liberal government.

Some of the indirect evidence on this topic in Canada is apparently related to normative restraints on admitting the possibility of interest-group-party interrelations. According to Engelmann and Schwartz:

> Both actors in, and observers of Canadian political life hesitate to face up to the realities of interest-party relations; until recently, they tended to maintain strongly that these were illegitimate, or non-existent.[39]

From the evidence available, it is still clear that interrelations are much more modest than in other Western democracies, yet there remains some sense of dissatisfaction at the sketchy information available. Both the uniqueness of the Canadian situation, and the values that appear to permeate understanding of interests in Canada make it necessary to consider our next topic, the consequences of the social and political milieu.

SOCIAL AND POLITICAL MILIEU

The very existence of interest groups, their scope of operation, and their possible impact are closely intertwined with the nature of the society in which they operate. It is in this context that the role of Canadian interest groups appears to differ from those in other countries. For example, Van Loon and Whittington consider interest groups in both the United States and Britain to have greater impact on political parties. Presthus, who has done a systematic comparison of interests in the United States and Canada, rates those in Canada as less active and less effective. His findings lead him to make a number of judgments about differences between the two societies.

> In the United States the system of interest group politics is more fully developed. Explanations include a more participative political culture; the separation-of-powers apparatus which provides more, and more effective, points of group access; and greater wealth and occupational differentiation which encourage a more intensive and well-supported interest group structure. As a re-

sult, lobbying activities are more common and group effectiveness seems to be generally higher, particularly regarding business
and welfare groups. Although labor is only marginally effective
in the American system, it is clearly more effective than its Canadian counterpart. American directors [of interest groups] tend to
have more political resources, which apparently rest upon a generally higher level of felt political efficacy. Since several of their
hard resources — for example, directors' education and occupation, experience, age, organization — are often no greater than
those of Canadian directors one must attribute this condition to
cultural differences, including American optimism, contrasted
with the somewhat pessimistic strain apparent in Canadian
thought and literature.[40]

We may look again for guidance from Dion on the issues relevant to a
cross-national comparison of the situation of interest groups.

Societal Factors

The first set of questions that need to be posed in evaluating the impact of
the societal setting on interest groups relate to groups in general. Fundamentally, we need first to ascertain whether groups have a legal basis. In
the short history of Canada, this concern can, for the most part, be disre-
garded, but it has been highly relevant in other countries.[41] Given the
right to organize, we need to consider the likelihood of voluntary associations existing and of sizable portions of the population affiliating with
them. The United States has often been seen as a nation of joiners, but
comparative research now calls into question whether this is unique to the
United States. As Curtis has recently demonstrated, there is little difference between Canada and the United States in the proportion of the
population belonging to voluntary associations, and this is also true of
multiple group affiliation.[42] While French and English speakers join associations in similar proportions, the former are much less likely to af-
filiate with civic associations.[43]

Given the existence of organizations and the likelihood of joining, we
must still determine the meaning attributed to participation. For joining
voluntary associations to be relevant to our concerns, there should be
some evidence that members attach importance to it as a means of exert-
ing influence on the political system, in contrast to valuing it for its
socializing opportunities, its ability to improve personal economic interests, or gain social status. Although the implications are only indirect, it
was found that a national sample of Canadians were more likely than a
comparable sample of Americans to believe that the actions of the ordinary citizen would have little impact on the conduct of government. It is
probably also noteworthy that Canadians were more cynical about politics, expressing greater lack of trust in political authorities.[44]

Legitimacy

If we focus directly on interest groups, two issues are especially important. The first concerns the legitimacy accorded to interest groups in their efforts to influence government. By legitimacy we do not refer to the legal right to organize but to the more subtle, yet every bit as essential, recognition that interest groups can appropriately engage in activities which result in pressure on political authorities. It is legitimacy that is typically problematic, since it immediately calls into question the role and independence of political representatives, the political insulation of the public bureaucracy, and the protection of the public generally from those subgroups that have the organization and other resources to make their positions politically dominant. Everyone who writes about interest groups in Canada faces a situation in which interest group activities in the political sphere are questioned, presented as nonexistent, or dismissed as illegitimate. "Lobbying," it is alleged, is an American activity, foreign to Canada . We have, in fact, seen that this is not the case, yet we must still recognize these reactions as reflections on the legitimacy of interest groups. One consequence has been a relatively small number of studies on interest groups and, as indicated in the discussion of relations with government and parties, considerable difficulty in breaking through the secrecy that surrounds their actions. One should not assume, however, that questions of legitimacy are raised only in Canada. These are general problems, endemic to all societies where interest groups exist. For example, Presthus calls attention to the absence of all political science writing on interest groups in Britain until 1955 as an indication of low legitimacy there.[45] Even in the United States, a so-called paradise for interest groups, serious questions remain. As indicated at the outset of this chapter, the whole tradition of muckraking literature in that country was premised on the dangers interest groups posed to the viability of American democracy. Dion also documents the range of literature demonstrating the continuing distaste for interest groups in the United States, and the pressures for interest groups to keep out of politics.[46] Without better comparative data, we can only suggest that legitimacy remains questionable in many societies, and this in itself does little to explain cross-national differences in the presence or effectiveness of interest groups.

Theories of Representation

One of the elements raised by the concept of legitimacy relates, as we have already stated, to the role and independence of political representatives. From the perspective of theories of representation, rather than interest groups, the question is: Whom do legislators represent, and how do group interests enter into their selection and deliberations? Out of the many possible ways in which theories of representation bear on interest groups, it is the theory of consociationalism that has recently received attention in Canada. Elaborated by Arend Lijphart from his analysis of the

Netherlands, the theory postulates that the stability of political systems, riven by deep social and economic cleavages, is maintained through the cooperative activities of elites representing the principal cleavages. The cleavages are themselves insulated from contact, while members trust their leaders sufficiently to let them bargain on their behalf.[47] Consociationalism was first applied to Canada by Noel,[48] and to the realm of interest groups by Presthus. On the question of applying consociationalism to Canadian society, Kenneth McRae provides a particularly balanced appraisal, noting that consociationalism is probably present, to a degree, in all societies with major social cleavages, but having said this, it becomes necessary to establish empirically that degree in any particular society. The special features of Canadian society, with its complex, sometimes overlapping, system of cleavages include the comparative lack of clear-cut organization along lines of greatest segmentation; an electoral and party system that does not divide along lines of cleavage; and a system of accommodation that takes place primarily, though not always successfully, within the federal cabinet.[49] In this sense, consociationalism is not a particularly apt model for Canada.

Also of increasing interest are models of corporatism, particularly as applied to the liberal state.[50] Liberal democratic corporatism differs from consociationalism in stressing the functional representation of socio-economic interests, the close ties between these interests and the state, and the reciprocal impact of the state on corporate groups. Panitch sees few corporatist elements in Canada,[51] though one aspect of corporatism, where the state calls on representatives of critical interests for consultation, may be present and corporatist approaches appear to be increasingly attractive.

Political Factors

If we move now to more narrowly defined political factors as these affect the emergence and operation of interest groups, Dion draws our attention to four. They include federalism, the nature and dispersion of power, the proliferation of governmental activities and agencies, and the constitutional separation of powers. In each instance, where there is more governmental activity, Dion hypothesizes greater scope for interest groups.

We have already discussed the impact of federalism on Canadian interest groups, and this requires no repetition. Of the remaining factors, Dawson provides a useful checklist of the ways in which the Canadian political system has had a different impact from either the British or the United States. In Canada, there is considerably less contact with parliamentary committees than in the other two countries, taking into account differences in their political systems and in the procedures of contact. There is also less contact with and effort to influence private members of Parliament. In Britain, interest groups maintain considerable contact with former cabinet ministers; in Canada, this is virtually nonexistent. This contrast is also evident in the case of parliamentary secretaries. When comparison is made with the United States, Dawson finds little scope here for the kind of venal lobbying that has characterized the worst abuses of interest group politics, although perhaps this has something to do with our own ignorance. With fewer appointments available outside the civil service, there is also less consultation with Canadian interest groups on personnel. The one exception to generally lower interest-group activity in Canada, tied by Dawson to differences in political structure, is the greater contacts made by Canadian interests directly with the prime minister. In Britain, such contacts are highly unusual.

LIMITS TO THE GROUP APPROACH

In concluding our assessment of the group approach, we must re-emphasize that this refers to a comprehensive, all-encompassing way of conceptualizing the political process, in which the life of groups is seen as the essence of politics.[52] Studies of particular interest groups, or even of interest groups generally, do not necessarily reflect such a group approach.

We can, first of all, dismiss the claim of those group theorists who argue that political processes need only a focus on groups to illuminate them. In an effort to explain everything through one approach or one framework, we could find ourselves explaining nothing, and be left with conclusions too general, and analyses too descriptive, to advance the study of politics in any significant way.[53] We can, moreover, isolate four more specific shortcomings.

The group approach, certainly in its most general form, tends to slight the effect of issues and events on the political process. This is true whether an accommodative or a conflict conception of the political process is used. In either case, we must consider the world of politics as struggles among social cleavages and the organized interest groups that emerge to participate directly in that struggle, as well as on more immediate circumstances that cleavages and interest groups do not necessarily shape. In this respect, we found the work of Paul Pross particularly useful, especially the emphasis on issues and events in his concept of "issue-oriented groups." Issues and events, however, do not only have an impact on specific interest groups whose goals are directly tied to them, but are also involved in the life of institutionalized interest groups. They provide the circumstances to which interests must respond, and the setting that shapes their daily life and the direction of their organization. In the example cited of the mining industry, proposed tax changes were the crucial stimulus to mobilizing an interest group. In Kwavnick's study of labor unions, changes in the market, in particular industries, and in the nature of the provincial and federal governments all affect interest group development. We find in these and similar case studies of Canadian interests that attention is paid to the impact of issues and events. At the same time, such individual studies do not necessarily represent a thoroughgoing group approach, where there is still a lack of emphasis on the impact of issues and events. Allied with this lack of concern for issues and events is a lack of attention to the impact of individual actors. Garson, in his criticism of the group approach, objects strongly to this omission in Bentley. He attributes it partly to Bentley's aversion to psychological interpretations, but this in itself is not of major importance. What is more significant is Bentley's lack of differentiation between elites and the mass of followers or members.[54] Yet even an emphasis on elites does not always result in the conception of a differentiated group life, one in which members have unequal access to decision makers, both within the interest group itself and in governmment. Again we have to turn to specific case studies, as in Kwavnick, to obtain a more effective measure of the role of individuals and the ways in which specific members of interest groups, along with individual members of government, make a difference to outcomes. The relationship between group structures, the interaction between interest groups and government, and the effect of individual actors are also brought home by Van Loon and Whittington in at least two ways. They note, for instance, the low level of influence mass write-ins have on government, attributable in part to the undifferentiated quality of mass pressure. This observation is confirmed in another way by Chant's study of Pollution Probe, an issue-oriented group that was aided by its connection with an existing university organization, and the high status and good contacts of its leaders. At the elite level, Van Loon and Whittington attribute prime importance to the network of relations between interest groups and government necessary for effective influence, and confirm the particularly advantageous position of specific individuals.

The rationale for a group approach to politics was a more effective way of describing and explaining how politics really works. One of the ironies of its development has been an underestimation of political factors, as some practitioners of the approach have turned away from concern with the role of political parties and government itself. As Dion points out, the structure of interest groups and their scope of action is largely dependent on the structure of government, and hence to ignore the political system leads only to an imperfect understanding of interest groups themselves.

We have already commented on some theoretical problems associated with distinctions between political parties and interest groups. The differences between the two, and the complexity of their possible relationship are affirmed by a prominent American exponent of the group approach, V.O. Key, Jr. At the same time, he finds it useful to consider that those aspects of party life associated with the core of the organization are a form of interest group.

> Political parties are differentiated from pressure groups; they, unlike pressure groups, nominate candidates who seek formal control of the government. In doing so, parties must appeal to the entire community rather than to a single interest. Yet in one respect the inner core of the party—the machine or the party organization—may be considered to be in the same category as a pressure group: like the Chamber of Commerce of the United

> States, the party machine wants to bring about certain types of
> governmental action and to prevent others on questions of im-
> mediate concern to it.[55]

It is here that we would part company with Key, since he now muddies the
distinction in several important ways. For one thing, Key's treatment of
political parties is unnecessarily restricted and bound to the experience of
the two broad United States parties. Many political parties are quite content to appeal to one or at least a small number of interests, and not the
total community. Even more serious, for our perspective, is the confusion
of the party organizational apparatus with an interest group. The absurd-
ity of this conflation lies in diverting attention away from the principal goals
of interest groups—influencing political agencies and decision makers in
ways favorable to the group—and their essential contrast with
political parties, which exist to gain governmental power. To the extent
that some small parties see their role as primarily one of influencing existing governments, they fall much more in the category of interest groups
than of parties. All organizations have, by definition, continuing structures with a life of their own, and a set of organizational imperatives that
become independent of other, even primary, goals. This does not make
party organization an interest group; all it means is that both parties and
interest groups have structures that can be expected to have many
similarities simply because they are organizations.

For the most part, we can say that the reasons for ignoring political
parties in the study of Canadian interests have much to do with the low
level of contact and impact that one has on the other. To the extent that
this has not been true for organized labor and the CCF and NDP, it has
also been carefully recognized by most students of the topic.

If downplaying political parties can be rationalized in Canada by the
apparently minor role of party-interest-group relations, although there is
no conclusive evidence on this, the same cannot be said where government is given a minor role. Government is simply not just a reflection of a
variety of interest groups, either contending for greater access to resources, as the pluralists might describe, or reflecting the dominance of
particular interest groups, as class analysts would allege. It may be this, it is
true, but it is also much more. Just as in the case of political parties, government as an institutional area, once in existence, continues largely in
response to its own imperatives. Members of Parliament are elected, government departments organized, cabinets formed, the day-to-day business of government met, even crises faced, through the structural
mechanisms that exist to meet these exigencies. Interest groups may have
an impact on them, but governmental activities are still independent of
interest groups in the most essential ways. Not to recognize this explicitly,
and not to take this into account in the study of interest groups, results in
an apolitical, if not mindless analysis. We must also acknowledge what
students of interest groups tell us about the difficulty of ascertaining the
actual impact of interest group efforts. We do know that prime ministers
and cabinet members weigh some of the pressures they perceive, reject

some, and are always mindful of their own special powers. It is instructive that a neo-Marxist theory of the state now argues that government must necessarily be autonomous if only to carry out the interests of the bourgeoisie.[56]

We do not question the value of studying interest groups in Canada. Many issues remain unexplored, and new theories for suggesting hypotheses and explanatory frameworks for data collected are needed. New methods need exploring to obtain data in areas where participants deny the existence or operation of interest groups. What is less clear is whether we need an all-inclusive group approach. To the extent that there are few in Canada who could be termed group theorists, as distinct from students of interest groups, this is probably all to the good. The group theorists made important contributions: freeing us from the undue rigidity of juridic and institutional analyses; redefining the nature of sovereignty; and continuing to direct us to fundamental questions about the nature of representative democracy and the place of the individual in the state. Fortunately, Canadian students of interest groups can benefit from all these contributions without being caught up in the serious short-comings of an all-inclusive group approach.

ENDNOTES

1. David B. Truman, "Political Group Analysis," *International Encyclopedia of the Social Sciences*, Vol. 12 (1968), pp. 241-245; Earl Latham, "The Group Basis of Politics: Notes for a Theory," *American Political Science Review*, 46 (June, 1952), pp. 376-397.

2. John D. Lewis, "Otto von Gierke," *International Encyclopedia of the Social Sciences*, Vol. 6 (1968), pp. 177-180.

3. Herbert A. Deane, "Harold J. Laski," *International Encyclopedia of the Social Sciences*, Vol. 9 (1968), pp. 30-33; G. David Garson, "On the Origins of Interest-Group Theory: A Critique of a Process," *American Political Science Review*, 68 (December, 1974), pp. 1509-1511.

4. Arthur F. Bentley, *The Process of Government* (Evanston, Ill.: Principia Press, 1935), originally published 1908 by The University of Chicago Press; Garson, "On the Origins of Interest-Group Theory," pp. 1511-1514; Richard W. Taylor, "Arthur F. Bentley," *International Encyclopedia of the Social Sciences*, Vol. 2 (1968), pp. 58-62.

5. Bentley, *op. cit.*, p. 180.

6. Louis Filler, *The Muckrakers: Crusaders for American Liberalism* (Chicago: Regnery, 1968).

7. See, for example, Charles Beard, *The Economic Basis of Politics* (New York: Vintage, 1957), originally published 1922.

8. Léon Dion, *Société et politique: La Vie des groupes* (Quebec: University of Laval Press, 1971), Vol. I, *Fondements de la société libérale*, Vol. II, *Dynamique de la société libérale* (1972).

9. Mancur Olson, *The Logic of Collective Action*, rev. ed. (New York: Schocken Books, 1971).

10. Richard Van Loon and Michael Whittington, *The Canadian Political System*, 2nd ed. (Toronto: McGraw-Hill Ryerson, 1976), p. 286.

11. Bentley, *op. cit.*, pp. 208-209.

12. We use "interest group" throughout, but it should be considered synonymous with "pressure group," "political group," or "lobby." Dion, *Société et politique*, Vol I., pp. 98-108.

13. For example, David B. Truman, *The Governmental Process*, 2nd ed. (New York: Knopf, 1971), pp. 511-515; V. O. Key, Jr., *Politics, Parties and Pressure Groups*, 5th ed. (New York: Crowell, 1964), p. 116.

14. F. C. Engelmann and M. A. Schwartz, *Canadian Political Parties: Origin, Character, Impact* (Scarborough: Prentice-Hall, 1975), pp. 71-92, 186-208, 263-282, 282-309.

15. Truman, *The Governmental Process, op. cit.*, pp. 66-108.

16. A. Paul Pross, "Pressure Groups: Adaptive Instruments of Political Communication," *Pressure Group Behaviour in Canadian Politics*, ed. A. Paul Pross (Toronto: McGraw-Hill Ryerson, 1975), pp. 9-12. I use "institutionalized" rather than "institutional" to stress both the patterned and regulative aspects of interest group organization and the process by which they become established in their ties with major institutional areas.

17. *Ibid.*, p. 19.

18. Interest group efforts to influence government are often termed "lobbying." I have avoided the term whenever possible because of its pejorative connotations.

19. Helen Jones Dawson, "National Pressure Groups and the Federal Government," in Pross, *op. cit.*, pp. 36-38.

20. D. A. Chant, "Pollution Probe: Fighting the Polluters with Their Own Weapons," in Pross, *op. cit.*, p. 66.

21. Engelmann and Schwartz, *op. cit.*, pp. 154-156.

22. Robert Presthus, "Interest Groups and Parliament: Activities, Interaction, Legitimacy and Influence," *Canadian Journal of Political Science*, 4 (December, 1971), p. 460.

23. Van Loon and Whittington, *op. cit.*, p. 298.

24. *Ibid.*, p. 295; Robert Presthus, *Elite Accommodation in Canadian Politics* (London and New York: Cambridge University Press, 1973), p. 211.

25. Presthus, *Elite Accommodation, op. cit.*, p. 197.

26. M.W. Bucovetsky, "The Mining Industry and the Great Tax Reform Debate," in Pross, *op. cit.*, pp. 89-114.

27. Donald Barry, "Interest Groups and the Foreign Policy Process: The Case of Biafra," in Pross, *op. cit.*, pp. 117-147.

28. For example, Dawson, *op. cit.*, p. 48.

29. *Ibid.*, p. 34.

30. Engelmann and Schwartz, *op. cit.*, p. 146. Apparent disagreement with Presthus's findings (*Elite Accommodation*, p. 113), is tied to his sampling methods, and his criteria for defining interest groups. These procedures result in the inclusion of many local, minor interest groups.

31. Dawson, *op. cit.*, p. 30.

32. Truman, *The Governmental Process, op. cit.*, p. 323.

33. David Kwavnick, "Interest Group Demands and the Federal Political System: Two Canadian Case Studies," in Pross, *op. cit.*, pp. 70-86.

34. Presthus, *Elite Accommodation, op. cit.*, p. 60.

35. Gabriel Almond, "Interest Groups and the Political Process," *Comparative Politics: Notes and Readings*, ed. R. C. Macridis and B. E. Brown (Homewood, Ill.: Dorsey Press, 1961), pp. 129-130.

36. Dion, *op. cit.*, Vol. II, p. 81. Examples of variations in the relationship can be found in Henry W. Ehrmann, ed., *Interest Groups on Four Continents* (Pittsburgh: University of Pittsburgh Press, 1958).

37. Van Loon and Whittington, *op. cit.*, p. 295.

38. David Kwavnick, *Organized Labour and Pressure Politics* (Montreal: McGill-Queen's University Press, 1972); Gad Horowitz, *Canadian Labour in Politics* (Toronto: University of Toronto Press, 1968).

39. Engelmann and Schwartz, *op. cit.*, p. 166.

40. Robert Presthus, "Interest Group Lobbying: Canada and the United States," *Annals of the American Academy*, 413 (May, 1976), p. 57. See also Robert Presthus, *Elites in the Policy Process* (New York: Cambridge University Press, 1974).

41. For example, it is a crucial variable in understanding the development of trade union organization. See Reinhard Bendix, *Nation-Building and Citizenship* (New York: Wiley, 1964), pp. 80-87.

42. James Curtis, "Voluntary Association Joining: A Cross-National Comparative Note," *American Sociological Review*, 36 (October, 1971), pp. 872-889.

43. Dion, *op. cit.*, Vol. I, pp. 243-244.

44. Mildred A. Schwartz, *Politics and Territory* (Montreal: McGill-Queen's University Press, 1974), pp. 207-210, 223-227.

45. Presthus, "Interest Group Lobbying," *op. cit.*, p. 45. See also Ehrmann, *Interest Groups, op. cit.*, p. 183.

46. Dion, *op. cit.*, Vol. I, pp. 294-297, 303-304.

47. Arendt Lijphart, "Consociational Democracy," *World Politics*, 21 (1969).

48. S.J.R. Noel, "Consociational Democracy and Canadian Federalism," *Canadian Journal of Political Science*, 4 (1971), pp. 15-18.

49. K.D. McRae, "Consociationalism and the Canadian Political System," *Consociational Democracy*, ed. K. McRae (Toronto: McClelland and Stewart, 1974), pp. 238-261.

50. Philippe Schmitter, "Still the Century of Corporations?" *The Review of Politics*, 36 (January, 1974), pp. 85-131.

51. Leo Panitch, "The Development of Corporatism in Liberal Democracies," *Comparative Political Studies*, 10 (April, 1977), pp. 61-90.

52. For example, Charles B. Hagen, "The Group in a Political Science," *Approaches to the Study of Politics*, ed. Roland Young (Evanston, Ill.: Northwestern University Press, 1958), pp. 38-51.

53. Garson, *op. cit.*, p. 1519.

54. *Ibid.*, p. 1513.

55. Key, *op. cit.*, p. 381.

56. Leo Panitch, "The Role and Nature of the Canadian State," *The Canadian State*, ed. Leo Panitch (Toronto: University of Toronto Press, 1977), pp. 3-27. See also, Ralph Miliband, *The State in Capitalist Society* (New York: Basic Books, 1969); Nicos Poulantzas, *Political Power and Social Classes* (London: Humanities Press, 1973).

SELECTED REFERENCES

BENTLEY, ARTHUR F. *The Process of Government.* Evanston, Ill.: Principia Press, 1935. Originally published by the University of Chicago Press in 1908, this is the classic statement on the group approach in the United States.

CANADA, LIBRARY OF PARLIAMENT, RESEARCH BRANCH. "Pressure Groups in Canda." *The Parliamentarian* LI (January, 1970), pp. 11-20. A useful compilation of pressure groups in Canada.

S.D. CLARK. *The Canadian Manufacturers' Association.* Toronto: University of Toronto Press, 1939. An early study, with continuing relevance, of one of the major interest groups in Canadian society.

DAWSON, HELEN JONES. "An Interest Group: The Canadian Federation of Agriculture," *Canadian Public Administration,* III (June, 1960), pp. 134-149. Dawson is the major student of farm organizations in Canada.

————. "The Consumers' Association of Canada." *Canadian Public Administration,* VI (1963), pp. 92-118. An analysis of organized consumers as an interest group.

DION, LÉON. *Société et politique: La Vie des groupes.* Vol. I, *Fondements de la société libérale* (1971); Vol. II, *Dynamique de la société libérale* (1972). Québec: Les Presses de l'université Laval. These two volumes present an analysis of the group approach and a thorough review of the literature, covering both Europe and North America. The extensive bibliography is a major source for further study of interest groups and the group approach.

————. *Le Bill 60 et la société quebécoise.* Montreal: Editions HMH, 1976. Educational change in Quebec and the impotence of interest groups.

ENGELMANN, F. C., AND M. A. SCHWARTZ. *Canadian Political Parties: Origin, Character, Impact.* Scarborough, Ont.: Prentice-Hall, 1975. Chapter 7 discusses the relations between interest groups and political parties.

GARSON, G. DAVID. "On the Origins of Interest Group Theory: A Critique of a Process." *American Political Science Review,* 68 (December, 1974), pp. 1505-1519. Critical of the group approach and useful in summarizing the positions of its early exponents, as well reviewing work in the United States up to the 1970s.

KWAVNICK, DAVID. *Organized Labour and Pressure Politics.* Montreal: McGill-Queen's University Press, 1972. A major study of trade unions as pressure groups.

MCRAE, KENNETH, ed. *Consociational Democracy.* Toronto: McClelland and Stewart, 1974. A collection of essays on consociational democracy, with direct relevance to the group approach in Canada.

MEYNAUD, JEAN. "Groupes des pression et politique gouvernementale au Québec," *Reflexions sur la politique au Québec,* ed. André Bernard. Montreal: Sainte Marie, 1968, pp. 69-96. A review of the position of interest groups in Quebec politics.

PRESTHUS, ROBERT. *Elite Accommodation in Canadian Politics.* London and New York: Cambridge University Press, 1973. A comparative study of interest groups in Canada that has been subject to critical attention and merits careful reading.

PROSS, A. PAUL, ed. *Pressure Group Behaviour in Canadian Politics.* Toronto: McGraw-Hill Ryerson, 1975. If one were to read only one book on Canadian interests, this would suffice.

TRUMAN, DAVID B. *The Governmental Process,* 2nd ed. New York: Knopf, 1971. This has been the major text on American government devoted to an elaboration of the group approach.

VAN LOON, RICHARD, AND MICHAEL WHITTINGTON. *The Canadian Political System*, 2nd ed. Toronto: McGraw-Hill Ryerson, 1976. Chapter 13 presents the role of interest groups in Canadian Politics.

16

Political Economy and Class Analysis: A Marxist Perspective On Canada

Philip Resnick[*]

Classical political economy has fallen into disrepute in recent decades. Where political economists like Smith, Ricardo, or Mill tried to uncover the laws of production, distribution, and consumption in relationship to the public as well as private spheres of capitalist society, twentieth-century economics and political science have gone their separate ways. Each of the social science disciplines—political science, economics, and sociology—at least in North America, has defined a specific subject matter, usually emphasizing technical, at times microscopic, problems at the expense of what may be called global, interdisciplinary concerns.

It is precisely these global questions that Marxist political economy raises and that this chapter will seek to explore. What has been Canada's place in a larger world capitalist system? What are the social classes in advanced capitalist society, and the implications of class relations for the political, no less than economic, process? What is the role of the state in contemporary and earlier capitalist development? What is the significance of nationalism, both in multinational societies such as Canada and between smaller and larger powers? What relationship exists between political ideology, educational curricula, or the mass media and the capitalist mode of production?

Those operating within a Marxist framework, to be sure, are not the only ones concerned with interdisciplinary questions. In the Canada of the 1920s and 1930s, for example, an important school of liberal political economists, principally Harold Innis, Donald Creighton, and their associates, sought to chart Canada's economic history in a broad, macroscopic perspective. Some of the themes they developed have been taken over by recent authors. Themes such as the role of metropolitan powers

*Assistant Professor of Political Science, University of British Columbia.
Author's Note: This chapter was written in October, 1976.

like France and Britain in stimulating staple production—cod, fur, wood, wheat—in the Canadian hinterland; the role of the state in fostering capitalist development for projects like canals and railways; or the shift in the early part of the twentieth century from a British to an American orientation in Canada's political economy, have attracted the interest of Kari Levitt, Mel Watkins, Cy Gonick, and Tom Naylor, all of whom write from a Marxist or neo-Marxist perspective. This renewed interest now provides an important foundation to the current revival of Canadian political economy.

The major strand in Marxist political economy, however, owes nothing to this earlier liberal tradition, which tended to a geographical determinism in which men and women were but secondary actors to the rivers and resources of a half-continent. Where Marxism breaks with liberal political economy is in positing class relations, in conjunction with material forces, as the determining factor in historical development, grounding political and social institutions in them.

> The history of all existing society is the history of class struggle.[1]

> The mode of production of material life conditions the social, political and intellectual processes in general. It is not the consciousness of men that determines their being, but, on the contrary, their social being that determines their consciousness.[2]

From these basic insights, Marx and Engels go on to postulate certain theses about the capitalist mode of production in particular: the role of the state as an instrument of bourgeois domination; the exploitation of labor power as the basis for capitalist accumulation; the tendency of the system to chronic and repeated crises of production and distribution; increasing polarization of society between that class owning the principal means of production, the bourgeoisie, and a class with only its labor power to sell, the working class.

Not every aspect of Marx's or Engels' analysis of nineteenth-century capitalism, with England as their model, holds good for twentieth-century capitalism. Nor is there universal agreement among twentieth-century Marxist writers on various developments in the political economy of capitalism, let alone the theory and practice of socialism. But if there is no single Marxist orthodoxy, and indeed it may be more accurate to speak of Marxisms in the plural, there is a kernel of Marxist political economy that holds good and for the purposes of this essay I would thus define: *Marxist political economy posits an integrated social science grounded in material relations and forces of production and embracing political, ideological, and social phenomena. Further, it looks beyond the parameters of capitalism to a classless society and world system in which unequal property relations and the institutions these give rise to will have disappeared.*

The utility of Marxist political economy to the study of Canadian politics has been relatively untested for the very simple reason that until recently very few researchers have been working in the Marxist tradition. Unlike continental Europe and later Asia, Latin America, and Africa which developed Marxist parties and movements of major importance, Canada, like Britain and the United States, did not. The Canadian Communist Party, for all its trade union and related activity from the 1920s through the 1940s, had relatively little impact on the mainstream of Canadian society and, with exceptions such as Stanley Ryerson, produced few intellectuals of note. The CCF/NDP, being staunchly Fabian, has had little use for Marxism, opposing the latter's vision of class conflict and revolutionary transformation with its own emphasis on gradualism and legislative reform. Most Canadian intellectuals calling themselves socialists in the last forty years have been social democrats, not Marxists.[3] This tendency was reinforced during the period of the Cold War (1945-1965 [?]), when, for many, Marxism came to be identified with Stalinism and the Soviet Union, further undermining its legitimacy in Canadian intellectual life.

The waning of the Cold War, the success of the Chinese, Cuban, and Vietnamese revolutions, the weakening of American imperialism and simultaneously of Soviet hegemony over the international communist movement, the radicalization of the student movements of the 1960s, and the emergence of a left-leaning variant of English-Canadian nationalism, have all played their part in making Marxism more atttractive to English-Canadian students and intellectuals over the last decade. Simultaneously, the breakdown of the old order in Quebec following the death of Duplessis, the so-called Quiet Revolution and rise of a modernizing nationalism and separatism, increasing university exchanges between Quebec and France, and the radicalization of the trade union movement, gave Marxism a constituency in French Canada where it had had almost none before. The result has been a veritable outpouring of articles, collections, theses, and books exploring Canadian and Quebec reality from a Marxist perspective.

Some of the principal themes of Marxist analysis have already been suggested in the opening paragraphs. For the moment, let me stress three major contributions that Marxist political economy can make to the study of Canadian and Quebec politics.

Firstly, in positing an integrated social science, it breaks with the jurisdictional boundaries erected among such disciplines as political science, sociology, and economics, stressing instead the underlying unity of capitalist development. It sees little use in discussing political institutions such as parliament or the party system divorced from the functions these have and continue to play in maintaining capitalist relations of production. Similarly, it finds little point in economic discussions that leave out the state, class conflict, or imperialism in their fanciful search for the perfect equilibrium point between demand and supply.

Secondly, in bringing to bear a larger international perspective on Canadian development and looking at capitalist and imperialist relations as part of a world process, it transcends the parochialism into which so much of the discussion of Canadian politics and economics descends. While there are certainly features of Canadian development that are unique, most are not: Canada is a capitalist society like many others; the mechanisms of accumulating wealth and exploiting labor are scarcely different; external capital is prominent here as in many Latin American countries; the Canadian state is not some neutral agency but, like all capitalist states, historically an instrument of bourgeois rule; and our contemporary class structure is analogous to that of other advanced capitalist societies. Once these facts are accepted, we can get down to the business of charting what is peculiar to Canada's political economy.

Thirdly, Marxist political economy does not share the system-defending focus of mainstream Canadian political science.

> The philosophers have only *interpreted* the world in various ways;
> the point, however, is to *change* it.

Marx argued the above in his eleventh thesis on Feuerbach. This commitment finds precious little support in most writings on Canadian government. That is quite natural given the liberal biases of Dawson, Ward, Corry and Hodgetts, Smiley, Mallory, or Van Loon and Whittington, to cite some of the major textbook authors of recent decades. For them, the real is the rational, and with timely reforms the Canadian political system an ideal system extending into the future indefinitely. A Marxist perspective cannot but look beyond the limits of a class-bound political system to a social order in which those who work with hand or brain exercise the dominant political and economic power. It is this commitment to revolutionary change, or at the minimum to radical transformation in class and power relations, that differentiates Marxist political economy from other approaches to Canadian politics.

The starting point for a Marxist analysis of Canada is twofold: on the one hand it recognizes the position that Canada, or its component parts, has occupied within a world capitalist system with its international division of labor among core states, semiperipheral states, and peripheral states;[4] and on the other hand it recognizes the economic relations of production within Canadian capitalism, in particular the domination the Canadian capitalist class or bourgeoisie, and more marginally in Quebec a small capitalist class and petty bourgeoisie, has over other social classes and over the political system as a whole.

As far as the first assertion is concerned we need to understand that New France and what was later to become Canada sprang up on the periphery of a world system centered in Europe, for several centuries playing the role of staple producer and resource supplier to that continent. The political systems of New France and the British colonies depended quite directly on those of France and Britain, while the mode of capitalist production favored mercantile pursuits over industrial into the late nineteenth century. Although in Quebec agriculture showed vestiges of feudal organization in the seigneurial system, it is more correct to speak of petty producers as the key group in Canadian agriculture through to the twentieth century.[5] Ideologically speaking, as befitted peripheral outposts of empire, Quebec and Canada resisted the revolutionary currents of the late eighteenth century, the American and French revolutions, coming instead to find in counterrevolutionary values and hinterland production the base for a regionally splintered state. As time went by, manufacturing, often foreign-controlled, came to play an increasing role, while the Canadian political economy, reflecting shifting international patterns, moved from the British to the American empire. The origin of the Canadian state in dependency vis-à-vis core areas continued to dog Canadian development into this century, while the unequal union of Quebec and English Canada undermined the possibilities of a Canadian nation.[6]

As far as the second assertion is concerned, we need to understand that Canadian capitalism, like all capitalist societies, has been based on unequal property relations between those who own the principal means of production, usually called the bourgeoisie, and those with only their labor power to sell, the working class. However, these have not been the only two classes in Canada. Farmers long played a crucial role in the politics and economics of the country; small proprietors have also been not unimportant; while self-employed professionals, joined in recent decades by large numbers of salaried professionals such as teachers, civil servants, scientists, and the like, have also played an important role.

There is still good reason to underline the role of the bourgeoisie as the dominant class in Canada. To be sure, the Canadian bourgeoisie has been more regionally divided than that of more centralized states in Europe or Japan; consider the friction between the regional bourgeoisies of Western Canada and the Maritimes and those of central Canada over the tariff. The existence of a separate national group in Quebec with a class structure parallel to, but in most respects separate from, that of English-speaking Canada further undercuts the national character of this class. Notwithstanding this, the Canadian bourgeoisie in its various guises, from the Family Compact and fur merchants through the railway syndicates and industrial and financial corporations of a later date, has controlled the Canadian economy, at least those parts not owned and controlled from the outside, and, in conjunction with the metropolitan bourgeoisies of Britain and the United States, set the priorities for the political system.

Those priorities have been geared to rapid accumulation of capital, intensive exploitation of resources, and repression of untoward dissent. As the muckraker, Gustavus Myers, argued as early as 1914, the state was the basis of the great Canadian-derived fortunes from the Hudson's Bay Company to the Catholic Church to the CPR.[7] Capital accumulation in a peripheral area was too risky to attract capitalists without major support from the state. If Canada has had an interventionist policy through much of its history, it has been applied to help socialize the costs of capitalist development, such as transportation systems, by subsidies and pilfering from the public purse.

It is symbolic that the godfathers of Confederation were the Baring Brothers of London with their large loan commitments to the Grand Trunk and other colonial railways,[8] and that Canadian capitalism and Canadian governments at all levels have, since Confederation, relied heavily on outside capital to meet their most pressing needs. Most importantly, this capital has not come without a price, namely, long-term Canadian specialization in staple production and resource extraction for international markets. The image of Canadians as hewers of wood and drawers of water for the outside world may be somewhat exaggerated even to describe the late nineteenth-century situation (else why the National Policy?), and is even more so for the twentieth. Nonetheless the mark of Cain that Jacques Cartier discerned on the landscape of this country is an apt metaphor for the minerals and primary resources that for so long defined Canada's position in the international capitalist system.

Bourgeois domination of the political system has been most evident in the repression of political dissent. The essentially petty bourgeois revolts of the 1830s in both Lower and Upper Canada ended in defeat as the Family Compact and Château Clique, in effect the commercial bourgeoisie of the day, rallied against revolt all that was most conservative in both Canadas. Confederation was an arrangement between British imperialism and colonial capitalist spokesmen such as George Etienne Cartier and John A. Macdonald aimed against the United States, but aimed no less definitely against an independent Quebec,[9] and against any radical challenge to property relations.[10]

As far as French Canada is concerned, Canadian history from the Riel Rebellion, to the Manitoba schools question, to the conscription crises of both World Wars, to contemporary Quebec nationalism, has often reflected diverging interests between the Canadian bourgeoisie, committed to a united predominantly English-Canadian state at almost any price, and more nationalist forces in Quebec. To be fair, however, Quebec history is not restricted to this conflict and the traditional Quebec ruling class—lawyers, professionals and French-Canadian entrepreneurs—has by and large collaborated with the Canadian bourgeoisie, sharing the latter's ideological commitment to capitalism. How else is one to interpret the procapitalist policies of successive Quebec governments from Honoré Mercier, to Alexandre Taschereau, to Maurice Duplessis, to Robert Bourassa?

Where threats to property are concerned, the century since Confederation has seen the use of state force, both the militia and army and in more recent years the police, against striking workers, and state intervention by executive, legislative, and judicial means against class-conscious trade unionism. Mackenzie King made things crystal clear in his 1903 Report on Industrial Disputes in British Columbia:

> With regard to these [radical] organizations we think they ought to be specially declared to be illegal, as their leaders have shown that they care nothing about the obligation of contracts or about the interests of their employers, against whom they are ever fomenting discontent; . . . that they at all times preach the doctrine of confiscation of property without compensation, and that society is divided into two classes, the toilers and the spoilers; that they justify the boycott and the sympathetic strike; that they do not disapprove of violence and intimidation.[11]

And from the mining and railway strikes of the early 1900s to the Winnipeg General Strike of 1919, from Duplessis's Padlock Law and antilabor legislation to Mitchell Hepburn's opposition to the Committee for Industrial Organization (CIO), there is a long history of repression in the policy of the Canadian state toward labor.

Where farmers were concerned, brutal class repression was less common. But tariff and railway policy largely did the trick, and it was only for a brief interregnum between the wars that farmers were able to organize themselves into protest parties with some limited effect on the political system. The dominant political parties since Confederation, the Liberals and Conservatives, have served the interests of commercial and industrial capitalism well, and though their policies toward different classes have varied over time, both have been resolutely committed to the defense of private property.

Yet capitalism evolves, and capitalist political economy in the post-World War II period has a number of specific features on which I would like to dwell. The most striking are the following: the rise and relative decline of American imperialism over a thirty-year period; the changing class structure of advanced capitalist society; the changing role of the state; the eruption of nationalism in industrialized, no less than Third World, countries; and the greatly increased importance of education and mass communications in the political economy of advanced capitalism.

Let us examine the implications of these features more carefully for Canada and Quebec.

Where American imperialism is concerned, the roots of American economic domination in Canada go back well before the turn of the century.[12] The Canadian bourgeoisie and Quebec petty bourgeoisie, like those of Latin America, welcomed American branch plants, while links with the United States gained in importance as British imperialism weakened between the wars. The crucial turning point came with the Second World War and the forging of a full-fledged military and political alliance at Ogdensburg in August, 1940.[13]

As American investment in the Canadian economy, especially in the resource sector, skyrocketed in the postwar period, the strategic importance of Canada to the United States increased. The simultaneous development of the Cold War turned Canada into a neocolonial appendage of the United States in both foreign and defense policy. A series of bilateral and multilateral agreements, such as the radar lines in the Canadian North, the North Atlantic Treaty Organization, the North American Air Defense Agreement, and the Defense Sharing Agreement, all reflected the shrinking margin of Canadian sovereignty, while the practitioners of quiet diplomacy lent support to American foreign policy, from containment of the Soviet Union to imperialism in Vietnam.[14]

In the heyday of the American empire, roughly 1945-65, the United States was the determining factor for much of the Canadian political economy. Through the branch plants, American capitalists were active coparticipants in shaping Canadian economic priorities; through radio and television programs, magazines, films, and the like, American culture set the tone for mass culture in this country; in the academic world, American universities were magnets for tens of thousands of Canadian graduate students, while American techniques and approaches spilled over into Canada, for example, behavioralism in the social sciences. If the Canadian political system, both federal and provincial, enjoyed formal autonomy through this period, the quid pro quo was a close alignment by governing parties, most notably the Liberals, with American positions. The one instance of hesitation, by the Diefenbaker government over nuclear weapons in 1962-63, ended in open American political, though not military, intervention and that government's quick demise.

Yet imperialism is not a once and forever proposition and in the decade since 1965 there has been evidence of a significant weakening in American hegemony over allies and client states. The rise of nationalism in the Third World and in such advanced capitalist countries as France under de Gaulle was one important factor; massive opposition within the United States to the Vietnam War was a second; the revival of Western Europe's and Japan's economic power a third; the increased influence of both the Soviet Union and China in world politics yet a fourth. The result, since the early 1970s, has been an American capitalism beset by balance-of-payments problems, bedevilled by the growing independence of energy-producing states, defeated in Vietnam, and generally less able to get its way in international forums.

This tendency has been no less operative in American-Canadian relations. If Canadian foreign policy has shown marginally greater independence in recent years, for example, the so-called third option in Canadian foreign policy, and if nationalism has become a more important force, then the chief explanation lies in the relative weakening of American power. I stress relative, for I certainly do not want to imply a wholesale reduction of what remains the major external operating force on the Canadian political economy. It is the shifting position of the United States within the international capitalist system and the structural changes to that system itself, which may well decide the future of Canadian capitalism.

Class is a crucial variable where Marxist analysis is concerned. Defined as the relationship of people to the means of production, it has often led Marxist theorists to stress two main classes: the big bourgeoisie, who own the principal factories, resources, and pools of capital on the one hand, and the working class, who have only their labor power to sell, on the other.

Marx and Engels proposed such a two-tiered class model in the *Communist Manifesto*, though Marx himself in such a work as *The 18th Brumaire of Louis Bonaparte* seriously modified it, talking of different types of capitalists, for example, financial and industrial, the peasantry, and the petty bourgeoisie, as well as the working class in nineteenth-century capitalism. A similar sophistication is required in any analysis of the class structure of twentieth-century capitalism.

Where contemporary Canada and Quebec are concerned, I would suggest that the chart in Figure 1 shows a comprehensive class model. There are two distinct, though parallel class systems, similar in most respects, though with a stronger capitalist class in the case of English Canada than of Quebec.

Figure 1

The Class Structure of English Canada and of Quebec American Imperialism

Canada

	English Canada		**Quebec**
Big Bourgeoisie: *(assets in excess of $25 million)*	Foreign-control—manufacturing, resources Indigenous-control—manufacturing, finance, transportation	Big bourgeoisie: *(assets in excess of $25 million)*	Foreign control—manufacturing, resources English-Canadian control—manufacturing, finance, transportation, resources Indigenous control—some manufacturing, finance, transportation
Smaller bourgeoisie: *(assets under $25 million)*	Foreign control as above Indigenous control as above	Smaller bourgeoisie: *(assets under $25 million)*	Foreign control as above English-Canadian control as above Indigenous control as above
Traditional petty bourgeoisie:	Farmers, i.e., independent commodity producers self-employed business self-employed professionals	Traditional petty bourgeoisie:	Identical to English Canada
New petty bourgeoisie:	Teachers, professors civil servants other salaried professionals	New petty bourgeoisie:	Identical to English Canada
Working class:	white collar blue collar unemployed	Working class:	Identical to English Canada

Source: Philip Resnick, *The Land of Cain: Class and Nationalism in English Canada 1945-1975*, (Vancouver: New Star Books 1977), chap. I.

The exact numbers of the big bourgeoisie in Canada as a whole are difficult to determine, though Corporations and Labor Unions Returns Act (CALURA) data for 1972 show 669 nonfinancial corporations with assets in excess of $25 million, some 63.2 percent of the assets of all nonfinancial corporations.[15] Throwing in the large financial corporations such as banks and insurance companies would give us a range of at least ten to twenty thousand principal directors and executives in the contemporary Canadian bourgeoisie. This is a good deal more than the roughly one thousand souls Porter and Clement describe in their books,[16] but then Marxist analysis, unlike elite theory, does not see the Canadian big bourgeoisie as a conspiratorial handful of individuals defined more by their prep schools and private clubs than by their structural relationship to the means of production. Some of these big capitalists are in the foreign-owned sector, some in the indigenous, yet both share a common allegiance to an open, expanding capitalist system.

The smaller bourgeoisie, that is, firms with assets under $25 million, are also important employers of labor, though at its lower levels this class shades over into the petty bourgeois entrepreneur, usually self-employed, and employing at most only a handful of laborers. Business proprietors and investors have constituted a stable 8.2 percent of all occupations, according to tax returns, since 1946.[17] Politically speaking, the influence of the big bourgeoisie, through such organizations as the Canadian Manufacturers' Association and the Canadian Chamber of Commerce, or directly on the major political parties and the state, is enormous, usually carrying smaller business in its wake. The smaller and even petty bourgeois entrepreneurs, however, also have their influence, particularly at the provincial and municipal level, and do not always see eye to eye with the big bourgeoisie. Consider, for example, the activities of the Canadian Federation of Independent Business in recent years, or the campaign waged by small businessmen and farmers for public ownership of electricity in Ontario in the 1900s.[18]

A class whose importance has declined are the farmers, almost 50 percent of the labor force in the late nineteenth century, down to 25 percent at the beginning of World War II, and to under 6 percent today.[19] Clearly, their political influence was greater in an earlier day, though even then the big bourgeoisie called the shots at the national level, than in the urban industrialized Canada of the 1970s.

Conversely, there has been a sharp rise in the number of professionals, especially salaried, in recent decades, to at least 12 percent of the total labor force.[20] With the new demands that capitalism makes in the scientific and technological fields, with the tremendous development of the educational system, with the increased importance of communications, and with the takeoff of the state sector, salaried professionals from research scientists to journalists, from academics to civil servants, have become an important force. From the Marxist point of view, they can be termed the new petty bourgeoisie; though not self-employed, they occupy a position intermediate between capital and labor, absorbing through their high salaries and other prerequisites part of the surplus value extracted by capital from labor.[21]

Elements of the new petty bourgeoisie have access to both ideological and political levers of power, and for all their vacillation, have at times attempted to redefine the political system in their own interests. Such, for example, is one interpretation of the Quiet Revolution in Quebec, the coming to power of a new urban French-Canadian middle class.[22] In English Canada as well, nationalist politics in recent years has been much influenced by members of this class, for example, the Committee for an Independent Canada or the Waffle. This is not to say that the new petty bourgeoisie in fact dominates the political system. But there is the possibility of class friction between the new petty bourgeoisie and members of the big bourgeoisie over the size of the state sector, the nature of state intervention, and so on; and doubtless such conflict will play an increasingly important role in late capitalism.

The working class, those who have only their labor power to sell, remain the vast majority of the population, though increasingly in white-collar rather than blue-collar occupations. While theoretically this class could challenge the big bourgeoisie for power, in practice the Canadian working class has seldom been class-conscious in the Marxist sense, especially not since World War II. Furthermore, only a third of the working class is unionized, and the influence of American business unionism in the Cold War years coupled with conservative currents within the Canadian trade union movement, has had a dampening effect on radicalism. It is significant that the major exception to this has been Quebec where radical trade unionism has taken root in recent years.[23] It remains to be seen whether a similar radicalization, spurred on by measures such as wage controls, will characterize the English-Canadian working class in coming years.

The analysis of the state should be at the very heart of political science, yet it is remarkable how little serious reflection there has been on this subject in Canada over the last thirty years. From the White Paper on Income and Employment of 1945 to Wage and Price Controls in 1975, the trend has been to ever-greater government involvement in the economy. Nor is this trend by any means confined to Canada.[24]

Marxist theory would argue that state intervention becomes necessary as capitalism fails to function, either through crises of overproduction or underconsumption. To be sure, the state has been involved in fostering capitalist accumulation for centuries, but in the period since the 1930s its role has become a good deal more one of planning and coordinating capitalist development as a whole. Left to individual capitalists, the system is too prone to generate crises.

Simultaneously, the broadening of the franchise since the nineteenth century means that the state has been forced to meet some of the demands of other classes, most notably the working class. The system must be made to appear legitimate to different classes in society, hence the legitimizing function of various social and economic programs.[25] It follows that the state in advanced capitalist society, if it is "a committee for managing the common affairs of the whole bourgeoisie," as Marx and Engels argued in *The Communist Manifesto*, must have a certain degree of autonomy to fulfill its role.

How great that autonomy is, is another matter. In Canada, the greatest part of the economy remains in private hands, and government intervention, from monetary and fiscal policy to funds for regional development or research, or to price and wage controls, is grafted onto a predominantly capitalist structure. The economic policies of Canadian governments, federal and provincial, are greatly circumscribed by the likes and dislikes of those who dominate the corporate sector, the big bourgeoisie, though that class does not always get its way. The state has a commitment to make the capitalist system function as a system, and this may take it into areas of activity that many individual capitalists may oppose, such as pensions, price controls. To use Rousseau's terminology for a moment, the state may be said to articulate the "general will" of capitalism rather than the "particular wills" of individual capitalists.

At the same time, the state must seek to accommodate other classes. This explains the move toward accommodation and integration, rather than overt repression, in the policies of both the federal government and most provincial governments toward labor since 1945. Labor relations boards, labor codes, and the like can be important carrots in winning labor support, though the stick of repression, physical no less than judicial, is always there. Similarly, social programs, from family allowances, to unemployment insurance, to Medicare, to the Canada Pension Plan, are ways of humanizing capitalism, without putting the underlying capitalist structure into question.

The figures on the growth of the state sector in postwar Canada are remarkable, though no more so than for other Western societies. (See Figure 2.) What they reflect is not a move toward socialism, as critics on the right are prone to suggest, but a move to statism, to ongoing involvement by the state in the running of the capitalist economy. This is, of course, a reversal from an earlier liberalism's commitment to the noninterventionist or "night-watchman" state, but it does not necessarily spell the beginnings of a transition from capitalism to socialism. It may be more correct to call it monopoly state capitalism, suggesting a partnership between the state and the largest corporations.

Even this is not the whole story. In some important ways those who work for the state or in state-financed institutions are, as I have argued above, salaried professionals or workers with class interests different from those of the big bourgeoisie. With some 22 percent of the labor force working in the state sector in Canada today, though not all of these, by any means, are new petty bourgeois, with many more people dependent on the state's social and welfare programs, the possibilities of a drastic weakening of the state's role are slight.[26]

A further consequence of these structural changes in capitalist political economy is that the state is relatively little affected by whichever political party is in power. The changes that a new government at either the federal or provincial level is likely to introduce are only marginal, for the factors affecting state behavior are secular and long-term. Within the limits of a capitalist economy, then, the areas of difference among such political parties as the Conservatives, the Liberals, the NDP or Social Cre-

Figure 2
Total Government Revenue as a Percentage of Gross National Product in Canada
(Federal, Provincial and Local)

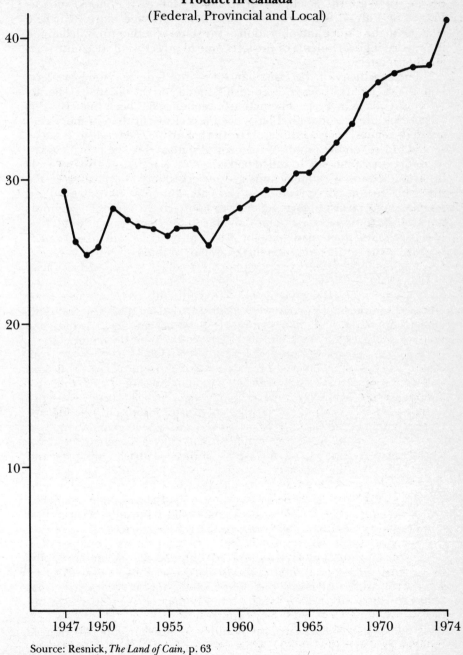

Source: Resnick, *The Land of Cain*, p. 63

dit are far less important than the sound and fury in the public arena might lead one to believe. All are forced to practise a greater or lesser measure of state intervention, while none is pledged to eradicate capitalist power. In Western societies with stronger Marxist traditions, such as France or Italy, it is theoretically possible to envisage more structural changes in the nature and operation of the state. Whether this will happen in practice if governments of the left come to power in those countries is another matter.

The specificity of the Canadian state—the federal system—reflects both the regional character of English Canada and the binational character of Canada as a whole. The main consequence has been that class differences at the national level have been less clear-cut than in more centralized polities, such as those of Western Europe. Federalism has also served to weaken the power of the central state and of the provinces vis-à-vis foreign capital, the so-called balkanization effect, though conversely it has tended to give state actions greater credibility and support in the different regions than would be the case under a more centralized scheme. For Marxist theory, federalism points to the underlying importance of the national question in Canada, and to the regional splintering of classes within the Canadian political economy. It does not, however, detract from the underlying capitalist character of that economy.

The national question in Canada principally involves Quebec's relationship to English Canada and Canada's relationship to the United States. Applying Marxist theory, we have little difficulty in recognizing that by the criteria of geography, history, language, and culture, both Quebec and English Canada constitute national entities and that, as a political consequence, each must enjoy the right to self-determination.

Marxism, however, does not separate the issue of nationalism from that of class. Rather, it recognizes that nationalism has a class basis and that as often as not, in advanced capitalist societies, this will give nationalism a reactionary rather than a progressive character. Evidence of national oppression in much of Quebec history would for the Marxist certainly bolster the case for Quebec's right to self-determination. Still, the Marxist would have to distinguish carefully between the clerico-conservative nationalism of the Abbé Groulx, Maurice Duplessis, and much of the traditional petty bourgeoisie that long ruled Quebec; the economic and political nationalism of the new petty bourgeoisie in recent years, such as the Parti Québécois, tending toward a technocratic capitalist state; and a more working-class-based nationalism putting socialism first on the agenda.[27] Clearly, Marxism would favor the third.

Where English Canada is concerned, Marxist theory would be hesitant to speak of an oppressed nation. Not only was there general support by Canada's bourgeoisie and by other social classes for Canada's ties, first with Great Britain, then with the United States, but in recent years Canadian capitalists themselves have become important participants in imperialist ventures in Third World countries.[28]

Nonetheless, Marxist analysis would recognize the subordinate role Canada came to play within the American empire after World War II, and would support an anti-imperialist form of nationalism aimed at weakening American domination in this country. In class terms, an anti-imperialist nationalism would have to embrace the Canadian working class and probably a significant component of the petty bourgeoisie, especially those new petty bourgeois salaried professionals who have been so important to the nationalist movements of the last ten years. On the other hand, the Canadian big bourgeoisie, ever more integrated into American and world capitalism, ever more interested in multinational ventures of its own, cannot but be the chief enemy of any progressive nationalism in this country.

Having acknowledged all this, Marxist analysis, in my opinion, would remain wary of forms of English-Canadian nationalism that did not place socialism first. In particular, it would reject the position that nationalism provides some kind of shortcut to socialism, or that one should downplay the latter in the name of some common national goals. Bourgeois and petty bourgeois nationalists would like nothing better. Important as the national question may be, it is not removed from class and class conflict, least of all in advanced capitalist countries. Anti-imperialism, while important, is only one part of what a Marxist analysis of Canadian political economy must stress.

"The ideas of the ruling class are in every epoch the ruling ideas, the class that is the ruling material force of society is at the same time its ruling intellectual force."[29] Marx and Engels wrote that back in 1845. In the capitalist mode of production, then, one would expect these ruling ideas to be those of the bourgeoisie, and that has indeed been the case throughout Canadian history. The "peace, order and good government" tradition enshrined in the BNA Act can be interpreted as a capitalist bill of rights, while the parliamentary tradition that our history and political science textbooks revere came out of centuries of struggle for power by the bourgeoisies of Europe and America. The bourgeois concept of representation reduces politics to the parliamentary arena at the expense of more direct and participatory forms of government.[30] Consider the overwhelming emphasis on electoral studies in contemporary Canadian political science.

The hegemony of bourgeois and prebourgeois values in Canada and Quebec has been fostered through religious and educational institutions, as well as through the mass media. In Quebec, until recently, the church, through its control of educational and other institutions, effectively eliminated all critical points of view. In English Canada, while the churches and school system were somewhat less monolithic, the results were much the same. The Canadian intelligentsia has been what John Porter aptly called a "clerisy,"[31] a group of establishment intellectuals strongly supportive of the state and state institutions:

> Our concern is with the deeply embedded beliefs that support and justify present day democratic [i.e. liberal] government, and with the rejection of these beliefs [e.g. Marxism] that has brought modern dictatorship to the fore.[32]

That this clerisy in important respects has been a branch-plant intelligentsia vis-à-vis Britain and the United States has only reinforced its native conservatism.

In the case of the mass media, much the same class that owns the principal means of production, the big bourgeoisie, owns the newspapers, private radio and television stations, theater chains, and so on. The capitalist state exercises very effective behind-the-scenes control over such institutions as the CBC, for example, the CBC directive cautioning against criticism of the government during the October Crisis. McLuhan notwithstanding, content is still the crucial feature of mass communications in advanced capitalist society. In the words of Ralph Miliband:

> It does not seem extravagant to suggest that radio and television in all capitalist countries have been consistently and predominantly agencies of conservative indoctrination and that they have done what they could to inoculate their listeners and viewers against dissident thought. This does not require that all such dissent should be prevented from getting airing. It only requires that the overwhelming bias of the media should be on the other side. And that requirement has been amply met.[33]

To return to the educational system, it remains, despite changes from an elite to a mass institution, particularly at the higher levels during the last three decades, firmly geared to capitalist values. As Harold Innis, no Marxist, recognized in a prescient passage: "The descent of the university into the market place reflects the lie in the soul of modern society."[34] The lie does not begin with university, but with the socialization that sets in from kindergarten on. The predominant values instilled by the educational system, individualism, consumerism, and so on, are bourgeois liberal to the core, while the bias of history and social studies, no less than literature and language texts, is toward middle- and upper-middle-class conceptions of the world.

To be sure, there are countervailing currents in the schools, as in the media; there are some radical teachers and journalists and a few left-wing periodicals and small publishing houses. There are slightly larger numbers of critics in Canadian universities and colleges today than was the case twenty or thirty years ago. The student movement of the 1960s has left some small imprint on university structures, such as student and faculty representatives on boards of governors, while the fiscal crisis of the 1970s is bringing salaried professionals closer to unionization. But these countercurrents are fairly weak and have failed to alter the class nature of educational institutions. Teachers and professors rarely identify with the working class against the big bourgeoisie, though here again there has been slightly more of this identification in Quebec recently than in English Canada.[35] At best, educational institutions, like the mass media, are potential arenas for class conflict. The tasks of any would-be Marxist intelligentsia in moving these institutions to the left or mapping alternatives to mainstream, for the most part bourgeois, Canadian culture and ideology are enormous.

It should be evident to the reader that there are limitations to a Marxist analysis of Canadian politics. The first difficulty stems from the ambitious character of the Marxist project, which attempts to explain the larger forces at work often at the expense of detailed investigation. This danger is compounded by the fact that Marxism as a theory first developed in reference to Europe, and its expansion to deal with capitalism in other parts of the world is not without its problems. Capitalism for the semiperiphery is not identical to capitalism for the center, and though Canada is a developed and not a Third World country, a Marxist political economy of Canada must take her position within the world capitalist system into account.

A second danger in Marxist analysis is dogmatism, a tendency to be more concerned with what Marx, Lenin, or other founding fathers wrote, than with what has actually been happening in twentieth-century capitalism. Certain of Marx's predictions have simply not come true, for example, the growing pauperization of the working class; other parts of his analysis, for example, the withering away of the state, are inadequate. Moreover, the distortions to which Marxist theory has been subjected in such ostensibly socialist societies as the Soviet Union (wholesale suppression of civil rights, establishment of work camps, retention of the worst features of the capitalist division of labor) make it all the more imperative to apply Marxist theory creatively and in a new way to those societies for which it was originally intended—the developed industrial nations.

Thirdly, there is the need yet again to underline the internationalist dimension of Marxism. There has been a tendency in English Canada for some spokesmen to reduce Marxism to a form of Canadian nationalism, or to attempt to graft Marxist political economy wholehog onto the liberal writings of the 1930s.[36] While there are features of the early political economy tradition worth retaining, the latter differs from a Marxist approach in terms of theory no less than practise. Similarly, nationalism may well have provided the environment in which Marxist analysis began to put down new roots in English Canada and in Quebec. But Marxist political economy is not simply a form of nationalism! While recognizing the reality of imperialism in the contemporary world, Marxist analysis does not dwell narrowly on the Canadian-American relationship at the expense of larger trends in the world capitalist system. Nor does it exaggerate the dependency factor in Canadian-American or Quebec-Canadian relations over the indigenous class structure of each, a class structure that bears close analogy to that of other capitalist societies. While, as I have just argued, Marxist political economy must pay close attention to Canadian specifics, it must be careful not to stress Canadian uniqueness at all costs. The road to hell is paved with such assertions.

I have tended to stress the differences marking Marxist political economy off from other approaches to Canadian politics, though acknowledging some similarities with the earlier liberal political economy tradition. Marxism poses an integrated social, political, and economic theory. It poses such large questions as imperialism, the class nature of Canadian and Quebec society, the nature of the state, the national question, and education and ideology, and addresses them in an integrated fashion. It looks beyond the limits of an existing capitalism and the political and ideological structures to which it gave birth, to a more egalitarian and democratic political and economic order. It is this combination of revolutionary commitment with cogent analysis of Canadian society that explains its growing attraction to younger people doing political and social science in Canada today. If Marxist political economy is gaining in adherents, is it not because competing paradigms have been found wanting?

ENDNOTES

1. Karl Marx and Friedrich Engels, "Manifesto of the Communist Party," *Selected Works* (London: Lawrence and Wishart, 1968), p. 35.

2. Marx, "Preface to A Contribution to the Critique of Political Economy," in Marx and Engels, *op. cit.*, p. 182.

3. See, for example, League for Social Reconstruction, *Social Planning for Canada*, repr. of 1935 ed. (Toronto: University of Toronto Press, 1975); or Michael Oliver, ed., *Social Purpose for Canada* (Toronto: University of Toronto Press, 1961), for two examples of social democratic thought.

4. See Immanuel Wallerstein's brilliant theoretical work, *The Modern World System* (New York: Academic Press, 1974), for a discussion of these three types of states and their relationship to the larger international system of capitalism.

5. See Denis Moniére, "L'utilité du concept de mode de production des petits prodocteurs pour l'historiographie de la Nouvelle France," *Revue d'Histoire de l'Amérique Francaise*, 29, No. 4 (mars, 1976). See also C.B. Macpherson's classical study, *Democracy in Alberta* (Toronto: University of Toronto Press, 1953) for an analysis of the "independent commodity producer" in Western Canada.

6. See Stanley B. Ryerson, *Unequal Union* (Toronto: Progress Books, 1968).

7. Gustavus Myers, *A History of Canadian Wealth*, 2nd ed. (Toronto: Lorimer, 1972).

8. Alfred Dubuc, "The Decline of Confederation and the New Nationalism," *Nationalism in Canada*, ed. Peter Russell (Toronto: McGraw-Hill, 1966), pp. 112-132; Tom Naylor, *The History of Canadian Business 1867-1914*, Vol. I (Toronto: Lorimer, 1976).

9. For a discussion of the opposition of Dorion and the *Rouges* to Confederation, see Jean-Paul Bernard, *Les Rouges: French Canadian Liberalism, Nationalism, and Anticlericism in the 19th Century* (Montreal: University of Quebec Press, 1971).

10. See John A. Macdonald's 1861 comment: "Unless property were protected, and made one of the principles upon which representation was based, we might perhaps have a people altogether equal, but we should cease to be a people altogether free." Cited in Ryerson, *op. cit.*, p. 355.

11. Canada, Royal Commission on Industrial Disputes in the Province of British Columbia, *Report* (Ottawa: King's Printer, 1903), p. 68.

12. H. Marshall, F.A. Southard and K.W. Taylor, *Canadian-American Industry*, repr. of 1936 ed. (New York: Russell and Russell, 1970), for a history of American investment since the early nineteenth century. See also Kari Levitt, *Silent Surrender* (Toronto: Macmillan, 1970), for a more radical and up-to-date analysis.

13. See Frank H. Underhill, "North American Front," *Forum - Canadian Life and Letters 1920-70: Selections from the Canadian Forum*, ed. J. L. Granatstein and Peter Stevens (Toronto: University of Toronto Press, 1972), pp. 191-193.

14. See Jack Warnock, *Partner to Behemoth* (Toronto: New Press, 1970); Charles Taylor, *Snow Job: Canada, the United States and Vietnam, 1954 to 1973* (Toronto: Anansi, 1974); or Philip Resnick, "Canadian Defense Policy and the American Empire," *Close the 49th Parallel, etc.*, ed. Ian Lumsden (Toronto: University of Toronto Press, 1970), pp. 94-115.

15. "In 1972 foreign controlled corporations with assets of over $25 million in the non-financial industries numbered 372 or about 6 percent of the total number of non-resident controlled corporations. They held $40 billion in assets or 71 percent of the assets of all non-financial foreign controlled corporations. The 297 Canadian controlled non-financial corporations in this asset size group represented less than 1 percent of the total number of domestically controlled corporations and had assets of $62 billion or 63 percent of the total assets under Canadian corporate control." CALURA, *Report for 1972*, Part 1, Corporations, 1975, p. 19. My 63.2 percent figure represents the share these 669 corporations have of the assets of both foreign and Canadian controlled corporations, including the many smaller corporations CALURA lists as "unclassified."

16. See John Porter, *The Vertical Mosaic* (Toronto: University of Toronto Press, 1965), Ch. 8 and Appendix II; and Wallace Clement, *The Canadian Corporate Elite* (Toronto: McClelland and Stewart, 1975), Ch. 4.

17. See Philip Resnick, *The Land of Cain* (Vancouver: New Star Books, 1977), Table 2.9.

18. H. V. Nelles, *The Politics of Development* (Toronto: Macmillan, 1974), Ch. 6.

19. See "Population in Nonagricultural and Agricultural Pursuits, 1881-1941," *Historical Statistics of Canada*, ed. M. C. Urquhart and Kenneth A. H. Buckley (Toronto: Cambridge University Press, 1965), p. 59; and *The Canada Year Book 1973* (Ottawa: Queen's Printer, 1973), Table 8.5, p. 356.

20. See discussion of the statistical size of the "new petty bourgeoisie" in Resnick, *op.cit.*, Ch. 2.

21. For a theoretical discussion of the new petty bourgeoisie, see Christian Baudelot, Roger Establet and Jacques Malemort, *La petite bourgeoisie en France* (Paris: Maspero, 1974); and G. Carchedi, "On the Economic Identification of the New Middle Class," *Economy and Society*, IV, No. 4 (November, 1975).

22. See Hubert Guindon, "Social Unrest, Social Class and Quebec's Bureaucratic Revolution," *Queen's Quarterly*, 71 (1964), pp. 150-162; Jacques Brazeau, "Les nouvelles classes moyennes," *Le pouvoir dans la société canadienne-française*, ed. Fernand Dumont and Jean-Paul Montminy (Quebec: Laval, 1966), pp. 153-163; Gilles Bourque and N. Laurin-Frenette, "Social Classes and Nationalist Ideologies in Quebec, 1870-1970," *Capitalism and the National Question in Canada*, ed. Gary Teeple (Toronto: University of Toronto Press, 1972), pp. 186-210.

23. See D. Drache, ed., *Quebec-Only the Beginning* (Toronto: New Press, 1972); Dianne Ethier, Jean-Marc Piotte, and Jean Reynolds, *Les travailleurs contre l'état bourgeois* (Montreal: L'Aurore, 1975).

24. For an excellent discussion of the growth of the state sector in all Western societies, see Ian Gough, "State Expenditure and Advanced Capital," *New Left Review*, No. 82 (July-August, 1975), pp. 53-92.

25. For a discussion of the legitimation function see James O'Connor, *The Fiscal Crisis of the State* (New York: St. Martin's Press, 1973); and for a Canadian application, Leo Panitch, "The Role and Nature of the Canadian State," *The Canadian State*, ed. Leo Panitch (Toronto: University of Toronto Press, 1977).

26. This figure is derived from Hugh Armstrong's excellent study, "The Patron State of Canada," M. A. Thesis, Carleton University, 1974, Table 5.9, p. 149.

27. See Bourque and Laurin-Frencette, *op.cit.*, pp. 186-210; and Stanley Ryerson, "Quebec: Concepts of Class and Nation," in Teeple, *op.cit.*, pp. 211-227.

28. See, for example, John Deverell and the Latin American Working Group, *Falconbridge: Portrait of a Canadian Mining Multinational* (Toronto: Lorimer, 1975); Daniel Jay Baum, *The Banks of Canada in the Commonwealth Caribbean* (New York: Praeger, 1974); "The Brascan File," *The Last Post* (March, 1973), pp. 28-39. For a somewhat dogmatic argument, see Steve Moore and Debi Wells, *Imperialism and the National Question in Canada* (Toronto: Author, 1975).

29. Karl Marx and Friedrich Engels, *The German Ideology*, ed. C. J. Arthur (New York: International Pubs. Co. Inc., 1970), p. 64.

30. See Philip Resnick, "The Political Theory of Extra-Parliamentarism," *Canadian Journal of Political Science*, VI, No. 1 (March, 1973), pp. 65-88.

31. Porter, *op.cit.*, pp. 491-494 *ff.*

32. J. A. Corry and J. E. Hodgetts, *Democratic Government and Politics*, 3rd ed. (Toronto: University of Toronto Press, 1959), p. 23.

33. Ralph Miliband. *The State in Capitalist Society* (London: Weidenfeld and Nicholson, 1969), p. 224.

34. Harold Innis, *Political Economy in the Modern State* (Toronto: University of Toronto Press, 1946), p. 76.

35. See, for example, the document published by the Quebec Teachers' Federation, the CEQ, "Ecole et lutte de classes au Québec," 1974.

36. This is my reading of the article by Daniel Drache, "Rediscovering Canadian Political Economy," *Journal of Canadian Studies* (August, 1975).

SELECTED REFERENCES

GENERAL

AMIN, SAMIR. *Accumulation on a World Scale.* New York: Monthly Review Press, 1974. An attempt to extend Marxist economic theory to the world system with particular reference to the Third World.

BARAN, PAUL AND PAUL SWEEZY. *Monopoly Capital.* New York: Monthly Review Press, 1966. An important updating of Marxist theory with particular reference to the United States.

FRANK, ANDRE GUNDER. *Capitalism and Underdevelopment in Latin America.* New York: Monthly Review Press, 1969. An analysis of metropolis-periphery relations with respect to Latin America.

GAMBLE, A., AND P. WALTON. *Capitalism in Crisis, Inflation and the State.* London: Macmillan, 1976. A discussion of the current economic crisis and its significance for the international capitalist system.

GOUGH, IAN. "State Expenditure in Advanced Capitalism." *New Left Review*, No. 92 (July-August, 1975). A discussion of the increased importance of state expenditure in various capitalist countries.

MAGDOFF, HARRY. *The Age of Imperialism.* New York: Monthly Review Press, 1966. An updating of the Marxist theory of imperialism to the age of the American empire and multinational corporation.

MILIBAND, RALPH. *The State in Capitalist Society.* London: Weidenfeld and Nicholson, 1969. A theoretical discussion of the role of the state in twentieth century capitalism.

PARKIN, FRANK. *Class Inequality and Political Order.* London: Praeger, 1971. A sociological study focusing on ongoing inequality in capitalist societies with a comparative look at Eastern Europe.

WALLERSTEIN, IMMANUEL, *The Modern World System*, New York: Academic Press, 1974. An important work in Marxist historiography examining capitalist development between 1450-1650.

CLASSICAL CANADIAN POLITICAL ECONOMY

CREIGHTON, DONALD. *The Empire of the St. Lawrence*, rev. ed. Toronto: Macmillan, 1970. A paean to the Montreal merchants of the eighteenth to mid-nineteenth centuries and to the political economy of the St. Lawrence River system.

FOWKE, VERNON. *The National Policy and the Wheat Economy.* Toronto: University of Toronto Press, 1957. An application of staple theory to the Canadian Prairies.

INNIS, HAROLD. *Essays in Canadian Economic History.* Toronto: University of Toronto Press, 1956. Essays by the key exponent of staple theory.

NELLES, H. V. *The Politics of Development.* Toronto: Macmillan, 1974. A discussion of the political economy of Ontario between 1850-1940.

SMILEY, DONALD, ed. *The Rowell-Sirois Report.* Toronto: McClelland and Stewart, Carleton Library, 1963. A classical treatment of federal-provincial relations up to World War II from a political economy perspective.

RADICAL AND MARXIST CANADIAN POLITICAL ECONOMY

BOURQUE, GILLES. *Question nationale et classes sociales au Québec, 1760-1840.* Montreal: Parti pris, 1970. A class analysis of the national question in Quebec from the Conquest through to the Act of Union.

CLEMENT, WALLACE. *The Canadian Corporate Elite.* Toronto: McClelland and Stewart, Carleton Library, 1975. An extension of Porter's 1965 study of the Canadian power structure with particular reference to the corporate elite.

GONICK, CY. *Inflation or Depression.* Toronto: Lorimer, 1975. A discussion of Keynesianism and its long-term failure to resolve some of the principal contradictions in Canadian and Western capitalism.

JAMIESON, STUART. *History of Industrial Strife in Canada*, Study No. 22. Task Force on Industrial Relations. Ottawa: Queen's Printer, 1970. A treatment of twentieth-century Canadian labor history which underlines the pervasiveness of industrial conflict and, at times, class consciousness.

KEALY, GREGORY S., AND PETER WARRIAN, eds. *Essays in Canadian Working Class History.* Toronto: McClelland and Stewart, 1976. Essays, principally on the nineteenth century, by some of the younger labor historians in Canada.

LAXER, JAMES, AND ROBERT LAXER. *The Liberal Idea of Canada.* Toronto: Lorimer, 1977. An analysis, by two former members of the Waffle, of postwar Canadian liberalism.

LEVITT, KARI. *Silent Surrender.* Toronto: Macmillan, 1970. A strong critique of the Americanization of Canada through the multinational corporation.

MACPHERSON, C. B. *Democracy in Alberta.* Toronto: University of Toronto Press, 1953. A classical study of Social Credit in Alberta, underlining the role of the petty bourgeoisie as a social class in Canada.

NAYLOR, TOM. *The History of Canadian Business, 1867-1914,* Vols. 1 and 2. Toronto: Lorimer, 1976. A carefully documented foray into Canadian business history between Confederation and World War I.

PANITCH, LEO, ed. *The Canadian State.* Toronto: University of Toronto Press, 1977. A major collection of essays on the Canadian state by some of the younger Marxist political economists in Canada.

PARK, F., AND L. PARK. *Anatomy of Big Business,* 2nd ed. Toronto: J. Lewis and Samuel, 1973. A study dating from the early 1960s, though by no means dated, of business interconnections in Canada.

PIOTTE, JEAN-MARC, et. al. *Les travailleurs contre l'état bourgeois.* Montreal: L'Aurore, 1975. An analysis of the 1972 Common Front strike in Quebec.

PORTER, JOHN. *The Vertical Mosaic.* Toronto: University of Toronto Press, 1965. An application of C. Wright Mills's power elite analysis to Canada.

PRATT, LARRY. *The Tar Sands.* Edmonton: Hurtig, 1976. A foray into regional capitalist analysis, in this case of Alberta and the Syncrude project.

RESNICK, PHILIP. *The Land of Cain: Class and Nationalism in English Canada, 1945-1975.* Vancouver: New Star Books, 1977. A class analysis of English-Canadian nationalism since 1945.

RYERSON, STANLEY. *Unequal Union.* Toronto: Progress Books, 1968. A work in Marxist historiography of Canada between 1837-1871.

TEEPLE, GARY, ed. *Capitalism and the National Question in Canada.* Toronto: University of Toronto Press, 1972. A collection of essays focusing on class structure, labor history, and the national question in Canada.

Subject Index

Name Index